# ETHNOLOGY
## OF
# ASIA, AFRICA & EUROPE

DESCRIPTIVE STUDY OF ALL RACES &
TRIBES IN THREE CONTINENTS

TWO VOLUMES

*By*

R. G. LATHAM

VOL. II

GYAN

Ethnology
of
Asia, Africa & Europ
Descriptive Study of All Races &
Tribes in Three Continents

R. G Latham

ISBN : 978-81-212-0003-5 (Set)

ISBN : 978-81-212-0160-5 (Vol. II)

First Published 1985, reprint 2013 in India by
Gyan Publishing House
23, Main Ansari Road, Daryaganj,
New Delhi - 110002
Phones : 23282060, 23261060

Fax : (011) 23285914
E-mail: books@gyanbooks.com
website: gyanbooks.com

*Printed at* : Sagar Color Scan, New Delhi.

# CONTENTS.

# DESCRIPTIVE ETHNOLOGY.

## CHAPTER I.

The Lithuanic Branch of the Sarmatian Stock.—The Old Prussians.—The Lithuanians.—The Yatshvings.—The Lets.

In beginning the notice of the Ugrian stock with the Finlanders a sacrifice was made to convenience. It would have been more scientific to have taken them last; inasmuch as they are the population most closely allied to the first members of the exclusively European group. Of this, the most eastern division is the Sarmatian; the Sarmatian stock falling into two branches: (1) the Lithuanic, or Prussian; (2) the Slavonic, Slavonian, or Slavic.

The present representatives of what was once the great Lithuanic family are only to be found in fragments. A few are Prussian subjects. The majority, however, belong to the Russian Governments of Kurland, Liefland (Livonia), Estonia, Witepsk, Vilna, and Grodno—further south than which latter Government they are not to be found. Nor yet are they to be found west of the Vistula. There are several Lithuanians in Prussia, but only in East Prussia. West Prussia has none.

In the eleventh, twelfth, and thirteenth centuries things were very different. All Prussia was Lithuanic; the parts on the Vistula as well as the parts on the Niemen—the parts even beyond the Vistula. All was Lithuanic as far as the frontiers of Pomerania; where it was Slavonic. Where, then, were the Germans? In Hanover, Westphalia, and the parts to the west of the Elbe. They had yet to conquer their present occupancies in the two Prussias;—the two Prussias, for when we write about the Lithuanic populations, the division into East and West is important. West Prussia was, and is, the more thoroughly Germanized of the two. In both, however, the present Germans are Prussians in the way that an Englishman is a Briton, *i. e.* not at all. An Englishman is a German upon soil originally British. A Prussian is a German upon soil originally Lithuanic.

The most Lithuanic parts of East Prussia are the parts to the east of the Pregel, the villages near Tilsit, Gumbinnen, Ragnit, and Pilkallen; the termination in *-allen* (*gallen* or *kallen*) being common—as are many other Lithuanic forms. As is also the use of two names, one Lithuanic and one German, for the same place. In Livonia we may find three.

I think *Prussia* and *Prussian* are native denominations, and that the Old Prussians who gave their name to the country were a separate substantive division of the family. That they differed from the others in language is known by the short specimens that have come down to us of the dialect of Samland, Nattangen, and a part of Oberland, as it was spoken about A. D. 1550.

In the twelfth century the Prussians were a powerful nation. In the second they bore the name Gothones, and occupied the amber country. The Germans called them *Esten*, or men of the east; this being the origin of the words Ωστιαῖοι and Æstyii, in Strabo and Tacitus. The Germans who conquered them called them Guddon. At the present time the name Pakul is to be found in songs and legends, which, in other respects, are purely German; Pakul being the name of the old Prussian god Pikullos.

As it was in the west so was it in the south. Individually, I believe that, in the time of Tacitus, a Lithuanic language was spoken as far south as Gallicia, and that it was that form of speech which Tacitus attributes to the Gothini and calls Gallic. Be this as it may, it is certain that the parts between the northern frontier of the present Gallicia and the boundaries of ancient Prussia, were occupied in the thirteenth century by a powerful nation which is sometimes called Pollexiani, but oftener Getuini, Jaczwingi, Jentuisiones, and Getæ, and which is especially stated by contemporary authorities to have been one of the four divisions of the Lithuanic name; the other three being the Prussian, the Lithuanic proper, and the Let. Of the Yatshving language we have no specimens—only a few proper names, *e. g.* Komatus, Mestor, Rausimodus, Taifal, and Podlakus, the latter being, in all probability, the individual from whom the present district of Podlachia bears its name.

The Yatsh-vings lay to the south of the East Prussians, and to the east of the Poles, in the present province of Sierdec, and in the Podlachia of the older maps. They are said also to have extended as far as the marshes about Pinsk at the head-waters of the Pripecz. At the beginning of the thirteenth century they were formidable to both Russia and Poland. This population, "vast and warlike, greedy of honour, allied in language, rites, religion, and customs to the Lithuanians, the Samogitians, and the Prussians, dedicated, too, like them, to the worship of idols, a population of which Drohyczyn was the metropolis, was so broken in a great battle against the Poles, under their Duke, Boleslav, in the year of our Lord 1282, as to become well-nigh extinct, a few only remaining; some of whom were attached to Poland, some to Lithuania. They never retreated, and never refused a battle, however unequal." This is the language of the chroniclers in speaking of the now unknown Yatshvings. The Poles were their chief conquerors.

Of the Lithuanian proper the district of Samogitia is the chief, though not the only, locality. As a general rule, however, it has been displaced by the Polish on the west and south, and by the Russian on the east It is a form of the Lithuanian proper, rather than one of the Prussian, that is spoken at the present time in East Prussia. Such, at least, is the general opinion. It is possible, however, that the difference between the two sections may be exaggerated.

The Lets are the Lithuanic occupants of Courland and Livonia, differing from the Lithuanians in dialect and in their external relations. Whilst the Lithuanian proper has been pressed upon by the Pole, it is the German who has encroached upon the Let—the towns of both Liefland (Livonia) and Kurland being German rather than Slavonic, as is the territorial nobility, the civilization, and the creed.

The Lithuanians have been pressed upon by the Poles and by the Germans. They seem, however, themselves to have pressed upon the Estonians. That the Liefs of Liefland were Fins has already been stated. So probably were the Koralli, Karelians, or Kurs, of Kurland. So also the populations who gave the Fin name *Suome* to the fenny districts of *Sam*land and *Sam*ogitia. It is possible that, at the present moment, no single representative of the Lithuanic family may stand on soil originally Lithuanic. What was originally Lithuanic is now Polish or German. What is now Lithuanic was originally Fin.

In their physical form both the Lets and the Livonians have many points in common with the Fins. They are light rather than dark, with undersized, rather than stout, bodies, flattish faces, and skulls (as far as they have been observed) somewhat truncate at the occiput. This may be accounted for by intermixture, or it may be accounted for by original similarity. To say nothing about the fact, just noticed, of the Lithuanic occupancies being originally Fin, the physical conditions of soil and climate are the same for both populations. So are the pursuits. The marshy flats of both Livonia and Estonia are rich in their produce both of corn and flax; and it is on the purely agricultural labours of the flax-dresser and the corn-grower that the industry of both the Estonian and the Let expends itself. As are the occupations, so are the ideas. The seed-time and the harvest are the chief times for festivity. The influences, imaginary as well as real, that affect the change of seasons, and determine the vicissitudes of the weather, are alike invoked on both sides of the Salis; for the Salis is the river of Livonia that divides the Let area from the Estonian.

Flax, oats, oaks, firs, aspens, willows—these give the imagery to nine-tenths of the popular poetry of the countries under notice.

As early as A. D. 1691 a fragment of the popular poetry of the Lithuanians found its way into print. It runs thus:—

> Ar asz taw ne mielas buwau?
> Su tawimi ruggelus pjowjau;
> Su tawimi szeneli grebjau;
> Su tawimi awiżeles riszau.

Or,

> Do I not become dear to thee?
> With thee the rye I cut;
> With thee the hay I raked;
> With thee the oats I bound.

In 1745 Ruhig added a few more specimens; which, attracting the notice of Lessing and Herder, appear in the work which, like the ancient ballads of our own language, has done so much towards the creation of a taste for the poetry of a natural life, the famous *Stimme der Völker*. Nothing, however, that could be called a collection preceded the publication of the Dainos, by Rhesa, A. D. 1825. Dainà, which is, word for word, the Daina of the Rumanyo, and, perhaps, the Duan of the Kelts, and, as such, a very remarkable term, means *song of the people—volksgesang*, as the Germans translate it. A *daina* (plural *dainos*) is secular in respect to its subjects, rather than ecclesiastic, a religious poem being called *gésme*. The dainos are handed down from father to son, are sung on all occasions and by every one, are simple in construction, without rhyme, and of no great length. They generally embody a sentiment, or exhibit an image; and are rarely sufficiently narrative to deserve the name of ballad.

They preserve more than one archaism, *e.g.* the horse of common life is an *arklys*, the steed of the dainos is a *źirgas*. They preserve, too, more than one relic of paganism. It is the Mother Earth, or the Goddess Zemyna, that gives the corn and flax. It is the sea-god Bangputys who raises the billows. It is Lamia who brings luck. The better known names of Perkynos and Pikullos are of frequent occurrence. This implies that the number of dainos is considerable. Rhesa gives eighty-five. In the collections, however, of Nesselmann and Schleicher, the two being taken together, they amount to about four hundred.

I have elsewhere* given my reasons for believing that a great deal of the history of the Goths belongs, not to the Germans, but to the Lithuanians; the main argument

* Native Races of the Russian Empire. The Germania of Tacitus.

in favor of this view, lying in the fact of the subjects of Alaric, Theodoric, and the other conquerors of the fourth, fifth, and sixth centuries having been Goths only as Englishmen are Britons, *i. e.* not at all. In Germany they never bore the name. They received it when they settled on the soil of the Getæ. If so, some portion, at least, of the old inhabitants of Dacia and Thrace were Lithuanic; a fact of importance when the remarkable relations between the Lithuanic and the Sanskrit come under notice.

Apparently, the Lithuanians are the most western members of the stock to which they belong. In Prussia they come in direct contact with the Germans; with nothing Slavonic in the interval. In Livonia and Estonia, they lie to the west of Russia. Yet it is only in appearance, that they seem to intervene between the Slavonians and the Germans. Germany has pressed up to their frontier. Russia has lapped round. Their real relations to the west are what they are in Lithuania; between which country and Germany the whole of Poland is interjacent, and to the east of which lie the Ugrians.

The clear and unequivocal history of the Lithuanic family, *eo nomine*, begins no earlier than the eleventh century; when the Teutonic Knights, the Knights of the Sword, and the Poles invaded East Prussia, Courland, Liefland, Lithuania, and the Yatshving country; the movement being from west to east.

In Poland the Yagellon dynasty was, more or less, Lithuanic. I say "more or less" because it is believed to have been Slavonic as well; the Lithuanians, as a general rule, being considered to be anything but a nation of conquerors. With the doctrine thus suggested, I differ *in toto*; having given my reasons elsewhere.*

* Native Races of Russia.

The present distribution of the Lithuanians of Russia is as follows :—

| | |
|---|---|
| In Kovno . . . | 568,794 |
| — Vilna . . . | 138,320 |
| — Courland . . . | 7,434 |
| — Grodno . . . | 2,338 |
| | 716,886 |

The Let population, on the other hand, runs thus :—

| | |
|---|---|
| In Courland . . . | 401,939 |
| — Livonia . . . | 318,872 |
| — Vitepsk . . . | 142,497 |
| — Kovno . . . | 6,341 |
| — St. Petersburg . . | 2,000 |
| — Pskov . . . . | 458 |
| | 872,107 |

| | |
|---|---|
| Total of Lithuanians . . | 716,886 |
| ——— Lets . . . | 872,107 |
| | 1,588,993 |

To these add certain members of the same stock in East Prussia.

## CHAPTER II.

The Slavonic Branch of the Sarmatian Stock.—The Russians.—Servians.—Lekh or Poles.—Tshek or Bohemians.—Bulgarians.—Panslavonism.—Original Slavonic Area.

THE Lithuanians are one of the two branches of the great Sarmatian stock. The Slavonians are the other.

The Slavonians fall into five divisions. I take the one which abuts upon Lithûania first. This is

1. *The Russian or Moscovite.*—In language, at least, it is closely connected with

2. *The Servian.*—The occupancy of the Servians Proper is, as we expect, Servia. But many other countries are, more or less, Servian. Bosnia, Turkish Croatia, and Herzegovna are Servian. Dalmatia is, in its essentials of blood and language, Servian. Carinthia, Carniola, and Croatia, the language of which is sometimes called Vend and sometimes Illyrian, are Servian. Montenegro is Servian. The Uskoks and Morlakians are closely akin to the Servians.

3. *The Polish.*—The Lekh, or Poles, are the Slavonians of the great central levels of Europe. Akin to them are the Serbs, or Vends, of Lusatia and the Circle of Kotbus, along with the now Germanized Linones of Luneberg, as well as the isolated Kassub of Rugenwalde in Pomerania.

4. *The Tshek of Bohemia.*—A German of the parts about Prague and Olmutz, a German of the country of

Huss and Ziska, is a Bohemian or a Moravian only as an Englishman is a Briton, or a Spaniard of the New World a Mexican, *i. e.* not at all. He is simply a German on Slavonic soil. The real *indigenæ* are the Tshek, for so they call themselves. Whether the term be native from the beginning is more than I can say. Word for word, it is Daci, of which we have the intermediate form Τζάκοι. The Tshek is the language of Bohemia and Moravia. Akin to it is the Slovak, of the southern part of the western Carpathians, in contact with the Magyar of Hungary.

5. *The Bulgarians.*—The language of Bulgaria is Slavonic. We may also add with safety, that its basis is something either Servian or Russian, or, if not this exactly, something between the two. The country over which it is spoken belongs to the area where the two forms are supposed to have graduated into each other. Yet the Bulgarian is as little purely Servian as it is purely Russ. It has more than one Turk sound, more than one Turk combination. The Turk, like all the Siberian forms of speech, prefer an inflection at the end, to one at the beginning of a word. The Bulgarian (in this respect standing alone amongst the Slavonic tongues) not only has a definite article, but incorporates it with the substantive to which it is attached, and, not only does this, but places it at the end of that word, rather than at the beginning. The Albanian does the same. So does the Rumanyo of Wallachia. So do the Norse languages. But no Slavonic tongue does so except the Bulgarian. Now the Bulgarian blood is pre-eminently mixed. It is Fin, Turk, and Sarmatian—certainly, more or less Slavonic; probably, more or less Lithuanic.

At an early period, the Scriptures were translated into Slavonic; from which it followed that the language into which they were rendered became written. Its alphabet was founded on the Greek; inasmuch as the Christianity which it conveyed was the Christianity of Constantinople, *i. e.* that of the Greek Church. The missionary who introduced it bore the respected name of Cyrill, and the alphabet is known as the Cyrillian. It is one of the best and worst in Europe. It is good because it is full, and contains, for each simple single sound, a simple single sign. It is bad because it is founded upon the capital letters only; and, so being founded, is fitter for inscriptions than for writing. Nevertheless, it is the alphabet of the Russian portion of the Greek Church; and how large that portion is I need not say. It is an alphabet by means of which more than one language of Caucasus, Siberia, and even Armenia, has been reduced to writing.

What modern dialect represents this Old, or Church, Slavonic? Some say the Russian, some the Servian, some the Bulgarian. It is certainly not the Bulgarian, and, probably, neither the Russ nor the Serb *exactly*. I believe it to be a dialect now extinct, but one which, originally, was spoken in some part of Hungary or Transylvania.

And now we may ask how these divisions and subdivisions of the Slavonic name are determined. Do they graduate into each other, or are they separated by broad and trenchant lines of demarcation? There are broad and trenchant lines of demarcation and there are the phenomena of transition.

The members of the southern division, the Servian and Russian (for the Russian, though at the present time spoken in both Siberia and America, originated in the parts about the Danube and the Carpathians), run into each other (the Russian being the most of an outlyer) but not into the members of the northern group, of which the Slovak is their nearest congener. Yet the Slovak affinities are

Tshek, Moravian, and Bohemian. The Serb of Lusatia is more Polish than Bohemian; not, however, without Bohemian elements. The isolated dialects of Luneburg and Pomerania are Polish. In one word, the affinities are just what the geographical relations suggest.

What applies to the language applies to the creed. The northern and southern divisions are natural, provided always that we consider the Russians as southern and Servian. At the same time, there are the phenomena of transition and intermixture.

The Germanized Slavonians of Luneburg, the Germanized Slavonians of Pomerania, the Poles, the Serbs of Lusatia, the Bohemians, the Moravians, and the Slovaks are either Romanists or Protestants; in other words, they took their Christianity from Rome rather than Greece. On the other hand, the Russians, the Bulgarians, and the Servians took their Christianity from Constantinople, and belong to the Greek, or Eastern, rather than to the Roman, or Western, Church.

In Illyria, by which I mean Croatia, Carinthia, and Carniola, there is (or rather there has been) an intermixture. The discovery of old writings in what is called the Glagolit alphabet has rewarded the industry and acumen of the investigators of the Illyrian, or Vend, dialects; the Glagolit alphabet being Greek in origin, and, as such, betraying a Constantinopolitan influence. It differs from the Cyrillian in detail only. Practically speaking, however, it is merely a literary curiosity. The Dalmatian, Carinthian, Carniolan, and Croatian dialects are written, when written at all, in Roman letters; the Cyrillian alphabet being Servian and Russian. The letters go with the churches.

One portion of the Slavonic stock is neither Protestant nor Romanist; neither Latin nor Greek. Bosnia, along with part of Bulgaria, is, to a great extent, at one and the same time, Slavonic and Mahometan.

It is an enormous mass—this great Slavonic stock, and we have (so to say) to distribute its component parts. We have done so in the way of language. We have done so in the way of creed. We have done so in the way of alphabet. We now consider its political analysis.

*Russia.*—The lion's share is Russian. To Russia belongs, with a small exception, everything that is Russ. To Russia, too, belongs the greater part of the Polish division. A few Servians, and few Bulgarians, are Russian.

The Russ division itself, however, falls into sections and subsections, both in respect to physical conformation and dialect. The Great Russian is spoken over the greater part of Russia, over Central Asia, and Siberia, over parts even of North-western America, with a *minimum* amount of dialectual difference, and with a *minimum* amount of difference between it and the written language. All this indicates the recency of its diffusion, combined with the homogeneous character of the form of speech diffused.

The White Russians belong to the Government of Smolensk, their frontier being Lithuanic, their original political relations Lithuanic, and (as such) some of their differentiating characteristics Lithuanic also. Haxthausen states that they are weaklier in body, and worse-looking in the face, than the others.

The Little Russians coincide with the Polish frontier, as it stood originally; the Ukraine and the south-west Governments being their chief area. They have the credit of being as much better-looking than the majority as the White Russians are worse. They extend into Austria, and in Hungary, Bukovinia, and Gallicia, are known as

Rusniaks or Ruthenians. Malorussian is their Muscovite name. A good deal more than I can either confirm or contradict, has been said about their separate nationality. It lies, I imagine, much within the same limits as that of the English and the Scotch—Kiev being the Malorussian Edinburgh.

Smolensk, Mohilev, Minsk, Vitepsk, Grodno, Vilna, and Bialystock are the White Russian; Pultava, Kharkhov, Tshernigov, Kiev, Podolia, Volhynia, Ekaterinoslav, Kherson, Bessarabia, and Taurida are the Little Russian Governments; the rest being Great Russian.

| | |
|---|---|
| Great Russians . . . | 35,000,000 |
| Little Russians . . . | 13,000,000 |
| White Russians . . . | 2,700,000 |
| Total . . . | 50,700,000 |

The Little Russians are the most purely Slavonic. From Kiev northwards and from Kiev eastwards, ran the lines of Slavonic occupancy; the valley of the Dnieper leading across the water-sheds to those of the Volkov and the Volga. Of some of the special Slavonic populations who thus extended themselves, Nestor gives the names. These were the Polyane, the Derevlyane, the Dregovitshi, the Polotshane, the Syevera, and others. The Desna, the Sula, and the Polota, are the rivers upon which they were more especially located; the present Governments of Kiev, Orel, Kaluga, Smolensk (partly), Novogorod (partly), being the eminently Russian localities. The Poles and Lithuanians pressed upon them on the west; the Pripecz being a Polono-Lithuanic river, rather than a Russian one. As to the southern Governments, they were Turk. So was the greater part of the Volga. The Ugrians, in Nestor's time, still predominated on the Oka and the parts beyond the Valdai hills. There were some Scandinavians in the north; but how they became Slavonized is uncertain.

Volhynia and Podolia were the battle-fields between the Russian and the Pole; the valley of Don, a battle-field between the Russian and the Turk. Of the Ugrian struggles in the north the history is obscure; though such struggles there were. Novorogod was the point from which the line of conquest in this direction originated; Olonets, Archangel, Vologda, and Viatka, the parts reduced.

The Slavonians of Russia outnumber all the others put together. They are almost all, however, Russians. If we look for representatives of the different divisions of the family we must look elsewhere. We must look towards

*Austria.*—The Tsheks of Bohemia are Austrian. So are the Tsheks of Moravia. So are the Slovaks of Hungary, on the north. So are the Croats of Hungary and Croatia on the south. So are the Carinthians. So are the Slavonians of Carniola and Styria. So are those of Dalmatia. So are the Poles of Gallicia. So are the Rusniaks, or Little Russians, of Gallicia and Bukhovinia.

*Turkey.*—Bulgaria belongs to Turkey. Turkish Croatia is what its name denotes, an Ottoman dependency. Upper Mœsia is but a part of Servia; yet it is (which Servia is not) Turk. So is Mahometan, but Slavonic, Bosnia.

*Montenegro.*—Montenegro, Czernogory, or the Black Mountain, lies between wind and water. It professes to be independent; but is in a state of chronic warfare with the Albanian part of Turkey, is menaced by Austria and subsidized by Russia. It belongs to the Greek Church.

*Servia.*—Independent.

*Prussia.*—To Prussia belong the Poles of the Duchy of

Posen. To Prussia, too, belongs the fragmentary population of the Kassub, of Pomerania, occupant of a portion of the Rugenwalde.

*Kassub Paternoster.*

Oytsche nasch, ktory ies w niebie. Swietsono badsch imie twe. Prsydsch twe krolestwo. Twa sie wola stani, iako w niebie, tako y na siemi. Chleb nasch powschedny day nam dschisja. Y odpusch nam nasche winy iako y my odpustschamy naschim winowaytsom; a nie wodsch nas w pokussenie; ale nas sbaw ob sljego. Bo twe iesta krolestwo, twoia moa, y potschesnosch (chwala) as na wieki wiekow. Amen.

To Prussia, too, belong the Serbs of the circle of Kotbus, divided only by their political relations from the Slavonians of

*Saxony.*—These are the Serbs of Lusatia, few in numbers, yet once occupants, not only of the whole of Saxony, but of much of the country beyond. It was their ancestors who, as the Vandali Silingi (Σίλιγγοι), or the Vandals of Silesia, are joined with the Goths who conquered Spain. It was the ancestors of these obscure Serbs of Lusatia who gave the name Andalusia (the Vandalland), to the finest province of the peninsula.

*Hanover.*—The Linones of Luneburg are now completely Germanized.

In the same works wherein the eastward prolongation of the Slavonic area is investigated, I have given reasons for believing that the southern Slavonians, of the very earliest historical period, extended as far westward as the Keltic frontier; in other words, that the Tyrol, the Vorarlberg, Bavaria, Wurtemberg, and even parts of Switzerland and Savoy, were what Bohemia and Carinthia are now, *i. e.* Slavonic occupancies. That the movement of the Slavonians in general has been from west to east, and from south to north, is certain. In the time of Charlemagne, there were no Germans to the east of the Elbe. In the sixth century, there were but few Russians beyond the Dnieper. The Slavonians have retreated before the Germans, the Ugrians before the Slavonians. Hence, the blood and language coincide but partially. Much of what belongs to the German language is Slave in blood. Much of what belongs to the Russian is Fin.

The influence of the Slavonic stock upon the history of the world is material rather than moral or intellectual, its great representative being Russia. Yet the Slavonic languages are spoken by, perhaps, eighty millions of human beings. At any rate, Schaffarik's tables give the following numbers:—

| | |
|---|---|
| Poles | 9,365,000 |
| Bohemians* | 7,167,000 |
| Lusatians | 142,000 |
| Illyrians† | 7,246,000 |
| Bulgarians | 3,587,000 |
| Russians | 51,184,000 |
| Total | 78,691,000 |

It is difficult to contemplate such a vast brotherhood in language as this, without asking why it is that the literary influence of the Slavonians is so little. It is certainly no fault of the language; the nearest congeners of which are the Sanskrit, the Latin, and the Greek. As little is it due to any inferiority of organization. The list of true and undoubted Slavonians who have walked in the first ranks of science is a long one, whilst, if it did but know, or would but own it, half Germany is Slavonia in disguise.

* This includes the Slovak of Hungary.

† This includes the Servian, Croatian, Dalmatian, Montenegro, and Carinthian.

Still, there is nothing that can worthily be called a national Slavonic literature. Why? The full details I am not prepared to give. I can only indicate two or three of the facts which have had most to do with the hindrance of one.

In the first place, the civilizing and the christianizing influences have had a divided origin. There were the Greek creed, the Greek alphabet, and the Greek way of thinking for the Servians and Russians. There were the Roman alphabet and the Latin models for the Bohemians and Poles. A Polish literature can scarcely be said to have had an existence, so thoroughly has Latin been the vehicle of Polish thought.

In the second place, the great material expansion of the Slavonian tongue has been towards the parts most remote from Europe, and from the quarter where the civilization is the least European. It is Russia that, at the expense of the Ugrians, has spread itself abroad. It is the Slavonism of Mecklenburg, Pomerania, Brandenburg, Bohemia, and Austria, which, under the pressure of Germanism, has receded, and is receding.

Thirdly, the Slavonic stock is most irregularly distributed, as may be seen from the following tables.

POLITICAL DISTRIBUTION OF THE SLAVONIC STOCK.

| | Russia. | Austria. | Prussia. | Turkey. | Cracow. | Saxony. | Total. |
|---|---|---|---|---|---|---|---|
| Great Russians.. | 35,314,000 | ... | ... | ... | ... | ... | 35,314,000 |
| Little Russians.. | 10,370,000 | 2,774,000 | ... | ... | ... | ... | 13,144,000 |
| White Russians.. | 2,726,000 | ... | ... | ... | ... | ... | 2,726,000 |
| Bulgarians ...... | 80,000 | 7,000 | ... | 3,500,000 | ... | ... | 3,587,000 |
| Servians and Bosnians ... | 100,000 | 2,594,000 | ... | 2,600,000 | ... | ... | 5,294,000 |
| Croatians ......... | ... | 801,000 | ... | ... | ... | ... | 801,000 |
| Carinthians ...... | ... | 1,151,000 | ... | ... | ... | ... | 1,151,000 |
| Poles ............... | 4,912,000 | 2,341,000 | 1,982,000 | ... | 130,000 | ... | 9,365,000 |
| Tshekhs ......... | ... | 4,370,000 | 44,000 | ... | ... | ... | 4,414,000 |
| Slovaks .......... | ... | 2,753,000 | ... | ... | ... | ... | 2,753,000 |
| Upper Sorabians | ... | ... | 38,000 | ... | ... | 60,000 | 98,000 |
| Lower Sorabians | ... | ... | 44,000 | ... | ... | ... | 44,000 |
| Total ......... | 53,502,000 | 16,791,000 | 2,108,000 | 6,100,000 | 130,000 | 60,000 | 78,691,000 |

RELIGIOUS DISTRIBUTION OF THE SLAVONIC STOCK.

| | Greek Church. | United Greek Church. | Roman Catholic. | Protestant. | Mahomedan. |
|---|---|---|---|---|---|
| Great Russians ...... | 35,314,000 | ... | ... | ... | ... |
| Little Russians ...... | 10,154,000 | 2,990,000 | ... | ... | ... |
| White Russians ...... | 2,376,000 | ... | 350,000 | ... | ... |
| Bulgarians ............ | 3,287,000 | ... | 60,000 | ... | 250,000 |
| Servians and Bosnians | 2,880,000 | ... | 1,804,000 | ... | 550,000 |
| Croatians ............... | ... | ... | 801,000 | ... | ... |
| Carinthians ... ........ | ... | ... | 1,138,000 | 13,000 | ... |
| Poles ......................... | ... | ... | 8,923,000 | 442,000 | ... |
| Tshekhs ............... | ... | ... | 4,270,000 | 144,000 | ... |
| Slovaks ..................... | ... | ... | 1,953,000 | 800,000 | ... |
| Upper Sorabians ...... | ... | ... | 10,000 | 88,000 | ... |
| Lower Sorabians...... | ... | ... | ... | 44,000 | ... |
| Total ......... | 54,011,000 | 2,990,000 | 19,359,000 | 1,531,000 | 800,000 |

Is this great language always to stand dumb in the world of thought? I can only answer this by stating, that there is such a word as Panslavonism. It is the creation of a literary man, and by the writings of literary men the doctrine which it embodies has chiefly been developed. It means that, with such a slight difference as actually exists between the extreme forms of the Slavonic speech, a literature should be developed, which all Slavonians should read; that in Austria and Posen it should replace the German; and that in Servia and Russia it should be national.

But Panslavonism has a political, as well as a literary bearing. This varies with the country. In Poland, it means absolute equality between the Pole and Russian, the two separate nationalities being merged under the great generality of Slavonism. In Russia it means the propagation of the Greek creed, and the displacement of such languages as the Turk and Rumanyo by the Russian or Servian. In Servia and Montenegro, it means dislike to all things Ottoman; and in Hungary, the denial of the right of predominance to the Magyar minority. It means, in short, different things in different places. It means, however, most especially, the non-recognition of the assumed superiority in literature and science on the part of the Germans, and the development of the Slavonic press, whose domain shall be co-extensive with the language. It began, as has been stated, in Bohemia, where the Slavonic civilization is the highest, and where the German contact is the least satisfactory to the Slavonian.

## CHAPTER III.

### The Skipetar, or Albanians.

At the present time the Albanian population is one of the most isolated in the world; being surrounded by Turks, Greeks, and Slavonians. But as the Turks, at least, are intrusive, and as the whole of the country to the north has, from the beginning of history, been the scene of continual invasion and displacement, the presumption is in favour of the ancestors of the present Skipetar (for so the Albanians call themselves) having once extended further northwards in the direction of Ugria, as well as further east in the direction of Caucasus.

Albania extends from Montenegro to the Gulf of Arta. Eastwards it reaches the back-bone of Turkey, or the watershed between the small rivers which empty themselves into the Adriatic and the larger ones which fall into the Ægean.

The occupants of this district fall into the following divisions, clans, or tribes.

1. The Ghegh, containing—

*a.* The proper Ghegh, conterminous with the Slavonian countries of Montenegro, Bosnia, and Herzegovna, bounded on the south by the river Drin.

*b.* The Mirdit, south of the Drin, in the province of Kroia.

2. The Toski.—In the mouth of a Ghegh, Toski is the name for the South Albanians in general. The true and proper Toski, however, in the limited sense of the word, are a tribe of the river Voyutsa. Another tribe which a Ghegh would call Toski, but which the Toski, in the limited sense of the word, call Lyap, calls itself Arb; its occupancy being the ancient Chaonia. The Dzhami touch the Greek frontier, Parga and Suli being two of their towns.

The Skipetar of the parts about Bérat, on the Ghegh and Toski frontier, are said to be, in respect to their dialect, intermediate, or transitional—Ghegh, however, rather than Toski.

The Ghegh proper, and the Mirdit, are more dark than fair, and more Christian than Mahometan; some belonging to the Greek Church, and some being Romanists.

The Toski have often light complexions and grey eyes. Like the Lyap and Dzhami, they are chiefly Mahometans. The Christian Toski are, almost wholly, of the Greek Church.

The tribe system is, perhaps, stronger in Albania than in any part of Europe; the Highlands of Scotland not excepted. This engenders no small amount of private war, arising out of blood-feuds. A Skipetar, even in time of peace, goes armed. Indeed, he belongs to a country that, though European, and (as such) supposed to be civilized, is to be compared with Circassia or Kurdistan, rather than with Scotland or Switzerland. The worst of the Turk garrisons, whether in Asia Minor or in Africa, are composed of Albanian, or, as they more usually called, Arnaout soldiers; and it is through these hard and unscrupulous men that the Pashas do their worst deeds. The state of hostility between the Montenegriners and the Albanians of their frontier is chronic.

Though shepherds, robbers, and soldiers, the Albanians must not be looked upon as exclusively landsmen. Those of the islands exhibit great naval aptitude. As sailors they are both bold and skilful.

They marry young; and become betrothed still younger. When this is the case the principals have but a small voice in the marriage preliminaries. The parents effect these long before the sons and daughters are adolescent. What Hahn calls Doric love, and considers innocent and proper, deserves a coarser and more disreputable name.

The best traits in the Skipetar character are their love of liberty, their love of their country, their courage, and their confidence in each other. Hence their chief representatives in history have been warriors; first and foremost of whom stands George Castriotes, Little Alexander, or Scanderbeg. That there was Skipetar blood in more than one of the heroes of antiquity is nearly certain. There was Skipetar (it would then be called Illyrian) blood in the veins of more than one of the kings of the Hellenic world. Pyrrhus, for instance, and the Temenids of Macedonia were, probably, more or less Skipetar.

It is the opinion of Hahn that the Ghegh division coincides with the Illyrians, the Toski with the Epirots of antiquity.

There are Albanians beyond the boundaries of Albania, *i. e.* in Greece, in the Banat, in Turkey, in Italy, and in the Ottoman garrisons wherever they exist. In like manner, there are many parts of Albania which are other than Skipetar. The parts about Ochrida are a Bulgarian occupancy. Greek districts indent the northern, Servian the southern, frontiers. Besides these, there is more than one Rumanyo or Wallachian settlement, both on the frontier, and in the heart of the country.

*Numbers of Skipetar.*

| | |
|---|---|
| In Greece, Attica, Megara, Salamis, the Piræus . . . . . . | 30,000 |
| Bœotia . . . . . . . . | 25,000 |
| Phokis . . . . . . . . | 5,000 |
| Valley of Sperchius . . . . . | 10,000 |
| Eubœa (South) . . . . . . | 25,000 |
| Andros (North) . . . . . . | 6,000 |
| Argos . . . . . . . . | 25,000 |
| Korinth and Achaia . . . . . | 15,000 |
| Acadia . . . . . . . . | 10,000 |
| Hydra . . . . . . . . | 12,000 |
| Spezzia . . . . . . . . | 10,000 |
| | 173,000 |
| In Austria, Clementines of Ninketze and Herkovtze in Syrmia . . | (?) |
| ——— Erizzo, a suburb of Zara in Dalmatia . . . . . . | 880 |
| ——— Pervi, near Pola in Istria | 210 |
| | 1,090 |
| In Russia (Bessarabia) . . . . | 1,328 |
| In Italy, Calabria Ulteriore . . . | 4,407 |
| ——— Calabria Citeriore . . . | 30,812 |
| ——— Basilicata . . . . . | 10,090 |
| ——— Capitanata . . . . . | 13,465 |
| ——— Terra d'Ottranto . . . . | 6,844 |
| ——— Abruzzo Ulteriore . . . | 220 |
| ——— Sicily . . . . . . | 19,713 |
| | 85,551 |

To which add a few families in Venice, chiefly or exclusively in the parish of S. Cassiano. Add, too, as areas more or less Albanian, some villages of the Monte Gargano in Italy, and those of Bronte, Biancaville, S. Michele, and S. Angelo in Sicily. Here, however, fusion has taken place, and the general character is Italian or Sicilian.

| English. | Skipetar.* | Romaic.† | Servian. |
|---|---|---|---|
| *Man* | nyeri | anthrôpos | tshovek |
| *Head* | koke | kefalê | glava |
| *Hair* | lyezh | mali | vlasi |
| *Eye* | su | omma | oko |
| *Ear* | vezhe | ôtion | uvo |
| *Nose* | khoundea | muti | nos |
| *Mouth* | goye | stoma | usta |
| *Tooth* | demp | odonti | zub |
| *Tongue* | gzoukhe | glôssê | yazik |
| *Hand* | dori | kheir | ruka |
| *Foot* | kame | podi | noga |
| *Sun* | dyel | helios | suntshe |
| *Moon* | khenne | selênê | mesestsh |
| *Star* | uli | astron | zvezda |
| *Fire* | zyarri | fôtia | ogany |
| *Water* | ouye | nêri | ooda |

One Albanian poet seems to be almost a classic. At any rate, he was no untaught bard. He wrote in his native tongue; but his poems are on the Turkish model, (itself but Persian at second-hand), and are full of exotic words. His name was Nesim Bey, and he was born at Premét. He compared the eyebrows of his mistress to the holy stone of the mosquè of Mecca, the Kaaba: and was maltreated as a blasphemer for doing so.

The popular poetry, though not without vigour, and though dedicated to the recital of warlike actions, has less of the ballad character than that of the Servians. A great deal of it is sentimental and exotic. Of the ancient mytho

* Toski dialect. † Modern Greek.

logy it gives us but little. At the same time, there is no lack of Skipetar superstitions. There is the belief in the evil eye; in the vampire; in men with tails; and, apparently, in lycanthropy. There is the belief in fairies, both male and female, fair in form, amiable in disposition. On the other hand, there is the fear of the Kore, a malignant baby-eater. The tutelary spirit of the house takes the form of a snake, that lives on the walls, shows itself but seldom, and rustles behind the wainscot when danger approaches. When all the males of the family die, it leaves. The Kutshedra causes droughts. The Sukyeneza has four eyes. The Lubra, like the Kore, feeds on the flesh of infants. The Ore takes note of the prayers and wishes of men. Mauthia shines bright in a dress of gold and jewels. Dif is endowed with more than mortal strength.

The area of the Skipetar has, doubtless, been greater than it is. In the direction of the southern Ugrians, and the most south-western Dioscurians, it probably extended far northwards. I think this, because the displacements in Thrace, the valley of the Danube, and Russia, are enormously great—and not only are they this, but they are old as well. The Getæ were possibly, the Scythians were certainly, intrusive—even in the time of Herodotus. Again, all Greece, the Morea included, seems to have once been Skipetar. This, however, was before the occupancy of the Hellenes; the origin of whom is suggested in the next chapter.

## CHAPTER IV.

The Latins or Italians, and the Greeks or Hellenes.—The Germans.—The Kelts.—The Euskaldunae, or Basks.

*The Italians and Greeks.*—Respecting populations so well known as the Romans and the Athenians, the Latins and the Hellenes, the Italians and the Greeks, I have little to say in the way of ordinary detail. Their early civilization, and their influence on the world's history, are palpable and patent. The physical conditions, both in the way of climate and sea-board, under which this civilization was developed, are amongst the earliest teachings in geography. Their southern physiognomy has been, over and over again, contrasted with the blonde complexions and light hair of the Germans; and their great intellectual aptitudes have been admitted to either accompany, or represent, a fine, and almost faultless, organization.

No one asks the descriptive ethnologist for a history of either Rome or Greece. Both Rome and Greece, however, have their ethnologies. In noticing these, I shall limit myself to the three questions which, in the present state of our inquiries, are the most important. These are—

I. The relations of the Greek and Latin groups to each other.

II. The relations of the division which the two groups constitute to the other families of Europe.

III. The relation of the modern Greeks and the modern Italians to the ancient.

I. *The relations of the Greek and Latin groups to each other.*—Roughly speaking, this is represented by the relations of the Latin and Greek languages; languages which have long been admitted to constitute branches of the same stock, or sub-sections of the same section, rather than separate classes or separate sections. The exact value of the class thus constituted is another question. The current phraseology sufficiently indicates likeness as well as difference, difference as well as likeness. What is the geography, what the history that accounts for this? Whence came the Greek that it is so like the Latin, whence the Latin that it is so akin to the Greek? Somewhere or other the two must have been in close geographical contact. At present they belong to two different peninsulas, with the sea between them in one direction, and a vast block of Albanian and Slavonic territory in the other. What was the original continuity? I have given elsewhere* my reasons for making even the most ancient Hellenes not only foreign to the soil of Greece (which was originally Skipetar), but also Italian in origin; a doctrine which implies not only a maritime migration, but also the high probability of the Hellenes having been, to a great extent, a population of half-bloods; Italian on one side, Albanian, Illyrian, or Epirot on the other. This is because no mode of migration is less favourable to the purity of the migrants than a sea-voyage; where space is limited and females an encumbrance.

Let Greece under the leadership of Agamemnon be as truly Hellenic as Kent and Essex were Anglo-Saxon in the reign of Alfred. What does it prove in the way of the occupants being aboriginal? As little as the English

* Ethnology of Europe, page 97, &c.

character of the counties in question at the time referred to. Four centuries (or even less) of migration may easily give all the phenomena that occur; for the area of Hellenic Greece is smaller than the kingdom of Wessex or Northumberland, and the country but little more impracticable.

II. *The relations of the Italians and Hellenes to the other families of Europe.*—If Apulia, Calabria, and Sicily were the occupancy of the ancestors of the Hellenes, it follows, from the position of those countries at the extremity of the peninsula, that the connection of the Greek language with the other tongues of Europe must be indirect, or through the Latin. If so, the Greek is what is called Indo-European only so far as it is Roman, Oscan, Umbrian, or the like.

Again, the Greek blood must be far less Hellenic than the language, the Greek relations, in the way of blood, being, more or less, Skipetar. In other words, the connection between the Kelts and Germans of Great Britain (whatever it was) repeats itself in that of the Albanians and the Hellenes.

The Greek language being spoken at the extremity of an area, has no congeners except on the north. In this direction it is suceeded by the Latin and its allied forms of speech, which lead up to the other three great members of the division called Indo-European, viz. the Keltic, the German, and the Sarmatian. Its connections with these are by no means equal. In Keltic elements the Latin has been shown to abound; but it has also been shown that these elements are intrusive, *i. e.* that they are Latin in the same way that the Norman elements of our own tongue are English. In their grammatical structure the Kelt and Latin are widely different.

That the Latin should be more Slavonic than German

is what we expect *à priori.* The untenable doctrine that the Slavonians of Carinthia and Carniola are recent settlers is, or ought to be, abandoned. This being given up, the southern Slaves and the northern Italians are in geographical juxtaposition.

III. *The relation of the modern Greeks and the modern Italians to the ancient.* (1.) *The Greeks.*—Why is it that when we compare a map of modern with one of ancient Greece, such a small proportion of the old classical names can be found? Such is, undoubtedly, the case. Yet, subject to Turkey as Greece, until the present century, has been, the majority of the new names is not Turkish. On the contrary, it is chiefly Slavonic.

As early as A. D. 582, movements set in towards Greece, Thrace and Macedon being overrun by Slavonians. The details here, however, are obscure, and there is an occasional confusion of the Slaves with the Avars. The latter nation, however, seems to have made no notable settlement in Southern Greece at least. In the latter half of the seventh century, Thessaly, Epirus, several of the islands, and parts of Asia Minor, were overrun. In the ninth, Macedon is called Sklavinia. In the eleventh, Athens is sacked, and the inhabitants driven to take refuge in the isle of Salamis. Under Constantine Porphyrogeneta, the presence of an Hellenic population is an exception. "In Macedon," he writes, "the Scythians dwell, instead of the Macedonians." Again, "the whole country is Slavonized."

But the most remarkable passage is the following, which shows that a Slavonic population is so far the rule that where an approach to the ancient population is found it is dealt with as a remarkable phenomenon; and that by a Greek writer:—"It must be known that the inhabitants of the settlement (κάστρον) Maina, are not of the race of the aforesaid Slaves, but of the old Romans, and even till the present time, they are called by their neighbours Hellenes, from having been originally pagans and idolaters like the old Hellenes."—*De Adm. Imp.* i. 50.

Latin writers, equally with the Greek, considered Greece to be Slavonic :—" Inde (*i. e.* Sicilia) navigantes venerunt ultra mare Adrium ad urbem Manafasiam in Sclavinica terra." By Manafasia, is meant Napoli di *Malvasia* in the Morea.

More than this. The details of some of these Slavonic populations are given ; so that we know that there were Ezeritæ and Milengi in the Morea, with Dragovitæ, Sagudatæ, Velegezetæ, Verzetæ, and others in Northern Greece.

So much for the Slavonic, the most important of the foreign elements, in the modern Greek blood. Others there are besides ; viz. Albanian, Italian, Turk, Bulgarian, Wallachian, Arab, and even French, and Catalonian.

To say that there is no blood-connection at all between the present Greeks and the old Hellenes, would be an over-statement. It is no over-statement, however, to say that the foreign elements of intermixture are both numerous and important. They are, probably, at their *maximum* in the Ionian Islands, and in Bœotia ; at their *minimum* in the land of the old Laconians, the truly Hellenic character of the Zakones having long commanded attention.

(2.) *The Italians.*—Ligurian, Etruscan, and, more or less, Keltic in the north ; Keltic, to some extent, in even the Umbrian, Sabine, and Samnite countries ; and Greek in the south ; Italy, in even the time of the Romans, must have been more Italian in language than in blood. And so it is now—the most Italian parts of it being the more inaccessible districts of its middle third of the peninsula.

the country of the Marsi, Peligni, Vestini, and similar allied populations. Yet even here there has, in all probability, been admixture from the time of the Republic to our own. Thus, in the second century of our era, Frontinus tells us of the Cornelian and Bæbian Ligurians in Samnium. These were the descendants of a colony transplanted from Liguria by P. Cornelius Cethegus and M. Bæbius Tamphilus. In the same Samnium (saving its Kelt elements one of the most Italian parts of Italy), there was a Bulgarian colony in the time of the Lombards. We know of these. Of how many other similar intermixtures may we be ignorant! The constitution of the Roman armies was pre-eminently heterogeneous; so much so, that, in speaking of a soldier of the Empire, it is better to call him a legionary than a Roman—so easily may he have been a Briton, a Gaul, a German, a Slavonian, an African.

Of the so-called barbarian inroads, some were Sarmatian, *e. g.* that of the Vandals and Gepidæ; some Turk, *e. g.* that of the Huns, Avars, (?) Heruli, and Skiri; some, perhaps, more or less Ugrian, *i. e.* that of the Bulgarians. The German settlements, however, are the most important. The conquest by Theodoric was not only permanent, but it was the first of three from the same stock. Themselves, probably, of mixed blood, having taken it up, during their various settlements on the Lower and Middle Danube, from the Slavonians and Turks of the countries with which they came in contact, the Ostrogoths, to the amount of not less than two hundred thousand, settled in the most favoured parts of the country. When Italy is recovered by Narses and Belisarius, more than one hundred and fifty years after, they are only ejected from power, not bodily put out of the land.

The Lombard dominion rapidly succeeded the Ostrogoth. Partial invasions of Bavarians, Suabians, and Alemanni were, for a time, successful. But the Lombards ruled over all Italy, with the exception of the Exarchate of Ravenna, till the conquest by Charlemagne, and over the Duchy of Beneventum till the conquest of Sicily by the Normans. Since then, there has been Spanish, French, Austrian, and Albanian intermixture. The main foreign elements, however, in Italy are those of the original Latin basis (Kelt, Etruscan, and Greek), and those of the German superadditions.

*Sicily, &c.*—Sicily and the extreme south of Italy deserve a separate notice. By hypothesis they were originally Greek; the mother-countries of what was afterwards Hellas. They then presented the phenomenon of what we may call a reflected colonization. Colonies from the colony came back to the mother-country, establishing cities like Naxos, Gela, Syracuse, &c.,—some Doric, some Ionic. Then, or concurrently, came settlers from Africa, some Libyan, some Punic. Then came the conquest by the Romans, before which, I believe, no one imagines that Sicily was, in any respect, Latin. Between A. D. 827–878 the island was reduced by the Arabs. By the end of the eleventh century the Normans (Scandinavian and French) had established themselves. French, Catalonian, modern Greek, and Albanian elements may all be found in Sicily. Of the amount of these we can only conjecture; and that very loosely. This uncertainty gives value to the few facts that have come down to us in a numerical form. One of these is the following. When the Norman power was broken up, 60,000 Saracens (Mahometans, though not necessarily Arabs) were removed from Sicily to Nocera in the south of Italy.

Of the 19,000 actual Albanians of Sicily the details are as follows:—

| | |
|---|---|
| In Contessa . . . | 3,000 |
| — Mezzojuso . . . | 4,623 |
| — Palazzo d' Adriano . | 5,450 |
| — Piana de' Greci . . | 5,920 |
| — S. Cristina . . | 720 |
| | 19,713 |

Besides these, there are several other villages where the blood is Albanian, the language Sicilian.

Is the intercourse between the two sides of the Adriatic, which these Albanian colonies imply, recent or old? Both. Migrations from the opposite coast—migrations other than Greek—modified even the early populations of Italy. The Chaonian name was common to both sides of the Gulf. Again, the Galabri, writes Strabo, are a "people of the Dardaniatæ, in whose land is an ancient city." Word for word, Galabri is Calabri.

Without being identical, the name of the Italian Iapyges (which was to all intents and purposes another name for Calabri) is closely akin to Iapodes; so that, in Italy, we have Calabri called also Iapyges, and, in Illyria, Iapodes near a population called Galabri.

Again, the Sallentines were partly Cretans, associated with Locrians and Illyrians.

Again, the district wherein the legends concerning Diomed prevailed is also the district of the Daunii, whom Festus connects with Illyria.

I conclude the notice of Italy with the following table, which gives the foreign elements of the countries south of the Alps, along with the islands of Sicily, Sardinia, Corsica, and Malta; all of which are, more or less, Italian, though it is doubtful whether they can all be properly called Italy. Malta, for instance, is Arab in speech, English in its political relations.

AREAS.

| | Germans. | Slavonians. | French. | Wallachians. | Albanians. | Greeks. | Catalonians. | Arabs. | Jews. | Gipsies. |
|---|---|---|---|---|---|---|---|---|---|---|
| Illyria | 1,200 | 190,000 | ... | 320 | 300 | 500 | ... | ... | 3,200 | 100 |
| Lombardy | 40,000 | 20,000 | ... | ... | 50 | 600 | ... | ... | 7,630 | 60 |
| Ital. Tyrol | 5,500 | ... | ... | ... | ... | ... | ... | ... | ... | 100 |
| Sardinia | ... | ... | 78,000 | ... | ... | 100 | 8,000 | ... | 6,820 | 100 |
| Parma | ... | ... | ... | ... | ... | ... | ... | ... | 680 | ... |
| Modena | ... | ... | ... | ... | ... | ... | ... | ... | 2,710 | ... |
| Tuscany | ... | ... | ... | ... | ... | 400 | ... | ... | 7,060 | ... |
| States of the Church | ... | ... | ... | ... | ... | 150 | ... | ... | 10,090 | 80 |
| Two Sicilies | ... | ... | ... | ... | 85,551 | 18,000 | ... | ... | 2,000 | 300 |
| Tessino and Valais | 800 | ... | ... | ... | ... | ... | ... | ... | ... | ... |
| Malta | ... | ... | ... | ... | ... | ... | ... | 130,000 | ... | ... |
| Corsica | ... | ... | ... | ... | ... | 640 | ... | ... | ... | ... |
| Total | 64,724 | 210,000 | 78,000 | 320 | 85,901 | 20,390 | 8,000 | 130,000 | 40,190 | 740 |

*The German Stock.*

The German area, as it exists at the present moment, contains—

1. The Germans of the German empire, the Dutch of Holland, and a portion of the Swiss.

2. The Germans of the Baltic provinces of Russia; by which is meant Kurland, Liefland (Livonia), and Estonia.

3. The English and Lowland Scotch of the British Islands, their colonies and dependencies, and the United States of America.

4. The Danes, Norwegians, and Swedes; along with

5. The occupants of the Ferö Isles and Iceland.

Add to these detached settlements in Hungary, Italy, Russia, and elsewhere.

The most northern occupants of the German area are the Norwegians of the parts about Vardö and Hammerfest, within the Arctic Circle. The most southern are the Germans of the Sette and Tredici Commune, in Italy. The Swiss occupy the Alps. The Hollanders lie on or below the level of the sea. If we take in the English colonies, the differences in the way of latitude and climate become still stronger.

In England no spot is a hundred miles from the sea. The same may, probably, be said of Norway. In Saxony and Bohemia we have the least maritime localities in Europe.

The German populations are, to a man, Christians; there being no such a combination as a German language and a Mahometan creed. They are also Christians of the Western Church; their present alphabets being exclusively of Latin origin.

Of their original paganism, all Christian nations retain more than they care to own. The Germans, however, retain less than the Sarmatians.

The German civilization is more uniform than the Slavonic, and the literature more developed.

Of the little real self-government that exists in the world the Germans have well-nigh the monopoly. It is not, however, on the soil of Germany proper that it has its growth. It must be sought for in Norway, in Great Britain, and in the United States.

The particular forms of speech that have developed themselves into literary and national languages are the English, from the Anglo-Saxon; the Dutch of Holland; the German; the Danish (which is the literary language of Norway as well as Denmark); the Swedish; and the Icelandic,—the provincial dialects being numerous. In Germany these fall into two divisions—the Platt Deutsch (Low German) and the Hoch Deutsch (High German). The Dutch of Holland belongs to the former; the literary German to the latter. The difference between them is less marked in reality than in books. The Hessian is the most northern of the High German dialects, of which one of the extreme representatives is the Bavarian. The

Frisian of Friesland, on the other hand (unless we treat it as a separate language), belongs to the Low German division; as did the Old Saxon and the Anglo-Saxon of Hanover and Holstein, the mother-tongue of the English. The Frank of the Carlovingian period was intermediate.

The Norse, or Scandinavian languages, form a separate division. They all have a middle or passive voice. They all have a post-positive article. Thus—*jeg kalle* = *I call;* whilst *I am called* is expressed by *jeg kalles.* Also—*en sol* = *a sun. The sun* is *sol-en* (*solen*). There are other distinctions, but these are the chief.

As a general rule, the German populations call themselves by the same name that they are called by us of England, *e.g.* a Swede calls himself a Svenske; a Dane, a Danske; a Norwegian, a Nordmand; a Swiss, a Schweitzer. There is, however, one remarkable exception. The names German and Germany are foreign to the Germans proper. They know them, indeed, to a great extent, because it is generally known that Germania was the Latin for Germany. The native name, however, for themselves, is Deutsche, and, for their country, Deutschland. The French called them Allemands, from the Alemanni; the Italians, Tedesci, from Theotiscus, a Latinized form of Deutisc, or Deutsch; the Slavonians, Niemce. Meanwhile, the Germans call the Slavonians Wends. Another German name for populations other than German is Welsh, from *wealh,* meaning *a foreigner,* and, in some cases, a slave. In the eyes of the old Angles, the older populations of our island, whether Roman or British, were Welshmen, and their country Wales. In the eyes of a German proper, Italy is Welschland, and the Italians Welschmen. So are the French of the parts about Liege, being known as Walloons. It was, however, the Germans of their neighbourhood who gave the name. The Valais, or Wallis district, in Switzerland, is Welsh. Of the two Danubian Principalities, the western is named Wallachia. Wallachia, however, is no native name, but, word for word, Wales, or Welschland.

The Germans are more blonde than dark, and are, probably, the tallest and the heaviest men in the world. Clear pink and white complexions are common amongst them. In the towns, however, brown hair and dark eyes preponderate. In Friesland and Sweden the number of light-haired individuals is the greatest. Whether there is anything like purity of blood anywhere to the north of the Baltic, the east of the Elbe, the south of the Mayne, or the west of the German Ocean, is doubtful. Scandinavia was originally Fin; Britain, Keltic; the remainder Slavonic.

*The Kelts*.—With the exception of a large district between the Loire and the Pyrenees, which was Iberian, and an irregular tract along the Rhine, the whole of the ancient Gallia was Keltic. So was, part, at least, of Helvetia, or Switzerland; part, too, of Batavia, or Holland. How much of the Piedmontese Alps was Keltic is uncertain. It is only certain that, at a very early period, the Kelt frontier was advanced far into Italy; into the valley of the Po, into the valley of the Tibur. A strong case may be made out for there having been a Kelt population in Umbria, in the Sabine district, and in Samnium. Much of the blood of the Romans was Kelt; and so is much of the Latin language. The further migrations of this population into Illyria, the valley of the Danube, and Asia Minor, though generally believed in, stand on very insufficient evidence. I am satisfied that the population which gave its name to ancient Gaul was different from the one which, according to Tacitus, spoke the Gallic language in the parts about Moravia and Upper Hungary; one being Gallic, the other Gallician—as different from one another as Lithuanians and Welshmen. Isolated settlements, however, of true Gauls seem to have existed in Pannonia. Though less ubiquitous than they are generally supposed to have been, the Kelts of Gaul were a conquering and an intrusive population. The details of their settlements in ancient Spain and Portugal are obscure. The importance of those in Italy has, probably, been undervalued.

The other great Kelt occupancy was the British Isles.

The Kelts of Gaul, with the exception of a remnant in Brittany, have been first Romanized, then modified by the Goths and Franks of Germany. From the Romans they have taken their language; from the Germans the name France.

The Kelts of Britain, with the exception of the Welsh, the Manxmen of the Isle of Man, the native Irish, and the Scotch Highlanders, have, after having first been modified by the Romans, been Germanized by the Angles. In Britain both the name of the country (England) and the language is German.

The blood, however, of even the most English parts of England must needs be more Keltic than the tongue; inasmuch as the probability of any notable amount of German females having been brought over in the ships of Angles is small. At the present moment, the diffusion of Keltic blood over the domain of the English language is great; the Irish migration into America being the chief agent.

The Kelts, however, with their full and complete characteristics of language and nationality, are a fragmentary population. They fall into two branches:—

1. *The British*, represented by the Bretons of Brittany

and the Welsh. The first of these constitute the Armorican, the second the Cambrian, section; the division being chiefly philological. To the latter belonged the now extinct language of Cornwall.

2. *The Gaelic.*—This division comprises the Manxmen, the Irish Gaels, and the Scotch Gaels.

The languages of the two divisions are mutually unintelligible. All the Gaels, however, can understand each other; and, with care and attention, a Welshman may understand a Breton. To the eye, the affinity between these two languages is greatly disguised by the difference in the orthographies. So is the affinity between the Gaelic and British branches in general.

The early civilization of the Kelts of Gaul, at least, was on the comparatively high level of the Iberians of the Spanish peninsula and of the northern Italians. They dwelt in towns, cultivated the land, submitted themselves to powerful chiefs, were capable of forming alliances and organizing campaigns. The chief creed was Druidism. Of their ancient paganism they retain in their present Christianity as little as any population in Europe. Deuce, meaning the devil, is Keltic.

The Kelts of Gaul were a light rather than a dark population. At the present time there are two types. In South Wales brunette complexions and black hair are common. So they were in the time of Tacitus. So they are in Brittany. In the Scotch Highlands red or sandy hair is common. The combination of truly blue eyes and black hair, which many say is a Kelt character, I have rarely met with anywhere. Under similar conditions, there is but little difference between the Kelt and the German. In Cornwall and in North Wales, hundreds of individuals of pure Keltic blood are not to be distinguished from the men of Hanover and Holstein.

The Bretons of the British branch are Roman Catholics, the Welsh Protestants. Of the Gaels, the Manxmen are Protestant, the Scotch Highlanders more Protestant than Romanist, the Irish, Romanist.

*The Euskaldunac, or Basks.*—The western extremity of the Pyrenees, where France and Spain join, gives us a locality rendered famous by the historical events of San Sebastian and the legends of Fuentarabia, with the provinces of Bearn and Gascony on the French, and Navarre and Biscay on the Spanish, side of the mountains. Here it is where, although the towns, like Bayonne, Pampeluna, and Bilbao are French or Spanish, the country people are Basques or Biscayans—Basques or Biscayans not only in the provinces of Biscay, but in Alava, Upper Navarre, and the French districts of Labourd and Soule. Their name is Spanish (the word having originated in that of the ancient Vascones), and it is *not* the one by which they designate themselves; though, possibly, it is indirectly connected with it. The native name is derived from the root Eusk-; which becomes Eusk-ara when the language, Eusk-kerria when the country, and Eusk-aldunac when the people are spoken of; so that the Basque language of the Biscayans of Biscay is, in the vernacular tongue, the Euskara of the Euskaldunac of Euskerria.

That the Euskara is no new tongue may be inferred from the fact of its falling into dialects, which Humboldt limits to three.

*a.* The Biscayan Proper.

*b.* The Guipuscoan is the western Biscayan.

*c.* The Laburtanian is the Euskarian of France, spoken in the parts about St. Jean de Luz; and which, in the district of Soule, is supposed to fall into a subdialect.

The general name for the numerous ancient populations, occupants of Hispania and Gallia, who are, on reasonable grounds, believed to be represented by the present Basks, is *Iberic*, or *Iberian*, from the old name of the Spanish peninsula. It is in the present Bask that many of the geographical names of the ancient Iberia are significant.

## CHAPTER V.

Populations, other than Italian, speaking a Language derived from the Latin.

THE populations other than Italian, and, as such, the occupants of a soil whereof the original blood was different from that of the pure and proper Italians, but who, nevertheless, have been sufficiently Romanized to speak a language of Latin origin, are the following:—

1. *The Sardinians and Corsicans.*—The exact relations of the earliest occupants of these islands is unknown. Before the Roman conquest, Carthaginian influences had been extensively at work. Since the break-up of the Romans, Spain has told most on Sardinia, France on Corsica. The language of both islands is, however, more Italian than aught else.

2. *The Spaniards and Portuguese.*—The aborigines of the Spanish peninsula were of the Iberian family, represented, as has been stated, by the Basks. There appears also to have been certain Kelt occupants. At any rate, there is the name Celtiberi. As it was in Sardinia, so it was in Spain. Before Rome, Carthage had effected settlements. Neither were Greek elements wholly wanting. Since the Roman period, the Goths and Arabs have been the chief intruders.

The Catalonian and Valencian forms of speech are

Provençal rather than Spanish proper. The Spanish proper is the Castilian dialect. Gallicia is Portuguese in language; the Portuguese itself being remarkable for its exhibition of nasal sounds; which, wanting, for the most part, in Italian and Castilian, appear in the French.

The most Arab part of Spain is Grenada; Catalonia the most German. Andalusia is Vandalusia, the country of the Vandali Silingi or Vandals of Silesia. The remains of an Alan (and, as such, a Turk) invasion have yet to be discovered.

Next to the Italian the Castilian is the most like the Latin.

Of the Spaniards beyond the frontier of Spain, the great areas are Central and South America; then, at a long interval, the Philippine, and Marianne, and Caroline Islands.

The Portuguese are to be found in Brazil, Africa, and India, and other less important localities.

Both Spaniards and Portuguese have largely mixed their blood with that of the populations with which they have come in contact.

*The French.*—The ethnological basis in northern and central France was Keltic, in southern, Iberian. The extreme forms of speech are the Provençal dialects of the south on the one side, and the Walloon of the parts about Liege on the other. In parts of Belgium the earlier population was German. Speaking, however, generally, we may say that the French blood is Keltic and Italian; the superadded elements being chiefly German, Gothic, Frank, Burgundian, &c.

The chief occupancy of the French beyond the frontier of France is Lower Canada; after that, Algeria.

What applies to France applies, in the main, to Switzerland and Savoy; though I think that, in some of the

Alpine localities, the original population was Slavonic. Different from one another as are the French of Paris and the Italians of Rome, there are Piedmontese dialects of which the position is equivocal; so thoroughly is the French like the Italian, or (changing the expression) the Italian like the French. *Mutatis mutandis*, the same may be said of the Catalonian of Spain, and the Provençal.

*The Rumanyo of Wallachia, Moldavia, and Bessarabia.*—The name by which a Wallachian, a Moldavian, or a Bessarabian designates himself, is a name which we find, in some form or other, widely spread elsewhere, in a variety of forms, and with no slight latitude of meaning. It is the name the Gipsies give themselves; which is Rommani. It is the name of the modern Greek language; which is Romaic. It is the name of the language of the Grisons; which is Rumonsch. It is the name of the old Romance language of France. It is the name of that part of European Turkey which corresponds with ancient Thrace, and of which Constantinople is the capital, viz. Rumelia. It is the name of a large portion of Asia Minor, Roum. It is a name as honourable as it is widely spread; for wherever we find it it reminds us of the old sovereignty of Rome.

The language does the same, as may be seen from the following extracts.

1.

| RUMANYO. | LATIN. |
|---|---|
| Bela in larga valle amblà, | Puella in larga valle ambulabat, |
| Erba verde lin calcà; | Herbam viridem leniter calcabat, |
| Cantà, qui cantand plangeà, | Cantabat, et cantando plangebat, |
| Quod tóti munti resunà. | Ut omnes montes resonarent: |
| Ea in genunchi se puneà, | Illa in genua se ponebat, |
| Ochi in sus indireptà; | Oculos sursum dirigebat; |
| Ecce, asi vorbe faceà: | Ecce, sic verba faciebat: |
| Domne, domne, bune domne. | Domine, domine, bone domine. |

2.

| RUMANYO. | LATIN. |
|---|---|
| Nucu, fagu, frassinu | Nux, fagus, fraxinus, |
| Mult se certà intra sĕne. | Multum certant inter se. |
| Nuce, dice frassinu, | Nux, dicit fraxinus |
| Quine vine, nuci cullege, | Quisquis venit, nuces lĕgit, |
| Cullegend si ramuri frange : | Colligendo ramos frangit : |
| Vaide dar de pelle a tua ! | Væ itaque pelli tuæ ! |
| Dar tu fage, mi vecine, | At tu fage, mi vicine, |
| Que voi spune in mĕnte tene : | Quæ exponam mente tene ? |
| Multe fere saturasi ; | Multas feras saturasti, |
| Qui prĕbĕne nu amblasi ; | At haud bene ambulasti ; |
| Quum se au geru apropiat | Quum gelu appropinquat |
| La pament te au si culcat, | Ad pavimentum te deculcant |
| Si in focu te au si aruncat, &c. | Ad focum projiciunt. |

3.

| English. | Rumanyo. | Latin. |
|---|---|---|
| *Heaven* | ceriu | cœlum |
| *Moon* | luna | luna |
| *Mountain* | munte | mons |
| *Lake* | lacu | lacus |
| *Sea* | mare | mare |
| *Bank* | ripa | ripa |
| *River* | rivu | rivus |
| *Smoke* | fumu | fumus |
| *Spark* | schinte | scintilla |
| *Light* | lumine | lumen |
| *Shadow* | umbra | umbra |
| *Wind* | ventu | ventus |
| *Lightning* | fulger | fulgur. |

The previous specimens are in Roman letters. The Roman alphabet, however, is strange to the Rumanyos. They took their Christianity from Constantinople ; so that the creed is that of the Greek Church, and their alphabet is Slavonic, like the Servian and Russ. This is as if the Latin were written in Greek characters. Were it so, it would be (what the Rumanyo actually is) strangely disguised.

It was the legions of Trajan, and the colonies introduced by that conqueror, that carried the Latin language into the Rumanyo area, which, in the second and third centuries, was co-extensive with the ancient province of Dacia,—Romanized by Trajan; abandoned by Aurelian.

After its abandonment hordes of barbarians overran it, displacing, in some districts, the Romanized population, in others modifying it. The invaders who did this were chiefly of the Turk or Ugrian stock, Huns, Bulgarians, Avars, Petshineks, and, lastly, Magyars. Even before the time of Aurelian these foreign elements had been partially introduced. Some of the Germans of Mœsia must have been in some part of the ancient Dacia; *i. e.* on the Sereth and Pruth—not to mention the original inhabitants, who, in my mind, at least, were Lithuanic.

The Rumanyo are dark-skinned, black-haired, and black-eyed; more tall than short, with prominent features, and faces more long than round. Their resemblance to the figures on Trajan's column has either been observed or imagined. Their Christianity is still redolent of heathenism. At the head of their Pantheon stand Smou and Smeone, mother and son. Smou, the son, can change his shape, and visit men in any form he likes. He does so sometimes, and makes love to mortal maids *incognito*. His dwelling is underground. Here his mother, Smeone, keeps house for him; upon the whole, being the better disposed being of the two: for Smou, though possibly more good than bad, is fickle and odd-tempered. It is his mother who keeps him steady and good-humoured.

Smou is as much good as bad; but Balduru is a being of unmodified evil. The fens, the bogs, the rocks, the glens, and the caverns, are his residences; and when men find any of these more suspicious-looking than usual, they tremble lest Balduru should lay hold of them.

Vilva is Wallachian, and Slavonic as well; in name, wholly; in attributes, but partially. In Servia she is the dark-eyed maiden of the night, with hair black and flowing, and eyes black and bright. In Wallachia she is half-dragon and half-snake.

Sina is the Goddess of Hunting; Sina, who is also called Dina and Diana. She may safely be identified with the Latin Diana. But it is by no means so safe to derive her from Italy. The Bohemians, far beyond the influences of Rome, had also a Diana, of which the classical mythologists take too little cognizance.

The Muma padura, the mother of the woods, is more good than bad, more kind than vicious, more old than young. When children lose themselves in a forest, she protects them.

The water, like the wood, has its divinities. When the Wallachian maid fills her vessel, she pours out a spoonful or two for the water goddess.

The Morii are ghosts in general. So are the Strigoi, in Latin Strigæ. When a child is born, the bystanders throw a stone behind them, saying, *this to the Strigoi.*

The Sinit (Sanctus) is the festival to the domestic genius special to each hearth, the Lar of the Romans, with his feast-day under a Christian designation.

The Murony is the vampire, in which every Rumanyo believes.

Priccolitsh is a Murony under a modification, being, like the vampire, a bloodsucker. It is, however, horses, goats, pigs, and sheep, rather than men, that he drains. And this he does only at night, and after changing himself from his usual form of a human being into a dog. A female Priccolitsh is a Priccolitshone.

There are Wallachians beyond the boundaries of Wallachia. The Wallachian colonists, called also Kutzo-Wallachians, are to be found in three localities—

1. In the mountains between Macedonia and Albania.

2. In the Pindus range between Thessaly and Albania.
3. In the highlands between Bœotia and Albania.

There are settlers, too, in Albania, and in Italy.

The Rumanyo of Russia are as follows:—

| | |
|---|---|
| In Bessarabia | 406,182 |
| — Kherson | 75,000 |
| — Ekaterinoslav | 9,858 |
| — Podolia | 7,429 |
| | 498,369 |

In the Principalities they may amount to 2,000,000. In Transylvania they number about 900,000, being more numerous than any other population. Thus:—

| | |
|---|---|
| Rumanyos | 900,000 |
| Magyar | 700,000 |
| German | 250,000 |
| Slavonians, Greeks, Jews, Armenians, Gypsies | 206,000 |
| | 2,056,000 |

*The Swiss of the Grisons.*—The Romance of the two parallel valleys formed by the streams of the Upper Rhine and the Upper Inn is in the same category with the Rumanyo of Wallachia. It is a separate and independent derivative of the Latin.

## CHAPTER VI.

The Dioscurians, or Caucasians of Caucasus.—The Circassians.

THE mountain-range of Caucasus must not be confounded with the Government of Caucasus. Neither must it be supposed that the term Caucasian as applied to one of the primary divisions of the human species is either accurate or convenient. The moment we have to treat of the Caucasus proper, as the occupancy of a very complex population, confusion arises.

The most northern of the Caucasians proper are the natives of Circassia. In this word the first *C* should be sounded as in Italian, *i. e.* as the *ch* in *chest*. Many actually write Tsherkes, instead of Circassia, and it would be well if the practice were general. In all probability the ordinary spelling, which is purely that of an Italian, is due to the Genoese of the Crimea, who first gave currency to the name.

This is not native. It is the Russians and Turks who talk of the Tsherkes of the Circassian part of Caucasus, not the Circassians themselves.

Word for word, *Tsherkes* is *Kirgiz*. Should any one doubt this, let him learn that another Turk name, Kasak, is also applied to the Circassians.

The really native names are Adigé and Absné. By these three divisions of the Circassian population speak of themselves, and of each other. A collective name for the whole group they have not—not, at least, a native one.

*The Adigé.*—Word for word, A-dig-é is Ζήχοι, the name under which the author of the Periplus of the Euxine, written in the reign of the Emperor Hadrian, speaks of one of the tribes of the coast. In doing this, he places them east of their present locality; which is more inland, to the north of the axis of Mount Caucasus, and on the drainage of the Kuban.

The division of which the Adigé are the representatives, although now exclusively mountaineers, was once spread, more or less, over the plains to the north of the Caucasus, as well as over the hills and valleys of the great range itself. No wonder. Both Turks and Russians have encroached on their area, once larger than it is at present. More than one map of the fourteenth century carries a Circassian population from the Straits of Yenikale to the mouth of the Don, along the whole eastern coast of the Sea of Azof; and Klaproth believes that the present Kosaks of these parts are, more or less, Circassian in blood.

Equally strong is the evidence to a Circassian population in the Crimea. The upper part of the river Belbek, in the south of that peninsula, is called Tsherkes-tüs, or the Circassian plain, to this day. On it stand the remains of the Tsherkes-kyerman, or Circassian fortress. The particular division to which these Tsherkes of the Don and the Crimea belonged seems to have been that of the Kabarda tribes.

*The Kabarda.*—There is a Great and a Little Kabarda, which lie on the Terek rather than the Kuban, and slope towards the Caspian rather than the Black Sea. The patriarch, or hypothetical father, of the Kabarda tribes is Inal.

*The Absné.*—The sea-coast between Sukhumkaleh and the Straits of Yenikale, along with the valleys of the rivers that descend from the western slope of Caucasus, is the occupancy of the Absné. So they name themselves. The Georgians, however, call them Mibkhaz and Abkhazi, their country being Abkhazeti. This ending in *-eti* appears and re-appears. It is the Georgian for *-land*; so that Abkhazeti is Abkhaziland. A Persian would call it Abkhazistan. The Adigé form is Abazi, and the Adigé name for the Absné is Kushkhasip Abasi, or the Abasi beyond the Mountain, the Transalpine Abasi. That Ab-sné and Ab-azi are the same words is probable. That Abazi and Abkhazi are the Greek and Latin terms Ἄβασγοι and Abasci is evident.

The Great Abaska-land, or Abkhazeti proper, extends from the frontier of the Adigé to Mingrelia and the Suan country—both Georgian. It contains the following tribes:—

| | |
|---|---|
| Netshkwadzha | Bakh |
| Abasekh | Tshegreh |
| Bzubbeh | Kasilbeg |
| Ubukh | Barrakai |
| Tubi | Midaveh |
| Bakh | Beshilbai. |

The six tribes of the Little Abaska-land call themselves Tepanta; being called by the Adigé Baskekh, and by the Turk populations of their neighbourhood Altekezik Abasi. Some are subject to Russia; some independent.

It is in Circassia where the feudal structure of society is the most strongly marked, and where the relation between the *vorkh*, or *noble*, and the *pshi*, or *retainer*, is the closest. The Circassians, too, are most in the habit of selling their daughters to the harem-masters of Constantinople and Egypt. If a Circassian maiden stays at home, she is sold in marriage to one of her own countrymen. If shipped to Constantinople she is sold to a foreigner.

The divisions of the Circassians are pretty distinctly marked by their dialects.

| English. | Tsherkes. | Abas. | Karatshai, or Turk. |
|---|---|---|---|
| *Man* (*homo*) | dzug | agn | keshi |
| —— (*vir*) | tle | katzha | erkhek |
| *Head* | shha | kah | bash |
| *Hair* | shhats | kuakokh | zadzh |
| *Eye* | nne | ullah | gös |
| *Ear* | takumah | lemha | kulakh |
| *Nose* | peh | pintsa | burun |
| *Mouth* | dzhe | utsha | ul |
| *Tooth* | dzeh | pitz | khurt |
| *Tongue* | bsa | ibz | tish |
| *Foot* | tle | shepeh | ayakh |
| *Hand* | ia | meppe | kol |
| *Sun* | dgeh | marra | gun |
| *Moon* | masah | mis | ai |
| *Star* | vhagoh | yetshua | üldus |
| *Fire* | mapfa | mza | ot |
| *Water* | pseh | dzeh | su |
| *Stone* | mivveh | kau | tash |
| *Tree* | dzig | adzh | ayadzh |
| *One* | se | seka | bir |
| *Two* | tu | ukh-ba | iki |
| *Three* | shi | khpa | utsh |
| *Four* | ptle | pshiba | dürt |
| *Five* | tkhu | khuba | besh |
| *Six* | khi | ziba | alty |
| *Seven* | ble | bishba | yedy |
| *Eight* | ga | akhba | sekys |
| *Nine* | bgu | ishba | tokus |
| *Ten* | pshe | zheba | on. |

## CHAPTER VII.

**The Dioscurians, or Caucasians of Caucasus.—Tshetsh and Lesgians.**

I HAVE objected to the term Caucasian. The term by which I propose here, as elsewhere, to replace it is Dioscurian.

Dioscurias is the name of one of those towns of the ucasian sea-coast which is not only mentioned by ancient writers, but mentioned with reference to one of the most remarkable characteristics of modern, as it also was of ancient, Caucasus. This is the multiplicity of languages and dialects. The business, says Pliny, of Dioscurias had to be transacted through the medium of thirty interpreters. Now, the number of interpreters that would be requisite for a similar function in modern Caucasus, is undoubtedly fewer, the Turkish being pretty generally understood, and serving as a kind of *lingua franca.* Nevertheless, the actual number of separate substantive languages, dialects, and sub-dialects, is still considerable.

The distribution of these numerous Dioscurians over their several localities is difficult or easy, according to the distinctness or indistinctness of the investigator's view of the physical geography of the parts whereof they are the occupants. Of primary importance in this matter is the direction of the axis of the Caucasian range, and next to this the river-system of the Caucasian drainage.

The axis of the mountains runs from north-west to

south-east, from the mouth of the Kuban and the parts opposite the Peninsula of Kertch in the Crimea to the Promontory of Baku on the Caspian.

The drainage, therefore, is double; one portion of the rivers falling into the Black Sea and one into the Caspian.

The Black Sea influents are the Kuban, and the minor rivers Enguri, Rion, and Tshorok, running westward.

The Caspian rivers are the Terek, and, of subordinate importance, the Kuma and the Koisu.

There is, then, the double drainage; and there is, of necessity, the watershed to match. Here the two great mountains of Elbruz and Kasbeck take prominence; the former dividing the Kuban from the Terek; the latter, the Terek from the Kur.*

With these preliminaries, and with the remark that the Circassians faced the Euxine, and that the Lesgians, when we come to them, will face the Caspian, we may consider the intermediate population of the watershed; a population truly inland; truly central; a population with affinities in the way of language which connect it with both its eastern and its western neighbours.

This population is called by the Russians Tshetshents, by the Turks, Tsherkes, and by the Andi Lesgians, Mizdzhedzhi. One of their tribes is named Kisti, the Georgian name for their area being Kisteti. Guldenstadt has used this name as a general denomination for the whole group; for which he is blamed by Klaproth. The word, however, has the merit of being pronounceable, which is scarcely the case with Klaproth's choice, Mizdzhedzhi. In the opinion of the present writer, Tshetsh, the Russian word divested of its non-radical elements, is the most eligible.

The Galga, Halha, or Ingush division of the Tshetsh,

* A good view of the physical geography of Caucasus is to be found in the fifth volume of the Westminster Review, pp. 480-519.

in contact with the Circassians of the Little Kabarda, are the most western members of the group. They call themselves Lamur, or Hillmen.

The second section is called

| | |
|---|---|
| By themselves . . | *Arshte.* |
| — the Tshetshents . | *Aristoyai.* |
| — certain Turk tribes | *Kara-bulakh.* |

They occupy part of the valley of the Martan, or Fartan.

The third section is that of the Tshetsh, or Tshetshents proper, in contact with and to the east of the Arshte.

| English. | Tshetsh. | Ingush. | Tsherkes. |
|---|---|---|---|
| *Man (homo)* | steg | stag | dzug |
| —— *(vir)* | maile | mairilk | tle |
| *Head* | korte | korte | shha |
| *Hair* | kazheresh | beshkenesh | shhats |
| *Eye* | berik | berg | nne |
| *Ear* | lerik | lerk | takumah |
| *Nose* | mara | mirha | peh |
| *Mouth* | bagga | yist | dzhe |
| *Tooth* | tsargish | tsergish | dzeh |
| *Tongue* | mot | motte | bsa |
| *Foot* | kok | kog | tle |
| *Hand* | kuik | kulg | ia |
| *Sun* | malkh | malkh | dgeh |
| *Moon* | but | but | masah |
| *Star* | seta | seta | vhagoh |
| *Fire* | tze | tze | mapfa |
| *Water* | khi | khü | pseh |
| *Stone* | kera | kera | mivveh |
| *Tree* | khie | khie | dzig |
| *One* | tza | tza | se |
| *Two* | shi | shi | tu |
| *Three* | koe | koe | shi |
| *Four* | di | di | ptle |
| *Five* | pkhi | pkhi | tkhu |
| *Six* | yalkh | yalkh | khi |
| *Seven* | uor | uor | ble |
| *Eight* | bar | bar | ga |
| *Nine* | ish | ish | bgu |
| *Ten* | itt | itt | pshe. |

The Tushi lie on the upper Alasani, within, or on, the Georgian frontier. They are the only members of the Tshetsh group of whose language we know the grammatical structure; of which the following is a sketch.

The declension of the personal pronouns is as follows. With a slight modification it is that of the ordinary substantive as well.

| Singular. | I. | Thou. | He. |
|---|---|---|---|
| *Nominative* | so | ḥo | o |
| *Genitive* | sai | ḥai | ox̣u |
| —— | —— | —— | oux̣ |
| —— | —— | —— | ox̣uin |
| *Dative* | son | ḥon | ox̣un |
| —— | sona | —— | oux̣na |
| *Instructive* | as | aḥ | ox̣us |
| —— | asa | aḥa | ox̣use |
| —— | —— | —— | oux̣se |
| *Affective* | sox | ḥox | ox̣ux |
| *Allative* | sogo | ḥogo | ox̣ugo |
| —— | —— | —— | oux̣go |
| *Elative* | soxi | ḥoxi | oux̣xi |
| —— | —— | —— | ox̣xi (?) |
| *Comitative* | soci | ḥoci | ox̣uci |
| —— | —— | —— | oux̣ci |
| —— | —— | —— | ox̣ci (?) |
| *Terminative* | sogomci | ḥogomci | oux̣gomci |
| *Adessive* | sogoh | ḥogoḥ | oux̣goh |
| *Ablative* | sogrodah | ḥogredah | oux̣gore |
| —— | —— | —— | oux̣goredah. |

| Plural. | We. | | Ye. | They. |
|---|---|---|---|---|
| *Nominative* | wai | ‘txo | su | obi |
| *Genitive* | wai | ‘txai | ṡui | ox̣ri |
| *Dative* | wain | ‘txon | ṡun | ox̣arn |
| —— | —— | —— | ṡuna | —— |
| *Instructive* | wai | a‘txo | aiṡ | ox̣ar |
| —— | —— | —— | aṡi | ox̣ra |
| *Affective* | waix | ‘txox | ṡux̣ | ox̣arx |
| *Allative* | waigo | ‘txogo | ṡugc | ox̣argo |
| *Illative* | wailo | ‘txolo | ṡulo | ox̣arlo |
| *Elative* | waixi | ‘tzoxi | ṡuxi | ox̣arxi |
| *Comitative* | waici | ‘txoci | ṡuci | ox̣arci |

| Plural. | We. | | Ye. | They. |
|---|---|---|---|---|
| *Adessive* | waigoh | ‘txogoh | ṡugoḥ | oẋargoḥ |
| *Inessive* (c) | wailoh | ‘txoloḥ | ṡuloḥ | oẋarloḥ |
| *Ablative* (c) | waigre | ‘txogre | ṡugre | oẋargore |
| ——— | —— | —— | —— | oẋardah |
| *Elative* (c) | wailre | ‘txolre | ṡulre | oxarlore |
| *Conversive* | waigoih | ‘txogoih | ṡugoiḥ | oẋargoih. |

That some of these forms are no true inflexions, but appended prepositions, is speedily stated in the text.

| Cardinal. | | Ordinal. | Cardinal. | | Ordinal. |
|---|---|---|---|---|---|
| 1. | cha | duihre | 8. | barl | barloġe |
| 2. | ṡi | silġe | 9. | iss | issloġe |
| 3. | ẋo | ẋalġe | 10. | itt | ittloġe |
| 4. | ahew | dhewloġe | 11. | cha-itt | cha-ittloġe |
| 5. | ṗxi | pxilġe | 12. | si-itt | si-ittloġe |
| 6. | je'tz | jeixloġe | 19. | tqeexç | iqeeẋcloġe |
| 7. | worl | worloġe | 20. | tqa | tqalġe. |

This last word the author of the grammar connects with the word *tqo* = *also, over again* (*auch, wiederum*), as if it were 10 doubled, which it most likely is. In like manner *tqeexc* is *one from twenty* = *undeviginti* :—

100 = ṗxauztqa = 5 × 20.
200 = içatatq = 10 × 20.
300 = ṗxiiæatq = 15 × 20.
400 = tqauziq = 20 × 20.
500 = tqauziġ ṗxauztqa = 20 × 20 + 100.
1000 = sac tqauziqa icaiqa = 2 × 400 + 200.

The commonest signs of the plural number are *-i* and *-si*. The suffixes *-ne* and *-bi*, the latter of which is found in Lesgian, is stated to be Georgian in origin. No reason, however, against its being native is given.

In verbs, the simplest form is the imperative. Add to this *-a*, and you have the infinitive. The sign of the conditional is *he* or *h*; that of the conjunctive *le* or *l*.

The tenses are—

(1.) Present, formed by adding *-a* or *-u* to the root: *i. e.* to the imperative form, and changing the vowel.

(2.) Imperfect, by adding *-r* to the present.

(3.) Aorist, formed by the addition of *-r* to the

(4.) Perfect; the formation of which is not expressly given, but which is said to differ from the present in not changing the vowel. However, we have the forms *xet* = *find, xeti* = *found;* (perf.) *xetin* = *found* (aorist). From the participle of the perfect is formed the

(5.) Pluperfect by adding *-r*.

(6.) The future is either the same as the present, or a modification of it.

I give the names of those moods and tenses as I find them. The language of the Latin grammar has, probably, been too closely imitated.

The first and second persons are formed by appending the pronouns either in the nominative or the instructive form.

The participle of the present tense is formed in *-in*; as *dago* = *eat, dagu-in* = *eating.*

The participle of the preterite ends in *-no*; as *xace* = *hear, xac-no* = *heard.*

There are auxiliary verbs, and no small amount of euphonic changes, of which one, more especially, deserves notice. It is connected with the gender of nouns. When certain words (adjectives or the so-called verb substantive) follow certain substantives, they change their initial. Thus hatxleen *wa* = *the prophet is,* hatxleensi *ba* = *the prophets are,* waso *wa* = *the brother is,* wasar *ba* = *the brothers are.*

Again—naw *ja* = *the ship is,* nawr *da* = *the ships are;* bstiuno *ja* = *the wife is,* bstee *da* = *the wives are.*

This is said to indicate gender, but how do we know what gender is? The words themselves have neither form nor inflexion which indicates it. Say that instead of gender it means sex, *i. e.* that the changes in question are regulated by natural rather than grammatical characters. We still find that the word *naw* is considered feminine—feminine and inanimate. This, however, is grammatical rather than natural, sex—"das weibliche Geschlecht wird bey *unbelebten* Gegenständen auch im Plural durch *j*-, bei *belebten* durch *a* ausgedrückt." Then follow the examples just given. How, however, do we know that these words are feminine? It is submitted that the explanation of this very interesting initial change has yet to be given. It recalls, however, to our memory the practice of more languages than one, the Keltic, the Woloff, the Kafre, and several other African tongues, wherein the change is initial, though not always on the same principle.

So, also, the division of objects into animate and inanimate recalls to our mind some African, and numerous American, tongues.

Such is the notice of the first of the Mizhdzhedzhi or Tshetsh (we may say Lesgian) forms of speech of which the grammatical structure has been investigated.

*The Lesgians.*—The Lesgian rivers fall into the Caspian. Daghestan and parts of Tabasseran are Lesgian. The drainage of the Koisu and Terek is, more or less, Lesgian. The Eastern Caucasians are chiefly Lesgian, the Western being chiefly Circassians.

The Lesgian area reaches the Persian districts of Shirvan, so that we find it spoken under the Persian name Lesgistan, or country of the Lesgians. *Lesgian* itself is believed to be, word for word, the Greek Λῆγαι. The Georgian form is Lekhi, the Iron Leki, the Armenian Leksi and Leker. Again, one Lekos, the fifth son of Targamos, is, according to the Georgian account, the eponymus of the Lesgian tribes. He dwelt between Derbend and Tarki.

Daghestan, Lesgistan, or the country of the Lesgi, is the ancient Albania; the country conquered by Pompey.

Lesgian, like Circassian, is no native name; for the Lesgians, like the Circassians, have no name which is at once native and collective. Its details are to be found in the hilly country out of which the rivers of Daghestan arise, the actual coast of the Caspian being Turk and Persian rather than Lesgian. It has been already stated that the Kara-kaitak are actual Turks. The rivers that most help us in our topography are the Aksu on the north-west, a feeder of the Terek, the Koisu on the north-east, falling into the Caspian (both with Turk names), and the Samar, to the south of Derbend.

*The Marul division.*—In the watershed between the Aksu and Koisu (Turkish terms) lie the tribes of the Marulat. Word for word, Marulat, the plural of Marul, from Mehr a hill, is the Greek Μάνραλοι. The Marulat tribes are—

| | |
|---|---|
| Khunsag | Burtuna |
| Kaseruk | Anzukh |
| Hidatle | Tebel |
| Mukratle | Tumurga |
| Ansokul | Akhti |
| Karakhle | Rutul |
| Gumbet | Tshari |
| Arrakan | Belakan. |

The Andi and Kabutsh are outlying members of this group. So are the Dido and Unso, whose districts lie as far south as the upper Samur.

*The Kasi-kumuk* lie to the east of the Koisu, in the Kara-kaitak district, and in part of Tabasseran.

*The Akush.*—The Akush and Kubitsh lie between the Koisu and the upper Manas and the Buam.

*The Kura*—In South Daghestan.

The Lesgians are called

| | | |
|---|---|---|
| By the Circassians | . | *Hannoatshe.* |
| —— Tshetsh | . . | *Sueli.* |

The Turk character of some of the names of their tribes is remarkable. It is probable that in the last part of the term Karakle (of which Hiddalte and Mukratle may be variations) we have the Turk *oglu* = *son*. Burtuna, though the name of a river, is, apparently, Turk. Tshari is decidedly so. One of the Tshulym tribes are so named. But the most important name is Chunsag, the name of the Cumanian Turks of Hungary, whose district now bears that name. Between the Danube and Theiss lie the Great and the Little Chunsag, *i. e.* the Great and Little Cumania. Hungary was once an occupancy of the Avars; of the Avars who came from the Russian Government of Caucasus; allied to the Alans, allied to the Cumanians, allied to a population mentioned but rarely, but still mentioned as being both Caucasian in its geography and Turk in its ethnology—the Savir (Σάβειροι). Now one of the terms applied to the Marul Lesgians, adopted by Klaproth, but pretermitted by the present writer because it appears to be other than native, is Avar; whilst the name by which the Suani, who also call the Karatshai Ows (As), designate the Iron is Sawiar. I think that some of the Dioscurians are Turks who have unlearned their language.

| English. | Avar. | Antshukh. | Tshari. | Andi. |
|---|---|---|---|---|
| *Man (homo)* | bâhardzh | tshi | tshi | —— |
| —— *(vir)* | tshi | bahartsh | bahartsh | heka |
| *Head* | beter | beter | beker | mier |
| *Hair* | sab | sab | sab | zirgi |
| *Eye* | beer | —— | beer | kharko |
| *Ear* | een | in | een | hanka |
| *Nose* | khomag | khumug | mushush | mahar |

| English. | Avar. | Antshukh. | Tshari. | Andi. |
|---|---|---|---|---|
| *Mouth* | kaal | kaal | kaal | kol |
| *Tooth* | sibi | sibi | sibi | solvol |
| *Tongue* | maats | maats | maats | mits |
| *Foot* | pog | pog | pog | tshcka |
| *Hand* | kwer | kwor | kwer | kazhu |
| *Sun* | baak | baak | baak | mitli |
| *Moon* | moots | moots | moots | horts |
| *Star* | zoa | zoa | zabi | za |
| *Fire* | tsa | tsa | tsa | tsa |
| *Water* | htlim | htlim | khim | tlen |
| *Stone* | itso | teb | khezo | hinzo |
| *Tree* | guet | —— | —— | tketur |
| *One* | zo | zo | hos | zev |
| *Two* | kigo | kigo | kona | tshego |
| *Three* | shabgo | tavgo | khabgo | khlyobgu |
| *Four* | ukgo | ukkgo | ukhgo | boogu |
| *Five* | sugo | shogu | shugo | inshtugu |
| *Six* | antgo | antlo | ankhgo | ointlgu |
| *Seven* | antelgo | antelgo | antelgo | ot'khkhlugu |
| *Eight* | mitlgo | mitlgo | mikgo | beitlgu |
| *Nine* | itshgo | itsgo | itshgo | hogotshu |
| *Ten* | anntsgo | antsgo | anzgo | khotsogu. |

| English. | Dido. | Akush. | Kasi Kumuk. |
|---|---|---|---|
| *Man (homo)* | —— | murgul | viri |
| —— *(vir)* | tsekvi | adim | tshu |
| *Head* | tkin | bek | bek |
| *Hair* | kodi | ashme | tshara |
| *Eye* | ozurabi | uhli | ya |
| *Nose* | mali | kank | mai |
| *Mouth* | haku | moli | sumun |
| *Tooth* | kitsu | tsulvo | kertshi |
| *Tongue* | mets | limtsi | maz |
| *Foot* | rori | kash | dzan |
| *Hand* | retla | kak | kua |
| *Sun* | buk | beri | barkh |
| *Moon* | butsi | baz | bars |
| *Star* | tsa | zuri | tsuka |
| *Fire* | tsi | tsa | tsha |
| *Water* | htli | shin | tshin |
| *Stone* | gul | kaka | tsheru |
| *Tree* | gurushed | kalki | mursh. |

## CHAPTER VIII.

The Dioscurians, &c.—The Georgians.—The Lazi.

THE most northern, and at the same time the rudest, of the Georgian populations, are the descendants of the Suani, lying inland, on the south-eastern frontier of the Absné Circassians, at the head-waters of the Zkhenistz-khali, Eguri, and Egrisi, between Sukhumkaleh and the Phasis. They call

| | |
|---|---|
| Themselves | *Suan.* |
| The Abkhas | *Mibkhaz.* |
| — Kartuelians | *Mkarts.* |
| — Mingrelians | *Mimrel.* |
| — Karatshai | *Ows.* |
| — Iron | *Sawiar.* |

The last two names, as has been shown, are important instruments of ethnological criticism.

*The Mingrelians.*—Like the Circassians, the Mingrelians face the Euxine, belonging to the drainage of the Phasis; the upper portion of which is

*Imeritian.*—Imerethi is the land of Imer, or Iber; word for word, the ancient Iberia. To the east of Imerethi lies the watershed of the Phasis and Kur, the occupancy of the

*Kartuli, Kartueli,* or *Kartulinian* branch of the Georgians. The Kartueli form of speech is the Georgian of

Tiflis; the Georgian of the literature and alphabet. It is also the dialect of Kakheti, and, according to Klaproth, of Imereti as well.

*Guriel* is connected, in the way of dialect, with Mingrelia, being, probably, transitional to the speech of that principality and

*Lazistan*, or the country of the Lazi. This extends along the sea-coast, from the parts about Batúm, at the mouth of the Tsorok, to Rizeh, east of Trebizond—perhaps further. Inland it extends over the country between Kars and the Black Sea. Its exact boundaries, however, are not known.

The Lazi are subject to Turkey, and are Mahometan in creed. The other Georgians are Christians, according to the Church of Armenia, and subject to Russia. Like some of the Tsherkes, the Lazi were originally Christian; their conversion having been effected about the seventh century. Even now, they abstain, to a great extent, from polygamy.

It is well known that the physical appearance of at least two of the Dioscurian populations, has been highly extolled, and that models of manly strength and female beauty are sought in the proverbially fine populations of Georgia and Circassia.

There is some exaggeration here. As compared with their neighbours on the side of Russia—as compared with their neighbours on the side of Turkey, the populations under notice are handsome and well-formed; and, as there is a vast traffic in female slaves for the harems of the Ottoman Turks, the best samples of the two populations find their way to Europe. From these the rest is judged. Again, the Circassian warriors represent the Caucasians of the north-west; and it is upon them that our ideas of the Circassian conformation are based. But Circassia (and this must be borne in mind) is a land of castes—of high-caste nobles and of low-caste plebeians. It is a land of caste and feudalism; war being, at one and the same time, the occupation of the nobles, and the means by which the greatest number of individuals are brought in contact with the nations of Europe. The evidence of those who have formed their opinions from residence in Caucasus rather than from the slave-markets of Constantinople is by no means over-favourable. Pallas, as quoted by Prichard, writes that the men, "especially amongst the higher classes, are mostly of a tall stature, their form being of Herculean structure. They are very slender about the loins, have small feet, and uncommon strength in their arms. They possess, in general, a truly Roman and martial appearance. The women are not uniformly Circassian beauties; but are, for the most part, well-formed, have a white skin, dark-brown hair, and regular features." He adds, "I have met with a greater number of beauties among them than in any other unpolished nation."

This is the language of fair and moderate encomium. Reineggs, however, so far denies their claim to superior beauty, as to write that he knows not "what can have given occasion to the generally-received prejudice in favour of the female Tcherkessians. A short leg, a small foot, and glaring red hair, constitute a Tcherkessian beauty."

The main *differentiæ*, however, of their organization lie in the statements of Klaproth—viz., that they have "long faces, and thin and straight noses."

Again, he writes that the Abassians, a tribe of the Circassians, are "distinguished by narrow faces; heads compressed at the sides; by the shortness of the lower part of their faces; by prominent noses, and dark brown hair."

A few of the Georgians proper are Mahometans; but they are scarcely the Georgians of Georgia. They are those of Abbasabad in Khorasan, where they were settled as colonists by Shah Abbas. A few of these only adhere to their original faith.

## CHAPTER IX.

The Dioscurians, &c.—The Iron.

THE distinction between the name by which a population designates itself, and the name by which it is designated by its neighbours, always important, is of pre-eminent consequence in the ethnology of the Iron; as was suggested when the Alans, or Osi, were under notice.

The population which now commands our attention calls itself Iron; but is called by the Georgians Osi. This name the Russians have adopted; so that, in their eyes, the Iron are Asetinzi, or men of Ose*thi* = Osi-*land*.

The population which the Greeks, Arabs, and Italians called Alan, called themselves As. They settled on the Georgian side of the Iron country, or (perhaps) on the Iron side of Georgia. They, probably, adopted, more or less, the Iron language, so as to appear, in the eyes of the Georgians, Iron; the actual Iron appearing as Osi. At any rate, Osi (as has been stated) is the Georgian name for the Iron; though by no means the native one.

By a blunder (for it is no less), excusable only because it is common, Klaproth identifies the two terms, and, by treating the Iron as if they were actually Osi or As, transfers much of the real, and some of the supposed, history of Alania, Bellad-Allan, or Alanland, to Iron-istan, or the country of the Iron. He also gives undue prominence to the foreign, or wrong, name; telling us, indeed, that it is other than native, but, nevertheless, using it as the ordinary denomination. Doing this, he has given currency to an exceptionable appellation.

The following is Klaproth's doctrine :—

> The Osset are the Yas of the Russians;
> ——————— As or Alan;
> ——————— Medes of Sarmatia;
> ——————— Medes of Herodotus.

Be it so. That the Osset are the Yas and As is true. But what is the evidence to their being Iron?

The Mede affinity rests on a different basis, *i. e.* that of the native name, which is, doubtless, a very interesting one. Iran is a name for Persia. The title of the Sassanian kings, as deduced from both coins and inscriptions, is *Malka Malkani Irân*, or Kings of the Kings of Iran, *Malka Irân wa Aniran*, or King of Iran and Not-iran. Whether the Iranian element of the Sassanian empire was Median or not, is another question.

I can give but little information concerning the Iron. Their language, of which there is a dictionary by Sjogren in Russian characters, falls into at least two dialects, one of which is the Dugorian. The people are Christian, and to a great extent Russianized. The great military road runs through their country, which lies to the north of Tiflis. In his account of Caucasus, Haxthausen gives several Iron legends. They do not, however, illustrate either a pagan or a heroic age.

## CHAPTER X.

### The Haik or Armenians.

THE name by which the Armenians are known in Europe is, I think, of Syrian origin. The populations to which it is applied call themselves Haik. Their chief occupancies are the Turkish province of Erzeroum, and the Russian district of Erivan, this being a new accession to the Russian empire; having, till lately, belonged to Persia. It is in Erivan where the chief monastery, Etshmiazin, the residence of the patriarch, lies. In Erivan also stands Mount Ararat, the centre round which the legends and superstitions of Armenia most especially collect themselves. The chief town, however, is Erzeroum. Here the native population assimilates itself in dress and manners to the Osmanli Turks; from whom the Armenians differ in language (though most of them can speak Turkish) and creed.

The Armenians are a pre-eminently Christian nation, with a native alphabet, a canon containing several books which the Western Church considers apocryphal, a ritual more Greek than Latin, and a system of monasteries that reminds us of the Buddhism of Tibet.

The influence of Armenia upon the world's history has been inconsiderable; limited, very nearly, to the neighbouring country of Georgia. The land itself has had periods of independence and even power. As a general rule, however, its political relations have been those of Persia. At present, as has been stated, they are Persian, Turk, and Russian.

But there are Armenians beyond the limits of Armenia. There is a colony in Persia near Isfahan, founded by Shah Abbas, the founder of the Georgian colony in Khorasan. There are Armenians in India, and many thousands in Constantinople. In *European* Russia their census is as follows:—

| | | |
|---|---|---|
| In the Government of | Astrakan . . . | 5,272 |
| ———————— | Bessarabia . . | 2,353 |
| ———————— | Ekaterinoslav . | 14,931 |
| ———————— | St. Petersburg . | 170 |
| ———————— | Stauropol. . . | 9,000 |
| ———————— | Tauris. . . . | 3,960 |
| ———————— | Kherson . . . | 1,990 |
| | Total . . . | 37,676 |

But the most important settlement is that of the Mechitarist monks on the island of St. Lazarus, in Venice. Here is the centre of the Armenian literature; with its library, rich in MSS., some published, some unpublished. Nine-tenths of the Armenian compositions that appear in print proceed from this Venetian press.

In figure the Armenians are more massive than the Persians. They have been likened to the Jews, the Turks, and the Afghans.

In the towns they show great commercial aptitude, and, with the Jews and the Parsis, both more or less strangers to the countries to which they naturally belong, may be classed amongst the communities who more especially attach themselves to the business of the banker and merchant, rather than the soldier, sailor, or agriculturist. In Armenia, however, they cultivate the soil, which is sub-Alpine in character. Erzeroum lies between 6000 and 7000 feet above the level of the sea.

Their language has been considered to be what is called

Indo-European, on, however, insufficient grounds. Its nearest affinities are what its geography suggests, *i. e.* with the Iron and Persian, and (more remotely) with the Arabic on the south, and the Ugrian dialects on the north. At the same time it is by no means closely connected with anything.

| English. | Armenian. | Iron. | Georgian. |
|---|---|---|---|
| *Man (homo)* | mart | moi | katsi |
| —— *(vir)* | air | lag | kmari |
| *Head* | klukh | ser | tavi |
| *Hair* | hyer | dzikku | tma |
| —— | lav | —— | —— |
| —— | mas | —— | —— |
| *Eye* | agn | tsaste | tvali |
| —— | atsk | —— | —— |
| *Nose* | untsh | findzh | tshkhwiri |
| —— | kit | —— | —— |
| *Mouth* | pyeran | dzug | piri |
| *Ear* | ungn | khus | kuri |
| —— | agantsh | —— | —— |
| *Beard* | morusk | botso | tsveri |
| —— | —— | rikhi | —— |
| *Blood* | ariyun | thuh | sizkhli |
| *Tooth* | adamn | dendag | khbili |
| *Hand* | dzyern | kukh | kheli |
| *Foot* | wot | kakh | phekhi |
| *Tongue* | tyesu | awsag | ena |
| *Heart* | zird | zerde | guli |
| *Sun* | aryev | khor | mse |
| *Moon* | luzin | mai | mtware |
| *Star* | azdegh | stal | varzklavi |
| *Fire* | hur | sing | tsetskhli |
| —— | grag | —— | —— |
| *Water* | tshur | dun | tzkhali |
| *Snow* | ziun | mit | towli |
| *Stone* | khar | dor | kwa |
| *Hill* | sar | khogh | mta |
| *Fish* | tsugn | kef | tevsi. |

Before their conversion, the Armenians were, more or less, fire-worshippers. In the eighth and ninth centuries Nestorianism took strong root amongst them, and many are Nestorians now. Some are Roman Catholics. One of the oldest translations of the Scriptures is in the Armenian. So is more than one work of the fifth, sixth, seventh, and eighth centuries; the history of Moses of Chorene being the chief. As may be expected, the language of these compositions is very different from the Armenian of the present time, with which many Turk elements are incorporated.

## CHAPTER XI.

The Semitic Populations.—The Arabians.—Syrians.—Samaritans

I NOW make a somewhat sudden transition, and prepare myself to give a sketch of the ethnology of south-western Asia and Africa, before I consider the remaining populations of Asia, viz. the Persian and the Indian.

*The Semitic group.*—A certain group of populations, currently believed to have been the descendants of Shem rather than of either Ham or Japhet, were called by (I believe) Eichorn, Semitic. They spoke languages all but mutually intelligible. They were on the confines of Africa; but they were not Negro. They were, in respect to their physiognomy and their influence on the world's history, what is called Caucasian rather than Mongolian. They formed a natural group. Whether it were a large one is a different question. In biblical criticism they were all important. Their language was that of the Old Testament, the Talmud, and the Syrian fathers. It was, in another form, that of the Koran. In other words, it was the language of the Judaic portion of Christianity, and of the primary source of Mahometanism. It was also the language of the earliest alphabet of Phenicia and the Punic colonies. It fell into the Aramæan, the Arabic, and the Æthiopic divisions. The Aramæan contained the Hebrew, the Samaritan, the Chaldee, and the Syriac of Edessa, Palmyra, Damascus, and other important and interesting cities. It was written when Greece and Rome were unlettered. It sounded strange to the Africans of the parts about Carthage, strange on the shores of many a Mediterranean island, strange in Spain. It was the language of enterprising merchants, bold mariners, monotheist priests. It was as much (and more) the language of the proper historian as of the ethnologist. Yet, like the Latin and the Greek, it will draw but little attention to the details of the men who spoke it—little in the present work. The present work is descriptive rather than historical. It is descriptive rather than historical because it deals with the existing rather than the by-gone state of things. It takes the populations of the world as it finds them; noticing them more or less fully in order that the description may serve as a basis for a certain amount of palæontological research. It relegates the earlier periods of their history to the civil historian. It does more. It passes *sicco pede* over the families which are supposed to be generally known. How little it said about the Greeks; how little about the Romans, the Slavonians, the Germans!

The present work says next to nothing about the Jews. It fails to find them as a pure Jewish population on Jewish soil. It finds them spread over many countries, and the writer of it believes that, in a general way, their history and distribution is understood. Of the Chaldee name the briefest notice would have to be preceded with pages and pages of preliminary criticism. The Samaritans it recognizes as the occupants of a single district. The Syrians are *eo nomine* and *eâ linguâ* nearly in the same category.

*The Arabians.*—The influence of the Arabian family upon the world's history, anterior to the time of Mahomet, is hard to ascertain. It appears, however, to have been far from inconsiderable. The notices in Scripture suggest the likelihood of the tribes of the Desert, at least, having been much what they are at present; saving, of course, the fact of their being pagans rather than Mahometans. They were independent and predatory. They were probably occupants of some districts in Ægypt; of some in Syria; of some in Persia. As a seafaring population they were known but little. The Mediterranean was the highway of the Greeks and the Phenicians; and the nature of both its trade and its colonies is well understood. Not so the details of the commerce with India and the eastern coast of Africa. The Indian Ocean and the Red Sea may have been traversed by fleet after fleet of adventurous Arabs; and yet no record has come down to us telling us what countries they visited, or with what populations they mixed their blood. That there was some maritime enterprize amongst the Arabians of the southern part of the peninsula is certain. How early it exhibited itself, and how far it went, is another question. It is assuredly unsafe to assume that the Arabs were exclusively a population of landsmen. They are not so now. They were not so at the beginning of the historical period.

Their early religion was what is called Sabæanism; the cultus of the heavenly bodies being its chief characteristic. It was, however, by no means free from idolatry; nor is it certain that it was the creed of the whole peninsula. Neither can we say what it borrowed from, or what it gave to, the neighbouring countries, *e. g.* Ægypt, Æthiopia, Chaldæa, Mesopotamia, Judæa, and Persia. In all these regions there are traces of influences from Arabia anterior to the time of Mahomet. With Mahomet, however, begins the æra of the Arab conquests, the Arab creed, Arab science, Arab literature. Before the time of the Prophet there were letters in Arabia. Before his time there was a partial amelioration of the original paganism; there was an incipient Christianity. The field, however, was narrow; and there was but little of what was Arab beyond the frontiers of Arabia—little compared with what there has been since.

At the present moment the Arabic alphabet is in use amongst all Mahometan nations; being that of the Turks, the Persians, the Malays, a portion of the Indians, and some of the Africans—some even of the Negroes, some even of the Negroes of America. It was not, however, indigenous to Arabia; but, on the contrary, of Syrian origin—as was much of the early Arab literature.

The Arab family is all but absolutely Mahometan. There were, however, Mahometan Slavonians in Bosnia; and, in a like exceptional manner, there are Christian Arabs in Malta. At any rate, the language of that island is Arabic.

The physical influence of the Arab stock upon the populations beyond Arabia is to be found in the history of the early conquests of the Prophet and his successors. It gives us, however, but a part of the whole; though it carries us as far as the Pyrenees on one side and beyond the Indus on the other. The actual range of either the Arab creed or the Arab commerce extends farther—farther by far. As far as twelve degrees, south latitude, Arab trade has advanced in Africa. There are Arab settlements in Bokhara and Khorasan. There are Arab habits and Arab letters in and beyond the Malayan Peninsula. Arab coins of the Caliphat have been dug up in large quantities in Siberia. The Mammoth of the Lena is, word for word, the Behemoth of the Nile.

There are several principles upon which the great mass of the Arab family, as it exists at present, may be divided. There is the difference between the Christians and the Mahometans; the former, as has just been stated, being extremely exceptional, and probably mixed in blood. Then there are the numerous forms of Mahometanism itself, some old, some new. There is the old schism between the Sunnites and the Shiites; the majority of the Arabs being Sunnite—not, however, exclusively. The sporadic intercurrence of Shiites exhibits itself on the very soil of Arabia, and in the very city of the Prophet. Then there is the modern sect of the Wahabis, puritans, and reformers, numerous in northern and eastern Arabia, numerous beyond the confines of Arabia.

In the way of politics, there are the Arabs of an organized government like that of the Imâm of Muskat, the Arabs of the sea-port town of Dzhidda, who are tributary to the Porte, the nominally dependent Arabs of Ægypt, the actually independent tribes of the Desert. Socially, there are the Arabs of the towns, who are mercantile rather than agricultural; the Arabs of the villages, who are fellahs or cultivators; the Arabs of the sea-coast, who are fishers; and the Bedawy, or Bedúins, who are spread over the Desert—sheep-breeders, camel-breeders, breeders of horses, warriors, robbers.

Lastly, there are the Arabs of the Arabian peninsula, and the Arabs of the parts beyond Arabia,—*i. e.* Syria, Palestine, Persia, Ægypt, Barbary, and many other countries; wherein, however, the population is less important, the characteristics more uncertain, the blood less pure. Such, amongst others, are Spain and India, along with Sumatra, and more than one other island of the Indian Archipelago.

Those travellers who have gone most minutely into the details of the geography of the peninsula and the genealogies of the Arab tribes, lay considerable stress upon a distinction, which, though it may possibly be real, is certainly different from the form in which it is usually exhibited. The Arabs of the south differ from the Arabs of the north, the former being the descendants of

Kahtan rather than Adnan, the latter being the descendants of Adnan rather than Kahtan. Meanwhile, Adnan is of the blood of Ishmael; whilst Kahtan is, word for word, the biblical Yoktan. Adnan, too, is akin to Yarab. This implies that the most Arab elements of the Arabian stock are those of the north. Be this as it may, the histories of the two regions are different. Of the northern Arabs the blood is that of the tribes allied to the Nabatheans and Idumeans, the social and political relations being with Syria, Palestine, Persia, and Ægypt. To South Arabia belonged the important empire of the Himyarites, or Homerites, occupants of a double line of coast; a line which on one side faced Æthiopia, and, on the other, fronted the Indian Ocean. India and Abyssinia are, or were, to the Kahtanians what Assyria and the Holy Land were to the Ishmaelites. Further notices, however, of this difference will appear as we proceed.

It is convenient to begin with the northern branch, the particular district in which it is first noticed being—

*Nedzhd.*—Nedzhd is Central Arabia. The frontier town, however, of even Central Arabia is treated by the writer who has best described it as Syrian, *i. e.* as belonging to the Syrian Desert. Algawf, writes Wallin, is sometimes called Bab el Nedzhd, or the Gate of Nedzhd, being the first place in that district. Its architecture is Syrian. The physiognomy of the population is Syrian. The intercourse with Syria is great. We have a full account of Algawf's very remarkable constitution. It consist of twelve quarters, or *suk*, each *suk* being divided and subdivided. Thus Algharb (a suk) has its six sections. Of three of these the chief occupants are Shammar Arabs of the tribe Hamúlet Almunâsibe. The inhabitants of a fourth were originally Ruwala nomads of the Eneze tribe; those of the fifth, Sirhan Bedúins.

Artisans from all parts of Syria and Arabia occupy the sixth. In Súk Ibn Alder the population is mixed, but the main tribe is an old one. It came from the S.E., *i. e.* from the Shakra. Gubbé lies between Shakra and Algawf. On the way the Shakra migrants seem to have passed through Gubbé. At any rate, a few families, older than the rest, profess a Gubbé origin. And the Gubbé people believe that their Algawf offset is in possession of certain old books in an unknown language. Two other *suks* are Syrian. In Khadma the blood is Bedúin, and the habits as nomad as residence in a town allows them to be. Ten families, the Mutawalladin, are more or less African. Algarawy consists of four families of artisans; Shammar in origin. Who founded Algawf? Soliman, the son of David, 800 years (*sic*) after the birth of Christ. This prominence of Solomon belongs to Northern rather than Southern Arabia. Every quarter has its own head, who decides differences. The sovereignty, however, is with the Shammar chief, to whom they pay tribute; as they do to the Bedúin sheiks of the parts around. At present the Algawf people are Wahabi. In the time of Mahomet they were Christians, Jews, and pagans. The evidence in favor of their having been the first is the strongest. The worship of an idol named Wud (love), is the fact from which (if real) we infer their paganism. Such are details of one town in Central Arabia. They serve to illustrate the general character of the others. The division into *suk* is common, though so many as twelve is a rarity.

The Dzhebel Shammar, or the Hills of the Shammar, are the occupancy of the most important tribes of the Nedzhd, bigoted Wahabis, but ignorant. The Alabde and Algafar are the chief tribes of the Shammar name on Shammar land. Two other, however, of its great divisions are occupants of a large district beyond the bounds of Arabia. There are the Sufuk and Alzakarit, with their sections and subsections, in Mesopotamia.

Even in Shammar, the present occupants are anything but aboriginal. The Beni Tamar, builders of cities now in ruins, in Syria as well as in Nedzhd, belong to the oldest stratum of the population; if, indeed, they be real. Then there is a local legend which derives the names of the two Shammar mountains, Aga and Selma, from two Amalekite lovers. Then there is the possibly historical account of two invasions; one from the Adnanian Hedzhaz which introduced the extinct Beni Asad and the existing Beni Temim as intrusive occupants into Nedzhd, and, after them, from Kahtanian Yemen, the Beni Tay and the true Shammar. If all this be true, there must be much intermixture, the elements being Adnanian and Kahtanian, not to mention those supplied by the aborigines. The Beni Temim represent the Adnanians. They occupy, to the amount of about 500 families, the largest village in the district; along with a few smaller ones. By certain "peculiarities of manner, appearance, and language," (what are they?) "they are easily distinguished" from the Shammar. They are agricultural and peaceful rather than nomad and warlike.

*The Hedzhaz.*—The Arabs of the Hedzhaz are the children of Adnan rather than the children of Kahtan.

The Arabs of Mekka and Dzhidda, the Mekkawy and the Dzhiddawy, notwithstanding the importance of their occupancies, are, by no means, to be considered as fair samples of their family. They are pre-eminently a mixed population; African, Turk, or Persian in blood, Arab in creed and language. As far, however, as a really native population exists, it is inconsiderable; belonging to the Bedúin tribes of the neighbourhood, converted into settlers. In the time of Mahomet the first of these was that of the Koreish; and of Koreish families, real or supposed, some few are still to be found. The Mekkawy tattoo their faces; the mark that they use being a sign of their origin. The Mekkawy skin is darker, and the Mekkawy figure somewhat lighter and more wiry than that of the men of Medina. In Medina, however, the population is mixed also; the representatives of the true Arab stock being the members of the Ocos, Kezredzh, and Beni Hossein tribes; the latter being Shias rather than Sunnites. Another section of the Medina Arab is called Khalifyi; being descended from the Abassides. In the other towns of the west coast, Mokha excepted, where the foreign intermixture is considerable, the blood is comparatively pure. It is, as a general rule, that of the neighbouring Bedúins, converted into settlers.

*Southern Arabia—Yemen, Hadramaut, Oman.*—The Arabs of Southern Arabia are the occupants of that favoured part of the peninsula known to the ancients as Arabia Felix. They are in contact with the Indian Ocean as well as the Red Sea. They are divided by a *minimum* amount of water from the Abyssinian part of Africa. They are opposite to a considerable portion of the Somauli coast. They are the children of Kahtan.

More or less Himaryite, or Homarite, in blood, history, and civilization, they are occupants, at the present time, of Mokha, Sana, Rodda, and Loheia, as townsmen, and of the southern third of the peninsula as Bedúins.

There are hilly districts in the Kahtanian area, and the Arabs of the hills are intermediate in character to the Arabs of the town and the Arabs of the Desert; rude in manners, and ignorant in respect to the details of their creed. The formula "there is but one God, and that Mahomet is his prophet," contains their whole doctrine. Of these tribes, a few out of many arrest attention. The Merekede, a branch of the Asyr, are accused of the habit attributed to the Jakuri Hazaras, *i. e.* that of prostituting their wives. Of the Beni Kelb, strange stories are believed in respect to their rudeness and the inarticulate character of their language. They bark like dogs (*Kelb*) rather than talk. They probably use an extreme dialect. The Dowâsêr are blacker than their neighbours. The Beni Yam, like the Beni Hossein, are mixed in creed, the Bedúin families being Sunnite, the settlers Shia.

Aden, the first town on the Indian Ocean, and now a British possession, has a mixed population. It was once a Turk occupancy. It contains Jews, Banians (from India), Somaulis, and other Africans. The Jews, to the amount of about 300, occupy a separate quarter, are artizans, are carriers, are labourers, but not soldiers. The tribes of the parts around are the Futhali (robbers), the Bareiki, the Beni Nayi, the Beni Dummiri, the Kaseidi, the Beni Goseidi, the Mahudi, and, further inland, the Dzhaffa, the Heshed, and the Bekeyl to the east of Sana.

Further to the east, on the sea-coast, at least, and for the parts about the town of Makulla, the physiognomy changes, and the men are black and undersized, almost as black and far shorter than the Somauli, who, at Makulla, are numerous. Makulla is the port of Hadramant, a valley some sixty miles in length, running parallel with the coast, with numerous towns and villages, ruins and inscriptions. The tribes further to the east are those of Mahara, Ad, and Amelik. At Hasek is the tomb of the prophet Hud, the fourth in descent from Shem. To the back of Hasek lie the Mahrah and Gara tribes, whose language is believed to bear a special affinity to the language of the Himyarite inscriptions.

| English. | Mahari. | Socotran. |
|---|---|---|
| *Back* | dara mothan | tadah |
| *Belly* | djof | —— |
| *Cow* | bakarôt | —— |
| *Donkey* | heir | —— |
| *Eyebrow* | ahajor | hajhar |
| *Fire* | sheewot | sheiwat |
| *Father* | heb | —— |
| *Fish* | seit | sodah |
| *Frog* | dthafzat | —— |
| *God* | bal | —— |
| *Hair* | shof | shif |
| *Knee* | barak | —— |
| *Milk* | ishakhof | huf |
| *Month* | warak | —— |
| *Nose* | nakhrir | nahir |
| *Red* | aufar | aufer |
| *Rice* | hiraz | arhaz |
| *Rope* | keiood | ket |
| *Sword* | shakee | ashko |
| *Sun* | heiom | shohum |
| *Star* | kabkob | kokab |
| *White* | âllabon | lebhem. |

Further east lie the Diyabi occupancies; the occupancies of a group of tribes or sub-tribes. Their government is patriarchal. Instead of Sheiks they have Abu, or elders, whose office is, for the most part, hereditary, but whose power is only what the voice of the majority in their meetings for the discussion of business allows. There are seven of these Abu to the Diyabi. There would be but one Sheik. For all thefts within his district the Abu is answerable, and, if the thief cannot, the Abu must, make reparation to the parties injured. If, however, the thief have property, the Abu claims a third of it over and above the amount restored.

It was through the Diyabi country that Lieut. Welsted

passed on his journey to the ruins of Nakeb el Hadzhar. The Arabs referred them to their pagan ancestors. "Do you believe," said one, "that these stones were raised by the unassisted hands of the Kaffirs? No! no! they had devils, legions of devils, to aid them." Wall inscriptions in a similar character were found at Hasan Gorab. There, however, they were ascribed to the Feringees (Franks).

From Cape Isolette, eastwards, dwell the Beni Geneba; whose Sheik lives at Sur. They fall into two classes. The first is that of fishers; generally a despised one. To the north of Dzhidda they are despised. The Huteim of the Peninsula of Sinai are despised. The Geneba, however, are not despised, and with the Bedúins of their neighbourhood they eat, they associate, and they intermarry. The pastoral tribes are, to a great extent, troglodytes. The date is their chief food.

Now come the tribes of Dzhailan, Oman, Dhorrah, and Batna, Oman being the province in which the metropolis of the Imam of Muskat is situated. The Muskattis are a mixed population—Persian, Biluch, Jewish, Indian, African—African most especially; inasmuch as the African island of Zanzibar belongs to the Imam. The towns, in the strict sense of the word, for these parts, are few. Muskat is built of brick and stone. So is Rostak. So are few, or none, of the others. Of the Bedúins, the most important are the Beni-Abu-Ali, said to come from Nedzhd,—Wahabis and enemies to the Beni-Abu-Hasan.

About Dzhebel Akdan the mountaineer character predominates, and the people, closely attached to their native valleys, rarely mix with either the Bedúins or the townsmen.

At the narrowest part of the entrance to the Gulf begins the pirate coast, and extends about 300 miles northwards. Though now reduced in power, the tribes of this part have been formidable from the dawn of their history. Ibn Haikal shows how old he considered their habits to be, when he writes that before the deliverance of the Israelites from the bondage of Ægypt a pirate king seized all the ships that passed his port. India was harassed by them. The Portuguese were harassed also. To the Imam of Muskat they have always been troublesome. In 1809 they brought upon themselves the heavy hand of the English rulers of India; and Ras in Khaimah and Leit on the island of Kishm, were destroyed.

The evidence of Lieut. Welsted to the existence of either a real or supposed superiority on the part of the Pirate Coast Arabs to both the Bedúins and the townspeople is decided. The former are tall, fair, active, and muscular. When not at feud with their neighbours, or when a north-westerly gale prevents them from putting out to sea, they employ themselves in fishing and diving for pearls; the season for the latter occupation being from June to September. In order to hold his breath the longer, the diver places across his nose a piece of elastic horn; which compresses the nostrils.

Of the northern portion of the peninsula I have little to say; believing that, upon the whole, the character of its inhabitants is that of the Arabs of Nedzhd.

Of the Arabs of the Syrian Desert something has been said already; those of the extreme south have been stated to be conterminous with the tribes of Algawf. Have we not written that that town was, in the eyes of the Syrians, the Gate of Nedzhd, *i. e.* the frontier town of Arabia? Have we not also written that the Algawf physiognomy is, more or less, Syrian? The distinction implied by this term may now be illustrated. Syrian features, Ægyptian features, Jewish features, are often associated by writers upon Arab tribes. The creed is Mahometan, the language Arabic, the frame Syrian, &c. This means that it exhibits a departure from the Bedúin type, which gives spare and wiry rather than square or massive figures; the latter being found amongst the undoubted Syrians, the Syrians who exhibit, over and above this particular physiognomy, the other characteristics of a language allied to that of the Syrian fathers and a Christian creed. How far they may denote Syrian blood, disguised by the use of the Arabic language, is another question. *Mutatis mutandis*, the same applies to the Ægyptians and the Jews. It is only certain that the Arab language is extended far beyond the domain of the Arab blood.

The tribes of the Syrian Desert belong also to the cultivated districts of Syria; inasmuch as, on the frontier, a definite division between the fixed and locomotive populations finds place. Some keep to the cultivated country throughout the year. Others change their occupancy with the season.

Of the locomotive tribes, the most important division is that of the Aenaze, Anase, or Aneze, of which the Wulad Ali, the El Hesene, the Raualla, and the Besher are sections; falling into subsections, viz. the Wulad Ali into five, the El Hesene into two, and the Besher into six. The parts about Palmyra, or Tadmor, are in the Anaze country. To the north-east, in the parts about Homs and Hama, lies a Turk district; the tribes whereof are called by the Arabs El Turkman.

To the southern section of the permanent settlers belong the Arabs of the Holy Land, a mixed population both in blood and creed. About Kerak, at least, near the Dead Sea, some of the tribes are Turk, some Christian.

In Hauran, Auranitis, Batanæa, or Bashan, the El Feheily, the Serdzye, the Ahl Dzhebil, and the Kerad tribes are intermediate in character to the migrants and the settlers. The true agriculturists, however, of the district are the Druses; the Haourans being pre-eminently a Druse occupancy. The parts between Hauran and Damascus belong to the Ledzha tribes, one of which, at least, El Turkman, is, what its name denotes, Turk.

In the Oases the population is more permanent than locomotive. In Khaibar the complexion of the occupants is very dark; a fact which Burckhardt expressly attributes to the heat and moisture of the locality. He adds that Jewish blood is believed to run in the veins of the Khaibar families; also adding that their language is decidedly Arab, as is every other character.

*The peninsula of Sinai and Ægypt.*—The southern tribes of the peninsula of Sinai are, more or less, fishermen; and, as such, a despised rather than a respected population. In the north they form an extension of the tribes of Syria.

In Ægypt the dialect changes. The Maazi tribes, however, to the south-east of Cairo, speak after the manner of the true Arabians, which the Howatut, to the north, and the Beni Wassil and Atouni, to the south, do not. About Kosseir, in 26° N.L., the blood changes, and that notably; and the names Bishari, Bedzha, and Ababde come in—all the names of tribes which are, at least, as much Nubian as Arab. Of these the Ababde are Arab, the others Nubian, in language. The northern Ababde belong to Ægypt, the southern to Nubia.

And now either the foreign elements increase, or the character changes. The Arabs of Syria and Palestine were on the soil of a population originally akin to them; the differences between the Arab and the Jew, the Arab and the Syrian, being, in many respects, unimportant. The Arabs, however, of Africa are on the soil of no less than three different families, varieties, or groups, viz. the Copt, the Nubian (in the widest sense of the term), and the Berber; not to mention the more distant settlements in the central and south-eastern parts of the continent.

The Sheyga of Sennaar are described as actual blacks; black in colour, Arab in blood—Arab in blood, inasmuch as the purity of their descent is especially borne witness to. The Arabs of Nubia and Kordofan are represented by the Kubbabish, and other less important tribes; Arab intruders being found in Darfur, in Borgu (or Waday), in Bornu, especially the parts about Lake Tshad, the occupancy of the Beni Sliman, or Sons of Solomon. Then there are the districts of the Abyssinian frontier, more or less African, but, at the same time, more or less Arab as well. Finally, there are the two divisions of

*a*. The Western Arabs, or the Arabs of Barbary, Morocco, and the Sahara; and

*b*. The South-eastern Arabs of the shores of the Pacific between the sea and the frontier of the Abyssinians, the Somaulis, the Gallas, and the northern members of the Kaffir group.

Less strongly contrasted with the natives of their several districts are the Arabs of Khuzistan and Irak Arabi, where the contact is with either pure Persians or Kurds. So it is in parts of Mesopotamia, where the frontier, besides being Kurd, is Turkish as well. In this latter district the chief tribe is that of the Shammar. In Khuzistan it is that of the Montefidzh. In the low levels about the mouth of the Euphrates the Arab becomes a fenman, and dwells in huts thatched with reeds in moist and malarious localities. The Beni Rechab bear a name which reminds us of the Rechabites of Jeremiah (chap. xxxv.), from whom they may or may not be descended. If, however, their name mean "sons of the stirrup," as Mr. Loftus, who visited them, suggests, Rechab is no true eponymic term, and Rechabites may exist wherever stirrups are in use. Rechabites are mentioned by Benjamin of Tudela. Their occupancy, however, lay in Yemen. As for those of Mesopotamia, they claim to be old inhabitants of the country; though, in more details than one, they differ from the surrounding tribes. Their prince or chief is an Emir, not a Sheikh. They are sullen and inhospitable; addicted to plunder; Jewish in physiognomy, and as such contrasted with the undoubted Arabs of their neighbourhood, the Kuzzeil, the Beni Lam, the Affedzh, and the Montefidzh.

*The Syrians speaking Syriac.*—A few families, occupants of Libanus, are stated by trustworthy travellers to be not only Syrian in blood (as are many apparent Arabs), but Syrian in speech as well.

A few others in the same category may perhaps be found in Mesopotamia. I am unable, however, to state whether the fact of their being able to speak Syriac (supposing it to be real) is evidence to the present existence of the Syriac as a living language. It may be spoken as Latin is spoken by certain Poles and Hungarians, *i. e.* as a dead language learned from books.

The scriptures of the Mendæans of the parts about Disful in Khuzistan are in Syriac.

In Syriac, too, are those of the Maronites, the Malabar Christians, and the Caldani, or Christians of Kurdistan, whose complexion is comparatively fair, whose eyes are gray, and whose beards are often reddish.

| English. | Arabic. | Syriac. | Hebrew. |
|---|---|---|---|
| *Head* | ras | rish | rosh |
| *Hair* | saro | shar | sear |
| *Eye* | ayn | eyn | ayn |
| *Ear* | adzn | adno | ozen |
| *Nose* | anph | hhatm | aph |
| *Mouth* | pham | phum | pi |
| *Tooth* | sen | sheno | shen |
| *Tongue* | lishan | leshono | lashon |
| *Hand* | yad | yad | yad |
| *Foot* | rigl | reglo | regel |
| *Sun* | shams | shemsho | shemesh |
| *Star* | kaukab | kukbo | kokab' |
| *Day* | yawm | yeum | yom |
| *Night* | laila | lailo | laila |
| *Fire* | anisat | eshotto | esh |
| *Water* | ma | mayo | mayim |
| *One* | akhad | hhad | ehhad |
| *Two* | thuna | tharin | shanim |
| *Three* | thaleth | tholth | shelosh |
| *Four* | arbat | arba' | arba' |
| *Five* | hhams | hhamesh | hhamesh |
| *Six* | sit | sheth | shesh |
| *Seven* | sab' | sheba' | sheba |
| *Eight* | samâra | thmon | shemoneh |
| *Nine* | tish | tsha | tesha' |
| *Ten* | ashar | 'sar | 'asar. |

*The Samaritans.*—The national existence of the Samaritans terminated B.C. 721, when the ten tribes were conquered by Shalmaneser. The extent to which this conquest put an end to the blood and language is another question. Some Samaritans were, doubtlessly, transplanted into some localities beyond the frontier of Samaria. Some as doubtlessly remained on their native soil. At the present time a few families calling themselves by the ancient name are to be found in the neighbourhood of Nablus. They preserve a copy of the Pentateuch of considerable but uninvestigated antiquity. A few, too, are said to dwell in Cairo.

## CHAPTER XII.

**The Semitic populations.—The Abyssinians of Tigré and Amhara.—The Agows.—The Falasha.—The Gafat.**

ARABIA leads to Africa; less, however, through the Isthmus of Suez than by the way of Abyssinia. For Abyssinia is in its essentials a truly Semitic country; Semitic after the fashion of Syria or Arabia itself. Whether it were always so is another question.

The country is mountainous, and, where not mountainous, a plateau. It scarcely touches the sea; the eastern slopes of its eastern range being the occupancy of the Danakil.

*The Tigré Abyssinians.*—Tigré, on the north, is rich in the remains of antiquity; the parts about Axum, its ancient capital, being of the most importance. The language is a derivative from the ancient Geez, in which was made the Æthiopic translation of the Scriptures. Allied to the Hebrew and Arabic, it differs in its alphabet, which is syllabic.

*Amhara.*—So is that of the neighbouring province of Amhara; the language whereof, with the same general affinities as the Tigré, is less closely a representative of the old Æthiopic.

Both the Amharic and Geez are written from left to right, not from right to left, like the Arabic, &c.

| English. | Amharic. | Tigré. |
|---|---|---|
| *God* | isger | esger |
| *Sun* | tsai | tsai |
| *Star* | quokub | kŏhhab |
| *Wind* | nefas | nefăs |
| *Rain* | zenam | zenab |
| *Clouds* | demana | debena |
| *Earth* | mider | midre |
| *Hill* | amba | amba |
| *Mountain* | tarara | amba |
| *Gold* | werk | wark |
| *Silver* | bir | beroor |
| *Grass* | sar | sare |
| *Fruit* | fre | fre |
| *Flower* | abbeva | ambova |
| *Bee* | niv | nebe |
| *Honey* | mar | mahar |
| *Wheat* | sinde | sindi |
| *Water* | waha | mi |
| *Well* (*water*) | azukt | azukte |
| *Horse* | feras | fras |
| *Ass* | hiyah | erge |
| *Mule* | bukalo | bugale |
| *Cow* | laam | laame |
| *Ox* | berai | bebherai |
| *Sheep* | bug | bugge |
| *Goat* | feel | tele |
| *Horn* | kund | kerne |
| *Lion* | anbasa | ănbasa |
| *Bird* | wof | wofeef |
| *Father* | abate | above |
| *Mother* | enate | onoo |
| *Friend* | wadadje | fetouye |
| *Head* | ras | rasi |
| *Hair* | tsegur | tsugure |
| *Eye* | ain | aini |
| *Nose* | afintcha | affinkyaha |
| *Mouth* | af | af |
| *Tongue* | melas | melhas |
| *Voice* | dimts | dimtse |
| *Beard* | tim | tehame |
| *Shoulders* | tekusha | kesa |
| *Arm* | edje | eed |
| *Bowels* | manta | amet |
| *Heart* | lib | libbe |
| *Blood* | dum | dam |

| English. | Amharic. | Tigré. |
|---|---|---|
| *Leg* | igger | iggere |
| *Year* | amit | ámet |
| *Month* | war | warre |
| *Week* | samint | summum |
| *Near* | kerib | kerub |
| *Far* | rook | rook |
| *Above* | lai | lab |
| *Below* | taich | takti |
| *Small* | tanash | nishte |
| *Short* | achir | atteer |
| *Dark* | tchelema | sellemat |
| *Heavy* | kubdal | kubbid |
| *Bitter* | memarar | murrur |
| *Sweet* | taffeet | toum |
| *Weak* | dekama | dukoom |
| *Red* | ki | kiyeh. |

Middle-sized, and well made, the Abyssinians vary in colour. Some are perfectly black; but the majority have a red tinge; and so come-out brown, nut-coloured, or copper-coloured. The features are often European, *i. e.* an aquiline nose stands out in prominent contrast to that of the typical negro. The cheeks are often sunk, so that the face looks elongated. The hair is dark and crisp, not to say curly. The limbs are well formed.

As is the Armenian in Asia, so is the Abyssinian in Africa. Both are Christian populations in contact with Mahometans. Both hold exceptional creeds. It was about A.D. 330 that Frumentius introduced the Gospel into Æthiopia. It is still retained. Abyssinia, however, is the rudest of all Christian nations.

*The Agows.*—Except that they are somewhat stouter in make, the physiognomy of the Agows is that of the proper Abyssinians. They differ, however, in language. They also differ in civilization. The little Christianity that is to be found amongst them is scarcely two centuries old. Damot and Lasta are the chief Agow provinces.

*The Falasha.*—The Falasha dialects are Agow rather than either Tigé or Amharic, the Falasha populations being sometimes highlanders, like those of the mountain-ranges of Samien, sometimes lowlanders, like the men of Dembea. The Kimmont hills to the north-east of Gondar (in the Amharic country) are Falasha. The Falasha greatly resemble the Jews in their habits and customs, and, by more than one writer, have been treated as actual Israelites. It is only certain that they exhibit many Jewish characteristics.

*Gafat.*—The Gafat language, akin to the Amharic, is rapidly disappearing. The Amharic displaces it; whilst the Galla, in many places, displaces the Amharic. A small district in the province of Damot is the Gafat locality.

Abyssinia, as we have said, is the rudest of all Christian nations. Its Christianity is not only imperfect and partial, but is complicated with Judaism and Mahometanism. The homely narrative of Nathaniel Pearce, an English sailor who was left in the country, at his own desire, by Lord Valentia, and who resided in it more than ten years, tells us that although the Abyssinians "are Christians, they are in some ways like Jews, and some ways like savages. For why they are like Jews is, they keep holy the Saturday as well as the Sunday, both equal alike. They also keep the three fast days of Nineveh, which they call the feast of Annernoi, or Jonah the prophet; and have a holiday yearly for Abraham and Sarah. And for why they are like savages, they eat the flesh whilst the blood is still warm in the veins. They keep very strict in their fasts; the fast of our Saviour or Lent, is fifty-six days, which begins in March and ends in May; the fast of Nineveh—the fast of the Apostles—the fast for the death of the Virgin Mary, &c. The priests of their separate parishes have a great feast at the end of every fast."

An account of one follows. It shows on unexceptionable evidence that the brutal habit of eating the warm, raw, and still-quivering flesh of animals is Abyssinian. The assembled guests take the sacrament, kill a cow, and "before the animal has done kicking, and the blood still running from its throat, the skin is nearly off one side, and the prime flesh cut off and with all haste held before the elders of the church, who cut about two or three pounds each, and eat it with such greediness, that those who did not know them would think they were starved; but at all times they prefer the raw to the cooked victuals."

Some of the women tattoo themselves. In no country are they married earlier. In no country is marriage more a matter of bargain. In no country is disparity of age less heeded. A man of sixty may marry a child of eight. "I have known," writes Pearce, "several girls given to men of that age, who have been born since I have been in the country; which is not yet ten years. Some girls have children at thirteen or fourteen years of age. You may by chance find a girl who is still a virgin at eleven or twelve years in the provinces of Tegri and Inderta (Enderta), but I can venture to say there is not one in the Ammerrer (Amhara) country above nine or ten. The king will give his daughters to any of his chiefs he thinks proper at the age of eight or nine. I, when a stranger amongst them, used to think it impossible that a child of that age could be fit for marriage; but I since find that it is their natural custom."

With all this, the analogue of the European nun is to be found in Abyssinia; inasmuch as a woman, on forswearing marriage, may wear a skull-cap like a man, and turn priest. She may not, however, enter a certain part of the church called Bethlem. She may also become possessed of a devil; as was Pearce's own wife. "She was five or six days very ill, and her speech so much altered that I could scarcely understand her. She then began to be continually hungry, and would eat five or six times in the night and never sleep." Then came a passion for begging, then the habit of addressing men as women, and women as men; then fits. And now her friends prepared to cure her. They hired trumpeters. They dressed up with all sorts of gewgaws. They called a meeting and feasted. They showed her to the company. Then she danced and jumped, and jumped and danced; ever and anon dropping one of her ornaments. When the sun set she dropped the last, and started to run. A young man with matchlock runs with her. She drops. He then fires over her body, and asks her name. She gives, having previously denied, it. Her friends then take her to church, when she is washed with holy water, and cured.

As are the women so are the men. Priests swarm. The little learning of the country is monopolized by them. They use this in the encouragement of superstitions. They fail, however, to check either the licence of the polygamist, or the profligacy of his wives and concubines. They fail, too, to enforce the sanction of oaths, which are broken as systematically and as ceremoniously as they are taken. Takely Georges acted thus:—a priest held up a cross, which was sworn by. The priest went his way. Then said Takely Georges—"Servants, you see the oath I have taken. I scrape it clean away from my tongue that made it." Thereupon he scraped his tongue, and spat away his oath. The men to whom he swore reminded him of it, saying—"Your majesty has perhaps forgotten what you swore to?"

*Takely Georges.*—"No, I have not; but, after you were gone, and before I had eaten or drunk, I scraped it from the tongue that made it, and this before all my house." Such are the methods by which perjury is organized in a land of nuns and priests. "If what I now swear to be not true, may God blow my soul away from me as I blow away the fire from this candle." The swearer then suits the action to the word, blows out the light, and keeps or forgets the imprecation as it best suits him.

As in many other parts of Africa, it is considered a misfortune for a woman to bear twins. It is not thought natural to breed like a dog; and children have been put to death in order that the reproach of so doing might be avoided.

Bad amongst the bad are the practices to which the Abyssinians resort in war. They always mutilate the dead body, and wear the parts cut off as a trophy. Sometimes they mutilate the living man. Pearce, who was constrained to join in one of their wars, killed some of the enemy in the "presence of the ras, but would not be so inhuman as to mangle a dead body; for which the ras was much displeased."

## CHAPTER XIII.

The Copts.—The Bishari.—The Nubians.—The Populations, &c., of Kordovan, of Darfur, of Sennaar.—The so-called Negroes of Abyssinia.—The Galla Family, *i. e.* the Danakil, the Somauli, and the Gallas Proper.

*The Copts.*—The Copts are the descendants of the ancient Ægyptians. As a separate population, with the full characteristics of language and nationality, they are wholly or nearly extinct. Much of their blood runs in Arab veins; and many a true Arab, on the strength of his frame being somewhat less wiry and spare than ordinary, has been put down for an individual of mixed blood. The analysis, however, is difficult. As a spoken language the Coptic is extinguished. As a written one it still exists. The Copts, who are Christian, still read a Coptic version of the Scriptures and other Coptic ecclesiastic writings. Many of the scribes or clerks of Cairo are Copts. In form they are somewhat massive, with fleshy limbs, heavy features, noses more flat than prominent, eyes somewhat oblique (so, at least, it is said), thickish lips, dark complexions; more yellow or brown than either black or white. The Copt language has been called sub-Semitic. It may be this without ceasing to be African. Indeed, it has numerous African affinities.

*The Bishari.*—The true Ægyptian area must not be supposed to transcend the eastern boundary of the valley of the Nile; the coast of the Red Sea being other than Ægyptian. In the parts about Kosseir a new element appears—new to the reader, old to the soil. The family to which the ruder aborigines of north-eastern Africa belong now comes into view. The Ababde are Bishari, the Bishari Ababde, with this difference—the Bishari preserve their own language, the Ababde speak Arabic. Such, at least, is the common statement; though I am unable to give the evidence on which it rests. I only know that the presumptions are in favour of its being true. The Ababde lie nearest the Nile; the Bishari nearest the sea. Both are to be found in Ægypt; both in Nubia. The Ababde, the northern members of the family, differ from the Arabs in colour and in the texture of their hair, which is either elaborately frizzled or curiously curled.

The Bishari proper are succeeded by the Adareb, whose best-known occupancy is the country about Suakin. One of these tribes reaches as far inland as the neighbourhood of Shendy. In Suakin the principal people affect an Arab origin; indeed, Burckhardt commits himself to the doctrine that, word for word, Adareb is Hadramaut.

*The Taka Tribes.*—The parts between the Mareb and the Atbara or Tacazze are the occupancy of the Hadendoa, Hammadab, Hallenga, and other tribes, known by the general name of Taka, Bishari in form, features, and complexion. They feed sheep and camels, hunt ostriches, collect senna, make occasional razzias upon Sennaar and Dongola, quarrel with the Ababde where the ground is debateable, deny that they eat raw flesh, but own to drinking warm blood.

*The Barea.*—The Barea, whose name is other than native, lie on the north-western frontier of Abyssinia. They are but imperfectly known, and not fully described. Mansfield Parkyns's is the work wherein they appear with most prominence. It describes them as formidable frontagers to the Abyssinians of Walkait, being bold, active, and predatory warriors.

*Nubians.*—The Nile ceases to be Ægyptian below Assuan, the ancient Syene. Where Ægypt ends Nubia begins. Upper Egypt and Lower Nubia touch. Both are full of ancient remains; those of northern Nubia being Ægyptian, those of southern being Æthiopic or Abyssinian, in character. The true Nubians lie along the river. Their language is neither Coptic nor Arabic. It is unintelligible to the Bishari and the Abyssinian. Its dialects are the Kensi in northern, the Nub (or Nubian proper) in middle, and the Dongolawy in Dongola or southern, Nubia. The Nubians are often called Barabbra, Berber, or Berberin. Subject to Ægypt, they are imperfect Mahometans; agricultural and commercial in their habits; not a little mixed in blood. Their hair is long and crisp; their colour brown rather than black. Rüppell calls the Dongolawi bronze-coloured; also stating that the Dongolawi face is oval, the nose curved, the lips thick. The Bishari have elongated faces, prominent noses, long and twisted hair.

*The Koldagi of Kordovan.*—The speakers of the Koldagi, one of the numerous languages of Kordovan, are, in language at least, closely allied to the Nubians.

*Darfur.*—The Fur, or Furians, of Darfur are imperfect Mahometans, who speak a language with Koldagi affinities. They are black, and far more like the ordinary negro than are the Nubians or Bishari. Many Arab tribes are spread over their country, which has been but little visited.

West of Darfur lies Darsaleh, an unexplored district, concerning which some of our notices come from the east, *viâ* Nubia and Kordovan, and others from the west, *viâ* Bornu, in connection with which kingdom I shall notice it.

Sennaar and the parts in contact with it now command

attention. As long as the Nile runs parallel to the sea, and keeps a straight course, the ethnology of the parts to the east of its valley is simple. South, however, of Nubia it makes a bend westward. It also receives feeders from the east, and the ethnology is complicated accordingly. There is a wider tract of alluvial soil, with a blacker set of tribes to occupy it. The dark skin of the Sheyga Arabs has already been mentioned. It is as black as that of the natives; though who the natives are cannot exactly be said. There has been conquest and intrusion in Sennaar. The intrusive tribes, however, coming, as they are believed to have done, from the neighbouring districts, are not likely to have been very different from the aborigines. The proportion they bear to the aborigines and Arabs is uncertain. The chief population is called Funge. We have no specimen of the Funge language *eo nomine*. It is probably akin to that of the Fazoglo tribes, whose language, as known through a vocabulary of Tutshek's, is that of

*The Qamamyl* of Cailliaud.

More remotely connected with both the Fazoglo and with each other are the languages named by Rüppel—

*Shabún* to the south of the Sennaar and Kordovan frontier.

*Denka.*—The Denka are pagans and idolaters.

*Shiluk.*—The Shiluk are pagans of the Bahr El Abiad; skilful in the management of canoes, who have woolly heads, and swear by the sun.

*The Tumali* country lies to the south of Obeid, between 11° and 12° N.L. It is divided into two kingdoms of unequal size, the smaller of which is the superior. Its name is Tumali Tokoken, and it is the seat of a Wofter, to whom the Ellot of Tumali Debili is subordinate, but who is himself subordinate to the king of Takeli, who is a vassal of the Viceroy of Ægypt. The Tumali of Tutshek is all but the Takeli of Rüppell, of which the Dai, or Daier, is a dialect.

| English. | Darfur. | Koldagi. | Shabün. | Shilluk. |
|---|---|---|---|---|
| *Man* | duedeh | kordu | le | uguilu |
| *Head* | tobu | oar | eldah | uidzh |
| *Eye* | kuli | kale | leg | uang |
| *Nose* | dormi | hein | nagul | ung |
| *Mouth* | udo | aul | keing | dok |
| *Tooth* | kaki | gehl | engar | lek |
| *Tongue* | dali | ghiadu | denkela | leb |
| *Ear* | dilo | uilge | neni | yib |
| *Hand* | donga | oshi | nimel | kiam |
| *Foot* | taroh | kuddo | ongi | lustiella |
| *Fire* | utu | eka | yah | maidzh |
| *Water* | koro | otu | knaf | fi |
| *Sun* | dulle | es | quedyude | kiong |
| *Moon* | dual | nundo | ciwah | goi |
| *Star* | uri | ondu | robah | kielo |
| *Tree* | kurru | saleg | yareh | yad |
| *Stone* | ditu | kager | kokol | niarkiddi. |

*Fertit* lies still further to the south.

| English. | Fazoglo. | Denka. | Takeli. | Fertit. |
|---|---|---|---|---|
| *Man* | meloko | moed | ead | koshi |
| *Head* | allo | nam | aik | kummu |
| *Eye* | are | ninu | undik | allah |
| *Nose* | kara | oum | endir | aue |
| *Mouth* | antu | tok | engiarr | ammah |
| *Tooth* | dovidit-ufuti | ledzh | nim | ensi |
| *Tongue* | halla | leb | auga | timi |
| *Ear* | ilai | yet | hennu | utai |
| *Hand* | raba | ruib | ora | adgianas |
| *Foot* | — | kwen | dakaak | tibrenu |
| *Fire* | mo | maid | ebe | ouwe |
| *Water* | fi | fiou | ek | ongou |
| *Sun* | mondzo | akol | ani | aloh |
| *Moon* | shig | fai | oar | ibue |
| *Star* | iso | kuol | lain | berabe |
| *Tree* | engoule | tiem | fa | donzu |
| *Stone* | bele | kur | arnan | ekbur. |

Within the frontier of Abyssinia, yet other than Abyssinian, are

*The Dizzela.*—This is the name of a tribe occupant of a portion of the Agow country.

*The Dalla.*—This is the name of a population on the Tacazze.

Both the Dizzela and Dalla are called Shangalla or Shankali; but this is a general term applied by the Abyssinians to the blacker and ruder populations of the western part of the country. That the languages, at least, are different, may be seen from the following list:—

| English. | Dizzela. | Dalla. |
|---|---|---|
| *Man* | gunza | kwa |
| *Woman* | inguffa | dukka |
| *Head* | Illukoma | annasunga |
| *Eyes* | Illikumah | wa |
| *Nose* | kotuma | bubuna |
| *Ears* | tsema | ukuna |
| *Teeth* | kuusma | —— |
| *Tongue* | kotettuma | —— |
| *Sun* | woka | wah |
| *Moon* | beja | terah |
| *Star* | beja | shunda |
| *Fire* | —— | tuma |
| *Water* | iah | —— |
| *Stone* | —— | uga |
| *Tree* | gea | —— |
| *One* | metama | illa |
| *Two* | ambanda | belle |
| *Three* | quokaga | sette |
| *Four* | zaacha | salle |
| *Five* | mankoos | bussume |
| *Six* | wata | erde |
| *Seven* | linyeta | barde |
| *Eight* | sugguata | quonqueda |
| *Nine* | sasa | quuntelle |
| *Ten* | chikka | quullakudde. |

About 17° N.L. the Bishari populations are succeeded by the most northern members of the great

*Galla* or *Ilmormo family*, containing

1. The Danakil.
2. The Somauli.

3. The Gallas proper.

1. The Danakil call themselves Afer, Danakil being an Arab name, word for word the same as Dongola—though the Dongolawy are Nubians. The country named Adel or Adaiel is Danakil rather than Somauli.

2. Word for word, Somauli (an Arab name) is Suwahili and Sofala. The Somauli area begins a little to the south of the Straits of Babelmandeb.

3. The Gallas proper belong to the interior rather than the coast, their area being of great magnitude and sinuous in outline. The Asubu tribes, for instance, have encroached on the Danakil, the Edjow upon the Amharas. Over all the southern part of Abyssinia the Gallas have spread far and are likely to spread farther.

Akin to the Bishari in form and habits, the Gallas are long-haired, dark-skinned, prominent-featured shepherds, robbers, and marauders; savage in their mode of warfare, yet not without commercial and maritime aptitudes when the neighbourhood of the sea and the trade with Arabia encourage them.

The Gallas fall into tribes and sub-tribes, and are almost exclusively pastoral. In the direction of Abyssinia they have encroached. The kingdom of Shoa is no longer Abyssinian, but Galla. So is that of Efat. The town of Ankober is a Galla capital, though mixed in regard to its population. In religion the Gallas are imperfect Mahometans, imperfect Christians, and pagans; the chief Christianity being in the districts conquered from Abyssinia. As warriors they are savage among the savage, delighting in the massacre and mutilation of their prisoners.

| English. | Bishari. | Nubian. | Dalla. | Galla. |
|---|---|---|---|---|
| *Man* | otak | itga | kwa | nama |
| *Woman* | tataket | ideynga | dukka | rete |
| *Head* | ogourma | ourka | annasunga | mata |
| *Hair* | tamo | shigertyga | anna | refensa |

| English. | Bishari. | Nubian. | Dalla. | Galla. |
|---|---|---|---|---|
| *Eyes* | tilyly | mainga | wa | hedzha |
| *Nose* | ogenuf | soringa | bubuna | funyan |
| *Tongue* | medabo | —— | —— | arruba |
| *Mouth* | oyaf | akka | ma | affan |
| *Teeth* | tongrek | nyta | —— | ilkae |
| *Ears* | tongy | okiga | ukuna | gura |
| *Beard* | hamoi | sameyga | —— | arreda |
| *Foot* | ragad | oyga | —— | fana |
| *Sky* | otryk | sema | —— | —— |
| *Sun* | toyn | mashakka | wah | addu |
| *Moon* | ondzhim | inatiga | terah | dzhea |
| *Star* | —— | windzhega | shunda | urdzhe |
| *Fire* | toneyt | ika | tuma | ibiddeh |
| *Water* | ayam | amanga | beya | beshan |
| *Tree* | —— | dzhollaga | illa | mouka |
| *Stone* | awey | —— | uga | dagga |
| *One* | engaro | werka | illa | toko |
| *Two* | molobo | onogha | belle | lumma |
| *Three* | mehay | toskoga | sette | sedde |
| *Four* | fadyg | kemsoga | salle | affur |
| *Five* | eyyib | didzha | bussume | shur |
| *Six* | essagour | gordzhoga | erde | dzha |
| *Seven* | essarama | kolodga | barde | turbah |
| *Eight* | essambay | idonoga | kwonkwedah | seddet |
| *Nine* | ogamhay | oskoda | kwuntelle | suggul |
| *Ten* | togaserama | dimaga | kwullakudde | kudun. |

Within the Galla area, as elsewhere in northern and eastern Africa, the great admixture of Semitic elements makes the analysis of both the blood and language of the numerous tribes a matter of no little difficulty. On the Bishari frontier, for instance, the Shiho form of speech is more Danakil than Amharic; whilst the Arkiko is more Amharic than Danakil.

| English. | Danakil. | Arkiko. | Shiho. | Amharic. |
|---|---|---|---|---|
| *Head* | ammo | ammo | ras | ras |
| *Nose* | sanna | san | anf | afincha |
| *Mouth* | afa | af | af | af |
| *Eye* | inte | inte | en | ain |
| *Teeth* | budena | ekok | enob | ters |
| *Sun* | aero | airo | tsai | tsai |
| *Moon* | alsa | alsa | werne | tkerka |

| English. | Danakil. | Arkiko. | Shiho. | Amharic. |
|---|---|---|---|---|
| *Star* | ettukta | ittuk | kokub | kwokub |
| *Fire* | gira | gera | essat | asat |
| *Water* | leh | le | mi | waha |
| *Stone* | data | dak | bunnet | dengea |
| *One* | innike | inek | ante | and |
| *Two* | lumma | lamma | kille | kwillet |
| *Three* | sudde | adda | selas | sost |
| *Four* | fere | afur | ubah | arrut |
| *Five* | konoyoie | kon | amús | aumist |
| *Six* | leheye | leh | sús | sedist |
| *Seven* | melhene | melhen | subhu | subhat |
| *Eight* | bahara | bahr | theman | semint |
| *Nine* | segala | suggai | tse | zatti |
| *Ten* | tubban | tummum | assur | assir. |

The Hurur vocabularies of Salt, Beke, and Burton, though to a great extent Semitic, have several Galla, Somauli, and Danakil names for even the most familiar objects, *e. g.*

| English. | Hurur. | Danakil, &c. | Arabic. |
|---|---|---|---|
| *Tongue* | arrat | arruba | lishan |
| *Sun* | ihr | airo | shams |

and others. These elements require a careful analysis; and even the Semite portion, when separated, requires a second elaboration. The Æthiopic words have to be kept apart from the Arabic

## CHAPTER XIV.

**The Tibbu.—The Bornúi and Howssa groups.—The Sungai.—The Amazig.—The Fula.**

*The Tibbu.*—The eastern part of the great northern desert is the occupancy of the Tibbu family, divided, like all the groups that have hitherto been noticed, into tribes and sub-tribes. They have not been very fully described. Lyon, who saw much of the families about Gatrone, speaks in high terms of their physical form. The females were light and elegant in shape, with aquiline noses, fine teeth, European lips, delicate feet and ankles, jetty skins. The men were slender and active. The tribes of the south of Fezzan are comparatively quiet and settled. Those of the desert, however, are thieves and pagans. They dwell in huts made of skins of animals and grass or palm-leaves, some being troglodytes. The female slaves sell at a high price, on account of their beauty; the men at a low one. They are ill-adapted for hard or continuous work. Dates and flesh are their chief food. They also eat the seeds of the *khandal* or colocynth apple.

Parts of Kanem, and certain districts along the shores of Lake Tshad, visited by Dr. Barth, are Tibbu; the Tibbu area being in contact with that of

*The Bornúi*, or men of the important kingdom of Bornu. As is the geography, so is the ethnology. Along with others, I expect that the more we learn concerning these two populations, we more closely we shall connect them. At present, however, the relations between the tribes of the desert and the occupants of that long zone of kingdoms or countries which, under the name of Kordovañ, Darfur, Darsaleh, Begharmi, Bornu, and Howssa, stretch from the Nile to the Niger, are obscure.

The Bidduma islanders of the Lake Tshad speak a language akin to the Affadeh dialect of the Kanuri.

*Howssa.*—Due west of Bornu, with which it is conterminous, lie the Howssa districts, succeeded by the country of which the great metropolis is

*Timbuktu.*—Some obscurity hangs over the details of the parts about Timbuktu. Caillié names the language of Timbuktu Kissour and gives a specimen of it, different from that of Denham, different from that of Hodgson (who agrees with Denham), different from that of Barth, whose specimen is headed Emghadesie. Upon the whole, however, they agree.

| English. | Sungai. *Hodgson.* | Kissour. *Caillié.* | Timbuctoo. *Denham.* | Emghadesie. *Barth.* |
|---|---|---|---|---|
| *Man* | harroo | harre | harree | berfua |
| *Woman* | owee | houi | weey | waei |
| *Head* | bonga | homo | bongo | benru |
| *Eye* | moo-ñg | nemode | moh-inka | mua |
| *Mouth* | meañg | mi | mey | mai |
| *Nose* | nenee | nini | —— | nini |
| *Hand* | kembee | lamba | kambah | kanba |
| *Foot* | kee | na-kidi | kay | kae |
| *Sun* | oinoo | ouena | ofitli | uênu |
| *Moon* | handoo | —— | idou | handu |
| *Fire* | monee | nounez | janee | horu |
| *Water* | haree | hari | hari | ari |
| *One* | afoo | afau | affoo | nifo |
| *Two* | hinka | ainka | nahinka | ahinka |
| *Three* | hinza | aindhia | nahinga | ahinza |
| *Four* | etakee | ataki | attakee | etthaki |
| *Five* | egoo | igou, horgou | aggoo | —— |

*The Amazig family.*—The fringe of the Mediterranean is Arab. The Sudanian area is Bornúi, Howssa, Sungai, and the like. But what is the desert that lies between? A part was Tibbu; but only a part. What is the remainder? Kabail, Amazig, or Berber; the latter being an inconvenient name. Have we not seen that the

Nubians were also called Barabbra or Berberin? At the same time, it is from the Amazig, or Kabail, Berbers that the States of Barbary take their name.

The Amazig area is the largest in Africa, extending from the confines of Ægypt to the Atlantic Ocean. More than this—the Canary Islands, until the extermination or fusion of their aborigines, were Amazig. This we know from the fragments of the Guanch language which represent the language of the opposite coast.

Again—the ancient Mauritanians and Gætulians were not only the occupants of the Amazig area, but of Amazig blood. Of Amazig blood were the native tribes with which the Greeks of the Cyrenaica came in contact. Of Amazig blood were the native tribes with which the Phenicians of Utica and Carthage came in contact. The subjects of Masinissa and Jugurtha occupied localities of which the ancient names are explained by means of the modern Amazig.

At the present time there are five names for five divisions of the Amazig populations, and seven names for the Amazig forms of speech. How far either series is natural is another question.

(1.) The Kabails, who speak the Kabail language, are the Amazig of the northern part of Algiers rather than Morocco.

(2.) The Showiah are the Amazig of Morocco rather than Algiers. They occupy, however, some of the central districts of Algiers; their language being the Showiah.

(3.) The Shiluk lie to the south of Morocco, their language being the Shiluk.

(4.) The Berbers belong to the south-eastern parts of Algiers, to Tunis, to Tripoli, and the corresponding parts of the Sahara. Their dialects are the Larua and Zenaitia.

Larua is the name of the Amazig of the Isle of

Dzherba, and of the Dzhebel Nfus (?) in Tunis. In Tripoli it is spoken in the town of Zuara. In Algeria it is limited to some of the oases, being especially stated to be spoken at Waregla, Temasin, and Tuggurt, collectively called Wadreag. Carrette observes, as Hodgson had done before him, that the Amazig population of Wadreag is extremely dark—almost as black as that of the negro, the features being other than negro. The Arabs of the same district are only brown.

The oasis of Twat is the locality of the Zenaitia form of speech.

(5) The Tuarik, who, perhaps should be less trenchantly separated from the Berbers of Wadreag and Twat, are the occupants of the rest of the Sahara, are bounded on the east by the Tibbu, and on the south by the Nigritian, or Sudanian, populations.

The oasis of Siwah, the ancient Ammonium, is Amazig.

The part of the Amazig area which is best known is (as may be expected) Algeria. For this we have the following statistics, taken from an elaborate work of Carrette on the origin and migrations of the principal tribes of Northern Africa.

PROVINCE OF CONSTANTINE.

| | Arabs. | Amazig. |
|---|---|---|
| Circle of Rône . . . | 10,340 | 900 |
| ——— Lacalle . . | 14,320 | — |
| ——— L'Edough . . | 7,230 | 4,780 |
| ——— Guelma . . | 6,340 | 34,490 |
| ——— Phillipville . . | 5,360 | 14,820 |
| ——— Constantine . . | 297,330 | 594,230 |
| ——— Setif . . . | 49,180 | —— |
| Kalifat of Medzhana . . | 115,650 | 7,950 |
| Eastern Kabilia . . . | —— | 130,900 |
| Total . | 505,750 | 788,070 |

PROVINCE OF ALGIERS.

| | Arabs. | Amazig. |
|---|---|---|
| Subdivision of Algiers . | 125,600 | 302,100 |
| ———— Miliana . | 33,800 | 52,400 |
| ———— Medea. . | 125,000 | 3,200 |
| ———— Orleansville . | 34,000 | 46,900 |
| The Sahara. . . . | 30,000 | 34,000 |
| Total . | 348,400 | 438,600 |

PROVINCE OF ORAN.

| | Arabs. | Amazig. |
|---|---|---|
| Subdivision of Oran . . | 50,300 | —— |
| ———— Mostaganem. | 52,500 | 34,200 |
| ———— Tlemcen . | 40,100 | 26,300 |
| ———— Maskara . | 96,200 | —— |
| The Sahara . . . | 185,400 | 3,200 |
| Total . | 424,500 | 63,700 |

RECAPITULATION.

| | Arabs. | Amazig. |
|---|---|---|
| Province of Constantine . | 505,750 | 788,070 |
| ———— Algiers . . | 348,400 | 438,600 |
| ———— Oran . . | 424,500 | 63,700 |
| Total . | 1,278,650 | 1,290,370 |

From Carette we get the following contributions to the history of the name. The Arab pedigrees are chiefly founded on the word Berber. One is to the effect that when Afrik, the son of Kis, the son of Saifi, invaded Africa from the Himyarite parts of Arabia, and heard what he thought was the patois of the native tribes, he exclaimed, "What a *berberat*" (*i. e.* jargon)!

Another derives the Berbers from Ber, the son of Kis, a king of Ægypt. A third makes them a colony of Amalekites, who murmured (*berberna*) at being taken so far from their country. A fourth gives the Berbers and the Ægyptians the same origin, *i. e.* one from Kobt, the son of Kanaan, the son of Ham, the son of Noah. A fifth makes Dzhalut, or Goliath, their ancestor and names one of the mountains near Siwah Dzhalut-el-Berber.

The Arab pedigrees attach themselves to the name Berber, the native to the name Amazig. Ber, the son of Kis, had a mother named Tamzigh. Mazigh was a descendant of Kanaan. The contrast between the two names is well shown in the following narrative. When Amru-ben-Aas, the first of the Mahometan conquerors who entered Tripoli, came in contact with the natives of that country, six men, with their heads shaved, presented themselves before him, and professed their readiness to adopt his creed. Amru sent them to Omar. Omar asked who they were. "Sons of Mazigh." "What does this mean?" His attendants answered, "It means the same as the sons of Ber, the son of Kis." "How do you live?" said Omar. "We breed horses." "Have you any towns?" "We never build."

Of all the indigenæ of the soil of Africa, the Amazig have been the most conspicuous (should we not rather say the least inconspicuous?) in history. Some of their tribes are prominent in the eighth and fifteenth centuries. The Senhadzha, for instance, take an active and influential part in the elevation of the Fatimite dynasty, eventually having dynasties of their own—the Zeirite and the Hammadite, both Algerian. Mohammed-Abdallah-ben-Toumart is the most conspicuous individual of the Masmuda, a deformed hero, whose thighs were joined together, so that his legs were only separated at the knees, which prevented his riding; but learned, enthusiastic, and brave. Half as prophet, half as warrior, *i. e.* in that semi-secular and semi-religious character which is so common in the history of the Desert tribes, he broke the power of the Almoravids, the power of the Almoravids itself being Amazig. If he really composed a work in the Amazig language, on the nature of God, and the duties of man to man, it must be the oldest composition in any African language, save and except the Æthiopic and Ægyptian. However, he died A.D. 1130, and appointed Abd-el-Mumed, warrior and insurgent, as his successor; warrior, insurgent, and conqueror. He reduced the power of the Almoravides, and the power of the Arabs. He invaded Spain, conquering Grenada. He was a conqueror and an administrator as well; the founder, too, of the Almohad dynasty, which lasted till A.D. 1269, when it was overthrown by the Beni Mrin of the Zenata division.

I have mentioned the Almoravids and their power. Who were they? Word for word, Al-*moravid* is *Marabout*, a Marabout being, in Morocco and the Mandingo countries, a Mahometan priest. The Almoravid is by far the most important of all the Amazig dynasties; and in a notice of the Amazig populations as an influence in the world's history, the Almoravid kings are to Africa what the lines of Tshingiz-khan, Tamerlane, or Togrul Beg are in Asia. It was the Almoravids who most especially carried Mahometanism into Nigritia, Sudania, or the black districts of Africa, as opposed to Ægypt and Mauritania. Timbuktu is an Almoravid foundation.

This presumes that the details of Carette in the difficult separation of the Amazig from the Arabs are to be taken as they are found. I have neither the will nor the way of taking exceptions to them in general. I only confess that, at times, I see a difference between the evidence and the doctrine. How little, too, is the criticism that has been expended on the details of African Mahometanism?

One contribution towards a clear view of them is the history of Amazig. Another is that of

*The Fula.*—Towards the end of the last century a vast number of wandering pastoral tribes spread over that part of Central Africa which is called Sudania, and underwent a change in respect to their social and political organization, which Prichard compares with that of the Arabs at the time of Mahomet. Many—but not all—of them embraced Mahometanism, and that with more than ordinar zeal and devotion. They visited the more civilized parts of Barbary, they performed pilgrimages to Mecca, they recognized in one of their sheiks, called Danfodio, a prophet with a mission, to preach, to convert, to conquer. Under his inspiration they attacked the pagan populations of the countries around—Guber to the north, and Kubbi to the south, Zamfra, Kashna, and parts of the Houssa country to the east. Their war-cry was *Alla Akbar;* their robes and flags were white, emblematic of their purity. Kano was conquered without a blow, so was Yaouri, so was the town of Eyo or Katunga on the Niger, so was part of the Nufi or Tapua country—even the frontier of Bornu was violated.

Danfodio's death, which took place in 1818, was preceded by fits of religious madness; not, however, before he had consolidated a great Fellatah kingdom, and become the terror to the States around. It was in vain that a portion of his conquests revolted. The present Sultan of Sakkatu is the most powerful prince of Africa, whether pagan or Mahometan.

Most of these Fellatas are Mahometans, some retaining their original paganism; but whether pagan or Mahometan, they are still the same people. Their features are the same, their pastoral habits the same, their language the same. This is one of the most isolated tongues of

Africa; with plenty of miscellaneous, but no very definite or special, affinities.

In Borgho, *i. e.* in the parts about Boussa, and Wawa, visited by Lander, there are two populations, one speaking a language akin to the Yoruba, one akin to the Fellatah; so that there are Fellata offsets in Borgho. But here, according to Lander, they have been in the country from time immemorial. Here, too, they hold themselves as a separate people from the Fellatas of Sakkatu, dominant and powerful as that branch is, and respectable as would be the connection. Such, at least, is Lander's statement. Their name, too, undergoes a slight modification, and is Filani. They have neither idea nor tradition as to their origin.

All this looks as if Borgho were the original country of the Fellata stock, the starting-point from which they spread themselves abroad. If so, their movement must have been from south to north.

But we have yet to hear the whole of their history. Under the names of Fula, Fulahs, Foule or Peule, they appear elsewhere. Where? As far north as the Wolof (or Jolof) country—as far north as the parts between the Senegal and the desert—as far north as 17° N.L. Here, between Galam and Kayor, is a vast Fula district—the district of the Fulas of the Siratik. Here, on the south bank of the river, lie the Fulas of Foutatorro, an elevated tract of land forming the watershed to the Senegal and the Gambia.

Thirdly, far in the interior, on the high ground over which Park passed from the drainage of the Senegal to that of the Niger, is a Fula-*du*, or country of the Fulas, between Bambuk and Bambarra.

Fourthly, there are the Fulas to the south of Bammakoo, in the parts called Wasselah, on the Niger itself.

Fifthly, in 11° N.L., on the head-water of the Rio Grande, is the large kingdom of the Fouta-jallo Fulahs, of which Timbu is the metropolis; surrounded by dry or rocky deserts and exposed mountain pastures, prolific with sheep, oxen, goats, and horses. Here, although the use of the plough is unknown, the occupants cultivate the soil and exercise more than one of the mechanical arts. They forge iron and silver, weave and tan, support schools and mosques. To the south lie the Sulimana tribes more or less akin to the Mandingoes. From these, Laing learnt, that the acquisition of the country about Timbu by the Fulas of Futa-jallo was an event of no great antiquity, having taken place about A.D. 1700.

There are other Fula, Fellata, and Filani localities (*e.g.* in Bornu), but an enumeration of the foregoing has been sufficient. It shows the vast space of ground covered by the population so-called.

The Fulas exhibit a decided physical and moral superiority over the ordinary negros; this being chiefly due to their Mahometanism. Although the particular shade of the particular colour which best suits the Fula is not a matter upon which authors write with unanimity, the testimony of all observers goes to the fact that, whether Filani or Fellata, Fellata or Fula, whether pagan or Mahometan, whether Sudanian or Senegambian, whether mountaineer or desert-born, the Fula is something peculiar. Sometimes his complexion is intermediate to that of the African and the Moor; sometimes he is described as being tawny, with soft hair, and with lips by no means prominent: sometimes the skin is of a reddish-black, the countenance being regular. "The tribe of Fulas," writes Golberry, "which under the name of Foules or Peuls, has peopled the borders of the Senegal between Podhon and Galam, are black with a tinge of red or copper colour; they are in general handsome and well-made; the women are handsome, but proud and indolent." Hence, to the Fulajallo Fulas the very definite and suggestive term Red Peuls has been applied; to which the name Black Peuls stands in opposition, this meaning the Fulas of the north bank of the Lower Senegal.

| English. | Tibu. | Berber. | Fulah. |
|---|---|---|---|
| *Man* | mar | alis | —— |
| *Head* | igrof | aghaf | hore |
| *Eye* | tiat | teit | yitere |
| *Ear* | tamazukt | temazug | nofuri |
| *Mouth* | imi | im | hundnko |
| *Tongue* | —— | elies | deurngal |
| *Tooth* | —— | tagumest | nyire |
| *Hand* | fus | afus | samere jungo |
| *Foot* | tishkunt | atar | teppere |
| *Fire* | isghraran | efeu | jeingol |
| *Water* | aman | aman | diyam |
| *Sun* | —— | ettij | nange |
| *Moon* | —— | ayor | leuru |
| *Star* | —— | atar | kandi. |

The extent to which the tribes of the present chapter agree or differ is a question of no little interest. So is the nature of their historical actions and reactions upon each other. That these have been considerable is certain; and it is also certain that the results have been important. Herein lies the justification of the manner in which they have been grouped. I am far from being certain that it is strictly ethnological. The Howssa populations are black, and have been compared to negros. The Amazig are liker to the Arabs.

The Amazig are Mahometans. Many of the Howssa people are pagans. In all this there is difference. At the same time there has been historical contact, and in this historical contact lies the natural character of the group. Timbuctoo is said to be an Amazig foundation. It stands, however, on Sungai soil. Sackatu stands on Howssa soil; but the dynasty that rules it is Fula.

Again—the earliest division of the Amazig tribes, evidently that of a logograph, rather than an actual observer, is that of Ebu Khaldun. He arranges the population under one of two divisions; (1) that of the Brani, and (2) that of the Medgras. This division is said to have had its origin in Eastern Algiers. In the province of Constantine is an ancient monument believed by the natives to be the burial-place of their oldest kings. It is called Medgrâsen. The valley of one of the rivers of Mount Aures (the Mons Aurasius) is called Wadi Branis. The name Branis occurs again in Morocco. Ksila, the most important opponent of the early Mahometan invaders, is said to have been a king of Aurba and Branis. The subdivisions of the Brani were—

1. Azdadzha.
2. Masmuda.
3. Auria.
4. Adzhisa.
5. Ketama.
6. Senhadzha.
7. Aurira.

Of the Medgras, also called El-Beter,

1. Addasa.
2. Nfusa.
3. Darîsa.
4. Leuta.

The subdivisions are again subdivided; *e. g.*:

The Aurira are divided into the Hauara, the Meld (or Lehana), the Mkhar, and the Feldan;

The Hauara fall into the Mhla and Kemlan;

The Meld into the Stat, Urfel, Mserta, Akil;

The Mkhar into the Maus, Zemur, Kebba, and Merisa;

The Feldan into the Kemsana, Urstif, Biata, and Bel.

Word for word, I believe Brani to be Bornu. Does this, then, mean that the history of the Algerian Brani is the history of a Kanuri population? Not necessarily. All that it necessarily means is that the gloss Brani was widely diffused.

Again—the darkness of the Tuarik skin has long commanded attention. What does it come from? From a southern occupancy, or from negro intermixture? Or from both? Future inquiries may give the answer.

The following is Dr. Barth's account of the oasis of Ghat. A freeman in the Berber there spoken is Amoshag, freemen being Imoshag. An unfree person, on the contrary, is Amghi, of which the plural is Imghad. This latter term, which the author first mistook for a Gentile name, afterwards proved to be a common term for subordinate populations in general. That there was a difference in form and feature between the Imoshag and the Imghad is expressly stated. It is also stated that this was greater with the women than the men. Many of these were almost black, and (as such) more or less like negros. The evidence that any difference of language coincided with this difference is by no means decided. "Many of the people, indeed, seem to be bilingual; but by far the greater part of the men do not even understand the Howssa language." Do the women? "I am persuaded that they were originally Berbers who have become degraded by intermixture with black natives." This may or may not be the case.

The Imghad, capable of furnishing about 5000 men, are divided into four sections—the Batanatang, the Farkana, the Segigatang, and the Warwaren. They live in the parts around Ghat rather than in the town itself.

*Amazig of Morocco.*—Except in the parts along the Mediterranean there are Amazig tribes over the whole of

Morocco. In the northern division the Girwan, Ait Imure, Zian, Gibbellah, and Zimurh-Shelluh are found to the west of Mekinez; chiefly in the mountain range. It is here, too, where they occur in the central district; of which the chief occupants are Arabs of the Duquella, Abda, Rahammena, and Shedma tribes.

On the other hand, in the southern division, or the provinces of Draha and Suse, it is the Amazig who preponderate; the tribes being those of the Emsekina, the Exima, the Idautenan, the Idaultil, the Ait-alter, the Kitiwa, the Messa, the Shtuka, and half the Ait-bamaran; the other half of which is Arab. The Suse population is warlike and independent. The Idautenan are free from tax and tribute. They shave the head in front, and wear their hair long behind.

It is the Suse tribes with which the Canary islanders have the most decided affinity. This extends to such minute details as the following:—

The common food of the islanders, writes Glasse, "was barley-meal, roasted, and mixed with goats' milk and butter, and this dish they called Asamotan." The same writes Jackson, "is the common food of the Shelluhs of Atlas, and they call it by a similar name—Azamitta." The extent to which the few fragments of the Lancerotta and Fuerteventura dialects agree with the Shelluh may be seen from the following table:—*

| English. | Canary. | Shelluh. |
|---|---|---|
| *Barley* | temasin | tumzeen |
| *Sticks* | tezzezes | tezezerat |
| *Palm-tree* | taginaste | taginast |
| *Petticoat* | tahuyan | tahuyat |
| *Water* | ahemon | amen |
| *Priest* | faycag | faquair |
| *God* | acoran | mkoorn |
| *Temple* | almogaren | talmogaren |

* Jackson, p. 232.

| English. | Canary. | Shelluh. |
|---|---|---|
| *House* | tamoyanteen | tigameen |
| *Hog* | tawaeen | tamouren |
| *Green Fig* | archormase | akermuse |
| *Sky* | tigot | tigot |
| *Mountain* | thener | athraar |
| *Valley* | adeyhaman | douwaman. |

The parts between Morocco and the drainage of the Senegal are chiefly Arab; perhaps wholly so in regard to language. At any rate, the Amazig elements have yet to be investigated.

The Tibbu language, originally placed in the same class with the Amazig, has since been separated—in my mind, prematurely.

## CHAPTER XV.

The Wolof or Jolof.—Serere.—Serawuli.—Felup.—Balantes.—Biafar.—Nalu.—Sapi.—Bagnon.—Bago.—Bissago.

*The Wolof.*—The Lower Senegal is the occupancy of the Wolofs, or Jolofs, who are black-skinned, tall, and well-made. The lips are but moderately thick, the forehead being prominent; sometimes remarkably so. Mahometanism has, as yet, made but little progress with the Wolof. At the same time they are intelligent and energetic. From the parts about Lake Kayor to the north of the Senegal, as far as to the parts about Cape Verde, the Wolof language is spoken. Akin to it is that of

*The Sereres,* the actual occupants of Cape Verde; who, like the Wolofs, are black pagans, with maritime aptitudes. Both Wolofs and Sereres may be found in London, having come over as sailors; the former being the commoner.

Not so

*The Serawuli.*—The Serawuli lie to the back of the Wolof area, and are a wholly inland population; pastoral rather than agricultural; black, well-made, and energetic. Kölle states that they are divided into six tribes, viz., the Gadsaga, the Gidemara, the Hanyaga, the Dzafunu, the Haire, and the Gangari. Galam, Kaarta, Ludamar, and parts of the Bambarra country, are, more or less Serawuli.

| English. | Wolof. | Serawuli. |
|---|---|---|
| *Man* | gor | yugo |
| *Woman* | dzhigen | yahare |
| *Head* | buob | yime |
| *Nose* | bokan | norune |
| *Eye* | bot | yare |
| *Ear* | nop | taro |
| *Mouth* | gemei | rake |
| *Tooth* | bei | kambe |
| *Tongue* | lamei | nene |
| *Sun* | dzhagat | kiu |
| *Fire* | sefara | imbe |
| *Water* | ndoh | dsi |
| *One* | wian | bane |
| *Two* | yar | fillo |
| *Three* | yat | sikuo |
| *Four* | yarint | narato |
| *Five* | dzudom | karago. |

*The Felup.*—The Felup country is a low alluvium between the mouths of the Gambia and Casamanca: the people being rude and savage. They file their teeth, and occupy but a small area. What applies to them applies, generally, to the populations of the coast trom the Gambia to the Mandingo frontier. Several mutually unintelligible languages are spoken within a comparatively small area. Such is that of

*The Papel,* at the back of the Portuguese settlements at the mouth of the Cacheo; also on one or more of the Bissago islands. Such is that of

*The Bagnon,* another population of the Cacheo. Such, too, is that of

*The Balantes* or *Bulanda,* spoken in part of the Bissago group, and also on the continent.

| English. | Felup. | Papel. | Bagnon. | Bulanda. |
|---|---|---|---|---|
| *Man* | aneine | nyient | udigen | nyendz |
| *Woman* | aseh | nyas | ndikam | gnin |
| *Head* | fokou | bene | bigof | ko |
| *Nose* | enyundo | bihl | nyankin | pfuna |
| *Eye* | gizil | pekil | kegir | fket |

| English. | Felup. | Papel. | Bagnon. | Bulanda. |
|---|---|---|---|---|
| *Ear* | gano | kebars | kinuf | gelo |
| *Mouth* | butom | montun | bure | psum |
| *Tooth* | finin | pinyi | harl | ksit |
| *Tongue* | furcrup | peremte | buremudz | demadn |
| *Sun* | bunah | ono | binek | lehu |
| *Fire* | sambul | buro | kuade | kledsa |
| *Water* | momel | munsop | mundu | wede |
| *One* | fanod | olon | nonduk | foda |
| *Two* | fugapten | ngepugas | hanuk | gsibn |
| *Three* | fufuaten | ngadsint | halal | kahn |
| *Four* | fubaregen | ngebakr | harenek | tasila |
| *Five* | futogen | kinyene | kiluk | kif. |

*The Nalu* extend to or beyond the Nunez; on which, I believe, reside

*The Sapi*, rude and pagan like the rest.

*The Bago.*—From Kölle's notice of the Bago I infer that the name is other than native. If so, it may easily be a name applied to different populations. Kölle writes that there are three different Bago countries, one of which is on the Nunez, and another on the Pongas. These may be Nalu or Sapi, since he also writes that the occupants speak closely-allied languages. But of these he has given no specimens, as the speakers prefer the independence of their native country to visiting Sierra Leone. Those of the first and second division are said to go naked—entirely so; so much so as to be remarked by the Bagos of the third group.

*The Bissago.*—The Bidsogo or Bidsoro of Kölle, is spoken, at least, on the islands Ankaras and Wan of the Bissago group. Word for word, Bidsogo seems to be Basare. If so, and if the Basare, as is stated, lie between the Bulanda and the Bagnon, we have their continental locality as well.

| English. | Biafada. | Nalu. | Bidsogo. |
|---|---|---|---|
| *Man* | —— | lamkiele | —— |
| *Woman* | —— | gnin | —— |
| *Head* | buofa | ko | bu |
| *Nose* | gandzini | minyeni | [illegible] |

| English. | Biafada. | Nalu. | Bidsogo. |
|---|---|---|---|
| *Eye* | agiri | nkiet | ne |
| *Ear* | gunufa | mineau | kono |
| *Mouth* | musu | misole | kana |
| *Tooth* | akede | mfet | kanyi |
| *Tongue* | wudema | milembe | nunume |
| *Sun* | wunari | miyakat | ibande |
| *Fire* | furu | met | munturo |
| *Water* | mambia | nual | nyo |
| *One* | numa | dendeg | modige |
| *Two* | bihe | bele | mundsuwe |
| *Three* | biyo | pat | isobe |
| *Four* | binehi | binam | wagene |
| *Five* | gubida | tedu | modewikoro. |

The Nalu has both Bagnon and Bulanda affinities.

## CHAPTER XVI.

The Mandingo Group.—Bago of Kalum.—Timmani.—Bullom.—The Vei Syllabarium.—Susu, &c.—Sokko, &c.—The Krumen.

*The Mandingos, Bembuk, Bambarra, and Dzhallunka populations.*—The western portion of the Sungai area is bounded by the most inland members of the great Mandingo family, some of which are to be found on the Dzholiba, some on the upper feeders of the Senegal, some on the Gambia, some on the sea-coast, along which they extend from the parts opposite the Isles de Los to Cape Mount; further too than this if, by moderately raising the value of the class, we include the Krumen amongst the Mandingos.

However, the most inland portion of the Mandingo country is Bambarra on the Dzholiba; west of which lie Bembuk and Dzhallunkadu, or Dzhallunkaland; then the proper Mandingo districts on the Lower Gambia.

All these populations are Mahometan, commercial, and, comparatively speaking, civilized; the differences of dialect lying within a small compass.

If so, why place them here? Why not have brought them in contact with the Amazig and Fulas of a preceding chapter? The answer to this lies in the fact of the family being a large one, and of the foregoing characteristics being applicable to only a part of it. Much of what is Mandingo, in the wider sense of the term, is pagăn, rude, and isolated.

At the mouth of the river Nunez some of these rude

members appear on the coast, which continues to be, more or less, Mandingo until we pass Cape Mount.

*The Bago of Kalum*, opposite the Isles de Los, speak a dialect, which along with that of the Landoma of Kölle, is closely akin to

*The Timneh, or Timmani*, to the east of Sierra Leone. Akin to which is

*The Bullom*, of which the Mampa or Sherbro is a dialect.

*The Vei.*—The parts about Cape Mount are the occupancy of the Vei.

The existence of what has been called a native alphabet in the Vei language must now be noticed. It has been known about nine years, and has commanded the attention of more than one investigator. The first notice of it was given in the beginning of 1849, by the commander of H.M.S. Bonetta, Lieut. Forbes, who enquired whether the missionaries of Sierra Leone had ever heard of a written language amongst the natives of the parts about Cape Mount. He also showed a MS., which was soon afterwards in England and in the hands of Mr. Norris, who decyphered and translated it. Meanwhile the Missionary Committee appointed Mr. Kölle to visit the country referred to by Lieut. Forbes and to make inquiries on the spot. This led him to the presence of a Vei native, named Doalu Bukere, about forty years old. He, assisted by five of his friends, invented the alphabet in question; the details being as follows:—

About fifteen years ago he (Doalu Bukere) dreamed a dream, in which a tall, venerable white man, in a long coat, appeared to him, saying, "I am sent to you by other white men."

*Doalu Bukere.*—What for?

*Man in the long coat.*—I bring you a book.

*D. B.*—Good; but what is its nature?

*Man in long coat.*—You must take it to the rest of the people; but neither you nor any one else who will read it must eat either dogs or monkeys, nor yet anything found dead, whereof the throat has not been cut. Nor must you touch the book on those days in which you have touched the fruit of the to-tree.

Look, Doalu, this sign means *i*, this *na*. Now read both together.

*D. B.*—*Ina*. What is the book?

*Man in long coat.*—Wait a little, and I will tell you bye and bye.

Whereon D. B. awoke, sad. His instructor, when telling him to spell *ina* (= *come here*), wrote the signs with his fingers on the ground.

Now D. B. had a brother named Dzhara Barakora, and four cousins, Dzhara Kali, Kalia Bara, Fa Gbasi, and So Tabaku, who all agreed that the dream was a divine revelation; indeed Kali Bara had a dream on the matter of his own.

The five, however, invented the alphabet, which is a syllabarium, and taught it, first in Dzhoudu, and afterwards in Bandakoru.

That D. B. was a man of no ordinary capacity I readily believe, without placing the invention of the Vei syllabarium amongst the more extraordinary instances of African ability. It is anything but an alphabet of wholly independent origin; though, at the same time, it has not been definitely deduced from any older one. It is not English, nor yet Arabic. In being a syllabarium, and written from left to right, it resembles the Æthiopic; butthe details of its affinities have yet to be worked out. It should be compared with the alphabet of the carved rocks of the Berber country.

The important point connected with its valuation as a proof of capacity, is the fact, that D. B. had learned, when a youth, to read English, and, afterwards, Arabic. A missionary had taught him when a boy, and the Koran was the creed of his people. When grown to be a man he was all but a regular letter-carrier. His masters, who were slavers and traders, despatched him to distant places as a messenger, and he told Mr. Kölle that the communication of distant events by means of the letters he conveyed struck him very forcibly. "How is this, that my master knows everything I have done in a distant place? He only looks at the book, and this tells him all. Such a thing we ought to have, by which we could speak to each other even though separated by a great distance."

Kalia Bara, too, speaks of the sense the Vei people had of the advantages of being able to write. "At that time my father Doalu Worogbe began to like books. And the people said the Poro (Europeans) have long heads; nobody has such a long head as the Poro. But some of our people did not believe this. Then I said to my father—'Why do you call what I maintain a lie? Can any Vei man write a letter to his friend, and that friend read it?'"

I think that over and above the wish of the Vei to have an alphabet, they wished also to have a peculiar one—one that the Arabs and English could not read, though the Vei could. That their language particularly required a syllabarium nowhere seems to have struck them; nor does it strike us. The Vei is a Mandingo form of speech, and to the ordinary Mandingo the Arabic alphabet has long been applied without inconvenience. Upon the whole, D. B.'s alphabet is a cypher, rather than aught else. At the same time, the conversion of an alphabet into a syllabarium is a work requiring some thought and ingenuity.

At the back of the Bullom, Timmani, and Vei districts, lie—

*The Susu,*

*The Kissi,*

*The Mendi* areas, wherein are spoken languages akin to the Pessa, Kossa, and other Mandingo forms of speech.

The details of the south-eastern extension of the Mandingo area are unknown. It is believed, however, that they extend over some portion of the Kong range, so as to lie behind not only the Kru country, but the parts to the back of the Ivory, and even part of the Gold, Coast. The dialects of these districts belong chiefly to

*The Sokko, or Asokko,* division.

I have just stated that by moderately raising the value of the Mandingo class we may include within it the Kru, or Krumen, populations. Indeed, the Gio and Mano dialects of Kölle are transitional.

*The Kru, Krumen, or Croomen,* speak the Dewoi (at the back of Cape Mesurado), the Basa, the Kra (or Kru proper), the Grebo, and the Gbe forms of speech of Kölle; akin to which are the Kanga, Mangri, and Gien, dialects of the Mithridates. They extend from Cape Mount to Cape Palmas.

The Kru has been called the Scotchman of Africa. He leaves, without hesitation, his own country to push a fortune wherever a wider field is to be found. He is ready for any employment which may enable him to increase his means, and ensure a return home in a state of improved prosperity. There the Kruman's ambition is to purchase one or two head of cattle, and one or two head of wives, and to enjoy the luxuries of rum and tobacco. Half the Africans that we see in Liverpool and London are Krumen, who have left their own country when young, and taken employment on board a ship, where they exhibit a natural aptitude for the sea. Without being nice as to the destination of the vessel in which they engage, they return home as soon as they can; and rarely or never contract matrimony before their return. In Cape Coast Town, as well as in Sierra Leone, they form a bachelor community, quiet and orderly; and in that respect stand in strong contrast to the other tribes around them. Besides which, with all their blackness, and all their typical negro character, they are distinguishable from most other western Africans; having the advantage of them in make, features, and industry. Hence, a Kruman is pre-eminently the free labourer of Africa; quick of perception and amenable to instruction. His language has been reduced to writing by the American missionaries of Cape Palmas.

| English. | Mandingo. | Bullom | Timmani. | Kru. |
|---|---|---|---|---|
| *Man* | ke | nopugan | wanduni | nyiyu |
| *Woman* | muso | noma | wunibom | nyiro |
| *Head* | ku | bol | rabump | debo |
| *Nose* | nu | umin | asot | mera |
| *Eye* | nya | lifol | rafor | gie |
| *Ear* | tulo | nui | alens | nogu |
| *Mouth* | da | nyen | kisen | nuo |
| *Tooth* | nyi | idsan | rasek | nye |
| *Tongue* | néú | limelim | ramer | me |
| *Sun* | tele | lepal | ret | giro |
| *Fire* | ta | dyom | nant | ne |
| *Water* | dsi | mem | mant | ni |
| *One* | kele | bul | pin | do |
| *Two* | fila | tsin | peran | so |
| *Three* | sawa | ra | pesas | ta |
| *Four* | nani | hiol | panle | nyie |
| *Five* | lolu | man | tomat | mu. |

## CHAPTER XVII.

Populations of the Ivory, Pepper, Gold, and Slave Coasts.—The Avekvom.—The Kouri, the Fantis, and Ashantis.—The Gha or Akkra and Adampi Tribes.—The Kerrapay.—The Dahomey, Yoruba, Benin. Ibo, Tapua, Old Calabar, Dualla, Isubu, Fernando Po, Ediya, and other Tribes.

THE Grain Coast is the country of the Krumen; the Gold Coast that of the Fantis and Ashantis. For the parts between we know little of the sea-board, less of the interior. The chief language of the Pepper and Ivory Coast is

*The Avekvom*, with miscellaneous affinities.

| English. | Avekvom. | Other Languages. |
|---|---|---|
| *Arm* | ebo | ubok, *Efik*. |
| *Blood* | evie | eyip, *Efik*; eye, *Yebu*. |
| *Bone* | ewi | ben, *Fanti*. |
| *Box* | ebru | brânh, *Grebo*. |
| *Canoe* | edie | tonh, *Grebo*. |
| *Chair* | fata | bada, *Grebo*. |
| *Dark* | eshim | esum, *Fanti*; ekim, *Efik*. |
| *Dog* | etye | aja, ayga, *Yebu*. |
| *Door* | eshinavi | usuny, *Efik*. |
| *Ear* | eshibe | esoa, *Fanti*. |
| *Fire* | eya | ija, *Fanti*. |
| *Fish* | etsi | eja, eya, *Fanti*. |
| *Fowl* | esu | suseo, *Mandingo*; edia, *Yebu*. |
| *Ground-nut* | ngeti | nkatye, *Fanti*. |
| *Hair* | emu | ihwi, *Fanti*. |
| *Honey* | ajo | ewo, *Fanti*; oyi, *Yebu*. |
| *House* | eva | ifi, *Fanti*; ufog, *Efik*. |
| *Moon* | efe | hâbo, *Grebo*; ofiong, *Efik*. |
| *Moskito* | efo | obong, *Fanti*. |
| *Oil* | inyu | ingo, *Fanti*. |
| *Rain* | efuzumo-sohn | sanjio, *Mandingo*. |
| *Rainy season* | eshi | ojo, *rain*, *Yebu*. |

| English. | Avekvom. | Other Languages. |
|---|---|---|
| *Salt* | etsa | ta, *Grebo.* |
| *Sand* | esian-na | utan, *Efik.* |
| *Sea* | etyu | idu, *Grebo.* |
| *Stone* | desi | sia, shia, *Grebo.* |
| *Thread* | jesi | gise, *Grebo.* |
| *Tooth* | enena | nyeng, *Mandingo;* gne, *Grebo.* |
| *Water* | esonh | usu, *Fanti.* |
| *Wife* | emise | muso, *Mandingo;* mbesia, *Fanti.* |
| *Cry* | yaru | isu, *Fanti.* |
| *Give* | nae | nye, *Grebo;* no, *Efik.* |
| *Go* | le | olo, *Yebu.* |
| *Kill* | bai | fa, *Mandingo;* pa, *Yebu.* |

*English*, one.
Avekvom, *eton.*
Kossa, *ita.*
Pessa, *tah.*
Kru, *du.*
Bassa, *do.*
Popo, *da.*
Haussa, *dea.*

*English*, two.
Avekvom, *anyu.*
Popo, *ono.*

*English*, three.
Avekvom, *aza.*
Uhobo, *ezza.*
Kossa, *shau.*
Pessa, *saua.*

*English*, four.
Avekvom, *ana.*
Mandingo, &c., *nani.*
Kru, &c., *nnie.*

*English*, five.
Avekvom, *enyu.*
Fanti, *enum.*
Ashanti, *inni.*

*English*, six.
Avekvom, *awâ.*
Ako, *effa.*

*English*, eight.
Avekvom, *etye.*
Ashanti, *auotui.*
Fanti, *auotui.*
Appa, *tita.*
Popo, *tatu.*
Moko, *tua.*

*English*, ten.
Avekvom, *ejiu.*
Fanti, *idu.*
Kissi, *to.*
Benin, *ti.*

The chief family of the interior is one for which I propose the name

*Kouri.*—The Kouri area, as I imagine, lies between the Kong mountains and the Niger, beginning where the eastern divisions of the Mandingo group end. It is also bounded by the Howssa and Ashanti areas. The country has not been explored by Europeans. Word for word,

I believe Kouri to be Goburi, Cumbri, Kafir, and Giaour.

*The Fantis, Ashantis*, and other allied populations of the Gold Coast, come now under notice. The most general name for the language of these parts is, according to Riis, who has published a grammar of it, Otshi. It is spoken by the Ashanti, Denkyira, and Vasa populations; also by the Fanti; also by the natives of the districts named Akim and Akwam (Akwambu); also by those of Akripon and seven other towns of Akwapim.

In the Otshi pantheon the supreme divinity is called Onjama, or Nyankupong, the latter word meaning the sky or heavens. Nyankupong is also called Odamangkama, or the Creator; Amosu, the rain-giver; Amovua, the sun-giver. The spirits of the hill, the forest, the rock, the river, &c., are called Obosom, apparently a derivative from the root *sum = shadow*, Abonsam being the evil demon, and Sasabonsam the god of the earth, more bad than good.

These points are noticed because we are now in a part of Africa where the Mahometan influences are at a *minimum*, and where the pagan observances are known to a fair degree of accuracy. We are in the region of the purest, *i. e.* the grossest and most unmodified, fetichism—snake-worship, medicine-men, obi-sorcerers, superstitious ordeals, devil-drivers, and Mumbojumbos. The inhabitants of a Fanti village meet at nightfall, with sticks and staves, to yell and howl. By doing this they fancy that they have frightened the devils from the land, which when they have done, they feast.

The yam custom is held in September. The king takes part in it. So do his medicine-men. So does every one else who can. A procession is formed; noisy, irregular; over which the king, seated in a basket, carried by his slaves, and with an umbrella over his head, presides. On reaching his dwelling, a sacrifice is made of eggs and fowls. It used (as is believed) to have been one of a human being. A yam is then tasted, and pronounced fit to eat. This having been done, the people consider themselves free to dig for them.

A fisherman will not go to sea on a Tuesday, nor will a huntsman enter the forest on a Friday.

A being named *Tahbil* resides in the substance of the rock upon which Cape Coast is built, and watches the town. Every morning, offerings of food or flowers are left for him on the rock. Most villages have a corresponding deity; and in earlier times there is good reason for believing that human beings were sacrificed to him.

If the survivors of a deceased Fanti be poor, the corpse is quietly interred in one of the denser spots of the jungles; and if rich, the funeral is at once costly and bloody; since gold and jewels are buried along with the dead body, and human sacrifices not unfrequently offered.

The administration of justice is rude and summary, the evidence consisting, for the most part, in either absurd ordeals or cruel tortures. The *dhoom* test is common over all western Africa. A poisonous or an emetic infusion is made. Innocence drinks and ejects, guilt swallows and dies of, it. That the priest, sorcerer, or medicine-man is often the detector of crime is what we expect. What is called "tying Guinea fashion" is one of the sharpest of their tortures. The arms are drawn together behind the back by a cord fixed half-way between the elbows and shoulders. A piece of wood is then inserted, by means of which the cord can be tightened or loosened. The African analogue of the boot is a block of wood and a staple. By driving in the staple any amount of agonizing pressure can be applied.

At the same time there is the exercise, among the Fantis more especially, of some little industry and art. The hardest workers are the fishers, who use a canoe of wood of the bombax, from ten to twelve feet in length, and strengthened by cross timbers. The net—a casting net—is made from the fibres of the aloe or the pineapple, and is about twenty feet in diameter (?). Next to these come the farmers, whose rough agriculture consists in the cultivation of maize, bananas, yams, and pumpkins; and lastly, the gold-seekers. Of this there is abundance; and where the European coin of the coast ceases, the native currency of gold-dust begins. Sums of so small a value as three half-pence are thus paid; smaller ones being represented by cowries. The highest of their arts is that of manufacturing gold ornaments, and this is the hereditary craft of certain families. These transmit the secret of their skill from father to son, and keep the corporation to which they belong up to a due degree of closeness, by avoiding intermarriage with any of the more unskilled labourers.

There is, too, a little weaving, and a little skill in pottery.

An African empire begins with a number of petty States with a little headman (by courtesy called king) to each. They quarrel with one another until some politician, stronger or more crafty than the rest, reduces them and consolidates an empire. The Ashantis have thus, within the last century, made themselves the ruling power in the domain of the Otshi language. In the Aquapim, and perhaps in many of the neighbouring, chieftaincies, the headmanship descends from the uncle to the sister's son, as is the case, over and over again, in India, in North-Western America, and elsewhere. In Congo the children of the females of royal blood succeed, the mothers being permitted to choose their husband, and to sell him if he fail to suit.

There is slavery everywhere. The worst form of slavery is that of the captive taken in war. His life is spared in order that he may be sold. A milder condition is that of the *adstrictus familiæ*. Here the servitude is domestic, and the slave is one of the family. Removal from the native soil is ensured against. Slavery of this kind is often voluntary. An able-bodied man may pawn his body, or borrow money on his labour. Of course debts may be worked out on this principle.

*The Accra, Inkra*, or, as the natives call it, the Gha language is nearly related to the Otshi, being spoken near Cape Castle, the Adampi or Tambi* being a dialect of it.

*The Kerrapay* is spoken in Abiruw, Odaw, Aokugwa (with Abonse), Adukrum and Apiradi, villages or towns of Akwapim, other than Otshi; in which, however, the Otshi, as the language of the dominant population, is generally understood.

*Date and Kubease.*—These, like Abiraw, &c., are Akwapim villages, whereof the language is other than Otshi. It is other than Kerrapong, Kerrapay, Kerrapi, or Krepee as well.

| English. | Akkrah. | Adampé. | Kreepé. |
|---|---|---|---|
| *Fire* | lah | lah | edjo |
| *Water* | noo | nўu | éché |
| *Sky* | n'wā | ë'om | jimmā |
| *Sun* | un | pun | āwā |
| *Moon* | yon'che'lé | ū'rammé | wālā |
| *Star* | ou'rahme | ū'rammé dodo'ë | rotev'e |
| *Air* | koy'ah | koīyo | av'vuvoh |
| *God* | mah'u | mah'wu | mah'nu |
| *Devil* | bo'san | az'zā | baīya |
| *Man* | bom'ma | nu'mu | n'chu *or* ammā |

* Not Tembu, which is a Kouri dialect.

| English. | Akkrah. | Adampé. | Kreepé. |
|---|---|---|---|
| *Woman* | yo | ye'o | yonno |
| *Boy* | bākā | jho'quā | deyvé |
| *Girl* | ob'bli'o | yā'yo | tubboquā |
| *Infant* | abbe'fah'o | jho'quā-borbio | vévé'ahjā |
| *White man* | blofonyo | blofon'o | yovo |
| *Wife* | n'yah | ā'yo | sun'no |
| *Head* | échu *or* écho | yé | tah |
| *Hair* | cchawë | yébuoh | dah |
| *Eye* | emay *or* hingmā | hingmāi | unku |
| *Nose* | gungo | gugon | watté |
| *Mouth* | narbo | nỹ'am | numé |
| *Teeth* | nĕoneĕng | lūn'go | addu |
| *Tongue* | lillā | lillā | addā |
| *Ear* | toë *or* toy | toë | etto |
| *One* | eku'me | kok'kā | dek'kah |
| *Two* | en'yo | en'yo | ā'vā |
| *Three* | ettā | et'tā | ātong |
| *Four* | edj'wā | ādj'way | en'nā |
| *Five* | en'nu'mo | en'nuo | atton |
| *Six* | ek'pah | ek'pah | ād'dā |
| *Seven* | pah'wo | m'pah'go | adderré |
| *Eight* | pah'no | pahn'yo | en'yé |
| *Nine* | nā'ing | nā | en'yeda |
| *Ten* | na'mah | nu'mah | ā'wo. |

*The Fot.*—This is the name for either the chief tribe or the chief language of Dahomey. Of all the countries of Africa, Dahomey has the credit of being the most truly savage. The greatest of the fetishes is the snake, which finds its way into both holy and secular buildings, and is feared, fed, and respected. Slavery, like superstition, is nowhere more general than in Dahomey. So is cruelty both in war and punishments. The Dahomey Amazons have commanded attention. The king is said to have a regiment consisting of four thousand of his wives. Strange as this (even allowing for exaggerations) appears to be, it is of a part with the institutions of the neighbouring countries. Where wives are married by the score or hundred, they must be utilized. Clapperton found the queens and half-queens of the King of Eyeo at long distances from the palace trading for him ; half-agents, half-housekeepers, with heavy loads on their heads, just like the wives of ordinary monogamists.

The King of Kiama's wives were something more. He showed himself to Clapperton with his train, in which were six spear-bearers, young girls from fifteen to seventeen years of age, with a fillet round their heads, strings of beads round their waists, and nothing anywhere else.

The following are translations of some of the Dahomey songs.

1.

When Yorubah said she could conquer Dahomey;
When we meet we 'll change their night into day;
Let the rain fall:
The season past, the river dries.
Yorubah and Dahomey!
Can two rams drink from one calabash?
The Yoribahs must have been drunk to say
Dahomey feared them,
They could conquer Dahomey.

2.

There 's a difference between Gezo and a poor man;
There 's a difference between Gezo and a rich man.
If a rich man owned all,
Gezo would still be king.
All guns are not alike;
Some are long, some short, some thick, some thin.
The Yoribahs must be a drunken nation,
And thus we will dance before them.

3.

Gezo is king of kings!
While Gezo lives we have nothing to fear.
Under him we are lions, not men.
Power emanates from the king.

4.

Let all eyes behold the king!
There are not two but one—
One only, Gezo!
All nations have their customs,
But none so brilliant or enlightened,
As those of Dahomey.
People from far countries are here:
Behold all nations, white and black,
Send their ambassadors.

AMAZONS' CHORUS.

With these guns in our hands,
And powder in our cartouch-boxes,
    What has the king to fear?
When we go to war, let the king dance,
While we bring him prisoners and heads.

GENERAL CHORUS.

Let the king grant war speedily!
Do not let our energies be damped.
Fire cannot pass through water.
    The king feeds us;
    When we go to war.
        Remember this!
We are clothed and fed by Gezo;
In consequence our hearts are glad.

*The Yoruba.*—The area of the Yarriba or Yoruba forms of speech succeeds that of the Fôt. It scarcely, if at all, touches the sea. The point, however, where it most nearly approaches it is the country about Badagry and the River Lagôs. Here it lies between Dahomey and Benin. Clapperton, who visited the capital of the kingdom of Eyeo, makes the natives a little less savage than those of Dahomey; he makes them, for instance, shocked at the extent to which the Dahomey people sacrificed human beings. At the same time his notice of their funeral is as follows. Over a poor man no ceremony at all. Over a rich man the firing of guns, and a feast in his house. Over a king the sacrifice of certain caboceers, certain women, certain favourite slaves. These were poisoned; the dose being administered by a fetish-man in a parrot's egg. If it failed to take effect the victim gained nothing by the failure. On the contrary, he was presented with a rope, and sent home to hang himself. In respect to the ordinary sacrifices made during the celebration of their customs it depends upon the fetish-man whether it be human or not. Something must be offered up; if a man, a criminal.

The land rises gradually from the sea, being strong and clayey, until it reaches a granite range of hills, between 400 and 800 feet above the level of the narrow, winding, and well-watered valleys. The hillier the land the scantier the wood. The women, who are, as usual, slaves and drudges to the men, are coarse-looking and plain. The men, however, "have less of the characteristic features of the negro than any I" (*i. e.* Captain Clapperton) "have yet seen; their lips are less thick, and their noses more inclined to the aquiline shape than negroes in general. The men are well made, and have an independent carriage."

In the province of Wawu the name Cumbrie appears; word for word, in my mind, Kaffir. When Clapperton asked the Sultan of Bowssa who were first inhabitants of the country, he answered: "The Cumbrie;" his own ancestors having come from Bornu, and the Sultan of Nike being descended from a younger branch. I understand this to mean that certain elements of the Bowssa civilization came from the east, *i.e.* partly from Bornu and partly from Howssa; the Howssa language being understood by even the Cumbrie.

The details of the Gha and Yoruba have been exhibited by native ethnologists; strange as the term may appear. More than one paper on the former nation has been published by Mr. Hanson, more than one edition of a Yoruba grammar by Mr. Crowther. On Mr. Hanson's notices more will be said in the sequel. Mr. Crowther's grammar gives us the following legend and proverbs:—

It is said by the Yorubans, that fifteen persons were sent from a certain region; and that a sixteenth, whose name was Okambi (an only child), and who was afterwards made king of Yoruba, volunteered to accompany them. The personage who sent them out presented Okambí with a small piece of black cloth, with something tied up in it; besides a fowl, a servant, and a trumpeter. Okinkin was the name of the trumpeter. On opening the gate of this unknown region, they observed a large expanse of water before them, through which they were obliged to wade. As they went on, Okinkin, the trumpeter, reminded Okambí of the small piece of cloth, by sounding the trumpet according to the instructions he had previously received from the personage above mentioned. The cloth being opened, a palm-nut, which was deposited in it with some earth, fell into the water. The nut grew immediately into a tree, which had sixteen branches. As the travellers were all fatigued from their long march in the water, they were very glad of this unexpected means of relief; and soon climbed up, and rested themselves on the branches. When they had recruited their strength, they prepared again for the journey; yet not without great perplexity, not knowing in what direction they should proceed. In this situation, a certain personage, Okikisi, saw them from the region whence they set out, and reminded Okinkin, the trumpeter, of his duty; on which he sounded again, and thus reminded Okambí of the small piece of black cloth, as before. On opening it, some earth dropped into the water, and became a small bank; when the fowl which was given to Okambí flew upon it, and scattered it; and wherever the earth touched the water, it immediately dried up. Okambí then descended from the palm-tree, allowing only his servant Tetú, and his trumpeter, to come down with him. The other persons begged that the might be allowed to come down; but he did not comply with their request until they had promised to pay him, at certain times, a tax of 200 cowries each person.

Thus originated the kingdom of Yoruba, which was afterwards called Ifè; from whence three brothers set out for a further discovery of better countries.

1.

Marks made with buje do not last more than nine days,
Marks made with inabí do not last more than a year.

2.

The farm-house will be after the farm,
The ridge of the roof will be after the house.

3.

If you have no money (to give), you may pay visits;
If you cannot visit, you may send kind messages.

4.

A pleader (with the gods) wards off death,
A pleader (with the judge) wards off punishment;
If the heat is oppressive
A fan wards off that.

5.

However a ruined mud wall may be garnished, the trouble will be useless;
But all trouble bestowed upon things made of wood is advantageous.

6.

The owner may broach his cask of liquid, or barrel of powder;
But he who is sent with it dares not broach the cask.

7.

He who sees another's faults knows well how to talk about them;
But he covers his own with a potsherd.

8.

Ordinary people are as common as grass;
But good people are dearer than an eye.

9.

Let the white pigeon tell the woodpecker,
Let bird tell bird.

10.

When there are no elders, the town is ruined;
When the master dies, the house is desolate.

11.

Beg for help and you will meet with refusals;
Ask for alms, and you will meet with misers.

12.

We wake, and find marks on the palm of our hand,
We do not know who made them;
We wake, and find an old debt,
We do not know who contracted it.

13.

If a needle fall from a leper's hand, it requires consideration (to pick it up);
If a great matter is before the council, it requires deep thought.

14.

No one can cure a monkey of squatting;
So no one can deprive a man of his birthright.

15.

A pistol has not a bore like a cannon;
A poor man has not money at his command as the rich.

16.

A wild boar, in the place of a pig, would ravage the town;
And a slave made king would spare nobody.

17.

The injury of a bag
Is (caused by) the injury of the pack-rope;
If the pack-rope breaks,
The bag will go down.

18.

To a liar a lie is natural;
Anything which a man is in the habit of doing is natural to him.

19.

The forest is very dark,
The night is very dark;
The darkness of the night is deeper than the darkness of the forest.

20.

The elephant makes a dust,
The buffalo makes a dust;
The dust of the elephant Hides that of the buffalo.

21.

Mouth keeping to mouth,
Lip keeping to lip,
Bring trouble to the jaws.

22.

Sacrifices were prescribed to the turkey-buzzard, But it refused to offer them,
Sacrifices were prescribed to the Akalla vulture, But it refused to offer them,
Sacrifices were prescribed to the pigeon, And it offered them.

23.

The locust will eat,
The locust will drink,
The locust will go away;
But where will the grasshopper hide itself?

24.

When the day dawns,
The trader takes his money,
The spinner takes her spindle,
The warrior takes his shield,
The weaver takes his batten,
The farmer wakes, himself and his hoe,
The hunter wakes with his quiver and bow.

The chief negros of Abbeocuta are Yoribanis.

| English. | Kouri. | Dahomey. |
|---|---|---|
| *Man* | abalo | sunu |
| *Woman* | alo | nyoni |
| *Head* | nyoro | ta |
| *Nose* | moro | awoti |
| *Eye* | esire | nuku |
| *Ear* | tingbanu | oto |
| *Mouth* | noro | onu |
| *Tooth* | gede | adu |
| *Tongue* | nsolumure | ede |
| *Fire* | gmin | zo |
| *Water* | lem | zi |
| *One* | kudum | ode |
| *Two* | nale | owe |
| *Three* | nadeso | ato |
| *Four* | nanasa | ene |
| *Five* | nanua | ato. |

*The Ibo Group.*—Conterminous with the Yoruba area lies that of the Ibo group, on each side of the Nun stream of the Niger. Here reside several of the kings and kinglings with whom our treaties have to be made against the slave trade; kings who give licences to trade, and who make the access to the interior part of the country practicable or the contrary. There are kings and caboceers —viceroys with kings over them—so that there is a sort of feudal chain of vassalage and sovereignty. King Emmery, for instance, was, at the time of the Niger Expedition, the chief of a village on the river Nun, himself being a subject to King Boy of Brass Town. Then there was the kingdom of Iddah, with its subordinate kingships, whilst Kakanda and Egga were the dependencies of a really consolidated monarchy at Sakkatu.

At best, however, the African monarch, except in the Mahometan kingdoms, is but a sorry potentate; a drunken, sensual, slave-dealing polygamist. When Drs. McWilliam and Stanger visited this same King Emmery, his dress was a uniform coatee that had belonged to a drummer in some English regiment, a plain black hat, and a blue cotton handkerchief for the lower man—a blue cotton handkerchief for drawers, trousers and stockings, collectively; the dress of the ordinary natives being limited to a simple shirt, with a cloth round the middle. In this we get one of the measures of the amount of English influence and trade.

The huts are of clay, arranged in squares rather than in rows; and when the soil is low and liable to be flooded, they are raised some feet from the ground on a foundation of wooden pillars; in which case a ladder leads to the principal opening. The king's palace is an assemblage of such huts; a miniature town; one side of the square which they form being the women's quarters. Here reside the numerous wives, half-wives, and ex-wives of the sovereign, the number of which is always considerable, since the rank of the man regulates it. The following table gives us, in the first column, the names of the different members of the Court of King Obi of Ibo in 1840; in the others, their age, and the numbers of their wives and families:—

| | | Wives. | | Children. | |
|---|---|---|---|---|---|
| | Age. | Living. | Dead. | Living. | Dead. |
| 1. Ajeh, king's brother | 40 | 80 | 40 | uncertain. | |
| 2. Amorara, judge and king's mouth | 40 | 4 | 2 | 2 | 6 |
| 3. Ozama, headman | 35 | 4 | 2 | 2 | 6 |
| 4. Omenibo, headman | 32 | 3 | 2 | 3 | 6 |
| 5. Amebak, headman | 28 | 4 | 1 | 3 | 6 |
| 6. Magog, bugler | 34 | 2 | 1 | 6 | 3 |
| 7. Ambili, headman | 35 | 3 | 2 | 3 | 11 |
| 8. Ogrou, headman | 30 | 3 | 1 | 2 | 2 |
| 9. Obi, king | 44 | 110 | uncertain. | | |

The nearer the sea the greater the amount of negro characteristics.

The Ibos of the Delta are extreme negros. Not so, however, the inhabitants of Iddah, where the greater "altitude of the district and the superior dryness operate in their favour. The people are in general well-made; the features are more softened and rounded than the Ibus. Their lips protrude, but are less thick; the forehead ample, though retreating. Altogether they have a look of superior intelligence."

When they touch the Yoruba and Nufi districts, the Ibo tribes come within the weak influence of an imperfect Mahometanism. As a rule they are Pagans. They are succeeded by the tribes who speak

*The Efik* and its allied dialects, occupants of the parts about the old Calebar River, but closely related to

*The Attam* or *Otam* populations of inland districts, the exact boundary of whose area is unknown. On the south the Efik and Attam tribes are succeeded by

*The Bimbia, Dualla, and Isubu tribes*, closely akin to which are

*The Amboise Islanders and the Ediya of Fernando Po*, men whose skins are yellow or coppery, rather than black; the island being volcanic.

*The Benga.*—The Benga inhabit the Islands of Corisco Bay and the two capes by which the bay is bounded. They amount to about 4000. Their language is spoken by a number of allied tribes to the north and north-east. To the Mbiko, Dibwe, Belengi, and the population extending southward it is unintelligible. The language of these is probably that of

*The Mpongwe*, or tribes of the lower Gabún, to the back of which lie

*The Akeli*, whose language is the Bakeli, and whose skins are lighter than those of the coastmen, darker than those of the mountaineers of the interior. Their bodies are said to be disproportionately long to the extremities. They fall into divisions and sub-divisions; are often at war; cultivate the soil a little; hunt and engage in trade when opportunities present themselves of acting as factors between the Mpongwe and

*The Pangwe*, a large tribe from the interior, occupant of the country behind the Sierra de Chrystal mountains.

We now return to the Ibo frontier, to the north of which lie the members of

*The Tapua*, or *Nufi*, *group*, with lighter skins, and more regular features than any of the tribes of the coast; pagans with a tincture of Mahometanism, and, like the Yoribanis, with whom they are conterminous, encroached upon by the Fulas.

| English. | Nufi. | Ibo.* | Udom. | Isubu. |
|---|---|---|---|---|
| *Man* | bagi | nuoke | manu | mome |
| *Woman* | isagi | ndiom | manka | moito |
| *Head* | eti | isi | esi | molofo |
| *Nose* | eye | imi | ntanauam | mbemba |
| *Eye* | eye | anya | lemar | liso |
| *Ear* | tugba | nte | eton | itoe |
| *Mouth* | emi | ono | anyo | mulongo |
| *Tooth* | eka | ezi | leman | isongo |
| *Tongue* | dzentara | ile | leliwe | yeme |
| *Fire* | ena | oko | ngun | moya |
| *Water* | nua | mmeli | alap | maliwa |
| *One* | wene | ote | dzidsi | yoko |
| *Two* | guba | abo | beba | wewai |
| *Three* | guta | ato | besa | pelalo |
| *Four* | guni | ano | bele | benen |
| *Five* | gutsu | isa | berom | betanu. |

The exact details of the Nufi area on its southern and western frontiers are unknown. The class is a large one, one to which several of the languages from the unexplored parts of Africa belong.

* The Isoama dialect of the Polyglotta Africana.

## CHAPTER XVIII.

### The Kafir and Hottentot Families.

AND now we are again on the sea-coast, just south of the equator, and in the parts between the Gabun and the Congo. The details here are obscure; but as we move southwards they improve. The European influences change. With the parts to the north of the equator the English have more to do than the Portuguese; though the influence of that nation is, even there, considerable. We know this as a matter of fact. We might, however, even without evidence, infer it. The oldest European words in the jargon of the West Africans are Portuguese, *e. g. savey* (*know*), *caboceer*, *fetish.* English, however, is rapidly gaining ground. The missionaries by whom the Bakeli, Mpoongwe and Benga languages have been reduced to writing are American, the Christianity which they introduce being Protestant. In Loango, however, it is the Romanist creed from the Portuguese teacher.

In Congo the Portuguese influence increases; and in Angola it is represented by the important metropolis of San Paolo de Loando. It extends as far inland as Cassange; and as far along the coast as 15° S.L., there or thereabouts.

Beyond this both the political and ethnological relations run south, *i. e.* in the direction of the Cape, where Dutch and English influences replace those of Portugal. These last, however, will reappear when the Cape has been doubled and the Kafir and Zulu districts, on the eastern side of Africa, have been passed. Inhambane and Sofala are Portuguese. More to the north, Arabia makes itself felt. Have we not spoken of the African possessions of the Imam of Muskat on the Zanzibar coast and in the area of the Suwaheli, or Sohili?

With these preliminaries I proceed to enlarge on the word Kaffir, Kaffre, or Kafir. It has two meanings. It means, in its more limited sense, the Kaffres of Caffraria, chiefly of the Amakosa tribe, the men who have given so much trouble to the Cape colonists. But it also has a wider or more general signification, and in this case it serves as the designation of a large family of allied populations—a very large family—one of the largest in Africa.

The connecting link between its numerous branches is the language, of which the structure has (amongst others) the following characteristics. Suppose that in English, instead of saying

*M*an's *d*og, we said *d*an *d*og,
*S*un's beam—*b*un *b*eam,
*F*ather's *d*aughter—*d*ather *d*aughter,
*D*aughter's father—*f*aughter father;

in such a case we should accommodate the sound of the word in the possessive case to that with which the word in the nominative case began. And if we did this, we should assuredly do something very remarkable in the way of speech. Now the Kaffre tongues all do this. It is done by the Amakosa, the Zulu, the Fingo, the Bechuana. It is done by the languages of Benguela, Angola, Congo, and Loango, &c. It is done by the languages on the eastern coast as well, as far as the Equator. It is done, so far as we know, by the languages of the interior. It is certainly done by the languages of the Great Lake Ngami.

The Kaffre division, then, is a large one; and it is based chiefly on similarity of language. In physical form, the range of difference is great. Some of the Kaffres are negro, others brown in colour, and with lips of moderate thickness.

On the other hand, more than one good writer has enlarged upon the points of contrast; and such there certainly are, if we take the more extreme forms—the typical Kaffre and typical Negro. In the latter, for instance, the skin (as aforesaid) may be brown rather than black. Then the cheek-bones may project outwards; and where the cheek-bones so project beyond a certain limit, the chin appears to taper downwards, and the vertex upwards. When this becomes exaggerated we hear of lozenge-shaped skulls. Be this as it may, the breadth in the malar portion of the face is often a remarkable feature in the Kaffre physiognomy. This he has in common with the Hottentot. Sometimes, too, the eye is oblique; the opening generally narrow.

In going over the details of the great Kafir family it is convenient to take them in the following order:—

1. The Portuguese districts of the western coast; from the Equator to 16° S.L., there or thereabouts.

2. The corresponding portions of the eastern side of the continent, *i. e.* the coasts of Zanzibar, and Mozambique, along with the Portuguese districts on the Pacific, or the countries of Botonga, Sofala, Imhambane, &c.

3. The Zulu and Kafir countries.

4. The interior.

1. *The Portuguese area on the west.*—In making the southern boundary of the Gabún tribes the frontier of the Kafir area, I consult convenience rather than accuracy. The line must be drawn somewhere, and when, although drawn where it is, it is, to a great extent, arti-

ficial, it would be just the same if it were carried further north. The physical formation of the Gabún and Cameroon tribes is that of the occupants of Loango. The alliterational system, though current throughout the Kafir languages, is, by no means, confined to them. The Benga, Dualla, Atam, and other groups, exhibit it as well. But as these graduate into the Tapua, Ibo, and their allies, nothing is gained by associating them with the Kafir forms of speech.

I repeat, then, the notice that the line of demarcation between the northern members of the Kafir, and the southern members of the Isubu, family, is provisional and artificial rather than definite and natural.

In Loango and Congo the men and women are more negros than aught else. The skin, however, is somewhat lighter. They are either pure pagans or imperfect Christians; their Christianity being due to the missionaries from Portugal. There is domestic slavery, and the slavery of the slave-merchants; quite as much of the latter as of the former.

Except that the Portuguese influence is greater in the latter countries, the ethnology of Loango and Congo is that of Angola and Benguela also; the parts best known being those on the coast. The particular tribe of the parts about Cassange, the most inland of the Portuguese settlements, is that of the Bangala; many of whom are imperfect Christians, and more or less Portuguese in blood. Of the Basongo, an allied tribe, Livingstone gives the following description:—

"All the inhabitants of this region, as well as those of Londa, may be called true negroes, if the limitations formerly made be borne in mind. The dark colour, thick lips, heads elongated backwards and upwards and covered with wool, flat noses, with other negro peculiarities, are general; but while these characteristics place them in the true negro family, the reader would imbibe a wrong idea, if he supposed that all these features combined are often met with in one individual. All have a certain thickness and prominence of lip, but many are met with in every village in whom thickness and projection are not more marked than in Europeans. All are dark, but the colour is shaded off in different individuals from deep black to light yellow. As we go westward, we observe the light colour predominating over the dark, and then again, when we come within the influence of damp from the sea air, we find the shade deepen into the general blackness of the coast population. The shape of the head, with its woolly crop, though general, is not universal. The tribes on the eastern side of the continent, as the Caffres, have heads finely developed and strongly European. Instances of this kind are frequently seen, and after I became so familiar with the dark colour as to forget it in viewing the countenance, I was struck by the strong resemblance some natives bore to certain of our own notabilities. The Bushmen and Hottentots are exceptions to these remarks, for both the shape of their heads and growth of wool are peculiar—the latter, for instance, springs from the scalp in tufts with bare spaces between, and when the crop is short, resembles a number of black peppercorns stuck on the skin, and very unlike the thick frizzly masses which cover the heads of the Balonda and Maravi. With every disposition to pay due deference to the opinions of those who have made ethnology their special study, I have felt myself unable to believe that the exaggerated features usually put forth as those of the typical negro, characterize the majority of any nation of south central Africa. The monuments of the ancient Egyptians seem to me to embody the ideal of the inhabitants of Londa, better than the figures of any work of ethnology I have met with."

The Kisama on the Coanga are still independent. The few seen by Livingstone reminded him of the Hottentots. The Libollo, their neighbours, are also, as yet, unsubdued, as are many others besides.

2. *The intertropical area on the eastern side of Africa.* —This extends from the equator to the tropic of Capricorn, or a little beyond. It comprises the coasts of Zanzibar, and Mozambik; where the influences are Arab, and where the population is called Sûaheli, Suwaheli, or Soheli, the language being the Kisuaheli. The most northern tribes are

*The Pocomo*, on the river Maro, or Pocomosi, who extend, perhaps, as far as the equator.

Then on each side of 5° S.L., to the north and west of Mombaz itself, come the Wanika, the Wakamba (or Merremengo), the Wataita, five days inland, the Taviati, further westward still, ending with the Msegua and Msambara, of the parts opposite Pemba Island and the river Pungani.

*The Wanika*, imperfect Mahometans, marry early, are described as drunken, thievish, and irascible, as disfiguring their bodies by filing their teeth and scarring their skins, as holding feasts, and pouring the blood of a slaughtered bullock over the graves of their dead.

*The Wakamba* are herdsmen, when at home, traders when abroad. They sell rather than barter, *i. e.* they know the use and value of money. They have long hair, which they twist into strings, Galla fashion, are patriarchal in their government, brew from the sugar-cane, and shoot with poisoned arrows.

These tribes are native, and comparatively un-
They all lie somewhat inland, and, so de-

tinguished from the population of the coast. This is of two kinds—native and Arab. The native is, in the essential elements of physical form and language, the same as the tribes just enumerated; or, if not actually the same, closely allied. Their name is, word for word, that of the Somauli under a modified form, and of Arab origin or application. Their creed is Mahometan. In short they are Pocomo, Wanika, &c., converted and turned maritime. Between them and the Arabs there are all degrees of intermarriage and intermixture. Some of the most abnormal and strange-looking blacks of the streets of London are Sohili half-bloods. Their face is full and flat, their skin brownish-black, their hair long and crisp rather than woolly, their extremities long, their nostrils patulous.

The island of Zanzibar is an Arab rather than an African settlement, belonging to the Imam of Muskat, who claims no small portion of the opposite coast. The population of the town is estimated at 200,000, the chief language being Arabic, the creed Mahometan, the government despotic. The slave-trade with foreigners is professedly forbidden under pain of death; the citizens, however, may purchase for their own use. The Africans thus brought over are called Sídís, or Murima. Amongst them are to be fonnd representatives of most of the tribes of Eastern Africa. A few children are annually exported to Persia.

The fringe of the Zanzibar coast is Sohili; the natives being to be sought inland.

The fringe of the Mozambique coast is also Sohili. Of the populations of the interior, of which the Makúa are the chief, it is safe to say that they are closely allied to those of the parts behind Zanzibar; and they seem, from specimens of their language and descriptions, to be, at least, as much akin to each other. The Maravi, Muntu, Meto, Matatan, Kiriman (Quilimani), vocabularies of the Polyglotta Africana, though some of them lie five degrees apart, are all members of the same section of the same division; all members, too. of the divisions which contain those of

| English. | Wanika. | Wakamba. | Msambara. | Sohili. |
|---|---|---|---|---|
| *Man* | muta | muntu | mgossi | mtu |
| *Woman* | mtsheta | muka | mdere | mtumke |
| *Head* | dzitzoa | mutue | mtoe | kitoa |
| *Eye* | dzityo | ido | yisso | dshito |
| *Nose* | pula | embola | pum | pua |
| *Tongue* | lammi | uimi | uraka | ulimi |
| *Tooth* | dzino | ino | zino | dzhino |
| *Ear* | sikiro | idu | gutui | shikio |
| *Hand* | mukono | mukono | mukono | makono |
| *Foot* | gulu | mudumu | emrondi | gu |
| *Sun* | dzua | kua | zua | dzhua |
| *Moon* | muesi | moi | muesi | muesi |
| *Star* | nioha | nioa | niniesi | niota |
| *Fire* | muotto | muagi | muotto | muotto |
| *Water* | madyi | mandzi | mazi | madzhi |
| *Stone* | dziwe | dziwe | ziwe | dzhiwe |
| *Tree* | muhi | mutte | muti | mti |
| *One* | emmenga | umue | mosi | emmodsha |
| *Two* | embiri | ili | kaidi | embili |
| *Three* | tahu | itatu | katatu | tatu |
| *Four* | enne | inna | kanna | ennc |
| *Five* | tyano | idano | kashano | tano |
| *Six* | tandaho | dandatu | ententatu | setta |
| *Seven* | fungahe | mama | fungate | sabaa |
| *Eight* | nane | munda | nane | nani |
| *Nine* | kenda | kenda | kenda | kenda |
| *Ten* | kumi | kumi | kumi | kumu. |

The Sohili words for *six* and *seven* are Arabic.

| English. | C. Delgado. | Maravi. | Sofala. | Lourenzo Marques. |
|---|---|---|---|---|
| *One* | mozi | modze | posa | tshinyua |
| *Two* | mbiri | viri | piri | ie-biri |
| *Three* | natu | tatu | tatu | tinaro |
| *Four* | ine | nai | shina | mune |
| *Five* | tanu | insanu | sano | klano |

| English. | C. Delgado. | Maravi. | Sofala. | Lourenzo Marquez. |
|---|---|---|---|---|
| *Six* | sita | intandu | tantatu | —— |
| *Seven* | saba | dzimbi | shinomoe | —— |
| *Eight* | nane | dwere | zere | —— |
| *Nine* | kenda | mwinda | fumbamoe | —— |
| *Ten* | kumi | kumi | gumi | kume. |

*Sofala* is the country of the Somali and Suhawili, under a slightly-altered name. Its name alone is sufficient to indicate an Arab influence, which, originally, was greater than at present. At present, the Portuguese possessions, beginning on the Mozambique coast, comprise all the Sofala country, and something beyond it.

In Imhambane we leave the tropic of Capricorn, and a little further to the south find ourselves in the neighbourhood of Dutch and English rather than Portuguese colonists.

The Arabs who called the northern and equatorial tribes of the eastern coast Somali and Suwahili, called those of the extreme south Kafirs or Infidels; from which we infer that, where the Kafir area begins, the Arab influence either ends or decreases. It either ends altogether, or is too weak to effect proselytism.

South of Delagoa Bay lie the Tambukis, succeeded by the Fingos and Zulus, or Amazulus, for the parts about Port Natal. Then come the Kafirs.

The extremity of the African continent is Hottentot; so is the greater part of the coast between Cape Town and Walwisch Bay. Hottentot but, more or less, Kafir also; as will be seen in the notice of the populations of the interior. This means the populations beyond the range of the Cape colonists, the populations of Lake Ngami, the populations of the parts between Cassange, and the Lower Zambesi—Cassange as a Portuguese settlement on the west, the Lower Zambesi as a Portuguese settlement of the east. It is needless to add that these lines give us the route of Livingstone. They also involve notices from Galton, Anderson, Cumming and others. The populations of the areas thus illustrated fall into two primary divisions; (1) the Kafir, (2) the Hottentot. Of these

*The Kafirs* present themselves under two types. Some are brown rather than black. Others, like the Angola and Mozambique tribes, are black rather than brown. The languages of all are closely allied. Also the creeds. As a general rule the browner varieties are found on the table-lands; the blacker along the watercourses.

*The Amakosas, &c.*—The eastern and north-eastern frontagers to the colonists of the Cape are the Kafirs in the limited sense of the term, the Koosa (or Amakusa), the Ponda (or Amaponda), the Tembu (or Amatembu), as the case may be; the Zulu (or Amazulu) being in the parts about Port Natal, with the Fingoes either on their frontier or amongst them.

Amongst the Kafirs the head man of the village settles disputes, his tribunal being in the open air. From him an appeal lies to a chief of higher power; and from him to some superior, higher still. In this way there is a long chain of feudal or semi-feudal dependency.

The wife is the slave to the husband; and he buys her in order that she should be so. The purchase implies a seller. This is always a member of another tribe. Hence the wish of a Kafir is to see his wife the mother of many children, girls being more valuable than boys.

Why a man should not sell his offspring to the members of his own tribe is uncertain. It is clear, however, that the practice of doing so makes marriage between even distant relations next to impossible. To guard against the chances of this, a rigid and suspicious system of restraint has been developed in cases of consanguinity; and relations must do all they can to avoid meeting. To sit in the same room, to meet on the same road, is undesirable. To converse is but just allowable, and then all who choose must hear what is said. So thorough, however, has been the isolation in many cases, that persons of different sexes have lived as near neighbours for many years without having conversed with each other; and such communication as there has been, has taken place through the medium of a third person. No gift will induce a Kafir female to violate this law.

The Kafirs belong to the hills on the side, rather than to the plateau in the centre, of the continent. The great name of the interior is that of

*The Bitshuana* or *Bechuana*, whose language is the Sechuana. They are bounded by the Kafirs on the East, and the Griquas and Bushmen on the south. On the west they extend into the Kalahari, a desert, where they become degenerate and under-sized; where, too, they come in contact with the Namaqua, and other, Hottentots. They either touch the frontier of the Ovaheriro or Dammaras, in the part between Walwisch Bay and Lake Ngami, or are divided from them by a strip of Hottentot ground. Their limits on the north are uncertain. It is only certain that, year after year, they advance themselves. The Bechuanas of the level country are more brown than black, the true Kafirs being more black than brown.

The tribes and sub-tribes of the Bitshuanas, writes Livingstone, "are named after certain animals. The term Bakatla means They of the monkey; Bakuena, They of the alligator; Batlápi, They of the fish; each tribe having a superstitious dread of the animal after which it is called. A tribe never eats the animal which is its namesake, using the term *ila*, hate or dread, in reference to killing it. We find traces of many ancient tribes in the country in individual members of those now extinct, as the Batáu, They of the lion, the Banóga, They of the serpent; though no such tribes now exist. The use of the personal pronoun, Ba, Ma, Wa, Va, or Ova, Am, Ki, &c., prevails very extensively in the names of tribes in Africa. A single individual is indicated by the terms Mo or Le. Thus Mokwáin is a single person of the Bakwain tribe, and Lekóa is a single white man or Englishman; Makóa being Englishmen."

The Bakwains, the Basuto, the Bamangwato, and other tribes of less importance, cover the country between Kuruman and the Lake Bakwain (word for word, Bichuana) lying beyond the Bichuanas and within the tropic. The former belong to the desert, the latter to the hill-country. The valley of the Zouga takes us to Bayeiye. This is what the indigenæ of the parts about the Lake call themselves; Bayeiye meaning men. Their conquerors call them Bakoba or slaves. The Bayeiye are more negro than Bichuana in appearance: sooty-skinned, and ill-featured, but robust; snuff-takers and drinkers of beer of their own brewing; polygamists, too, and superstitious. Their women smoke dakka. They are said to have owned herds before the Batoana took them away. In their damp and humid soil they suffer from rheumatism, ophthalmia, and fevers; being also subject to the small-pox. Their conquerors are hunters, herdsmen, and warriors, recent intruders, and Bichuana in language. Sebituane, a man of mark in many respects, led them. The whole district is subject to inundations, so that the houses of the small villages stand on mounds. The Barotse country, when under water, looked like a vast lake.

*The Balonda Tribes.*—The river which runs through this leads to the watershed between the Congo and the

Zambesi; the occupants of the Congo districts being members of the Balonda group. The Balonda or the occupants of Londa, are woolly-headed blacks of the true negro type, and they are contrasted in many respects with the Bichuana tribes to the south. Their women are allowed no little influence, mix in their politics, and are capable of succeeding to the captaincy. They swear by their mothers; the Bichuana swearing by their fathers. Near every village may be seen some rude idol, the image of a lion or alligator, before which they lay offerings and beat drums in cases of sickness, or when the chase has been unsuccessful. The Balonda frontier touches Angola.

Such the line which takes us from the Lake Ngami westwards. What do we find in the east? What lies between the Lake and Pacific?

*The Batoko and the Batonga.*—The Batoka are in the same category with the Bayeiye. They lie within the area of Sebituane's conquests; pagans, savages, head-hunters. At a hamlet belonging to the son of a chief named Moyara, a "number of stakes are planted in the ground, and I" (Dr. Livingstone) "counted fifty-four human skulls hung on their points. These were Matabele, who, unable to approach Sebituane on the island of Loyéla, had returned sick and famishing. Moyara's father took advantage of their reduced condition, and, after putting them to death, mounted their heads in the Batoka fashion. The old man who perpetrated this deed now lies in the middle of his son's huts, with a lot of rotten ivy over his grave. One cannot help feeling thankful that the reign of such wretches is over. They inhabited the whole of this side of the country, and were probably the barrier to the extension of the Portuguese commerce in this direction. When looking at these skulls, I remarked to Moyara, that many of them were those of mere boys. He assented readily, and pointed them out as such. I asked why his father had killed boys. 'To show his fierceness,' was the answer. 'Is it fierceness to kill boys?' 'Yes, they had no business here.' When I told him that this probably would ensure his own death if the Matabele came again, he replied, 'When I hear of their coming I shall hide the bones.' He was evidently proud of these trophies of his father's ferocity, and I was assured by other Batoka that few strangers ever returned from a visit to this quarter."

The Batoka tribes, like the Australian, knock out the upper front teeth of their children when they arrive at puberty. "This is done by both sexes, and though the under teeth, being relieved from the attrition of the upper, grow long and somewhat bent out, and thereby cause the under lip to protrude in a most unsightly way, no young woman thinks herself accomplished until she has got rid of the upper incisors. This custom gives all the Batoka an uncouth old-man-like appearance. Their laugh is hideous, yet they are so attached to it that even Sebituane was unable to eradicate the practice. He issued orders that none of the children living under him should be subjected to the custom by their parents, and disobedience to his mandates was usually punished with severity; but notwithstanding this the children would appear in the streets without their incisors, and no one would confess to the deed. When questioned respecting the origin of this practice, the Batoka reply, that their object is to be like oxen, and those who retain their teeth they consider to resemble zebras. Whether this is the true reason or not, it is difficult to say; but it is noticeable that the veneration for oxen which prevails in many tribes should here be associated with hatred to the zebra, as among the Bakwains; that this operation is performed at the same age that circumcision is in other tribes; and that here that ceremony is unknown."

The Batoka of the valleys are dark; those of the hills light—"of the colour of coffee and milk." They smoke hemp.

Word for word, Batoka is Batonga. The Batonga men of the eastern districts go naked, and when they salute a stranger roll themselves on their backs and slap the outside of their thighs. Most of the Kafir tribes are curious and careful with their hair. With the Bashukolompo "a circle of hair at the top of the head, eight inches or more in diameter, is woven into a cone eight or ten inches high, with an obtuse apex, bent, in some cases, a little forward, giving it somewhat the appearance of a helmet. Some have only a cone, four or five inches in diameter at the base. It is said that the hair of animals is added, but the sides of the cone are woven something like basket-work. The headman of this village, instead of having his brought to a point, had it prolonged into a wand, which extended a full yard from the crown of his head. The hair on the forehead, above the ears, and behind, is all shaven off, so they appear somewhat as if a cap of liberty were cocked upon the top of the head. After the weaving is performed it is said to be painful, as the scalp is drawn tightly up; but they become used to it."

Tete is in Batonga what Cassange is in Angola, viz. a town of the Portuguese frontier.

*The Dammaras.*—A third line has yet to be followed; one from the Lake to Walwisch Bay, illustrated by Galton and Anderson. On the sides of this lie the Ovaheriro, or men of the Heriro language, who, until lately, were described as Dammaras. It is in their habits that the Ovaheriro (with whom we may join the Ovampantieru) and Ovampo chiefly differ. Both have a fine frame of body, well-shaped limbs, regular features for Africans, and a fair facial angle of about seventy degrees. But the Ovampo, who are agricultural, are more orderly and more honest than their southern neighbours. Their capital, Ondonga, is laid out in neat farms of corn and pasture. Their laws against theft are severe. The king rules mildly but despotically. They possess the entire carrying trade between the Ovaheriro and the Portuguese. All this looks like regular industry, to which their fertile country in no small degree contributes. The Ovaheriro are drawn in more unfavourable colours. A tree is supposed to be their ancestor—or rather two trees, one at Omaruru and one on the road to Ovampo. They practise circumcision.

The ethnological relations of the Ghou and Soun Damup will be considered when the Hottentot division comes under notice.

*The Hottentots.*—The Saabs, or Bushmen, are the Hottentots of the most unfavoured parts of the Cape, who, being destitute of flocks and herds, live the life of miserable troglodytes, subsisting on what they find in the chase. It is the Saab upon whose unfavourable exterior we found our opinion of the form and features of the Hottentot family in general. He is under-sized, being often little more than four feet high. He is a starveling, too, in bulk his limbs being slight, his body light, his frame weak. Hi cheek-bones project; his eyes are oblique, small, black bright, and wild; his skin yellow or brown; sometimes lik parchment, sometimes like weak coffee. His hair grow in small tufts, showing interspaces of scalp between th twisted knots, which have been compared to a curled shoe brush. His small skull, like that of the African in gene ral, has a long diameter from fore to aft, with a conside able development of the occipital portion. The nates ar often steatomatous.

*The Gonaqua* occupy the watershed between Great Fish and the Orange Rivers, of which latter

*The Korana* hold the middle portion; the lower being the occupancy of

*The Namaquas.*—How far north do these extend? At least as far as the tropic; beyond which the ethnology becomes obscure. In the first place, there are numerous Namaquas who are recent intruders, and, as such, in contrast with the native inhabitants. These are called by the general name of Bushmen; being, for the most part, Nareneen, Ounip (or Topners), and Kubabees, all specifically stated to be Hottentot. The district to which they belong is, more or less, Heriro or Kafir. Some part of it is called the Dammara land.

The authority for the following statements is Galton. The native form of the word Dammara is Damup; the language to which it belongs being the Hottentot. In this it has three meanings:—

1. It denotes the occupants of the country in general, whether Ovaheriro, Ovampantieru, or aught else.

It denotes two specific populations:—

2. The Ghou Damup, and

3. The Soun Damup, allied in language, appearance, and superstitions, but different in locality.

The Ghou Damup are hill-men, the range of mountains between 19° and 23° S.L. being their occupancy. They are considered as an inferior population by the Heriro. The Hottentots who preceded the Heriro despised them. This they did so long as they were themselves powerful. Since, however, the Ovaheriro have encroached upon them they have been humbler and more friendly. In some instances they have been driven to the same fastnesses as the Damup, and where this has been done intermarriage has taken place.

The Soun Damup lie on the drainage of the Lake, on

or within the frontier of the Mationa (*i. e.* Bitshuana), to whom they are field-labourers. They are specially stated to be in the same class with the Ghou Damup, whatever that may be.

Mr. Galton considers them to be degenerate Ovampo. His evidence requires criticism. He separates them from the Ovaheriro and Ovampantieru, with whom "they have nothing in common." He connects the Soun Damup with the Ghou Damup, and likens both to the Ovampo. Yet he makes the former "a peculiar race of negroes, speaking the Hottentot tongue."

Whatever may be the ethnology of these obscure tribes it is certain that the northern Namaquas and the Bushmen most allied to them are by no means the half-starved Saabs of the desert; but, on the contrary, an active people, who not only hold their own against the Ovaheriro, but actually encroach upon their area.

It is probable that there are members of the Hottentot family as far north as 19° S.L., and as far west as the parts about Lake Ngami.

*The Oerlams* are chiefly of mixed blood, Hottentot and Dutch. So are

*The Griqua,* called also Baastaards, a pastoral population, upwards of 15,000 in number, on the north side of the great bend of the Orange River. They are the descendants of Dutch fathers and Hottentot mothers.

A mixture of Griquas and Hottentots occurs also on the Kat River, a feeder of the Great Fish River, in the district of Somerset, and on the Kafir frontier. Here they are distributed in a series of distinct locations, amid the dales and fastnesses of the eastern frontier. Many of them are discharged soldiers; so that, in reality, like the borderers of old, they form a sort of military colony.

## CHAPTER XIX.

Certain populations belonging to the unexplored parts of Africa to the South of Abyssinia.—The Gonga Family.—The Eloikob.

THE following populations agree in the negative character of being neither decidedly Abyssinian nor decidedly Galla, though they exhibit both Galla and Abyssinian affinities. Neither are their relations to the tribes of the south ascertained. They lie on or within the frontier of the *terra incognita*. The present position, then, is provisional.

*The Gonga Group.*—Moving from the Galla and Amharic areas towards the interior, we meet with a population whose languages are known through Dr. Beke's vocabularies under the names of Kaffa, Woraita, Wolaitsa, and Yangaro. They all belong to one and the same class.

This we call Gonga. The Gonga tribes, as noticed by Ludolf, dwelt to the south of the Bahr-al-Abiad, about 10° N. L. The language of Enarea was Gonga. There, however, it has been displaced by the Galla.

*The Eloikob.*—I describe the population which comes now under notice by its native name, which is Eloikob; partly because, as a general rule, the native names are the best, and partly because something will be said in the sequel respecting the name itself. Eloikob is one of those words, so common in the East African, and not wanting elsewhere, whereof the plural is the simpler, the singular the more complicated, form. They are generally collectives, the limitation of them to a single object being exceptional. In the instance before us the Loikob or Eloikob is the name of the nation; Oloikŏban or Oloikabani, that of a single member of it. I call these forms singular and plural, though in reality they are collective and individual.

The Wakamba change the name Eloikob into Akabi and Mukabi, singular and plural, and by the time the word reaches the missionaries, merchants, and travellers of the sea-coast, it has become Wakuafi (plur.) and Mkuafi (sing.); the name of the language being Kekuafi.

It is under these designations that the two fullest notices of them are given, Mr. Pickering's and Dr. Krapf's. The former derived his information from slaves at Zanzibar, where they are numerous; the latter from one at Mombaz, who gave the following account of the origin of his nation.

In the beginning a man resided on Oldoinio Eibor, or the White Mountain. Engai placed him here.

He was superior to all other beings:

His name was Neiterkob.

On Mount Sambu lived Enjémăsi Enauner, with his wife, whose name was that of Mountain on which they resided, or Sambu.

Mount Sambu is high, but not so high as Oldoinio Eibor. Oldoinio Eibor has white matter on the top; which Mount Sambu has not.

When Enjémăsi heard of Neiterkob he visited him, and took with him his wife, who conceived of Neiterkob, and bore children.

Neiterkob also taught Enjémăsi the taming of wild oxen.

At length he disappeared from Oldoinio Eibor and Enjémăsi returned to Mount Sambu.

I interpret this account somewhat differently from the learned missionary whom we have to thank for it. I see no necessity for making (as he does) the white matter on the Oldoinio Eibor snow. It may much more easily have been white limestone, of which definite mention is made in the sequel, and which is specially stated to belong to the Eloikob district.

In the name Neiter-kob I see that of the eponymus of the Eloi-kob; and that of Enge-Masi that of the neighbouring Masai. At any rate there is the special statement that Mount Oldoinio Eibor is the primitive home, or head-quarters of the former, Mount Sambu that of the latter. To this add that the two tribes, though hostile, are said to be allied in manners, form, and language.

The name of their highest deity is Engar, or Angayai, between whom and the Eloikob, Neiterkob acts as a mediator.

The Eloikob, who are circumcised polygamists, of all things hate and despise the tiller of the soil, so thoroughly are they a population of herdsmen. Lemasegnot, the slave to whom Krapf addressed himself for information, boasted that he had defied his master to inure him to agriculture, and had succeeded in his defiance. He would rather die than use a hoe.

The Eloikob are either intrusive conquerors in some part of their area, or the owners of imported slaves; since they employ the service of, at least, two subordinate castes, the Elkonono and the Wandurobo. The former are smiths, the latter hunters of elephants and procurers of ivory. Whether these have a language of their own remains to be proved; Dr. Krapf writes that "it appears that they have."

The Eloikob, themselves, watch their cattle, hunt for game, fight against their neighbours. In this they find the great business of their lives. The warriors of the nation are the young unmarried men between seventeen and twenty-five, who remain in their parents' houses, and form a sort of Eloikob militia. At the head of the State are the aged men who carry neither spear nor shield about with them, but only the bow and stick. The shield and spear are the arms of the youths. They fight bravely, and spare but few, neither giving nor asking quarter. They fight, too, with skill and cunning, and consider their spear and club as equal to the muskets of the coastmen.

Some of the tribes perforate the lobe of the ear, the highest aristocrats having the largest borings.

Their festal beverage is a kind of hydromel or mead called *olmarua;* honey being abundant in their country. Butter they use as an ointment rather than as food. They have several dyes.

Earthquakes they ascribe to the movements of a cow that supports the earth.

They have an ordeal of chewing. When an accused Oleikobani makes an oath, the priest, medicine-man, or Oleikon, boils some roots, mixes them with his meat, gives him the mess to eat, and watches whether he swallows it. Should it stick in his throat he is guilty.

The following are the names of some of the Eloikob tribes,—Enganglima, Burrabuyu, Modoni, Tigerei, Kiwia, Koppe-koppe, Elburgineji. In a Suaheli account the Wandurobo take the appearance of a separate substantive population called Máu and Wamáu.

## CHAPTER XX.

Certain populations belonging to the imperfectly-explored parts of Africa. —The Mobba, &c., of Darsaleh.—The Bagirmi.—The Mandara.—The tribes between the Mandara and the Nufi.—The Battas, &c.

EXPLORATION from the west has reached but little beyond Bornu; exploration from the east but little beyond Kordovan. Hence the intermediate countries are known, at first hand, only on their frontiers. Nevertheless, something has been collected respecting the centre, means being supplied by the writings and relations of such Arabs as have used their opportunities for observation.

I begin with the districts that fill up the parts between Darfúr and Bornu; Darfúr being followed by Darsaleh, and Bagirmi; Bagirmi by Mandara. Mandara will lead to Adamowa, and the tribes along the Tshari; which will, in their turn, bring us to the Nufi districts; these giving an area which has already been noticed.

*Darsaleh, Borgho, Waday, or the Mobba country.*—Darsaleh is, like Darfúr, imperfectly Mahometan. Like Darfúr it contains numerous Arab tribes. Whether many Fulas have reached it is doubtful.

The Mobba is the chief language of the tribes of Waday proper.

The Menagon, Manarit, Tama, Gnorga, Darna, Kubu, Sungori, Mimi, Moewo, Kasheméré, and Korunga (or Karinga) are members of a group called Abú Sharíb, the most western members of which lie on, or within, the Darfúr frontier.

I imagine that the Ko-runga of Barth are the people of Dar-runga as described by Browne—partly negros, partly of a red or copper colour; honest men and cleanly (there being abundance of water in their country), but pagans, and inordinate slave-dealers.

Some of these tribes shoot poisoned arrows. Others use red-hot spears. These the women supply. They light a fire behind the line of combatants, and exchange the heated ones for the cooled. Cannibalism is laid to the charge of some. So is the practice of wearing, on their hands and heads, the skin of their enemies. They make their own arms; and that of iron. They then heat the head, stick it in the trunk of a certain tree, and bring it out poisoned.

| English. | Dar-runga. |
|---|---|
| *Man* | kamere |
| *Woman* | mimi |
| *Eye* | khasso |
| *Ear* | nesso |
| *Hand* | tusso |
| *Foot* | itar |
| *Sun* | agning |
| *Water* | tta |
| *Fire* | nissiek |
| *One* | kadenda |
| *Two* | embirr |
| *Three* | attik |
| *Four* | mendih |
| —— | —— |
| *Six* | sabotikeda |
| *Seven* | ow |
| *Eight* | sebateis |
| *Nine* | atih |
| *Ten* | bûf. |

The Dar-runga word for God is *Kinga*, and Kingago is a Dar-runga exclamation. Compare the Eloïkob *Enga*.

The Tibboo frontagers (on the north) belong to the Zokhawa and Guraan tribes; the Arabs of Waday itself to those of the Mahamid, the Beri Helba, the

Shiggegat, the Sebbedi, the Sefeddin, the Beni Hassan, the Missiríye Zoruk (black), the Missiríye Homr (red), the Kozam, the Zoyud, the Dzhattena, the Zabbade, and the Abidiye, the Nuwaibe Sabalat, the Korobat, the Kolomat, the Terjem, the Welâd Rashid and others.

Of the numerous terms applied to the kingdom under notice—

*Waday* is applied by the Bornúi.
*Bargu* ———— Furians.
*Darsaleh* ———— Arabs.
*Mobba* being probably native.

Word for word, I believe that Saleh = Shiluk. As this term appears and re-appears in different parts of Africa, it is, probably, Arab. It by no means implies affinity between the populations to which it is applied. This may, or may not, exist.

The phenomenon, of which we have undoubted evidence in the Fula and Mandingo countries, is said to be repeated in Darsaleh. A number of tribes are red rather than black. Such are some of the Darkulla populations. Such, too (as we infer from the names) are some of the Arabs. Such, too, certain members of the Mobba division. That the difference of hue coincides with a difference of soil and sea-level is probable *à priori*; whilst the little evidence we possess on the question is in favour of such being actually the case.

*Bagirmi.*—The writers who have been furthest beyond the frontier of Bagirmi are Denham and Barth. The latter expressly states that the form of the natives is favourably contrasted with that of the Kanuri of Bornu. He compares it with that of the Fula, adding that the skin is darker—indeed that it is black. Of their morals he speaks less favourably; and more unfavourably still of the great extent to which slavery and slave-hunting prevail. The kingdom is a Mahometan one; the creed, however, is rude and imperfect. Much of the original paganism shows through it. Much exists in a purely unmodified form. The general surface of the soil is level, lying at a height of about 900 feet above the sea, with considerable rivers, numerous watercourses, and swampy districts not a few. There are large plains of black argillaceous soil, which lie under water during the rainy season. There are large collections of conical huts dignified by the name of towns and capitals. There are cultivated tracts of sorghum and other grains. There are flocks and herds of cattle, These, when the dry season sets in, are removed from place to place in search of water. There is, then, both grazing and tillage; the former giving rise to habits more or less locomotive. Arabs, too, there are from the East, and Fulas from the west, the former being called Shiwa. They chiefly belong to the Salamat, Beni Hassan, Welád Musa, Welád Ali, and Deghaghera tribes. They lived scattered over the country, occupants, in some places, of whole villages.

*The Mandara group.*—The occupancy of the divisions and sub-divisions of the Mandara group lies to the south and south-east of Bornu. The only Europeans who have set foot upon it are Denham and Barth. The latter expressly states that the inhabitants of Kotoko belong to the great race of Masa, to which the people of Logon, the Musgu, and the Mandara proper, also belong. Meanwhile, his map carries Kotoko to the Lake Tsad, whilst the text gives to that province the Affadeh language; the Affadeh language being Bornúi. With these elements of uncertainty I suspend my judgment as to the exact details of the area under notice. It may possibly be prolonged to Lake Tshad. If so, it is interjacent to the Bornúi and Bagirmi areas. It is more probably, however, a southern language, *i. e.* a language belonging to the parts on each side 10° N.L.

Whatever may be the ethnology of Kotoko and Logone, provinces in close contact with Bornu and Bagirmi, more or less Mahometan in creed, more or less Fula and Arab in population, and not deficient in civilization, the difference between them and

*The Musgu* is decided. The Musgu lie between 11° and 10° N.L., being pagans. The evidence, however, that their language is Mandara ratner than Affadeh is capable of improvement. The following extract from Barth gives us their physical form :—"The village we had just reached was named Fákalá, and is one of the most considerable places in the Músga River. A large number of slaves had been caught this day, and in the course of the evening, after some skirmishing, in which three Bornú horsemen were killed, a great many more were brought in; altogether they were said to have taken one thousand, and there were certainly not less than five hundred. To our utmost horror, not less than one hundred and seventy full-grown men were mercilessly slaughtered in cold blood, the greater part of them being allowed to bleed to death, a leg having been severed from the body. Most of them were tall men, with not very pleasing features. Their forehead, instead of shelving backwards, was generally very high, and the line of the face straight; but their thick eyelashes, wide, open nostrils, thick lips, high cheekbones, and coarse bushy hair, gave them a very wild appearance. The proportions of the legs, with the kneebone bent inwardly, were particularly ugly; and on the whole they were all of a dirty black colour, very far from that glossy lustre which is observed in other tribes. Most of them wore a short beard. The ears of several were adorned with small copper rings, while almost all of them wore round their necks a thick rope made of the dúm-bush or ngílle, coarsely twisted, as a sort of ornament.

"This female slave was certainly worthy of a sketch, as she was one of the most stately women I saw here. But I entertained some suspicion that she was not of Musgú origin, but belonged to the Marghi; for in the whole of the Musgú country I had not observed a single individual of red colour, but all were of the same dirty black, approaching to what the French call *café au lait*, while this woman was of a red complexion. She certainly wore in her uader lip the large bone, the national emblem of the Musgú females; but this custom she might have adopted. As for herself, she would neither give me any information with respect to her origin, nor sit still in order to allow me to finish my sketch. She was tall and well-grown, with the exception of the legs, which were rather crooked; and being still a young woman, her breasts had not yet attained that bag-like shape which is so disgusting in the elder females of this country. Her features were only a little disfigured by the bone in the under lip. Her neck was richly ornamented with strings of beads, but these were as little peculiar to her as the cotton cloth round her loins, having been given her by the new master into whose hands she had fallen. The national dress of the Musgú females consists of nothing but a narrow bandage, formed of bash, twisted like a rope, which is fastened between the legs and round the waist like a T bandage."

*The Marghi* tribes are, perhaps, favoured in the way of form and feature beyond their congeners. The hair of a youth most especially admired by Dr. Barth "was short, curled, but not woolly. He, as well as his mother and the whole family, was of a pale or yellowish red complexion, like rhubarb." A thin metal plate was stuck through the mother's under lip. Other individuals were, more or less, copper-coloured. Some of them were just Mahometan enough to be able to repeat a few formulas, and to cover the native nakedness of their semi-adult offspring with an apron of cotton.

The Babur, akin to the Marghi, are somewhat less modified by Mahometanism.

The Marghi and Musgu pay great respect to the memory of their ancestors.

"There was one object which attracted my attention in particular, as it testified to a certain degree of civilization, which might have shamed the proud Mohammedan inhabitants of these countries. For while the latter are extremely negligent in burying their dead, leaving them without any sufficient protection against the wild beasts, so that most of them are devoured in a few days by the hyænas, here we had regular sepulchres, covered in with large well-rounded vaults, the tops of which were adorned by a couple of beams cross-laid, or by an earthen urn. The same sort of worship as is paid by these pagans to their ancestors prevails in a great part of Africa, and however greatly the peculiar customs attached to the mode of worship may vary, the principle is the same; but I nowhere more regretted having no one at hand to explain to me the customs of these people, than I did on this occasion. The urn most probably contains the head of the deceased; but what is indicated by the cross-laid beams I cannot say."

So writes Dr. Barth, who passed through the land of the Marghi to that of

*The Batta*—occupants of Adamawa, where his personal explorations ended. The Batta tribes lay on each side of the Tshadda, where they were succeeded by those of Hamaruwa, the Domo and the Mitshi made known to us by the expedition of 1854 under Dr. Baikie.

| English. | Begarmi. | Mandara. | Batta. |
|---|---|---|---|
| *Man* | gaba | yili | mano |
| *Woman* | —— | muksi | metshe |
| *Head* | geujo | ire | bodashi |
| *Eye* | kammu | ishe | bashi |
| *Mouth* | tara | we | bratshi |
| —— | —— | tihi | —— |
| *Nose* | amo | uktere | ekilo |
| *Teeth* | nganah | sare | nesudabtse |
| *Tongue* | —— | erakha | —— |
| *Foot* | njanja | iyagãga | —— |
| *Sun* | kaja | bishiya | motshe |
| *Moon* | —— | tiri | —— |
| *Star* | —— | trioko | motshekan |
| *Fire* | peddu | kara | be |
| *Water* | mane | yawi | die |
| *One* | keddi | pale | hido |
| *Two* | sub | bua | pe |
| *Three* | mattah | kaji | makin |
| *Four* | soh | ufade | fat |
| *Five* | mi | ilivi | tuf |
| *Six* | mika | nkohe | tokuldaka |
| *Seven* | tshilli | vuyi | tokulape |
| *Eight* | marta | tisi | farfat |
| *Nine* | doso | musdmani | tambido |
| *Ten* | dokemi | kalawa | bu. |

We may now take a retrospect with a special view to the general questions connected with the ethnology of the great continent over which we have travelled. How slight the influence of Africa upon the history of the world has been is known to the most cursory reader. It is only so far as the Semite populations are African that it has any notable position at all. A little influence may be given to the Ægyptians, a little to the Berbers; provided always that the Almoravids be as Berber as they are represented. South, however, of the Berber area, nothing is to be found in Africa which has ever affected either Asia or Europe, in the way of either conquest or civilization. Where the Gallas, the Furians, the Bornúi, the Howssa populations, the Sungai or the Mandingos have encroached, they have done so at the expense of their neighbours. Of distant conquests they have known but little; of conquests beyond the Mediterranean and the Isthmus of Suez nothing. Neither have their arts or inventions spread abroad. They have had none to spread. From others they have taken a little. To none have they given. The amount of invention involved in the Vei syllabarium has been considered.

Lying beyond the pale of both Brahminism and Buddhism, the original mythologies of pagan Africa have been affected by only three of the great religions—Judaism, Christianity, and Mahometanism. In respect to the first I am unable to form a satisfactory opinion. There are Jewish customs, more or less general, and more or less decided, all over Africa. The Falasha of Abyssinia have been actually called Jews. Upon the Gha or Akra nation (a nation whose occupancy lies as far west as the Gold Coast) we have a careful and instructive paper by Mr. Hanson, himself of Gha origin. It tells us of the existence amongst his countrymen of, not only the practice of circumcision, but of numerous *minutiæ* as well—too striking to be what is called accidental. How are they to be explained? Has actual Judaism ever extended itself in Africa? Have points of Mahometanism been mistaken for things Judaic? Or is Judaism itself much more African than is generally supposed? I incline to this last doctrine. I only, however, incline to it. The details of tribe upon tribe are still desiderated.

Christianity in Africa is both old and new. It is of old standing in Ægypt and Abyssinia. Within the domain of the European missionaries it is new. So far as these are from Portugal it is Romanist. So far as they are from England, America, Holland, or Denmark, it is Protestant. One of the most interesting investigations in the history of African civilization is that of the corruptions of the early Christianity. Dr. Beke has committed himself to the opinion that certain Galla tribes are relapsed Christians.

More, however, than it is Jewish, more than it is Christian, is Africa Mahometan. It is, in one respect, more Mahometan than pagan. The area over which the Koran to some extent or other is recognized, is (I think) larger than that of the purely heathen populations. Not one of the countries to the north of 10° N.L. is without a tincture of Mahometanism; the zone which they form being carried across the very broadest part of Africa. Then come the districts of the west; amongst which Yoruba, the Ibo country, and the Nufi country exhibit a more or less imperfect and partial Mahometanism; a Mahometanism which again shows itself amongst the Somaulis and the Suwahelis of the Pacific. As the Mahometans are in the habit of calling the unconverted populations with which they come in contact by the name of Kafir, we may find in the geographical distribution of this term, a rough outline for the boundary lands between the Mahometan and the pagan. As a preliminary, however, we must remember the numerous changes of form which the word can undergo; also remembering that when it gets taken up by the tribes to which it is applied, it accommodates itself to the phonesis of a new language—and that an African one. Considering then that, word for word, it is Guebre and Giaour in Asia, I am prepared to believe that it is Cumbri and Kouri in Africa. I think, too, that it may be Yaouri, and, not impossibly, Yoruba. If so, however, the *-ba* may be the

*-be* in Ful-*be*, the Howssa form of Fula. Be this as it may, it is certain that where names of this kind occur, there is Mahometanism on one side, and paganism on the other. It is also certain that the name, in the first instance at least, is other than native. It is the name by which such and such populations are designated by their neighbours rather than the name by which they designate themselves. What applies to Kafir applies to other words as well. I think that *Fulah, Felup,* and *Wolof* are the Arabic *Fellah.* I think, too, that *Shiluk* (*Shiluh*, or *Shilha*) and *Berber* must be Arabic words. They apply to populations which, except that they are in contact with an Arab occupancy, have nothing in common sufficient to account for the identity of name. As an instrument of criticism, the principle of which the terms under notice are examples may be enlarged on. Here, however, they are noticed as measures of the influences from Arabia.

To the settlements effected in Africa by the Phœnicians, the Greeks, and the Romans, I merely allude. They belong to the civil historian, and the archæologist. On those of the Vandals I lay little stress; though much speculation has been set afloat by them. The light skin of certain mountaineers of the Atlas has been referred to a European origin.

For the languages of Africa a careful criticism is most especially needed. The alliterations of the Kafir languages are so remarkable that their value as a characteristic has been exaggerated. But they are found beyond the Kafir area. They are found in the Bullom, the Timmani, and other languages. What do they mean? Do they mean that, notwithstanding a considerable difference of vocabulary, and decided affinities in another direction, the dialects in which they appear are Kafir or South African? No. They merely remind the cautious investigator that classes in philology are, like classes in botany or zoology, unnatural when founded on a single characteristic.

Another caution. Of the numerous divisions of the African family that which is the best known to learned men is the negro; inasmuch as nine out of ten of the Africans seen in either Europe or America belong to it. The slaves are chiefly negro. Some, indeed, are Fulas, some Kafirs—some, but few. The mass is from a single district, the coast of Guinea. That this gives us a fair sample of the varieties of the African physiognomy is unlikely. It may possibly give us the exception rather than the rule. And this is what it actually does. The extreme negro is found on only a few areas. He is found on the coast between the Senegal and the Congo; and he is found to some distance in the interior. He is found in the parts about Lake Tshad, in Sennaar, and in several isolated spots besides. But he is not found in the vast tract occupied by either the Berbers of the north, or the Bitshuanas of the south. He is not found in the highlands of Æthiopia. He is not found amongst the widely-spread Fulas. All these tribes are expressly stated to be other than negro. Then come the Bishari, the Nubians, and the Gallas; who, by their length of hair and prominence of feature, are easily separated from the true negro; though negro-like in many respects. Let these represent a second class of Africans. Let them stand between the typical negro and the Berber.

Let the physical geographer now be called in, and let him divide the continent of Africa into the dry plateaus and the moist alluvia. The men of the Fula type will belong to the former, the true negros to the other. To say that there are no light-coloured men in swampy localities would be inaccurate. It would also be inaccurate to deny that some negros are to be found on high levels. As a general rule, however, the negro conformation and the alluvial soil go together. Read any work upon the ethnology of the water system of the Nile. Read the descriptions (not always free from exaggeration) of the fine Caucasian (so-called) Abyssinians; of the half-African Copts; of the negro-like (but not negro) Nubians; and finally of the Sennaar blacks.

Mark, on a map, the areas over which these several varieties are spread. Compare it with the geological chart of Russegger; and the closeness of the coincidences will, perhaps, surprise you. The blacks are found on the tertiary and recent deposits. The primitive and volcanic tracts will give the European faces. The intermediate conformations will be found on the sandstones. Read Livingstone. The same results will present themselves, and the author himself will draw attention to them. The negro is an exceptional African.

## CHAPTER XXI.

The Persian group.—The Kurds.—The Persians proper.—Talish, Tajiks, and Iliyat.—The Gypsies of Persia.—The Seistaunis.

FROM Africa back to Asia. From Arabia, where the two continents join, to the valley of the Tigris. From Armenia to Persarmenia. From the empire of the Turkish Sultan to the empire of the Persian Shah. From Arabia to Persia; and, afterwards, from Persia to Hindostan.

We shall find that this arrangement is convenient. We need only remember that, with the exception of the Indians, all the populations which come in contact with the great Persian area have already been described—on the north, the Turks and Dioscurians; on the west, the Armenians; on the south, the Arabs.

Of this great Persian area the most western part is the occupancy of

*The Kurds;* by which I mean the Kurdistan, or Kurdland, of the maps—this and something more. Both north and south of the Kurdistan of the maps Kurds are to be found, and that in considerable numbers—both north and south, both east and west. For the population is not only spread continuously over a large area, but is sporadic as well. There are Kurds in eastern Persia, Kurds in Asia Minor, Kurds in Syria, Kurds elsewhere.

The Kurds are, to a great extent, a population of the frontier; some being within the Turkish, others within the Persian, boundary. Many of them, however, are but nominal subjects to either Persia or Turkey. Where the hill ranges are high, and the country is impracticable, the chiefs are all but independent. Could they but be united, they would be wholly so; for their spirit is high, their temper hot, their character energetic, their habits martial. They keep up a chronic state of warfare with each other. They levy black mail after the fashion of borderers. Like the Skipetar of Europe, whom they resemble in character, they always go armed; ready to fight, ready to rob; ready to serve as an escort against robbers like themselves. They are wiry and bony in make, with extremely prominent features, elongated faces, and dark skins. Mahometans in the way of creed, they are but too ready to sharpen their swords for onslaughts upon their Christian frontagers; and of Christian frontagers there are many. In the north there are the Armenians; the Kurds being numerous in Armenia, the Armenians in Kurdistan. In the central districts lie the Caldani, Christians in creed, Syrians in respect to the language of their liturgy. In the south there is little but Mahometanism; the Mahometanism of the Turks and Arabs of Mesopotamia, the Mahometanism of the Arabs and Persians of Khuzistan. Lastly, there are the Kurds of the Russian empire in Erivan, in Karadagh, in Karabagh, and in the south parts of Georgia.

The family, then, comes in contact with Dioscurians, Armenians, Turks, Caldani, and Arabs on the west, with Persians on the east.

The Kurds are a population of tribesmen; falling into divisions and subdivisions. Thus the Bulbassi contains, as sections, the Kabaiz, the Manzun, the Mamash, the Piran, the Rummuk, and the Sinn and Taafah. The Bulbassi chiefs are called Muzzin. When a Muzzin dies, the strongest and bravest of his sons succeeds; birth being only a presumption in favour of the eldest. A chief, once nominated, cannot be deposed. The women marry within their own tribe. Blood feuds may be extinguished by the payment of so many oxen. A certain number of thieves is attached to each tribe, whose business is to rob for the chief.

The Jaf, the Bebber, the Sindjavi, the Afshar, are similarly constituted; each with its chief, its district, and its private wars.

The southernmost members of the Kurd family are exclusively Persian; Lak tribes, Faili (Feili) tribes, or Buktiyari tribes, occupants of the parts to the south of Kirmanshah, which are, for the most part, mountainous.

The analogue of the Tajik (of whom more will be said in the sequel) is to be found in Kurdistan. The existence of the tribe is the rule; its absence the exception. Yet certain subordinate populations, the Guraan and the Kelowspé (white caps), are said to be tribeless. They are, perhaps, extra-tribual, *i. e.* beyond the pale of the recognized and ascertained divisions.

As a general rule, the Kurds are Mahometans. At any rate they are more Mahometan than aught else. The Yezids are this; the Yezids, who have improperly been called Devil-worshippers. They simply conciliate Satan. He is powerful. He is easily offended. Hence, they speak of him either not at all, or with respect; eschewing the name in all imprecations and oaths; pained when they hear others use it.

The name *Kur*d is historical. Word for word, it is *Gordiæi*. Word for word, it is *Kar*duchi. Word for word, it may possibly be *Kha*sdim and *Chal*dæi. That the Karduchi, however, of the Anabasis, the men whose bows and slings inflicted more mischief upon the Ten Thousand retreating Greeks than all the armies of Arta-xerxes, were the ancestors of the present Kurds, is generally and reasonably believed. Again — the famous Saladin seems to have been a Kurd of the Ayubite division of the Rawadiæi; as was also the historian Abulfeda. I write this after Gibbon; who suggests, however, the likelihood of the blood of both the sultan and the philosopher having been mixed. The orthodox Arabs, who saw with grief and shame that the tribe under notice was infected with the heterodox doctrine of the metempsychosis, "insinuated that its descent was only on the mother's side, and that its ancestor was a stranger who had settled amongst the Curds." This is likely enough. The name Ayub is Arabic. The chief qualities of both Saladin and Abulfeda were those of an Arab. The Kurd frontier, in their time (as it is now), was Arabian.

*The Persian proper.*—Conterminous on the west with the Kurds, the Persians proper extend both eastwards and northwards; their area being one of great magnitude and irregular outline. It contains, as may be expected, a great deal of what is purely Persian. It also comprises many tracts wherein the language, at least, is intrusive. The Persian, for instance, of Erivan, and a great part of Aderbijan, is spoken on a soil originally Armenian; the Persian of Shirvan on a soil originally Dioscurian. Daghestan, to the north of the great axis of Caucasus, is a Persian name, meaning the land of the Dahæ. Yet its speech is, to a great extent, Persian; which, to the north, is succeeded by the Turk of Tartary. The details of its extension in the east will be seen in the sequel. At present it is sufficient to say that the blood and language by no means appear to coincide. The former must be, in Daghestan, more or less Lesgian; in Shirvan, Lesgian or Georgian; in Aderbijan, Armenian.

*The Talish.*—Between the mouth of the Kur and

Ghilan, a narrow tract of land, of which a part seems to be mountainous, and a part fenny, is the occupancy of the Talish.

They are spare, raw-boned men, strong, but not tall, hardy, active, and devoted to their chiefs. They reminded Frazer—as so many mountain tribes remind North Britons—of the Scotch Highlanders. One young man takes charge of his chief's firelock, another of his cloak, a third of his pipe. A fourth stands by his horse's head as he mounts.

Their country extends from the Suffid-rood (there or thereabouts) to the point whereat the mountain subsides into the plain of Moghan; part being Russian, part Persian. There are, I believe, some Turk and some Mongol families amongst the Talish. The data, however, for an accurate ethnology are wanting.

The Talish country runs along the side of the Caspian. So do the provinces of

*Ghilan and Mazenderan*, to the back of which lie the mountains of the Elburz range, whilst the parts along the coast are alluvial, fenny, swampy. Hence, we find that some of the occupants are mountaineers, others marshmen. As a general rule, they are rude and hardy; agriculturists along the lower levels, herdsmen in the hills. They are by no means of pure blood.

There are the Dioscurians at the one end of their area; the Turkomans at the other. There are certainly Turks in the central districts; and, I believe, a few Mongols. Asterabad and the northern part of Khorasan belong, in the way of ethnology, as much to Tartary as to Persia.

*Aderbijan.*—Aderbijan, in contact with the Dioscurian, Armenian, and Turk districts of Kars, Erivan, and Karabagh is Turk on its northern, and Kurd on its western frontier; is the hilly occupancy of a rude and hardy population; is believed to be, in respect to its ancient history, Mede rather than Persian; is believed to be the land in which the religion of the Magi most especially flourished; is believed to be the country wherein the local dialects give the nearest approach to the ancient language. In Dizmar, for instance, it has been specially stated that Pehlevi is spoken.

The remaining provinces belong, more or less, to the great central desert; for we must remember that when the broken country of the north, the low levels that fringe the Caspian, and the drainage of the Tigris have been subtracted, Persia, notwithstanding its ancient glory, and its poetic associations, is neither more nor less than a barren steppe, to the north of which lies Tartary, to the south, Arabia—steppe and desert also; steppe and desert; the one continuing itself northwards into the tundras of Siberia, the other becoming intertropical, equatorial, African.

From each of these quarters exotic influences have been brought to bear upon Persia; morally and materially, materially and morally. The blood of most, perhaps of all, the Persian dynasties has been Turk. Arabia gave the Koran.

The inhabitants of the towns are, as a general rule, of mixed origin. In language they are Persians. They are also, for the most part, Persians in physiognomy and habits. Their being, however, all this is perfectly compatible with their being, more or less, Indian, Turk, Mongol, Arab, or Dioscurian in blood. In the first place, the whole land has been overrun by foreign conquerors (chiefly from the north), over and over again. In the next, it has always been the custom of Persian and Turkish sovereigns to found cities, and (as a means of doing so) to transplant populations. Thirdly, there are the effects of trade; fourthly, the necessities of government. These introduce the foreign merchant and the strange soldier. Hence, the natives of towns like Heraut or Ispahan are Herautis or Ispahanis rather than simply Persians.

The extent to which names like these imply a difference between the citizens who bear them and the ordinary Persians of the country around depends upon the circumstances of each particular case.

The Persian of the villages is called by a name which has already been noticed—the name Tajik. A Tajik in Bokhara is a Persian as opposed to an Uzbek. A Tajik in Persia proper is a countryman as opposed to a townsman. It is not, however, every occupant of a rural district who is a Tajik. In order to be this he must be a tiller of the soil rather than a feeder of flocks; a farmer rather than a grazier; a man of fixed residence rather than a locomotive migrant.

Being this, the chances are that he will be a Persian also; a Persian in language, and a Shiite in creed. On the other hand, the migratory populations of the country, numerous as they are, are, as a general rule, not only other than agricultural in habits, but other than Persian in language.

The opposite to a Tajik is an Iliyat, the Tajik being a Persian, a cultivator, and a Shiite; the Iliyat being a Sunnite, a herdsman, and a Turk, an Arab, or a Kurd, as the case may be.

To one of these three classes can all the Iliyat, or locomotive tribes of Persia, be referred. The extent, however, to which they are Kurd, Arab, or Turk exclusively is by no means accurately known. I am not aware that, with the exception of the Aimauks, (who are scarcely to be classed with the sporadic tribes now under notice) there are any actual Mongol Iliyats on Persian soil. At the same time, I believe that there is much Mongol blood in the veins of men whose language is other than Mongol.

Then there are the Indians of the towns, especially the Banians, whose business is trade, and who, as a general rule, intermarry with one another.

Then there are the gypsies, who, in Persia, as elsewhere, are Indians in blood, and, to a great extent, Indians in language also. They hang about the towns; in this respect differing from the Iliyats who prefer the open country. They hang about the towns, being, in craft or profession, tinkers, horse-jobbers, fortune-tellers. They rarely marry out of their own bands or taifehs; are known under the names Duman, Kaoli, Gáobáz, and Ghurbat, or Khurbat, and are very imperfect Mahometans.

Kurbat is the name of a division of the gypsies of Syria, whose language, which is reasonably believed to be nearly the same as that of the Khurbat of Persia, is as follows:—

| English. | Kurbat. | Duman. |
|---|---|---|
| *Head* | sir | murras |
| *Hair* | val | khalluf |
| *Ear* | kan | priuk |
| *Eye* | akki | jow |
| *Tooth* | dandeir | ghiólu |
| *Hand* | kustum | dast |
| *Sun* | gaham | gaham |
| *Moon* | heiuf | heiuf |
| *Star* | astara | astara |
| *Fire* | ag | ar |
| *Water* | pani | how |
| *I* | man | man |
| *Thou* | to | to |
| *He* | hui | hui |
| *One* | ek | ek |
| *Two* | di | di |
| *Three* | turrun | sih |

| English. | Kurbat. | Dumau. |
|---|---|---|
| *Four* | tshar | tshar |
| *Five* | penj | penj |
| *Six* | shesh | shesh |
| *Seven* | heft | heft |
| *Eight* | hest | hest |
| *Nine* | na | na |
| *Ten* | das | deh. |

In no province of Persia is the population wholly Persian. There are foreign elements everywhere. There are foreign elements even where we omit the sporadic Iliyats. There are foreign elements because the frontier is, in all cases, overstepped by some portion of the populations of the neighbouring areas. Thus—Aderbijan is not only Persian, but also Armenian, Kurd, and Turk. Irak is (on its western frontier) Kurd. Khorasan is Turk, Afghan, and Hazareh. Khuzistan is Arab. Arab, too, are the eastern parts of Fars and the parts along the Persian Gulph. Arab, too, are the southern districts and maritime fringes of

*Kerman* and *Mekran*.—Of these the inner districts are Persian; not, however, without Turk, Biluch, Brahúi, and Afghan elements.

Biluchistan will be considered by itself. It contains, as opposed to the true Biluches, several settlements of Tajiks, who are called by the true Biluches, Dehwaur.

The northern division of the Persians beyond the frontier of Persia proper has yet to be noticed. To some slight extent it has been noticed already; the Uzbeks of the Oxus having been described as intruders into a region originally Tajik. This they were in Balk. This they were in Kunduz. This they were in Khost, in Inderaub, in Taulikhaun, in Huzrut Imaum, in Khullum, in Meimuna, in Andkhu, in Shibbergaun, and in Bokhara. In all these districts, large or small, weak or powerful, there are mixed populations of Uzbeks and Tajiks; and in all of these the Uzbeks are the newer, the Tajiks the older, population. Whether they are the aborigines is another question.

The natives of Aderbijan were said to represent the Medes rather than the proper Persians. The Tajiks of the parts under notice are occupants of the ancient Bactria; Bactria and Sogdiana. Their land is the Transoxiana of the classical, the Mahawulnaher of the Arabic, writers. In Bokhara they are called Sarts.

In Persia proper a Tajik is a Tajik as opposed to an Iliyat; the Iliyat being an Arab, a Turkoman, or a Kurd, as the case may be.

On the Oxus a Tajik is a Tajik as opposed to an Uzbek; who, besides being a Turk and a nomad, is also a political superior.

In Afghanistan a Tajik is a Tajik as opposed to an Afghan or Hazareh.

In Biluchistan he stands in contrast to the Biluch and Brahúi.

The names are

| | |
|---|---|
| In Persia . . . . . . . . | Tajik. |
| — Bokhara . . . . . . . | Sart. |
| — Afghanistan . . . . . | Deggaun. |
| — Biluchistan . . . . . | Dehwaur. |

A Tajik is also called, in the non-Persian countries, a Parsiwan.

Tajiks may be found as far from Persia as Chinese Turkestan—even further. Dr. Falconer tells me that, when in Cashmir, he met with one from the drainage of the Irawadi.

In the villages round all the great towns of Afghanistan Tajiks abound. Those on the Caubul river are specially called Caubulis. In

*Seistaun* the mass of the population is Tajik. The very

oldest occupants, however, either in fact or by hypothesis, are the fenmen of the great lake. They are said to differ from the ordinary Seistaunis both in form and habits. They are big, black, and ill-featured. They dwell in hovels of reed. They employ themselves in fishing and fowling. They are probably the ordinary inhabitants under certain physical conditions—the conditions that, in Africa, give us negros.

As Aderbijan was Mede, as the Oxus was Bactrian, as Fars is Persian in the stricter sense of the term, so is Khorasan Parthian; and as the Parthians were, in all probability, Turkomans from Tartary, it is likely that the blood of even the Tajiks is mixed; the mixture being of ancient date.

I follow Elphinstone in calling the Seistaunis Tajiks. Whether, however, they have all the Tajik characters is doubtful. In the desert district, their occupations and habits must be, more or less, those of the Iliyats. It is only certain that they are Persians rather than either Afghans or Biluches.

I am unable to say what latitude may be given to the term. As long as we have the Persian tongue, the Shiite creed, and the settled habitation, along with an Iliyat neighbour, with whom he may be contrasted, we have a full and perfect Tajik. But what if, with one characteristic retained, we lose another? What if we have men whose language and blood are more or less Persian, but whose habits are pastoral? What if we find them the sole occupants of their area, instead of being in contact with Iliyats? What if they be independent? What if they fall in tribes? What if their speech be akin to that of Persia rather than actually Persian? What if—we may go on asking questions of this kind far faster than they can be answered. And after all they may be questions concerning names rather than facts. The fact that we must best understand is the following: viz. that there are certain populations in contact with the Afghans and the Uzbeks who are more Persian than either Uzbek or Afghan. *Pro tanto,* they are Tajik.

In the Gilzye portion of the Afghan country lies the occupancy of

*The Buruki* of Logur and Butkauk. Tradition, or what passes as such, not only makes the Buruki foreign to their present localities, but gives, as the date of their settlement, the eleventh century, it being the Sultan Mahmud who settled them. Whence did he transplant them? This is unknown. Some deduce them from the Kurds. They themselves claim an Arab extraction. They fall into tribes, each tribe with a chief of its own, and with separate lands and strongholds. They are good soldiers, and, as such, respected by the Afghans. Eight thousand families is about the number of the Buruki.

*The Purmuli,* or *Fermuli,* whose numbers are about equal to those of the Buruki, reside in the Kharoti country; the parts about Orghun being Fermuli. Others live to the west of Caubul. They are brave and warlike, carrying on unceasing hostilities with the Kharoti tribes around them. Some, too, are soldiers in the regular army of the Amír. Many are engaged in trade; more in husbandry. Their origin is obscure.

*The Shulmani* seem to have moved from south to north, from the banks of the Korrum, which was their earliest locality, to the parts about the Tira range. At the end of the fifteenth century they are in Hustnugger, whence they are expelled by the Eusofzye. There are still a few who retain a peculiar form of speech, of which I have not seen a specimen.

*The Tiri* are a small tribe in the Shainwari country.

| English. | Buruki. | English. | Buruki. |
|---|---|---|---|
| *Head* | sar | *Village* | gram |
| *Nose* | neni | *House* | ner |
| *Eye* | tsimi | *Egg* | wolkh |
| *Ear* | goi | *Milk* | pikakh |
| *Tooth* | gishi | *Fish* | mahi |
| *Sun* | toavi | *One* | she |
| *Moon* | marwokh | *Two* | do |
| *Star* | stura | *Three* | ghe |
| *Day* | rosh | *Four* | tshar |
| *Night* | gha | *Five* | penj |
| *Fire* | arong | *Six* | ksha |
| *Water* | wokh | *Seven* | wo |
| *Stone* | gap | *Eight* | antsh |
| *Tree* | darakt | *Nine* | noh |
| *City* | kshar | *Ten* | das. |

*The Sirdehehs* are a small tribe who live at Sirdeh to the south-east of Ghuzni.

All these populations either now lie or originally lay to the south of the Caubul river; indeed, with the exception of the Shulmanis of the Hustnugger district, all do so, even now.

# CHAPTER XXII.

## The Biluch Tribes.

*The Biluch.*—Biluchistan is the land of the Biluches, just as Afghanistan is that of the Afghans, and Hindostan that of the Hindus.

The Biluch are all but Persians in language. Yet they are not Tajiks any more than the Kurds are Tajiks. They are tribesmen. They are herdsmen. They are, more or less, migrant, and not a little predatory. In habits they are Iliyats. The Kurds are this; and, except that Kurdistan lies to the west, and Biluchistan to the east of Persia proper, a Kurd is a Biluch, and a Biluch a Kurd. There are, of course, differences between the two. They are, however, unimportant. The skin of the Biluch is dark. The thirtieth parallel, which (there or thereabouts) bounds the Biluch country on the north, limits Kurdistan on the south.

Some of the Biluches live in mud houses; others even invest themselves in forts; but the usual lodging is the tent, or gedaun as it is called. This is made, like that of the Afghans, of black felt or camlet, stretched over a frame of wicker-work made of the tamarisk. An assemblage of gedauns constitutes a tumun or village, the occupancy of a kheil, the same word we have so often met with in Afghanistan. So many kheils form a tribe. As the locality of a Biluch tumun may vary, the name of the kheil may vary also; the name itself being taken from the locality, from the head-man in it, or from some real or accredited quality of the members of which it consists. In Western Biluchistan we may find one half of the kheil in gedauns, the other in huts.

A nation that lives in tents must needs be pastoral, and it is well if it be not predatory also. No Biluch is free from the character of a robber; least of all the Biluch of the west. Mounted on camels, frugally furnished with dates, bread and cheese, and a little water in a leathern bag, the depredators ride on with as few stoppages as possible till they come within a few miles of the spot upon which the attack is determined. Here they rest their camels. At night they remount, accomplish the small remainder of their journey, and make their merciless attack. The spoil being attained, they prefer to return home by a fresh route; always returning expeditiously. There is no care for camel flesh, and journeys of from eighty to ninety miles are often made within the four-and-twenty hours. The number of beasts exceeds that of the men; one of whom may manage as many as ten or twelve—all laden with spoil, and in danger of either pursuit or attacks by the way. At first the lot of such slaves as may have been taken is pre-eminently miserable. They are blindfolded as soon as caught, and tied on the camel that conveys them to the country of their future masters. The women's heads and the men's beards are then shaved, and the hair extirpated with lime. This is to disgrace them in the eyes of their countrymen should they succeed in returning to them. However, when once made safe, they are treated kindly, and soon become reconciled to their lot, attached to their masters, and (it is the master that speaks) so unwilling to change their condition "that the severest punishment we can inflict upon them is to turn them about their business."

The representative of the Biluches, in the way of politics, is the Khan of Kelaut. The field in which they show with the greatest historical prominence is North-Western India, as will be seen when we treat of Sind. How far, however, either the annals of the Khanat, or the records of the (so-called) Biluch conquests of Sind and the neighbouring countries, are Biluch in the strict ethnological sense of the word, will be considered when the Brahúi tribes come under notice.

At present it is enough to say that a man may be a Biluchistani, or native of Biluchistan, without being a true Biluch, just as a man may be a native of Great Britain without being of British (*i. e.* Welsh or Cornish) blood.

# CHAPTER XXIII.

The Afghans.—The Western Tribes.—The Durani.—The Ghilzyes.—The Eastern Afghans.

AFGHANISTAN is the country of the Afghans; whose language is the Pushtú or Pukhtu.

In India this last name takes the form Patan; and an Afghan of India is a Patan.

*The Western Afghans.—The Durani.*—The western Afghans are more of a pastoral people than the eastern; not that the former are all shepherds, nor yet that the latter are all agriculturists. Neither assertion would be accurate. Even with the western Afghans, it is only certain that the extent of land devoted to flocks and herds is greater than the extent under the plough or spade. That the number of shepherds is greater than that of the settled villagers and townsmen is by no means certain. Elphinstone considers that it is less. Many tracts are highly cultivated. The summer station is called the *Eilauk*, which is a Turk word. The winter station is called the *Kishlauk*, which is a Turk word also. The tent, however, is called by a native Afghan term, *Kizhdee*. It is of coarse camlet and black in colour, so that the Turks call it *Karaullee*, and the Persians *Siahtshaudur*, both of which words mean *black tent*. The less a tribe moves the better its tent. Some, indeed, have two sorts, one spacious and commodious for the chief residence, the other lighter and less bulky for the migrations.

There are nine Durani tribes—the Mauku, the Khougani, and seven others, the names whereof all end in *-zye*. This means the same as *Beni* in the Arabic and Hebrew genealogies, or *Mac* in the Scotch. Hence (*e. g.*), the Baurik-*zye* are the *Beni Baurik*, the *Mac Bauriks*, or the *Children of Baurik*, a mode of expressing relationship which by no means implies the personal existence of any real individual so-called. Some, perhaps all, of these nine tribes are divided into *kheils;* thus the Suddo-zye is a division of the Popul-zye. Amongst these *kheils*, one has, generally, a pre-eminence, and supplies the chief, or khan, of the higher denomination. The Suddo-zye is the *Khan-kheil* of the Popul-zye, so far as the subordination of the former to the latter is a reality. So great, however, are the privileges of the Suddo-zye that it may pass for a separate clan rather than a branch of any tribe.

Following, however the classification of Elphinstone, we find that the names for the nine Durani tribes are as follows:—Popul-zye, Allekko-zye, Baurik-zye, Atchík-zye, Noor-zye, Ali-zye, Iskhauk-zye, and the two others first named, Khougani and Mauku. Of these, the first is the largest, the two last the smallest. The influence of the Amír is more visible among the Duranis than amongst the other tribes, and the nearer a Durani district is to Candahar the greater it is. With the more distant tribes, that of the Sirdars exceeds that of the Central Government.

In person the Durani are stout and well made, with a considerable variety of feature. Some have round and plump faces; with others the countenance is strongly marked; with most the cheek-bones are prominent. The beard is an object of care. The young men clip it into shape. All, however, encourage its growth. Some of the shepherds let their hair grow loose and to its full length, so as to present a wild and shaggy aspect. It is more usual, however, to dress it with some care. A shaven stripe down the middle of the head is the common fashion. Long curls are occasional.

They rarely go out armed, except for long journeys, a matchlock being the ordinary weapcn. And this prepares us for a comparative absence of inter-tribual feuds so common amongst the eastern Afghans. The influence of the female is considerable, and few restraints are put upon her freedom. When the family is by itself, the men and women eat together; but at parties they separate. In a caravan in which Mr. Foster travelled a lady Afghan took the absolute command. Men marry between eighteen and twenty, women between fourteen and sixteen. The Durani dance is called the Attun. It is danced, almost every evening, with songs and tales to accompany it. This is when the business of the day and universal amusement of the chase is over. It is also after the duties of religion have been performed. In these the Atchikzye tribe alone is negligent; all the other Duranis being religiously given—religiously given, but not intolerant. There is no encampment without a Mollah, and no member of it who omits his prayers. The creed is Sunnite. Few of the lower orders read. Of the higher, many are familiar with the compositions of the Persian poets.

The love of his country is one of the strong passions of the Durani Afghan, and holy amongst the holy places of his land is the Durani city of Candahar. It is in Candahar that the powerful men of the tribe are chiefly buried; and, even when they die at a distance from Afghanistan, their bodies are carried thither to be entombed. As a general rule, however, a Durani travels but little, and rarely as a merchant or adventurer.

Their character is drawn favourably both by Elphinstone and others, and, what is more, the evidence of the rest of the Afghans is cited in confirmation of their good qualities. The tribes that least like their rule speak of them with respect, and praise them as compared with any third ruler, actual or possible. It is a merit of the Durani in the eyes of the other Afghans that they have replaced and keep out the Ghilzyes; for the Ghilzye rule is generally deprecated, and the Ghilzye ascendancy dreaded. Even the Ghilzyes themselves admit the hospitality and bravery of the Duranis.

From this favourable character one tribe must be excepted—that of the Children of Atshik or the Atchikzye, a tribe whose highest numbers are under 5000. They are pre-eminently pastoral, keeping their flocks in the valleys and heights of the Khojeh Amram and the high country of Toba, and their camels in the sandy plain of Shorabuk, where they are conterminal with the Baraitshes. They wear their beards unclipped, their clothes unchanged for years; are large, strong, quarrelsome men; inhospitable; without mosques or Mollahs, careless in the performance of their religious duties (but withal intolerant), and inveterate robbers. The Durani, unwillingly owning them as kinsmen, admit their courage, their fidelity, and their value as soldiers.

*The Ghilzye* is the second great name in Afghanistan. The number of its divisions is eight, the Ghilzye analogues of the Populzye, &c., being as follows:—

1st and 2nd—the clans of Hotuki and Tohki, from the first of which have sprung the kings, from the second Vizirs, of the Ghilzye dynasty.

3rd, 4th, 5th, 6th, 7th—the clans of Solimaun-kheil Ali-kheil, Suhauk, Under, and Turruki.

8th—the Kharoti.

To these add the division of the Shirpau, no true kheil or clan, but an association formed out of the other eight.

Of these, the Solimaun-kheil is by far the most important, amounting to between 30,000 and 35,000 families. The following are its subdivisions:—

The Kyser-kheil and Summul-zye (or Ismael-zye) who live in a state of comparative independence, and with migratory habits, to the south and east of Ghuzni;

The Staunizyes, and the

Ahmed-zyes—the former agricultural, the latter pastoral.

The Ghilzyes of the Durani frontier resemble the Duranis, with whom they most especially come in contact. Thus—it is chiefly in their form of government that the Tohki and Hotuki are other than Durani. The Turruki recede still more from the Durani type, and the Unders more than the Turruki. The direction of the Ghilzye country is from north-east to south-west, the Kyser-kheil and Kharoti being the most eastern, and the Ahmedzye, the Suhauk, and the tribes about the city of Caubul, being the most northern. Ghuzni, too, is Ghilzye, lying between the occupancies of the Unders and the Alikheil.

I have remarked that the first distinction drawn between a Ghilzye and a Durani is a political one. The Governments of the two divisions differ. Among the Durani, though the power of the Amír and the authority of the Sirdars were, to a great extent, in the inverse ratio to each other, there was, still, a large amount of authority on both sides. The Ghilzyes are much more lightly ruled. Their constitution, however, is less democratic than that of Eastern Afghans, the chief of whom are

*The Berdurani tribes.*—The Berduranis are the Afghans

of the north-eastern parts of Afghanistan, occupying the lower course of the Caubul river, and the parts between the Indus, the Hindu Cush, and the Salt Range. The Ghilzyes bound them on the west. On the north they touch the populations akin to the Siaposh, on the east the Indians of Hindostan. As a general rule, the Indus is their boundary. Here and there, however, there is a Berdurani occupancy beyond it. Peshawur is the chief Berdurani town.

The tribes of the parts about Peshawur are the following five—the Children of Mahomed, the Children of David (Mahomed-zye and Dawúd-zye), the Momunds, the Guggiani, and the Khulíls. The Mahomed-zye and Guggiani, strictly obedient to the Amír and their own chief, occupy the parts about Hust-nugger, or the Eight Villages. The Momunds of the plain, or Lower Momunds, are also British subjects; in this differing from the Upper Momunds, who will be noticed in the sequel.

The Khuttuks (British subjects) lie to the south of the Caubul river, and to the west of the Indus; a portion of them having extended itself into Hindostan. They fall intc two divisions. The further they lie south the greater their independence. The northern Khuttuks are fairer in complexion than the tribes of Peshawur, though more or less Indian in dress and habits. The southern Khuttuks occupy a more impracticable country, and are ruder.

The Bungúsh (British subjects) occupy the valley so-called.

The Khyberis are the tribes of the famous Khyber Pass. Word for word, I believe their name to be Kafir. I think that the name is well explained by supposing that, after the infidels of the parts around them had thrown off their infidelity, the men of the inaccessible ranges of the

Khyber mountain continued to retain theirs, just as, at the present moment, the Kafirs of Kafiristan do. There is another point connected with this name that deserves notice. A supposed connection between the Afghans and the Jews has commanded no little attention from more learned men than one. Now, one of the points that favour, or are supposed to favour the doctrine, is the similarity between the words Kyber and Heber (Hebrew). The Khyber division consists of three independent tribes—the Shainwairis of little, the Urukzyes of great, and the Afridis of very great, political importance.

The Urukzye are herdsmen and soldiers, soldiers and herdsmen—herdsmen who are, more or less, migratory in their habits. In the winter they live along the lower levels of the Kohaut and Tiri hills. In the summer they drive their flocks and herds to the mountain tops. Three of the divisions—(*a*) the Shíkhan, (*b*) the Mishtí, and (*c*) the Rabewkheil, occupy districts on the British boundary.

The most important, however, of our frontagers are the Afridis, who are wholly independent, fierce, factious, inaccessible, and strong—said (and, perhaps with reason,) to be faithless.

The Afridis are important from their numbers. They are also important from the passes of which they are the custodians. They cut in between the British districts of Peshawur and Kohat, so that the road between them runs through the Afridi country. It runs through two passes, the Kohat, and the Gulli or Jewaki. Each of these has been the subject of more than one quarrel between either the Afridis amongst themselves, the Afridis and some neighbouring tribe, or the Afridis and the British Government. The tribes thus mixed up with the politics of the frontier are (besides the Bungush, already mentioned, and the Jewaki, Bori, Bussikheil, and Bustikheil sections of the Afridi name), those of

The Sipah . . 500 }
— Buzotu . . 300 } fighting men.

Small as these tribes are, they are independent.

The Khyber pass itself, to the west of Peshawur, is about twenty-five miles long, rugged, narrow, tortuous, and often enclosed by precipitous and perpendicular walls of rock. Essentially predatory, the tribes on each side of it are largely paid for the permission to pass; largely, but not always sufficiently; a Khyberi escort being, by no means, sufficient to ensure a safe passage through the Khyberi country.

The Khyberis are lean, but muscular, dark-skinned, with prominent cheek-bones and high noses. This is also the Kurd physiognomy. In the vallies they have the terraced houses so common in Afghanistan; in the mountains, movable huts of mat. In some parts they are truly troglodyte; occupants of excavations in the rock. A dark turban, a dark blue tunic, and sandals of straw—this is the dress of a Khyberi, whose arms are a sword, a short spear, and a matchlock with a wooden fork to serve as a rest. Their habits make them excellent marksmen and good soldiers, so far as they can be relied upon for keeping their hands from plunder; for they love this better than fighting, and may fall upon the baggage of the army to which they belong, if they find it unguarded. This they did in the battle that lost Shah Shujah his crown.

*The Children of Joseph—the Eusof-zye*—are, perhaps, the most uncontrolled of all the Afghans. They are also amongst the most quarrelsome. Divided into numerous small communities, chiefly democratic, their form of government is eminently patriarchal. Contrasted with the feudalism of the Duranis, the Eusofzye system reminds us of the Lesgian and Mizhdzhedzhi communities of eastern Caucasus as opposed to the Circassian aristocracies of the west.

The Eusofzye division is numerous—numerous, but closely packed; for it is agricultural rather than pastoral, and it occupies warm and fruitful valleys rather than bleak and barren mountains. Its eastern limits touch the Indus, and, at one point, cross it; for the district of Drumtour on the eastern side of that river is Eusofzye, just as another district, lower down, is Khuttuk. The limits of the Eusofzyes touch the Indus on one side and the Punjkora on the other. On the south they extend to the Caubul. The northern part of the plain of Peshawur is Eusofzye. So is the valley of Bunír. So also those of Swaut, Punjkora, and Chumla. In all these the Eusofzyes have been encroachers, and in all of them the older population, although it has retired, is still represented. As a general rule, the higher the level of the valley the more aboriginal and the less Eusofzye its character. Let us remember this; also remembering that between the valleys there are hill-ranges as well as at the head of them. The plain belongs to the Afghan, the hill-range to the tribes he has dispossessed.

Swaut, Bunír, Punjkora, and the Eusofzye part of the valley of the Caubul, are the lands of the Akkozye, the Mullezye, and the Lawezye. Each clan owns his share of the soil, to which the original occupant is bound as a serf, under the denomination of fakir. The principle upon which the land is divided is so remarkable that I shall give it *in extenso*, and in the very words of Elphinstone:—"Each of these clans divided its lands among its khails at a general meeting of the clan, and this arrangement was repeated throughout all the subordinate divisions.

Each of the khails receives its lands in perpetuity; but a different arrangement was adopted within itself. The lands of each of its divisions were allotted only for a certain number of years, and were to be changed at the end of that period for those of some other, so that each might share equally in the fertility or sterility of the soil. Thus, each independent division of the Khauzoozyes retains the lands assigned to it at the original distribution; but the subdivisions interchange their lands, in a manner which I shall endeavour to illustrate by the example of the Naikpeekhail, a division of the Khail of Khauzoozye, and clan of Accozye, which is now an independent Oolooss, divided into six clans.

"The lands of the Naikpeekhail are divided into two parts, equal in extent, but, of course, not exactly equal in fertility; the Oolooss is also divided into two parts, which draw lots every ten years for the choice of land. If the lot falls on the half which is already possessed of the best share, it retains its possession; but if it falls on the other half, an immediate exchange takes place. The two half Ooloosses meet every ten years to draw lots, at a village which lies on the borders of the two shares of lands. Vast numbers of people attend to witness the ceremony; but as the exultation of the victors, and the anger of the vanquished party, would produce tumults in such an assembly, the Mulliks put off drawing the lots on various pretences, till the people get impatient, and return to their homes. When the crowd is dispersed, the chief of the whole Naikpeekhail draws the lots, and announces the result, which is received in the victorious party with public distributions of charity, firing of matchlocks, and all other marks of rejoicing. The change of lands is accomplished without much trouble or confusion; each clan of one half Oolooss is paired with a clan of the other, and the two thus paired, cross over into each other's lands.

"When the lot has determined that the half Ooloosses are to retain their former lands, the three clans of each cast lots among themselves for a new distribution of their share, which is divided into three portions.

"On the two last occasions, when lots were drawn among the Naikpeekhail, the half which had the worst share was successful each time, and, in consequence, there have been two complete interchanges of land within the last fourteen years. It is impossible not to suppose that the uncertain tenure on which the lands are held under this institution, must be a great bar to improvement; but, in spite of this obstacle, the Eusofzye country is cultivated with great industry and success, and the villages, watercourses, and other immovable property, are as good as in most parts of Afghaunistaun. It might also be expected, that there would be a civil war in the Oolooss, as often as the land was to be exchanged; and, in fact, at the expiration of the last term but one, the half of the Naikpeekhail which was in possession of the best lands, refused to submit to the usual custom of drawing lots. The Mulliks of the other half complained loudly of this injustice, and called on all the other Accozyes to prevent the subversion of the ancient custom of the tribe; so many Ooloosses declared in their favour, that their opponents were forced to give way, and to draw lots as usual.

"This custom is called Waish. It prevails through the whole of the Eusofzyes, and also among the Mahommedzyes. The period for which the lands are to be retained, however, varies throughout. In Boonere, for instance, the Waish is performed annually. Among the Jadoons, a branch of the Eusofzyes, individuals interchange among themselves, but there is no Waish among clans. With the Otmaunkhail, on the contrary, the whole tribe cast lots every twenty years. Among the Gundehpoors in Damaun, also, the lands are divided into six shares, corresponding to the number of clans in the tribe, and all the clans draw lots for the order in which they are to choose their shares. The period at which this ceremony is to be renewed, is not fixed permanently as among the Eusofzyes, but while one Waish is taking place, it is determined in the council of the tribe, when the next is to happen; the term is generally from three to five years. What is most surprising is, that all these transactions take place among the lawless Gundehpoors, without quarrels or bloodshed.

"None of the eastern Afghauns but those already mentioned, and two or three clans of the Oorookzyes, have this custom. There are some traces of its having prevailed among some tribes in Khorassaun, but the only remaining instance of its existence that has reached me, is among the Baraiches, where village sometimes draws lots with village, or man with man, but without any Waish among clans."

One of the Eusofzye saints pronounced upon his countrymen that they should always be free, but never united. And his prophecy has been true. Few communities are more anarchic. No Eusofzye chief has authority equal to a constable in England.

"I shall illustrate the above observations by an account of the proceedings of a part of the Ghalleekhail, one of the clans of the Naikpeekhail.

"The part of the Ghalleekhail which I am to speak of, inhabits at present the village of Galoche, which is shared by portions of three other clans. Each clan lives separately under its own chief (who is called Mushir, and who is subordinate to the Mullik of his own clan), and these quarters of the village are called Cundies. All the relations of each Cundy are to its own clan, and it does not seem more connected with the other Cundies in the same village, than if they lived in different parts of the country. The Mushir of each Cundy maintains a public apartment, where all councils are held; here also the men meet to converse and amuse themselves; and here they receive guests and transact all public business, unmixed with the members of the other Cundies. Such an assembly of discordant materials into one spot, cannot take place without frequent convulsions. Accordingly, scarce a day passes without a quarrel: if there is a dispute about water for cultivation, or the boundaries of a field, swords are drawn, and wounds inflicted, which lead to years of anxiety and danger, and end in assassination. Each injury produces fresh retaliation, and hence arise ambuscades, attacks in the streets, murders of men in their houses, and all kinds of suspicion, confusion, and strife.

"As these feuds accumulate, there is scarce a man of any consequence who is not upon the watch for his life. In every village are seen men always in armour, to secure them from the designs of their secret enemies, and others surrounded by hired soldiers, to the number of ten or twelve, and sometimes of fifty or a hundred.

"Anwur Khaun, the Mullik of the Ghalleekhail, always sleeps in his Hoojra, or public apartment, away from his women, surrounded by his male relations; his servants all sleep round, except four or five, who keep watch; all have their arms ready by them, and if one of them goes beyond the threshold of the apartment, he must be guarded by four or five armed men. I have been told by Mozirrib Khaun (the nephew of Anwur Khaun, a lad about eighteen years old), that he has seen several attacks on this apartment by one of the Cundies of the same village, but they failed from the alertness of the defendants."

Of the more anarchic clans the Naikpeekhail seem to be the worst. The following is a sample of their quarrels. The father of a Naikpeekhail Eusofzye, named Mozirrib, "had a dispute with a man named Sirundauz, about the boundaries of their lands: high words passed, and in the end Mozirrib's father was wounded. Anwur Khaun, his brother, and uncle to Mozirrib, is the head of all the Ghalleekhail, yet he had no means of redress beyond those possessed by any other individual. A Jeerga was held on the occasion, which does not seem to have had much effect. A few days afterwards, when Anwur Khaun went to the Hoojra, accompanied by Mozirrib, then only sixteen, and ten or twelve of his relations, some well armed, and others having only their swords, they found Sirundauz there, with twenty of his friends in full armour. This did not deter Anwur Khaun from reproaching him with his behaviour; his attack brought on the usual consequences, a desperate affray took place, in which Mozirrib received a severe cut on his head, and Anwur Khaun was covered with wounds; many of his relations were also wounded. A son of Sirundauz, and another of his partisans, were killed. As Anwur Khaun had killed the first man, he was considered to be in the wrong, and was obliged to fly with all his family. At last he was wearied with his exile, and submitted to Sirundauz, giving him his sister and his niece (a sister of Mozirrib's). Sirundauz behaved with courtesy; he said he considered Anwur's sister as his own, and restored her to her relations; but he kept the other without marrying her (for the Naikpeekhail never marry a woman given in price of blood), and from that day Mozirrib saw his sister no more. The pursuit of blood had, indeed, been put an end to, but no intercourse took place among the families; Sirundauz and Anwur never meet when they can avoid it, and when they do, they turn their heads away. Mozirrib, in answer to a question, what he would do, if he met Sirundauz alone, replied that he would instantly attack him, that he might anticipate the assault which Sirundauz would assuredly make on him. Such fury after a reconciliation would be blamed even among the Naikpeekhail, but says Mozirrib, 'A man's heart burns for his relation that was killed.'"

One of the commoner causes of war between tribe and tribe arises out of the abduction of a woman from one Ulus to another, or from an elopement from a man's own Ulus to another; abduction being common, and sanctuary in the case of elopement never being denied. Thus—"The wife of a Fakeer of the Naikpeekhail eloped into the lands of the Bauboozyes. The Fakeer followed with some of his relations to kill his wife; and as he was lurking about for this purpose in the night, he was set upon and killed, with one of his relations, by the person who had carried off the girl, and some of his new protectors. When the news reached the Naikpeekhail, their Khaun sent a drummer to summon the Mulliks of the six clans, and consulted with them on the propriety of a war. The Mulliks returned to their clans, and conversed with the heads of Cundies, who took the sense of the people at meetings in the Hoojra; all were eager for revenge, and in three days the whole Oolooss assembled in arms, and marched on the same night to an embankment which turned part of the river of Swaut into the lands of the Bauboozyes. They broke down the embankment, and erected a redoubt to prevent its being rebuilt.

"The Bauboozyes, who saw the water cut off from their cultivation, immediately assembled, and marched against the redoubt. The Naikpeekhail were six thousand, and the Bauboozyes much more numerous. Both sides had some horse, and some hundred Jailumees (champions distinguished by a fantastic dress, and bound to conquer or die).

"The rest were a mob, some in thick quilted jackets, some in plate armour, some in coats of mail, and others in leathern cuirasses; all armed either with bows or matchlocks, and with sword, shields, long Afghaun knives, and iron spears.

"When the armies came in sight, they at first fired on each other; afterwards the Jailumees turned out, and engaged with the sword; at last the main bodies came into close combat. The brave men on each side were mixed together, and fought hand to hand; the cowards, who were much the greater number, hung back on both sides, but joined in the general clamour; every man shouted and reviled his adversaries with as loud a voice as he could. Even the women of the Fakeers (for those of the Eusofzyes could not appear in public) stood behind the line, beating drums, and distributing water to refresh the weary. At last both sides were exhausted, and retired to their homes.

"Numbers on both sides were killed and wounded. It was, says my informant, a tremendous battle; songs were made on it, and the news went to Peshawer to the king.

"It led, however, to no important result; the redoubt remained, the lands of the Bauboozyes were ruined for want of water, the war continued for three years, many other Ooloosses joined each side, and the whole country up to the mountains was embroiled. At last many Khauns of neutral Ooloosses interposed, and meditated a peace."

In making the Naikpeekhail the most lawless of the Eusofzyes we have shown that there are degrees in their anarchy. In some cases, indeed, there is an approach to an organized consolidation of power in the hands of some powerful or astute chief. Such a one was Kaussim Khan, chief of Mullizyes, who succeeded in making for himself a power of life and death over his Ulus, and of abolishing private warfare. Some of this power he obtained by policy, some by war against the Kafirs of his frontier.

The whole number of Eusofzyes, including their fakirs and dependants, may amount to 900,000, though Elphinstone is unwilling to carry it higher than 700,000. The fakirs form more than half. Some of these are of Afghan blood, who have been reduced to migrate from their own district and become serfs in the country in which they found refuge. Some are of Indian origin—Hindkis and Cashmirians. The majority, however, are the old occupants of the land—Deggauns and Swautis.

Many of the Eusofzyes have fair complexions, grey eyes, and red beards. They are stout and brave; quarrelsome, as has been said; proud, as living as masters among slaves. Their morality is best in the high country; worst in the plains, where it is bad; very bad—where idleness induces vice, gambling, bang-eating, opium-eating, and worse. The influence, on the other hand, of the Mollahs is great—tyrannical. For an omission of the regular prayers, or neglect of the fasts, they either inflict bodily punishment, or disgrace the offender by public exposure on an ass. The intolerance is in proportion to their immorality.

When an Eusofzye becomes impoverished, the spirit

of clanship steps in to save him from disgrace. A subscription is raised to set him up again. Sometimes (though this is discreditable) he goes the round of the villages, and, stopping outside each, waves his *loongee.* This ensures a contribution. Or he may go on a pilgrimage to Mecca, or he may seek his fortunes in India. And this is a common resource. Notwithstanding the love of their country so general to mountaineers, and which is not less strong, but rather stronger, in Afghanistan than elsewhere, the numbers of Patans (for so they are called in India) in Hindostan, sometimes mixed with the native Indians, sometimes collected together under their own chiefs, is very great. Of the Afghan settlements in India by far the most important is that of the Rohillas, a settlement which will require a separate notice.

Next to the Eusofzye come the Turkaun (or Turcolauni) and the Othmankail, the former in Bajour, the latter in the hills between Bajour and Swaut. The Bauz, or chief of the Turcolauni, has great power over his tribe. There are no fakirs in the Turcolauni country.

The Upper Momunds are connected with the Khyberis rather than the Momunds of the plain of Peshawur, or Lower Momunds. They occupy the hill-range between the Punjkora, and the Kuner rivers. The Currapa, between Peshawur and Jellalabad, is in the Upper Momund country. Mulliks have considerable power over their separate clans, but not so much as to dispense with references to the Jirgas. The Khan is only powerful through his influence with the Mulliks, except in the time of war. He has no revenue from his tribe at all. He has, however, a salary from the Amír, from whom he also holds lands. This is the price for the Currapa pass being kept passable, and for a contingent to the royal army. A single Momund, as an escort, ensures the safety of a traveller through the Momund country. Without one you are sure of being robbed. Two kheils of the Upper Momunds are nomad, and move in the spring with their camels and black tents to the head waters of the Helmund.

For the remaining tribes we have no longer any general name like Berdurani, Ghilzye, or Durani. We may, however, for the sake of convenience, designate the majority of them as the Afghans of the Punjab frontier; some of them being the Afghans of the Damaun—the Damaun meaning the eastern skirt of the Solimani range. Others are true mountaineers.

The Turis touch the Upper Bungush; the Jaujis the Turis; the frontier being a scene of inveterate hostility. The Turis are Shiah, rather than Sunnite Mahometans. Some of the Jaujis live in houses half sunk in the earth.

The Esaukheil occupy not only the banks of the Indus, but some of its islands; cultivators of wheat and occupants of villages, but still lawless robbers.

In the valley of Bunnú, which belongs to British India, the population is mixed in origin. It has a bad name. Before the conquest of the Sikh empire there was chronic warfare along the whole Bunnú frontier; for the warlike Viziris were continually making raids upon the valley. The effect of this was to coop-up the Bunnúches in small high-walled villages, and to limit their locomotion to the parts immediately under their shelter. It is evident that Mr. Temple, from whose report the newer notices of the frontier tribes is, for the most part, taken, lays great stress upon what he calls "the propensity inherent in the Bunnúches to surround themselves with walls," and the "morbid desire to wall themselves in" as physical influences. He says that, as a general rule, they have lived, from their childhood, "within four square walls twenty-feet high;" and that many of them have never been more than a few miles from their native village. Hence, they stand in an unfavourable contrast to their neighbours. Hence, they are under-sized, and sallow-skinned. As is the body, so is the mind. Their moral qualities are of the worst. They are capable of reckless perjury, of deliberate assassination. It is admitted, however, that they are quiet, orderly, and regular in revenue matters. It is suggested, too, that some noble characters have arisen amongst them. Upon the whole, however, their name is a bad one. The first settlement of the affairs of the Bunnú valley was effected by Major Edwards; in whose Year on the frontier of the Punjab the first full account of the Bunnú population is given.

Bunnú is British, Dour is independent; or rather the Amír of Caubul is free to take it to himself. It has not been treated as a portion of the Sikh empire. Its population, like that of Bunnú, is mixed.

The Viziri is one of the more important names of Afghanistan. The tribes it embraces (divisions and subdivisions) are numerous. The men who bear it are brave, active, warlike, and predatory. They are amongst the rudest of the Afghans. They have the credit, perhaps, of being ruder than they are. Their occupancy is in the mountains, to the back, and on each side, of Bunnú and Dour. They may muster, perhaps, 30,000 men. They quarrel, however, amongst themselves; so that the whole force of the name is scarcely destined to be ever enlisted in the same cause.

I have said that the Bunnú valley has been the scene of inroad after inroad. It has, for the most part, been the Viziris who were the aggressors. Indeed, some of them have effected permanent settlements in the valley, transforming themselves into agriculturalists. These are British subjects. A few of their mountaineer brethren may admit the authority of the Amír of Caubul. The mass, however, is, both in practice and theory, thoroughly independent.

The chief division is into the Ahmedzyes, and the Othmanzyes. To the former belong

| | |
|---|---|
| The Hatti . . . kheil | The Sirke . . . kheil |
| — Sudun —— | — Omerzye |
| — Mohmund —— | — Paenduh kheil |
| — Bezund —— | — Bodín . . . —— |

To the latter

The Bukki | The Jani
The Nurmi.

Other divisions are, the Toroe, the Khojul, the Gunge, the Husein, the Taze, and (more important, from the circumstance of their having been mixed up with the quarrels of the frontier) the Muhsúd, and the Kabulkheil.

The Murwuts are, I believe, wholly British. They are stout active men, of mixed habits (*i. e.* they are, more or less, agricultural as well as pastoral) who have been once more predatory than they are now.

The Damaun tribes are more or less migratory. Many, too, are more or less mercantile This gives a greater mixture of manners than we find amongst the Berduranis. Their dress is more Indian than their look; for many of them are fair rather than dark.

Of the particular tribes each has something characteristic and differential.

The Gundehpoors are, perhaps, the rudest; the Baubutrs the most civilized. They have among them not only merchants but capitalists; and properties as large as £30,000, an immense treasure for these parts, are perfectly safe. A portion of the Bauburs live in Sehra, beyond the Solimani range, contiguous to the Shirauni, whom they resemble.

The Damaun tribes put a control upon their natural lawlessness by the election of temporary and responsible magistrates, armed with power sufficient to keep the peace, but not sufficient to endanger the freedom of the tribe. They are selected from each kheil in such proportions as to make up the number of forty in all; whence they are called Chelwashtis, from the Pushtu word chelwasht = forty. Their head, or fore man, is styled the Amír of the Chelwashtis. The whole tribe bind themselves by oath, on his election, to support his authority; being at the same time fully prepared, both to watch its exercise, and to check its abuse. The Meankheil has four Amírs, and suffers from the division of power and responsibility accordingly. The Chelwashti system, though a characteristic of the Damaun tribes, is by no means either universal throughout the Damaun, or limited thereto. Of the Damaun tribes two dispense with it. Of the tribes other tha Damaun two or more adopt it—the Shiraunis, and the Gilzyes of Kuttawauz. The Chelwashti system has been noticed as Tajik. It is also Nausser.

The Meankheil tribe is remarkable for being but incompletely Afghan, inasmuch as one out of the four parts of which it consists is Baktiari, the Baktiari being Persians.

The Storianis are so thoroughly a frontier tribe that part of their area has been conquered from the Biluches. This serves as their winter station, their summer one being in the high country belonging to the Mussakheil Caukers. A quarrel, however, with one of the tribes whose land lay between the two points made the migrations impracticable. So half the tribe sold its flocks and took to tillage at once; and the other half, with the exception of two clans, did the same soon afterwards. These two pastoral clans of the Storiani have Spusta, on the south-western skirts of the Tukt-i-Soliman, as their summer settlement.

The Sheraunis are the occupants of the Tukt-i-Soliman. They are pre-eminently agricultural, cultivating wheat, practising irrigation, keeping but few horses or camels and more oxen than sheep—hardy and frugal. They have bold features, grey eyes, and high cheek-bones. They never kill an ox; but, should one die, cut its throat with certain ceremonies prescribed by their religion, and eat it in defiance of their religion; for the Koran forbids the use of flesh of animals that die of disease as human food. They marry late; and the father gives his daughter a dowry instead of selling her (as is usually the custom) for a price. They have no serfs, no domestic servants. The few artificers and tradesmen of their country are Hindus or settlers from the Damaun. All the tribes that make their annual migrations through the Sherauni country have to fight their way: a traveller, however, with a native escort may pass through it in safety. The chief of the Sheraunis is called Nika or grandfather. He is elected as the head of the oldest Sherauni family, and is believed to be under the special guidance of Heaven. From every keeper of sheep he receives a lamb annually; from every keeper of oxen a calf; to omit the payment of which is to ensure some misfortune to the family of the defaulter. The Nika is the only true and legitimate judge. He hears the case, puts up a prayer to be enabled to decide justly, and is sure of his injunction being obeyed, for the fear of divine punishment is its sanction. The Chelwashti system is most in force in the parts distant from the Nika's residence; the two authorities being in the inverse ratio to each other. There is a Mullah in each village, who takes a tythe.

The Khan of Murhail is under the Nika of the Sheraunis, the Murhai country being Spusta. The tribe itself is pre-eminently pastoral, and resides in tents.

The tribes of Hurrepaul and Kuppeep are branches of the Sherauni.

Where the Sherauni portion of the Solimani range ends, the Zmurri portion begins. The Zmurris are said to rob less than the Sheraunis; but in other respects to resemble them. They are the most southern Afghans of the main ridge of the Solimani range.

## CHAPTER XXIV.

Certain equivocal Afghans.—The Baraich.—The Terins.—The Caukers.—The Naussers.

SEISTAN lies on the rivers Helmund and Furrarúd. Shoraubuk, due east of Seistan, lies on the Lora. It is the occupancy of the Baraich.

East of Shoraubuk, and higher up on the Lora, is Pishín. Pishín is the occupancy of the Tor Terín.

East of the Terín districts lies the land of the Caukers.

1. *The Baraich* are divided into four clans, each of which has a Khan at its head, who, acknowledging the supremacy of the Amír of Cabul, pays a tribute of a hundred horses. The Baraich are great camel-breeders.

2. *The Tor,* or *Black Terín* occupy Pishín.

3. *The Spín,* or *White Terín* reside in the valley of Zawura, and in the open plains Tull and Chutialli. Stretching into Cutch Gundava, they well nigh touch the Indian frontier. The statement that they resemble the Durani Afghans is by no means conclusive evidence to their being actually Afghan. I place them in the present group provisionally. They are, more or less, isolated, the population by which they are separated from the Tor Terín being that of

4. *The Caukers.*—The head-waters of the Lora lie within the Cauker country, which is wild and inaccessible. It forms a square of about 180 miles, between the Atshik-

zye country, the Spín Teríns, the range of Sōliman, and Biluchistan; beginning at the Siona Daug, a high, cold, and barren plain, fitted only for pasturage, but improving as we move southwards into the valleys of Tor Murgha, Nureen, Togye, Hunna, and Burshore.

This is the district of the Caukers of Afghanistan; but as all the Caukers are not within the limits of the Afghan country, a political division must be made between the ones just noticed and those of their southern frontier. The valley of Shawl, granted by Ahmed Shah to Nusser Khan, Prince of the Biluches, is no longer considered as part of the Afghan country. The name of the particular branch of the Caukers that occupies Shawl, the name of the Caukers of Biluchistan, is *Cassye*, or *Casía*—word for word, the same as the name *Casía* on the frontiers of Arracan and elsewhere in many places. *Casía*, indeed, and *Cauker*, are both words which may appear and re-appear as often as such words as *Highlander*, *Dalesman*, or *Mountaineer* in England.

The clan of Punnee, occupant of Seewee, in Seeweestan, is Cauker.

The Caukers of Burshore closely resemble the Teríns; the other elements of the Cauker name bear no exact resemblance to any of the populations around them. They are divided into at least ten clans, and these are subdivided. Their manners are by no means uniform. In Cunchogye they live in tents, and a single family may constitute an encampment. In Boree there are villages with terraced houses, the use of the tent being occasional. All the Boree Caukers belong to one tribe — that of Saraun. Yet they fall into as many as twelve independent communities, often hostile to each other. Each village is under its own Mushir, and it is only during a war that the several Mushirs acknowledge any single chief. Within the villages the jurisdiction of the Mushirs is limited. He calls a Jirga on weighty matters. Minor ones take their course.

The rudest part of the Cauker country is the centre. To go half naked is contrary to the notions of decency of an Afghan. A Cauker of the middle district, however, goes naked from the waist upwards during the summer. In some places they are said to live in caves, being troglodyte, like some of the Khyberis.

5. *The Naussers* are specially stated to speak Pushtu, or the language of the Afghans. At "the same time," writes Elphinstone, "their features and expression certainly indicate a race distinct from that nation." The kindred which they claim with the Afghan Hotuki is one which the Hotuki themselves deny.

The Naussers have no fixed habitation at all. In spring they are to be found in small encampments of some four or five tents in the Tohki and Hotuki countries. As the season advances, they congregate more numerously, and their encampments enlarge themselves to the amount of a hundred or more to the village—if so it may be called; the migration consisting of short stages in quest of grass for the flocks. These, however, change their character when autumn commences; for, then, there is a meeting in council, a striking of tents, and a general movement for a more distant locality. This is the Damaun, between which and the summer quarters lies the hostile country of the Viziris. For passing this, the whole body divides itself into two divisions, each of which makes for Kunzoor, on the banks of the Gomul; Kunzoor, on the banks of the Gomul, which is the general rendezvous for the whole Nausser body—a body amounting to some 30,000 souls, not to mention flocks of sheep and herds of camels. The tumult that ensues at the approach to Kunzoor is not decreased by the occasional quarrels that often ensue between hostile sections of the immigrants, crowded as they are, towards the end of the march, in one narrow valley—tents, cattle, and men—men, cattle, and tents. When all are assembled, they appoint Chelwashtis, and march onwards; the power of the Chelwashtis having suppressed all feuds, and determined the order of march as well as the means of defence against the now prepared, and always hostile, Viziris. No Viziri gives quarter to a Nausser. At length, after a dangerous march through narrow defiles, beset with ambuscade, they emerge into that part of the Damaun which lies north of Scind, and south of the Murwut country. Each horde has its own allotted ground, on which it encamps in circular groups of tents, within which the cattle are shut up at nights. The women work, the men idle or hunt. When the snow on Tukt-i-Soliman melts they prepare for returning to their spring and summer quarters, appoint Chelwashtis, and (what is more important) a Khan as a general dictator over the whole body, break up their camps, and turn their faces westwards. The appointment of a Khan is all-important; though only during the Nausser migrations. When collected in the larger encampments, they are governed by their own Mushirs. A Khan undertakes to organize and direct them during their migrations; out when they are spread over the country in the small detachments that have been spoken of, they go on as nearly as possible without any government at all. A measure of a Khan's value during a march is found in the following piece of conduct of Jurrus Khan. He was anxious to remain in the Damaun with 300 or 400 of his kinsmen. The expedition, however, was stopped till he could be prevailed upon to accompany it. The Khan and Mushirs are elected from the chief Nausser families, and are subject to deposition for incompetency. The Mushir (or Mullik) settles all disputes, can expel an offender from the camp without an appeal to the Jirga, and is absolute director in respect to all camp and quarter movements. Any four or five individuals may advise him. He is free, however, to act in defiance of their advice.

## CHAPTER XXV.

The Paropamisans of the Oxus.—Cohistanis.—Kafirs, &c.

I NOW come to a class for which I propose the name Paropamisan, its chief area being the parts between the southern slope of the Hindukush and either the main stream of the Indus itself or that of its feeder the Caubul river. To these drainages, however, it is by no means limited. Some of its members are on the water system of the Oxus, some on that of the Yarkend river, some (perhaps) on that of the Amur. They are all mountaineers, most of them being independent, and some being either actual Kafirs (*i. e.* infidels) or imperfect converts to Mahometanism. Our knowledge of them is eminently imperfect. For this reason it is far from unlikely that some of the populations now coming under notice may be more properly denominated Tajik.

The language, however, of a Paropamisan is Indian rather than Persian. The language of a Tajik is Persian rather than Indian. If so, the class under notice is transitional. This I believe it to be. I repeat, however, the statement, that it is one concerning which our details are of the scantiest.

The valuable, though fragmentary, journal* of Mr. Gardiner, gives us the following account of the superstitions of the Therba and Shuli tribes.

*Time*—February 24th, 1830.

* Journal of the Asiatic Society of Bengal, vol. xxii.

*Place*—E. or N.E. of Bamían, near a place called Dror, where the new and intrusive population is that of the Kalzubi Turkoman, the aboriginal that of the Thur, or Thurba, and Shu, or Shuli, tribes.

A small pool at the bottom of a deep valley is the site of Moh's death. It is believed to be bottomless. The water is bitter and bituminous; bubbling up with sulphuretted hydrogen, and surrounded by incrustations of sulphur. Lambent flames are said to occasionally play over its surface. Near it is a dark cave, and in this cave are the remains of idols—more than one. The chief of these represent Moh and his wife, Mábún, deities whom even the Mahometans of the district reverence. No one enters the cave with his shoes on.

Two other caves are dedicated to Sheh, the destroyer, and Zhei, the God of Fire. At each new moon the Therba (who reckon by months rather than years) make a fire-offering to Zhei.

Two other caves are dedicated to Hersh and Maul.

Small beads of gold and stone, found in these parts by natives who dig for them, are called Solomon's grains.

Moh created the earth, and his wife Mábún created the wilderness. From them sprung the first giant race. They slept alternately for 999 moons, and reigned 450,000 moons. After this period, three sons rebelled, viz. Sheh, the life-destroyer, Zhei, the fire-god, and Maul, the earth-quaker; and by their combined efforts, Moh was buried beneath the mountains. Confusion lasted 5000 moons, after which the three victors retired each to his own region for 10,000 moons. Maul was lost in darkness of his own creating, Sheh fled with his family towards the sun, which so much enraged Zhei, that he caused fire to spread over the earth; this was quenched by the spirit of Mábún, but not till the whole giant race was destroyed, and the earth remained a desert for 3000 moons. Then Hersh and Lethram, originally slaves of Moh, and great magicians, emerged from the north, and settled in these mountains. By some Lethram is considered as the incarnate spirit of Mábún and the Queen to whom Hersh was vizier. Hersh had three sons,* Uz, Muz, and All. These he left in charge of all their families, while with a large army he travelled toward the sun in pursuit of Sheh, who was supposed to be still living. So the three sons of Hersh and their descendants reigned happily for 18,000 moons, till Khoor (Cyrus?) invaded and conquered the country, but after many years' struggle, they expelled the invader, and retained the name Khoorskush (Cyrus killed) now Khirghiz. The descendants of Hersh continued to reign for 10,000 moons more till Khoondroo (Alexander?) invaded the country, after which no separate legend of them seems to be recollected.

In the same district stands the fort of Khornúshí, to which you ascend by a series of steep steps on hands and feet. Then comes a narrow ledge of rock, from which a ladder of skin-ropes, or a basket and windlass, takes the explorer upwards. At the top, a basin of bubbling brilliant water, hot in the winter and cold during the summer, always full, and never overflowing, gives rise to the following legend—an echo of remarkable clearness adding to the mysterious character of the spot.

When Noah was at Mecca, Khor, the chief of the district, went to pay homage to him. Thereat Noah was well pleased, and promised to grant him any favour for which he should ask. So Khor asked for water. But the voice

* Whose names seem retained in the Uztagh, Muztagh, and Altai mountains.

in which he spoke was rough and loud, and his manner coarse. At this the patriarch was offended. So that instead of blessing the land of Khor he cursed it, and condemned it to become solid rock. Nevertheless, he kept his promise in the matter of the water, and sent his grandson Shur to carry it into effect. The grandson cried Nu Shu. Echo answered Nu Shu. The sound Nu Shu reached Mecca. And now Nu Shu is the sound which the water murmurs, and which echo still conveys to Mecca; the place retaining the name of the three parties concerned—Khor, the prince who spoke so rudely; Noah, the patriarch who disliked Khor's manners; and Shu, the grandson who did the work in opening the basin and calling out the words which echo delighted in repeating.

Wood's legend of the valley of Meshid is to the effect that, in former days, it was overrun with scorpions, and that to avoid them a certain king whose name was Soliman, whose throne was the Tukt-i-Soliman, lived on the top of a hill, but had his meals prepared in the valley. A line of men handed up his dishes. In one of them, a spider was concealed in a bunch of grapes, which stung and killed him. The valley, now containing scarcely 100 families, once held 100,000 workmen.

Gardiner gives the following account. Esh is a desert. Its localities suit these parts. Its chief city was depopulated by snakes, that took the colour of the rocks on which they were found—blue to blue, green to green. The pass at the end of the valley really abounds in serpents.

Again, the Koh Umber mountain, central to Taulikhaun, Kunduz, and Huzrut Imaum, was transported to its present site from Hindostan; as a proof of which all the herbs indigenous to India, are to be found on its sides.

Again, the undulating plain of Reikshan is associated by a Badakshi with all the misfortunes of its country. Khan Khoja, a Mahometan fugitive, at the head of 400,000 men, cursed it. It was to be three times depopulated. It has, already, twice been conquered by the Uzbeks.

In the same districts are legends to a great amount, which Wood, *pudicitiæ causâ,* withholds.

I read all this thus:—there was a barren tract with Hindu legends.

Again, putting together, as I best can, the details of Gardiner, so as to give a geographical result, I come to the conclusion that, the following are the western Paropamisans, *i. e.* the Paropamisans of the Oxus, occupants of the parts to the west of the Belut Tagh.

| | | |
|---|---|---|
| 1. | Kafirs of Esh, calculated at . . | 15,000 |
| 2. | ——— Ushah . . . . . | 12,000 |

These are generally called Kafirs.

| | | |
|---|---|---|
| 3. | Khâl (Kheil ?) Kru . . . . | 12,000 |
| 4. | Gob or Gabr (Guebre ?) . . | 12,000 |
| 5. | Ghar . . . . . . . | 12,000 |
| 6. | Lah or Lashi . . . . | 12,000 |
| 7. | Udú . . . . . . . | 12,000 |
| 8. | Phaluth or Phah . . . . | 12,000 |
| 9. | Shuli, or Shu . . . . | 15,000 |
| 10. | Khuruk, or Kru . . . . | 12,000 |
| 11. | Therba, or Thur . . . . | 12,000 |

These are other than Mahometan, but, still, not called Kafirs.

| | | |
|---|---|---|
| 12. | Bhur . . . . . . . | 25,000 |
| 13. | Mhar . . . . . . . | 40,000 |

These are Nimchi Mussulmen, half Mahometans, or Mahometans with a certain amount of heathenhood.

Moguls are met with in the northern portion of this area.

The tribes who own these superstitions are especially stated to be connected with each other. Their language is specially stated to differ from both the Persian and Arabic; whilst Sanskrit affinities are suggested. That it is other than either Turk or Mongol, is shown in the context. I have but little doubt as to the ethnological place of the men and women who speak it. Their geographical position is obscure. A few may belong to the north-western part of the Cohistan of Caubul. The mass, however, are on the western slope of the Belut Tagh, on the Kafir frontier of Buduskun, and on the drainage of the Oxus. The most northern tribes appear to be in contact with the Paropamisans of the Yarkend river, of whom more will be said hereafter.

I now turn to

*The Cohistanis* of Caubul, occupants, more or less partially, of the valleys of the Ghorebund, the Punjir, the Nijrow, the Tugow, the Alishang and Alighur, and the Lower Kuner.

*The Pushai*, or *Pushye* is one of their dialects, but little different from

*The Lughmani* of the district called Lugman, and

*The Deggauni.*—The name Deggaun applies to the tribes of the lower Kuner. It applies to others as well. The Deggauns, however, in the limited meaning of the word, are the natives of the valley of the Kuner, in the parts about its confluence with the Caubul river.

| English. | Lughman. | Pushai. | Kashkar.* |
|---|---|---|---|
| *Man* | adam | panjai | moashi |
| *Woman* | mashi | zaif | kumedi |
| *Head* | shir | sir | sur |
| *Nose* | matht | nast | naskar |
| *Tongue* | jub | jib | legin |
| *Eye* | aneh | anch | ghach (?) |
| *Ear* | kad | kad | kad |
| *Hand* | atth | ast | —— |
| *Tooth* | dan | dan | dond |
| *Foot* | —— | pae | pong |
| *Sun* | thur | —— | —— |
| *Moon* | mae | mae | —— |
| *Day* | lae | dawas | chhoi |
| *Night* | vell | vyal | paniya |
| *Fire* | angar | angar | ingar |
| *Water* | warg | wark | ugh |
| *Tree* | kati | kadi | —— |
| *Stone* | wad | wad | —— |
| *Fish* | mach | macch | —— |
| *One* | i | i | i |
| *Two* | do | do | ju |
| *Three* | te | te | trui |
| *Four* | char | char | chod |
| *Five* | panj | panj | punj |
| *Six* | khe | she | chui |
| *Seven* | that | sat | sut |
| *Eight* | akht | ash | ansh |
| *Nine* | no | no | nehan |
| *Ten* | de | de | jash. |

*The Punjkora* and *Lundye Valleys.*—East of the Kuner lies the country of the Turcolaini, Othmankheil, and Eusofzye, Afghans. It lies, however, in the valleys rather than the hills; the valleys of the Punjkora and Lundye rivers. The skirts of mountains, and the mountains themselves, however, preserve the remains of an older class of occupants, Swautis of the valley of Swaut, &c., of which the details are obscure. The evidence that their affinities are with the tribes to the north is satisfactory.

* Spoken in Chitral, or upper part of the Kuner river.

I imagine that the following short vocabulary of the speech of the highlanders of Der best represents the Swauti language.

| English. | Deer. | Tirhai. |
|---|---|---|
| *Man* | mish | —— |
| *Woman* | is | —— |
| *Head* | shish | —— |
| *Foot* | khor | —— |
| *Eye* | achhi | achha |
| *Nose* | nistur | nasth |
| *Tongue* | jib | zhibba |
| *Tooth* | dand | danda |
| *Hand* | thoho | hast |
| *Lip* | dudh | —— |
| *Ear* | kan | kan |
| *Day* | dus | das |
| *Water* | wahe | wa |
| *Milk* | shid | dudh |
| *One* | yak | ik |
| *Two* | do | du |
| *Three* | shta | tra |
| *Four* | chor | tsor |
| *Five* | panch | pants |
| *Six* | sho | kao |
| *Seven* | shat | sat |
| *Eight* | pasht | akt |
| *Nine* | noh | nao |
| *Ten* | das | das. |

The Puraunchehs are, by Elphinstone, who only knows them as a class of carriers, called Hindki. He adds, however, that Baber gave them a separate language. I have been told that this is still spoken by a few families.

*Kafiristan.*—And now comes a vast block of mountainous country, imperfectly explored, imperfectly converted to Mahometanism. It is bounded by the Belut Tagh districts on the west. On the east it touches Chinese Turkistan and Little Tibet. To the south lies Afghanistan, and to the north Kokan or Fergana, where the population is Tshagatai Turk. It is eminently, pre-eminently, a Cohistan, or country of mountains; for the Hindukush and the Belut Tagh, along with other ranges more mysterious, still belong to it. It is a land of gorges and valleys; of short streams and of long rivers. These, as we expect, belong to different drainages. They will, probably, be our best landmarks in the perplexed geography of these parts.

Some of them are carried into the Indus. Of these one series is received by the Caubul river; another by the Shayuk.

The best measure of the inaccessibility of the country is to be found in the name of one of its districts, Kafiristan. What this means we have already seen. Is it not the land of the Kafir, Giaour, or Infidel, whereunto Mahometanism, triumphant elsewhere, has failed to penetrate? If such spots exist in western Asia, they must be few and far between. They must be defended by either the most impracticable conditions of nature, or the most fanatic obstinacy of man. Be this as it may, there is within a day's journey of Shiite Persia, of Sunnite Turkistan, of Buddhist Tibet, and of Brahminic India, a true Kafiristan, whither no Mahometan can with safety penetrate.

Kafiristan and Kafir are of course Mahometan designations; a name which is, at one and the same time, native and general, being wanting. Other names there are, Afghan and Mahometan also, though not impossibly native as well, as, Siaposh, Speen (white) Siaposh, and Tor (black) Siaposh.

The following " are the names of some of their tribes.

' 1. Traiguma, Gimeer, Kuttaur, Bairagullee, Chainaish, Dimdeau, Waillee Wauee, Cauma, Cooshteea, Dhaing, and Wauee, called Puneeta by the Mussulmauns.

" 2. Caumojee, Kistojee (whose chief town is Muncheeashee), Moondeegul, Camtoze (half of whom are towards Budukhshaun, and half towards Lughmaun), Puroonee (whose capital is Kishtokee), Tewnee, Poonooz, Ushkong,

Umshee, Sunnoo, Koolumee Roose Turkuma (to whom belong Kataur and Guinbeer), Nisha, Chumga, Wauee, Khoollum, Deemish, Eerait, &c., &c.

"3. Wauee Daiwuzee, Gumbeer, Kuttaur, Pundect, Khoostoze, Caumozee Divine, Tsokooee, Hurunseea, and Chooneea."

Again :

"The common names at Caumdaish were Chundloo, Deemoo, Hazaur Meeruk, Bustee, and Budeel. The names of certain men at Tsokooee were Gurrumbaus, Azaur, Doorunaus Pranchoolla, Gemeeruk, Kootoke, Oodoor, Kummur, and Zore. Those of certain women were Meeankee, Junailee, Maulee Daileree Jeenoke, Zoree Puckhoke, Malkee, and Azauree. The names of four men at Kuttaur were Toti, Hota, Gospura, and Huzaur, and of one woman Kurmee."

The Caumdaish call their chief god Imra ; the Tsukooe Kafirs call him Dagun. Their Paradise is Burry Le Bula ; their hell, Burry Duggur Bula. Buggish is the god of the waters. Mauni expelled Yúsh, or the Evil Principle. Seven brothers bore the name Paradik. Their bodies were of gold. So were those of the seven brothers named Purron. One or more of their gods was called Shee Mahadeo.

They have idols of stone and wood, male and female, mounted or on foot. One in particular is mentioned as having been erected by a Kafir magnate during his own lifetime. He purchased the privilege of doing so by giving a series of feasts to the village. Fire is used at their sacrifices ; blood also ; the blood of cows as well as of other animals. The details of a sacrifice are as follows :—

"There is a stone set upright about four feet high, and in breadth about that of a stout man. This is the Imrtan, or holy stone, and behind it to the north is a wall. This is all the temple. The stone represents God. They say, 'This stands for him, but we know not his shape.' To the south of the Imrtan burns a fire of Kauchur, a species of pine which is thrown on green, purposely to give a great deal of smoke. A person whose proper name is Muleek, and his title Ota, stands before the fire, and behind him the worshippers in a row. First, water is brought him, with which he washes his hands, and taking some in his right hand, throws it three times through the smoke or flame on the Imrtan, saying every time Sooch, that is, pure; then he throws a handful of water on the sacrifice, usually a goat or cow, and says Sooch. Then taking some water, and repeating some words (meaning, 'do you accept the sacrifice?' &c.), he pours it into the left ear of the sacrifice, which stands on his right. (Moollah Nujeeb saw two sacrifices, one to God and one to an idol.) If the animal now turn up its head to heaven, it is reckoned a sign of acceptance, and gives great satisfaction; afterwards water is poured in the right ear, and a third time on the forehead, and a fourth on its back. Each time Sooch is once said. Next throwing in some fuel, he takes a handful of dry wheat-flour, and throws it through the fire on the stone; and this flour they reckon a part of God; and again he throws both hands full of Ghee *into* the fire; this also is a portion of God. They do not in either of these ceremonies say Sooch, but now the priest says with a loud voice, He! and after him three times the worshippers and he say He Umuch! that is, accept! This they accompany each time with a gesture. They put their palms expanded on the outside of their knees, and as they raise them in an extended position, say He Umuch! The priest now kills the goat with a knife, and receiving in both hands the blood, allows a little to drop into the fire, and throws the remainder through the fire on the Imrtan (or idol, in case of an idol), and again three 'He Umuch!' The head is now twisted off (to the left), and thrown into the fire, but no 'He Umuch!' Wine is then brought in a bowl, and the priest dropping a little into the fire, throws the rest through it (the ghee, too, was thrown out of a bowl), and three He Umuch! The priest now prays God, 'Ward off the fever from us! increase our stores! kill the Mussulmauns! after death admit us to Burélebóola, or paradise!' and three He Umuch are said. The priest now brings forward and places before himself a Pusha, or person possessed by a spirit, who, after stretching forward his head into the smoke, and shaking it in it, turns up his eyes to heaven, and prays as before; the priest and worshippers three times say loudly He Umuch! Next each man puts the fingers of each hand together to his mouth and kisses them, next to his eyes, and lastly to his head: then all retire, and sit or lie down in one place. They now put the blood of the victim, with a little water, on the fire, and after it has simmered a little, put in the flesh, which is soon taken out half raw and eaten. But if the victim be a cow, it is divided, and each man carries his own home. The priest gets a double share in both cases. During the meal they sip some wine, mixed with a deal of water, and furnished by the person who gives the victim. The bones are now burnt. The circumstances are the same when the sacrifice is before an idol, but the only one of this sort seen by Moollah Nujeeb, was to Koomy, an idol some distance to the south of the village, on a height of difficult access; they contented themselves with throwing those things towards it. They had no Kibla, and their idols face always indifferently; but Moollah Nujeeb cannot now tell whether in all the

Umrtans and Umrumas the worshippers face to the north. A cow is struck one blow with an axe on the forehead, of which it dies."

They hate the Mahometans, who "frequently invade their territories in small parties to carry off slaves, and once or twice have undertaken more important expeditions against them. About thirty years ago there was a general crusade (if I may be allowed the expression) against them. The Khaun of Budukhshaun, one, at least, of the princes of Kaushkaur, the Paudshah of Coonner, the Bauz of Bajour, and several Eusofzye Khauns, confederated on this occasion, and met in the heart of the Caufir country; but notwithstanding this success, they were unable to keep their ground, and were forced to evacuate the country, after suffering considerable losses. The arms of the Caufirs are a bow about four feet and a half long, with a leathern string, and light arrows of reeds with barbed heads, which they sometimes poison. They wear also a dagger of a peculiar shape on the right side, and a sharp knife on the left, with which they generally carry a flint, and some bark of a particular kind, which makes excellent tinder. They have also begun to learn the use of firearms and swords from their Afghaun neighbours.

"They sometimes go openly to attack their enemies, but their commonest mode is by surprisals and ambushes, and they expose themselves to the same misfortunes by neglecting to keep watch by night. They often undertake remote and difficult expeditions, for which they are well suited, being naturally light and active; when pursued, they unbend their bow, and using it as a leaping pole, make surprising bounds from rock to rock. Moollah Nujeeb saw the men of Caumdaish march out against another tribe. The rich wore their best clothes, and some put on black fillets ornamented with cowry shells, one for every Mussulmaun whom the wearer had killed. They sung a war-song as they marched away, in which were the words, *Chera hi, Cheri hi, Mahrach,* and he learned that when they had succeeded in coming on an enemy unprepared, they set up a loud whistle, and sing a song, of which the chorus is *Ushro oo Ushro:* on such occasions they put every soul to death. But their chief glory is to slay the Mussulmauns; a young Caufir is deprived of various privileges till he has performed this exploit, and numerous distinctions are contrived to stimulate him to repeat it as often as may be in his power. In the solemn dances on the festival of Nummi-naut, each man wears a sort of turban, in which is stuck a long feather for every Mussulmaun he has killed: the number of bells he wears round his waist on that occasion is regulated by the same criterion, and it is not allowed to a Caufir who has not killed his man to flourish his axe above his head in the dance. Those who have slain Mussulmauns are visited and congratulated by their acquaintances, and have afterwards a right to wear a little red woollen cap (or rather a kind of cockade) tied on the head; and those who have killed many may erect a high pole before their doors, in which are holes to receive a pin for every Mussulmaun the owner has killed, and a ring for every one he has wounded. With such encouragement to kill them, it is not likely the Caufirs would often make Mussulmauns prisoners: such cases have happened when the Caufirs were defending their own village, and they then made a feast with great triumph, and put the unfortunate prisoner to death in much form, or perhaps sacrificed him to their idols.

"They, however, have sometimes peace or truce with Mussulmauns. Their way of striking a league is as strange as their mode of war. They kill a goat and dress the heart, bite off half, and give the rest to the Mussulmaun; the parties then gently bite each about the region of the heart, and the treaty is concluded.

"Though exasperated to such fury by the persecution of the Mahommedans, the Caufirs are in general a harmless, affectionate, and kind-hearted people. Though passionate, they are easily appeased: they are merry, playful, fond of laughter, and altogether of a sociable and joyous disposition. Even to Mussulmauns they are kind when they admit them as guests, and though Moollah Nujeeb was once obliged to be kept by the other Caufirs out of the way of a drunken man of their nation, he was never threatened or affronted on account of his religion by any man in possession of his faculties."

The Koh-i-ghar Kafirs shave the head; but when they kill an enemy allow a lock to grow. The Koh-i-kaf and Koh-i-loh tribes reverse this process. The hair grows naturally, but has a lock taken away from it when a Mussulman has been slain. Hence, whilst the Koh-i-ghar heroes rejoice in long locks, those of the Koh-i-kaf and Koh-i-loh may be bald shavelings. A party of Bhuri, with some Kafir girls for sale, had one of extraordinary beauty; the price asked for her being about half an ounce of silver. This tells us the state of the frontier. The Mahometans steal the Kafir women; the Kafirs kill the Mahometan marauders. The country is one which suggests legends and superstitions of all kinds. Sometimes the torrent disappears in some mysterious chasm leading to vast caves. Sometimes the caves themselves bear signs of human occupancy, excavated in labyrinthine windings, intricate, sculptured, and carven into pillars, the pillars themselves being figured.

In some of the chasms it is customary to consecrate certain medicinal herbs. Down one, near the Ziárat of Abba Shah, it is customary to hang a sort of gentian, and to leave it suspended for a month. After which it serves as a panacea.

Then there are the ruins of old cities; some of the monuments of which apparently bear inscriptions. About a mile and a half north of Esh, a Kafir district, bare and barren, is a colossal horse in pitchstone, measuring fifty-five feet from ear to hoof, forty-two from chest to tail. Nor is it the only one. Two others—like the first, in ruins—lie on the other two sides of the town.

The basaltic rocks, as is their habit in similar countries, assume fantastic shapes; sometimes that of a man, or man-like being. When this is the case, the Mussulman of the neighbourhood sees a petrified Kafir; and if asked who effected the petrifaction, answers Abraham. One of these, the Babo Bulan, is about twenty-five feet high, with red eyes, and an aquiline nose. Art has here, most probably, assisted nature. The Babo Bulan is an object of mysterious awe.

The fort of Ustam is said to have been built by Rustum, whose name is that of the great Persian hero. However, the legend makes him a son of Timur. Such are the elements of the Kafir fictions, and such their mixture. Half the inhabitants of the parts about Ustam are Mahometan, half Akaa. The foundations of the fort are Cyclopean, *i. e.* they consist of vast blocks of more than twenty feet in length.

Of the Akaa, the most Mahometan tribe is that of the

Ujuem. Elsewhere the belief in the Koran is but slight. The men are short, stout, hardy, and clothed in skin; the women plain.

The Keiaz tribe seem to be among the rudest. The caves of the highest peaks are their occupancies. They hunt, eat raw flesh (which is unlikely), and are said to be cannibals, which is more unlikely still. Their women are handsome. When a Keiaz lover wishes to marry, he lays his bow at the foot of the fair one. If she take it up, kiss, and return it, the knot is tied, and she is his wedded wife. By varying this practice she can divorce herself, *i. e.* by taking her husband's bow and flinging it on the ground before him. Thirdly—she may make the offer herself, by unslinging one from the shoulder of the man she selects. On the other hand, their husband can sell them. He can also make them over to his visitor; who, if he be a Hindu devotee, may have the choice of the whole Keiaz wifedom; for the credulous mountaineers venerate these impostors, and believe that such progeny as their wives or daughters may bear to them are more or less divine.

The ruins of Mahu are in the Akaa country; the Turks of the neighbourhood being of the Kibi tribe.

Ma and Hu were twin brothers, descendants of Toth, Emperor of the East. Ma was a righteous prince; but Hu was wicked. Hu murdered Ma by burying him alive.

Before his death, however, Ma invoked the same fate on Hu. So the mountain tumbled down upon him and his. This is the account of the origin of the vast excavated tumulus of Ma-hu.

Such are the fragmentary notices of the northern Kafirs, and their congeners, the half-Mahometans, as taken from an appendix to Elphinstone's Caubul, and a paper of Dr. Gardiner's in the Asiatic Transactions of Bengal.

The following vocabularies for the parts nearest the Tibetan frontier are from Cunningham's Ladakh. The Khajunah of Hunz and Nagar is a very remarkable form of speech. All that can be said is that its nearest affinities are Paropamisan.

| English. | Shina. | Arniya. | Khajunah. |
|---|---|---|---|
| *Man* | musha | rag | hir, er |
| *Woman* | grin | kamri | gus |
| *Head* | shis | sur | yetis |
| *Eye* | achhi | ghach | ilchin |
| *Ear* | kund | kad | iltumal |
| *Nose* | noto | naskar | gomoposh |
| *Mouth* | anzi | diran | gokhat |
| *Tooth* | duni | dond | gume |
| *Hand* | hath | hast | gurengga |
| *Foot* | pa | pang | goting |
| *Blood* | lohel | le | multan |
| *Sky* | agahi | asman | ayesh |
| *Sun* | suri | —— | sa |
| *Moon* | yun | —— | halans |
| *Star* | taro | satar | asi |
| *Fire* | agar | ingar | —— |
| —— | phu | —— | phu |
| *Water* | wahi | augr | chil |
| *River* | sin | sin | sindha |
| *Stone* | bat | —— | dhan |
| *Tree* | tum | kan | —— |
| *Wood* | katho | jin | gashil |
| *One* | ek | i | hin |
| *Two* | do | ju | altas |
| *Three* | che | triu | usko |
| *Four* | chhar | chod | walto |
| *Five* | push | punj | sundo |
| *Six* | shah | chui | mishando |
| *Seven* | sat | sut | talo |
| *Eight* | ast | ansh | altambo |
| *Nine* | no | neuhan | huncho |
| *Ten* | dahi | jash | tormo. |

As far as their blood goes, some of the Little Tibetans may be Paropamisan. When I wrote my notice of Bultistan I had no reason to believe that this was the case. I have since, however, seen several casts of Bulti faces brought into this country by the brothers Schlagentweit. They are anything but Bhot. They are, on the contrary, more Persian than aught else. How far they may represent the average physiognomy is another question. Assume that they do so, and it becomes probable that, in the Mahometan districts of Tibet, the blood and language differ. If so, it is the Bhot tongue that has encroached. If so, the dialects which it has displaced are, in all probability, Paropamisan in the south, and Turk in the north; Turk in Kheris, Khapalu, and Chorbad. This, however, is a suggestion rather than a doctrine. Dard is the name for the Paropamisans of the valley of the Indus, and of the mountains on each side. Indeed, Cunningham uses the term in a generic sense, and calls his Shina, Armiya, and Khajuna vocabularies specimens of the Dard language. The term is convenient. It is also old. The Indian Puranas speak of the Daradas, the classical writers of the Daradæ. Whether it be sufficiently general is another question. The tribes, on the other hand, of Chitral and Gilghit are called Dunghers; Dungher being, also, a Hindu word. The Dangri vocabulary of Vigne represents the language of these Dunghers; word for word, the two names being the same.

That certain Paropamisans are, in the way of creed, either actual Hindus or Buddhists is specially stated by Gardiner; whose table I give as I find it. I hang a doubt, however, upon the last name of the list, Bhoti. What is the evidence that the Bhoti are not the ordinary Bhots of Tibet? The list, however, runs thus:—

*Kafirs (Paropamisans) on the borders of Turkistan, Hindus or Buddhists.*

| | | |
|---|---|---|
| Bu, or Buli, | calculated at | 12,000 |
| Kahuz, or Huhi | ——— | 12,000 |
| Phah, or Phagi | ——— | 12,000 |
| Aspah | ——— | 12,000 |
| Kúlis | ——— | 12,000 |
| Muklu | ——— | 12 000 |
| Maha | ——— | 12,000 |
| Kalesh, Malesh, Lesh | ——— | 12,000 |

*Chinese Subjects.*

| | | |
|---|---|---|
| Beh, or Behel | calculated at | 12,000 |
| Plahi, or Plaaghii | ——— | 12,000 |
| Bhoti | ——— | 12,000 |

And now we turn to the west; to the parts above Budukshan (which is an ordinary Tajik district), and the drainage of the Oxus. The highest habitable district on the river is

*Wakhan, the occupancy of the Wakhani.*—By *habitable* I mean *permanently habitable,* and I draw attention to the qualification, because, although the first seventy miles of the river have no fixed residences upon them, they are the summer resort of the Kirghiz nomads, as has been stated in the sketch of that population. Where the stream from the Sir-i-kol meets the stream of the Durah Mastodzh, *i. e.* about the points named Issar and Langerkish in Wood's Map, the highest part of the fixed occupancy of the Wakhani begins, and it stretches downwards as far as the frontiers of Badakshan and Shugnan. Shugnan succeeds Roshan; and below Roshan comes Durwauz, all on the very stream of the Upper Oxus. North of Durwauz lies Karategin.

I think that these States are all in the same category; notwithstanding a statement of Wood's that the Shugnani or Roshani language is peculiar. Saving, however, any exception that may arise out of this difference, the States of the Upper Oxus form a convenient and not unnatural division.

They are Tajik as opposed to the Kirghiz and Uzbek countries of the north and east of them.

They are Tajik with a *minimum* admixture of Uzbek elements, a point which distinguishes them from Kunduz and Bokhara. *Politically*, however, they are more or less Uzbek, *i. e.* subject to the Khan of Kunduz.

They are on the drainage of the Oxus rather than the Caubul and Indus. This separates them from the Cohistanis of Caubul, whose political relations are with Afghanistan rather than Turkistan. Also from the Chitrali, &c. Finally—

They are Mahometans rather than pagans; though in other matters closely akin to the Kafirs of Kafiristan, with whom the Badakshi and Wakhani are conterminous on their southern frontier.

So scanty is the population of Wakhan that the whole number of the subjects of the Wakhani Khan is 1000—there or thereabouts. This is distributed over a few small villages, for which we have the names Kila Khoja, Pullu, Issar, Ishtrakh, Langerkish and Kundut, the latter under a monarch over fifteen families. At present the chief objects of tillage are barley and peas—both grown in quantities insufficient for the consumption of the Wakhani, who supply the deficiency by importations from the districts lower down; a deficiency due to the want of skill and industry as much as to sterility of the soil or the harshness of the climate. At one time the population was thicker, and a considerable trade passed through Wakhan in the way from Kunduz to Yarkend. This supplied a revenue. So did (and does) the slave trade. The Shak-durah, a mountain valley to the north of the Wakhan, is the land upon which the Mahometan Wakhani foray, the Shak-durah people being themselves Mahometan. The unhappy wretches thus kidnapped in the veriest violation of the Koran, which forbids the sale of true believers, are chiefly bartered for horses with the Uzbeks, who, in their turn, sell to the Chitrali. To the Uzbek Khan of Kunduz, too, the Wakhani owe their very imperfect allegiance.

Of fifteen Wakhani measured, the tallest stood five feet seven inches and a half, the shortest five feet one inch and three-quarters. This is taller than the Ladakhi Tibetans. The physiognomy is Tajik; "there is nothing peculiar in their facial line nor in their eyes and hair."

The sheep of a Wakhani constitute his chief wealth. The goat of the country gives a wool equal to the famous Tibetan staple, so valuable for the manufacture of the Cashmir shawls. The dog is like a Scotch colly, of the Chitrali breed, vigilant and courageous. The chief tree, or rather shrub, is the red willow. In April the seed is sown, in July reaped. There are some so-called Kafir forts in Wakhan.

*In Roshan and Shugnan* the natural strength of the country, which is accessible only at midsummer, and that through treacherous passes, protects the inhabitants against invading armies, but not against murderous forays. Shugnan, for instance, a little before Wood's journey, had lost 500 out of its 1000 families, the nominal population of both it and Roshan. The two districts pay a joint tribute of fifteen slaves to the Khan of Kunduz. Stone fruit grows abundantly in Shugnan and Roshan; so does wheat.

*Durwauz*, besides wheat, grows cotton. Its independence is complete. The Durwauzi are Sunnites.

*Karategin*, to the north of Durwauz, vacillates in its allegiance between Kunduz and Kokan. After Karategin, the country becomes Turk.

In speaking of the Little Tibetans I stated that their chiefs pretended to be descended from Alexander. Many of the Paropamisans do the same.

Baber enumerates the tribes who, in his day, inhabited Caubul. In the plains were Turks, Aimaks, and Arabs. Are these last, *eo nomine* and *eâ linguâ*, still existing?

In the hills were Hazarehs, Afghans, Kafirs, and Togderris. What are the Togderris?

The languages were Arabic, Persian, Turk, Moghul (Mongol), Hindi, Pushtu (Afghan), Pushai, Purâncheh, Gubri (Kafir), Buruki, and Degghâni. We have specimens of all these except the Purâncheh.

It is scarcely necessary to enlarge upon the interest and importance of the Kafir and half-Kafir countries. Nor are they inaccessible. Contiguous to the British districts of Caubul, they are, though closed to the Mussulman, accessible to the Frank and Hindu. That the physical difficulties are insurmountable is unlikely. The Belut Tagh is neither higher nor more abrupt than the Himalayas. The value of the fables about Alexander is worth investigation. The possibility of Macedonian and Bactrian remains should stimulate the energy of the archæologist. The analysis of the mythology of the only population in the Persian portion of India whose creed is older than Mahometanism, would be a well-rewarded labour. To the physical geographer the mountains give a quaquaversal watershed; some of its waters falling into the Indus, some into the Oxus, some into the Amur, some into the river of Yarkend. How sadly indefinite are the boundaries of the countries marked Kashgar, Gilgit, Chitral, Astor, Hunz, and Nagor in the ordinary maps!

From two quarters can knowledge best be sought—from Caubul and from Cashmir. Ladakh has been reduced by the Sikhs. More than this, it has been made the basis for offensive operations against the Paropamisans of the Bulti frontier. The power of Gulab Singh has been felt in Astor, Hunz, and Nagor.

To follow up the Kuner from Jellalabad to its head waters; to turn eastwards; to cross the watershed, and follow the largest of the rivers that reach the Indus, would be at once practicable and pregnant with results. The account in Elphinstone is that of Mullah Nujib, who penetrated into Kafiristan from Punkjora on the east and reached Cumdaish, within three days of Badakshan, on the west.

## CHAPTER XXVI.

### The Brahúi.

WITH few populations is the consideration of their language of greater importance than with the Brahúi; and with few has its value been more utterly ignored. That it differed from that of the Biluches, and equally so from the Pushtu of the Afghans, was known to both Elphinstone and Pottinger—for both state the fact. Both, however, treat the Brahúi as Biluches with certain differential characteristics; neither asking how far some of these may be important enough to make them other than Biluch. This is because the political term Biluchistan has concealed one of the most important and interesting affinities in ethnology.

A short specimen of the Brahúi language in Leach's vocabularies commanded the attention of Lassen, who, after enlarging upon its difference from the Persian, Biluch, and Pushtu, drew attention to some notable similarities between the numerals and those of the South Indian dialects. Following up this suggestion, the present author satisfied himself, much to his surprise, that the Brahúi tongue was, in many respects, Tamul, an opinion which others have either recognized or been led to form from their own researches.

In the country, however, which they now occupy, the Brahúi consider themselves aboriginal; the Biluch admitting that they are themselves of foreign origin. The rugged and impracticable nature of the Brahúi mountains favours this view. Of any creed anterior to the introduction of Mahometanism no traces have been discovered, though, doubtless, discoverable. As Mahometans, they consider themselves favoured, inasmuch as the Prophet, mounted on a dove, paid them a visit one night, and left a number of saints behind him for their guidance. Forty of these lie buried under a mountain to the north of Kelaut, called *The Mountain of Forty Bodies*,* a place held sacred and visited not only by Mahometans other than Brahúi, but by the Hindus also. The particular form of the Brahúi Mahometans is the Sunnite, in which they agree with the Biluch.

They differ from the Biluch most in language, as been stated already.

They differ from the Biluch also in physical form, and that notably. To this Pottinger speaks most decidedlv —"The contour of the people of these two classes is as unlike, in most instances, as their languages, provided they be the descendants of a regular succession of ancestors of either." He adds that the two populations intermarry. Again,—"It is impossible to mistake a man of one class for a member of the other. The Brahúi, instead of the tall figure, long visage, and raised features of their fellow-countrymen, have short, thick bones, with round faces and flat lineaments;—in fact, I may assert that I have not seen any other Asiatics to whom they bear any resemblance; for numbers of them have brown hair and beards." They are hardy; for they tolerate the scorching sun of Cutch Gundava equally with the cold frost of their own proper mountain-range. They are hardier, perhaps, than the Biluch. They are also more migratory than the Biluch, changing their pasturages several times in the year. They are harder workers; many of them in the plains to the south of Kelaut being

* Is not this the tale of page 257?

agricultural labourers. The product of their industry—which they dispose of to the occupants of the towns—along with the sale of a few coarse blankets and felts, forms the bulk of their traffic. Of their moral character I find a favourable account. They are less revengeful and less quarrelsome, though not less courageous, than the Biluches. Their chiefs have considerable power. Their women are but slightly, if at all, secluded. Their arms are the sword and the matchlock, in the use of which they excel, rather than the spear, for which they profess a kind of contempt. Their dress is the same for summer and winter. They are great eaters, especially of animal food. This they consume both fresh and dried. The drying is done by exposing the meat to the sun, after which it is smoked over a fire of green wood.

The division into tribes is Brahúi even as it is Biluch, Afghan, Turk, Arab, &c., the number of the tribual divisions being great. Pottinger gives the names of seventy-four; for fifty-two of which he gives the number of their fighting men. That of the Mingul, amounting to 10,500, is the highest. The lowest is that of the Jyanee, which is no more than sixty.

The list of Brahúi tribes could be doubled. "Were it answering my purpose I could enumerate twice as many more, but the foregoing list includes the principal ones in point of numbers, and will suffice to prove the multiplicity of the Brahooé, to say nothing of the absolutely innumerable *keils* into which they are subdivided." About one-fourth of the names end in *-zye*, as Jumul-*zyee*, Samo-*zyee*, &c.

The Kumburani tribe has two distinguishing characters. It only partially intermarries with the others, *i. e.* it receives wives from them, but not husbands, a common form of exclusiveness.

It is also divided into three distinct ranks,—(1) the Ahmedzyes, (2) the Khani, and (3) the Kumburani in the limited sense of the term

| English. | Brahúi. | Bilvch. |
|---|---|---|
| *Head* | katumb | —— |
| *Hair* | pishkou | phut |
| *Eye* | khan | tsham |
| *Ear* | khaff | —— |
| *Tongue* | duvi | zawan |
| *Tooth* | dandan | dathan |
| *Nose* | bamûs | phonz |
| *Foot* | nath | path |
| *Sun* | dey | —— |
| *Moon* (*new*) | nokh | nokh |
| *Star* | istar | —— |
| *Fire* | khakar | as |
| *Water* | dir | aph |
| *Tree* | darakht | darashk |
| *Stone* | khall | sing |
| *I* | I | ma |
| *We* | nan | mà |
| *Thou* | ni | thau |
| *Ye* | num | shumâ |
| *One* | asit | yak |
| *Two* | irat | do |
| *Three* | musit | shai |
| *Four* | tshar | tshyar |
| *Five* | pandzh | pantsh |
| *Six* | shash | shash |
| *Seven* | haft | hapt |
| *Eight* | hast | hast |
| *Nine* | nu | nu |
| *Ten* | dah | dah. |

The following is a Brahúi legend.

" A frugal pair, who had been many years united in wedlock, had to regret that their union was unblessed by offspring. The afflicted wife repaired to a neighbouring holy man, and besought him to confer his benediction, that she might become fruitful. The sage rebuked her affirming that he had not the power to grant what Heaven had denied. His son, afterwards the famed Hazrat Ghaos exclaimed that he felt convinced that he could satisfy the wife ; and casting forty pebbles into her lap, breathed a prayer over her, and dismissed her. In process of time she was delivered of forty babes, rather more than she wished, or knew how to provide for. In despair at the overflowing bounty of the superior powers, the husband exposed all the babes but one on the heights of Chihil-tan Afterwards, touched by remorse, he sped his way to the hill, with the idea of collecting their bones, and of interring them. To his surprise he beheld them all living, and gambolling amongst the trees and rocks. He returned and told his wife the wondrous tale, who, now anxious to reclaim them, suggested that in the morning he should carry the babe they had preserved with him, and, by showing him, induce the return of his brethren. He did so, and placed the child on the ground to allure them. They came, but carried it off to the inaccessible haunts of the hill. The Bráhúis believe that the forty babes, yet in their infantile state, rove about the mysterious hill. Hazrat Ghaos has left behind him a great fame, and is particularly revered as the patron saint of children. Many are the holidays observed by them to his honour, both in Bilochistan and Sind. In the latter country, the eleventh day of every month is especially devoted as a juvenile festival, in commemoration of Hazrat Ghaos." -*Masson's Journeys in Balochistán, Affghanistan, &c.* vol. ii. pp. 83—5.

The representative of the Brahúis, in the way of politics, is the Khan of Kelaut. The extent to which his dominions are Brahúi rather than Biluch will be considered in the sequel.

## CHAPTER XXVII.

Ancient History and Antiquities of Persia.—Relation of Persia to India. —The Religion of Ancient Persia.—The Parsis.

THE populations more or less akin to Persia, have now been enumerated in detail. The relations of Persia, however, as a preliminary to the ethnology of Hindostan, still stand over for notice. Of these two countries, the histories are inseparable. There were numerous Indians on the soil of Persia and Afghanistan, and there was scarcely a town of Caubul without its Hindus.

The literary language of India, allowance being made for a difference of dialect, is the inscriptional language of Persia.

Again,—Persian armies and Persian immigrants have, over and over again, occupied portions of India. They have done this so much, that even the strongest partisans of Indian autonomy and Indian self-development have admitted that, in analysing the ethnological elements of Hindostan, some part, at least, of Persia must be taken into account. But what do we gain by doing this, as long as Persia itself has been unsubmitted to analysis? What if, while Persia is an ingredient of India, Turkistan, Arabia, Armenia, Caucasus, and even parts of Europe, are ingredients of Persia? It is clear that an analysis is needed.

We have two instruments for effecting this, history and archæology. I begin with tne first.

The general presumptions in favour of a Turk intrusion into the land of Persia have been already considered. They constitute the preliminaries to many questions in ethnology in general. To the particular ethnology of Persia they are a preliminary with which no ethnologist can dispense.

I consider that the ordinary notices of the once formidable Parthians suggest the belief that they were of the Turk stock, *i. e.* that they were what the classical writers would have called Asiatic Scythians; the Persians, Sacæ; the Mongols and Tibetans, Sok. If so, the Arsacidæ were what most of the Persian dynasts of the true historical period have been, foreigners to the soil over which they ruled, but not foreigners to the soil which, from the Caspian to the Paropamisus, lies parallel with that of Persia. Let Persia be called (as it is called at the beginning of its history), Iran, and let the parts beyond its frontier be called (as called they were) Turan, and the Arsacidæ were Turanians. Turanian, however, was scarcely the word for the Latins and the Greeks. They used, instead of it, Scythian. Few of them, however, paid much attention to language as an instrument in ethnological criticism. For this reason the special statement of Justin, that the speech of the Parthians "was midway between the Scythic and the Mede, and consisted of a mixture of the two," is valuable. Amongst modern writers Erskine unhesitatingly commits himself to the doctrine, that "the Parthians were a foreign race, who never fully assimilated with the native inhabitants." The Parthian coins have Greek legends. The particular Parthian province was Khorasan.

I now submit the following inference from the similarity of the names *Parthia* and *Persia*; which are as much alike as the Greek words, πάρθω and πέρσω. I submit that, word for word, Parthia is Persia, and Persia Parthia; one being the name of a particular district, and, as such, implying a local conquest; the other being the name of a kingdom in general, and, as such, conveying the idea of a consolidation of power and a ruling dynasty. Just what is supposed to have taken place with these instances, has actually taken place with the word Frank. There is the particular Burgundian conquest of Franche Compté. There is the general French conquest of France. Both, however, were German; just as, *mutatis mutandis*, both Parthia and Persia are held to be Turanian. Let this be admitted, and the dynasty of Cyrus may have been Turanian, even as was that of the Arsacidæ. It was certainly other than Mede. The consideration, however, of the Mede and Macedonian dynasties stands over for the present.

Meanwhile, let those of Cyrus and the Arsacidæ bring us down to the epoch of the Sassanidæ. Word for word this seems to give us the Mongol title Zaisan. I do not, however, press this. I believe that current opinion is in favour of the Sassanidæ having been foreign dynasts.

They are succeeded by the Caliphs; out and out Arabian. But before the ninth century is over, the disturbances of the Turkish guards (the Turanian prætorians to an Arab court) have broken out, and Bagdad is in their hands. The Caliphat is shaken. The Taherites are nominally subordinate, practically independent. They govern in Khorasan, and they have come from the other side of the Oxus. This, however, is only a presumption in favour of their being Turanian. The Soffarids, who only reign from A.D. 872 to A.D. 902, may, not improbably, be Persians. The Samanids, who succeed them, like the Taherites, are from the north. They "passed the Oxus with 10,000 horse; so poor that their stirrups were made of wood, so brave that they vanquished the Soffarian army, eight times more numerous than their own." * The Bowids (from 933 to 1055) are said to have introduced the title of Sultan, a Turk term.

From the Bowid period to the present time, every king of either Persia, or any part of Persia, who consolidates a power with any pretension to stability, is either a Turk or a Mongol. Sebectegin, Mahmúd of Ghizni, Togrul Beg, Malek Shah, Alp Arslan, are all Turks. The Temuginian conquerors are Mongols; the Timurian, Turks.

It must be admitted, then, that the presumptions are in favour of the negative, and, therefore, hazardous, statement that the soil of Persia has never been permanently ruled by a native dynasty.

The doctrines suggested by names like Sacastene † and Indoscythæ have already been noticed.

That a Turanian dynasty interposed between that of the Macedonians in Bactria, and the Arsacidæ, is shown by coin after coin, illustrative of the parts on the drainage of the Oxus during the first and second centuries of the Christian era.

Such is the *primâ facie* evidence (independent of that of the arrow-headed inscriptions which will be noticed hereafter) in favour of an influx of influential Turanians into Persia, beginning early and ending late. Such, too, the notice of the influences from Arabia. The Caliphat gave them. But Arabia is not the only Semite country which has told on Persia. Assyria has done the same. So has Media. So also Macedonia.

As the notice of both Assyria and Media involves a special line of criticism, it is only Macedonia which now arrests our attention. Alexander's army, so far as we see in it a civilizing influence and a vehicle for the thought

* Gibbon, chap. lii. † Vol. i. p. 515.

and learning of Eastern Europe, was an army of Greeks. Its captain was a reader of Homer. One, at least, of its generals was a historian. A geographer accompanied it. A philosopher or two might be found among its court elements. If we look at it, however, as a mere material force (and in this light the physical historian ought to view it), it was a Macedonian medley of half-barbaric Hellenes, Thessalians, and Illyrians. It may have had in its ranks Getæ and Thracians. Should any of its members be, at the present moment, represented by any of the mysterious tribes of the Paropamisus, the chances are against their being Greeks. Skipetar blood is more likely to be found amongst the Kafirs and Wakhanis than Hellenic. This, however, is but a speculation. Nevertheless, it is one which illustrates the case out of which it grows. Materially speaking, the Macedonians were, to a great extent, other than Hellenes. Morally and intellectually, they were Greeks. It was in north-eastern Persia that their power and language lasted longest. Soon after the death of Alexander it took root. By the end of the first century it was shaken by the Turanians.

The general import of the arrow-headed, or cuneiform, inscriptions is now pretty widely known. They represent three forms of speech. One of these, akin to the literary language of India, will be noticed ere long. The other two find their place here. Of these one is Semitic, and one Turanian. The simple existence of the Semitic record tells us this much, viz. that in the reign of Darius, as well as earlier and later, there was a sufficient amount of Assyrian blood within the limits of the Persian empire, to make it either necessary or convenient for public inscriptions to be written in the Assyrian tongue. The details tell us much more. This, however, is enough for the present question; which merely asks whether the foreign influences that have acted on Persia are great or small, new or old, homogeneous or composite. Our answer is, that they are both multiform and ancient. They are not only Semite as well as Turanian and Greek, &c., but they are Semite in two ways. Arabia gave the Koran; but one thousand years before the birth of Mahomet, Chaldea gave something else. There have been the older and the newer elements. And, in the time of the Sassanians there is evidence to an intermediate series of influences.

Respecting the Turanian inscriptions Mr. Norriss, whose opinion I am fully prepared to adopt, has laid down the following doctrine. They are not Turk; as we may possibly expect *à priori*. They are not Mongol. They are rather Ugrian or Fin. If so, we must suppose that, just as certain southern members of the great Fin family penetrated into Hungary in the tenth century, so did certain of their congeners, some fifteen hundred years earlier, penetrate into Persia. Be this as it may, the elements of the ethnology of Persia were, in the time of Darius, as well as before and after, sufficiently complicated to require two languages other than native for the rock inscriptions of royalty.

Roughly speaking, the arrow-headed inscriptions represent the times of Darius and his successors.

To one who holds that Persia was in the same category with Parthia and that Parthia was Turanian, the language of the inscriptions, which is other than Turanian, and, at the same time, not Semite, is more likely to be Mede than aught else—Mede rather than Persian.

Meanwhile the only remaining dynasty, the last in the order of notice, but the first in time, calls us; the dynasty of Deioces, Phraortes, Cyaxares, and Astyages. Now Deioces was a Mede, a Mede of a nation to which the Bysæ, the Parêtakæni, the Strukhates, the Arizanti, the Budii, and the Magi belonged, as opposed to that of the Persians, who were, according to their γένεα, Pasargadæ, Maraphii, Maspii, Panthialæi, Derusiæi, Germanii (a Turk gloss), Dai, Mardi (a Ugrian gloss), Dropiki, and Sagartii. That there were actions and re-actions of the kind suggested by the previous remarks in the time of Deioces, is evident from the text of Herodotus. The Assyrians had held the Medes in subjection. The Medes had not only been successful in throwing off the yoke from themselves but had reduced the Persians. The Scythians and Cimmerians were overrunning not only Media and Persia, but Syria and Palestine as well. Let the history, then, of Persia speak to the great extent to which that country is the land of a mixed population.

It is Mede; it is Persian proper; it is Turanian.

More than this, the Cimmerii were Europeans; so that it has not been from Asia alone that its foreign elements have been derived.

The Cimmerii were Europeans. And so, in one sense, were the Scythians mentioned by Herodotus. They were the Skoloti of the southern parts of Russia rather than the Sakæ of independent Turkistan. They entered Media by the way of Caucasus. The Parthians, though equally Turk, entered Persia from the parts between the Caspian and the Paropamisus.

More unequivocally European than either the Scythians or the Cimmerii were the Thracians. It is impossible to study the campaign of Darius on the Danube without admitting that, notwithstanding all our tendencies to draw broad and trenchant lines of demarcation between the east and west, the early history of the Thracians, the Getæ, and the south-eastern Sarmatians is, to a great extent, that of Media—of Media rather than Persia. I am far from thinking that the Danubian principalities of the Great King were mere outlying possessions. I think that, of Media as opposed to Persia, they were central and integral parts, and that Macedonia was Persian quite as much because it was Thracian, as because it was Greek.

The influence that Greece exerted upon not only Persia in general, but that part of Persia in particular which lay nearest to India, is a matter of ordinary history. The influence of Rome is less distinctly seen. By Rome I mean the Rome of the west; Latin Rome; Rome proper rather than Greek Rome, Byzantine Rome, Constantinopolitan Rome. From the time of Lucullus to that of Julian there were either Roman proconsuls, or kings protected by Rome along the whole of the north-western frontier. There were Roman wars against the Seleucidæ, and Roman wars against the Arsacidæ. In after times there was Rome at second-hand from Constantinople.

It is chiefly through their early Christianity that Syria and Armenia (the former more especially) have acted on Persia. Persian Christianity, however, was short-lived. Yet it passed across the land so as to reach Turkistan, India, and even China.

The preceding analysis has been given because it is only when we undervalue the relations betwen Persia and Europe on one side and the relations between India and Persia on the other, that the phenomena presented by the ancient language and the ancient literature of Hindostan become mysterious; for mysterious they must be in the eyes of those who maintain that the Vedas are three thousand years old, and that the undeniable affinities between the Sanskrit and the languages of the west are explained by deducing the Russian, the German, the Latin, and the Greek from Asia. Any two points may be isolated by ignoring the interjacent area. The archæology of Persia is, to a great extent, the archæology of Hindostan. Persia has acted both morally and materially on India. Turkistan, Arabia, and Europe have similarly acted on Persia. Something was found on the land; something was brought into it; something was given off from it. This is the ordinary procedure when populations act and re-act on each, or where one acts on a second and the second on a third. What has been brought into Persia is, in some cases, extremely clear. It is clear, for instance, that one, at least, of the languages of the cuneiform inscriptions was an importation. So was Mahometanism. So were a great many other things.

The religion of the ancient Persians may or may not have originated on the soil of Persia. It is certain that it was from Persia that it more especially spread itself. It is also certain that, if foreign, the date of its introduction was early. Fire-worship, however, may have been Median rather than Persian proper, inasmuch as Media was (and is) a land where inflammable gases issue in mysterious currents in several localities. One, especially, near the city of Baku, is a nobject of devotion to the Guebres, who make pilgrimages to the spot, where "a blue flame, in colour and gentleness not unlike a lamp that burns with spirits," rises from the earth, and is supposed to be eternal. It may also, if we look at it on its sidereal, rather than its igneous aspect, have been Chaldaic or Arabian; for Sabæanism, as it is called, or the worship of the stars and planets, is pre-emimently Semitic.

I shall call the creed under notice Parsiism or Zoroastrianism indifferently. The chief *data* for its investigation are of three kinds:—the evidence of ancient authors other than Persian; the Parsi scriptures themselves; the practices and belief of the present fire-worshippers.

The Persians, writes Herodotus, think it foolish to

build temples. Yet they sacrifice. They sacrifice on the higher mountains. They sacrifice to the sun, the moon, the earth, to fire, to the winds. They have learned, of late, from the Assyrians and Arabians, to worship the deity called Mylitta by the former, Alytta by the latter, Mithra by themselves. The priest, girt with a wreath of myrtle, divides the victim, lays the parts on herbs, of which the trefoil is the chief, sings a hymn, and prays for all the Persians and the King of Persia. Lepers and white pigeons are not allowed to be near the sacrifice. He may not defile a river by even washing his hands in it. A Magus officiates. The bodies of the dead are first torn by dogs and birds, then interred. Previous to interment the body is smeared with wax. A Magus kills no animals except for the purpose of sacrificing. White is the colour of the sacred horses, of Nisæan breed. When Cyrus crossed the Gyndes one of the white horses plunged into the stream, whereon the king swore that from that time forward the river should not wet even the knees of a woman. So he turned off the main stream into 180 channels. Xerxes flogged the Hellespont, and threw fetters into it. Again, at sunrise he poured a libation from a golden cup into it, and prayed. Having finished the prayer he threw into the waves a golden cup and a scimetar. He also sacrifices white horses to the Strymon. Again,—" the Persians look upon fire as a god, and think it wrong to burn a dead man in a divine flame." Again, Xerxes sacrificed to the winds. Again, Darius wished to have his statue placed on the temple of the Ægyptian Vulcan, and Xerxes sacrificed to the Trojan Minerva. Dates forbade the fleet to approach Delos because it was the birth-place of Apollo and Diana. Xerxes buried certain boys and girls in honour of the god underground. The Magi, a γένος of Media, interpreted dreams, prophesied, and performed incantations. Ctesias makes Darius Hystaspes build an altar to the God of the firmament. Xenophon kills bulls, horses, and other victims according to the direction of the Magi. Strabo makes it unlawful to breathe on fire, according to whom the Cappadocians kept up a perpetual fire.

All this is the worship of the elements; especially is it fire-worship and sun-worship. It is not, however, Zoroastrianism in full. It is not the religion of the two principles. Of this, however, Xenophon gives an inkling. "I have two souls," says Araspes to Cyrus, "for a single soul cannot be bad and good at the same time," &c. Plutarch, from Theopompus, gives us Oromazes and Areimanius opposite and antagonistic to each other, the former of whom makes benevolence, truth, equity, wisdom, and joy; the latter their opponents. The former, too, makes the stars, and appoints Sirius guardian. He also makes twenty-four gods, and puts them in an egg, when Areimanius makes twenty-four others, who crack the egg, and out comes good and bad mixed. The heresy of Manes is stated by more than one of the early ecclesiastic writers to be Zoroastrian.

This gives us the great Dualism, along with a host of minor deities, who are, more or less, abstractions.

The next testimonies are those of the early Syrian and Armenian Christians. These give us a picture of fire-worship as it existed under the Sassanians. Elisæus in his History of the Religious Wars of the Persians and Armenians (as translated by Neumann) gives us the following proclamations and notices:—

"All peoples and tongues throughout my dominions must abandon their heresies, worship the sun, bring to him their offerings, and call him god; they shall feed the holy fire, and fulfil all the other ordinances of the Magi."

Again—

"Mihrnersch, Grand Vizier of Iran and Daniran, to the Armenians abundant greeting:

"Know, that all men who dwell under heaven and hold not the belief of the Mastesens, are deaf and blind, and betrayed by the devil-serpent; for, before the heavens and the earth were, the great god Zruan prayed a thousand years, and said: 'If I, perhaps, should have a son, named Vormist, who will make the heavens and the earth.' And he conceived two in his body, one by reason of his prayer, and the other because he said *perhaps.* When he knew that there were two in his body, he said: 'Whichever shall come first, to him will I give over my sovereignty.' He who had been conceived in doubt passed through his body and went forth. To him spake Zruan: 'Who art thou?' He said: 'I am thy son Vormist.' To him said Zruan: 'My son is light and fragrant breathing; thou art dark and of evil disposition.' As this appeared to his son exceeding harsh, he gave him the empire for a thousand years.

"When the other son was born to him, he called him Vormist. He then took the empire from Ahrmen, gave it to Vormist, and said to him: 'Till now I have prayed to thee; now thou must pray to me.' And Vormist made heaven and earth; Ahrmen, on the contrary, brought forth evil; and thus they divided themselves among creatures; the angels are of Vormist and the devils of Ahrmen: All good, in heaven and here below, is from Vormist; all evil, which is done here and there, is produced by Ahrmen. And thus, whatever is good on this earth, this has Vormist made; and whatever is not good, that has Ahrmen made: as, for example, Vormist has made men; Ahrmen has made sorrows, sufferings, and death; all misfortunes and mournful events which occur, as also lamentable wars, are the work of the evil being; as fortunate events, riches, fame, honour, and health of body, beauty of countenance, eloquence in speech, and length of years, all have their being from good; but all which is not so is the corrupt working of evil."

Again—

"The Persian troops which had been in the land of the Huns are marching hither, with many other troops which had been placed at the gates. Besides these, they are accompanied by three hundred learned Magi, who are to disperse themselves throughout the land, convert every one, pull down the churches, and force all to conform to the king's command. These Magi say: If you receive our faith of your own free will, *then shall you receive from the king honours and presents, from the court* also a remission in the taxes; but if you receive it not freely, we have orders to construct fire-temples in the boroughs and cities, to kindle the fire Behram, and to appoint Magi and Mogbeds learned in the law throughout the land. Should any one attempt resistance, he will suffer death, and his wife and children will be regarded as aliens, and banished."

The following gives us an insight into some of the more serious absurdities of the creed.

"Again, the Magi assign the following cause for the origin of light—they overturn what has just been said, and give another ground for the creation of the sun. They say: 'Ahrmen invited Vormist to a banquet. Vormist came, but would not partake of the meal till their children had fought against each other. Now after the son of Ahrmen had overthrown the son of Vormist, and they required an umpire and could find none, then they created the sun, that he might be the umpire between them.' Now they infer from this that Ahrmen is omnipotent even with regard to the sun, and contend that he took part in the creation of light. But was there, in reality, no other umpire present?—could they not have gone to the Father, or to Him to whom the Father and Son, according to their mythology, had addressed their prayers?

"And wherefore, then, were they in enmity against each other, Vormist and Ahrmen, who had been confined in one womb, who were about to banquet together, and who, by mutual co-operation, created the sun and set him up as umpire? But one Ssaratashd teaches the following disgraceful doctrine, that the Sun and the Light were made in maternal and sisterly embraces, and taught the nation that they might perpetrate the same atrocity: and to veil this disgrace it was given out that they (the Sun and the Light) were created for the office of umpire: for as their doctrines of belief are not contained in books, they sometimes say this, and at others they say that, and mislead the ignorant by it. But if Vormist was God, he was in a situation to create the sun, as well as the heavens and the earth, out of nothing, and not through a crime, or because there was no umpire at hand."

This is from Esnik, who is the chief evidence to the doctrine that both Ormuz and Ahriman are only secondary creations, the primary entity being Zeruan Akerane, *i.e.* Time Increate.

"Before yet anything was made, either the heavens or the earth, or any creature whatsoever which liveth in the heavens or on the earth, was one named *Zeruan*, a word signifying the same with *destiny* or *fame*. A thousand years he offered sacrifice that he might obtain a son, who should have the name Ormisd, and should create heaven and earth and all things in them. After a thousand years of sacrifice he began to reflect, and said, 'The sacrifice which I have performed, does it conduce to the end, and shall a son, Ormisd, be born to me, or do I strive in vain?' While he thought thus, Ormisd and Ahrmen were conceived in the body of their mother. Ormisd was the offspring of the sacrifice, and Ahrmen of the doubt. Zeruan knew this, and said,—'Two sons are in the mother's womb: he who shall first come forth to me will I make the king.' Ormisd knew his father's thought, imparted it to Ahrmen, and said, 'Our father Zeruan intends to make him king who shall first come to him;' and Ahrmen, hearing this, pierced through the body of his mother, and stood before his father. Zeruan, looking on him, said, 'Who art thou?' And he said, 'I am thy son.' Then Zeruan spoke to him: 'My son is of odoriferous breath and resplendent appearance, but thou art dark and of an evil odour.' While they were thus speaking together, Ormisd was born at his proper time, and he was bright-shining and sweet-breathing. He went forth and came before Zeruan: and when Zeruan looked upon him, he knew that this was his son Ormisd, for whom he had offered sacrifice. He took the vessel which he had in his hand, and wherewith he had sacrificed, gave it to Ormisd, and said, 'Hitherto I have sacrificed for thee, now and henceforward thou mayest sacrifice for me:' and hereupon Zeruan gave his vessel to Ormisd, and blessed him. Ahrmen saw this and said to Zeruan, 'Hast thou not taken an oath, whichsoever of the two sons shall first come to me, him will I make king?' Zeruan, that he might not break his oath, said to Ahrmen, 'O thou false and evil-doer! to thee be dominion given for nine thousand years; but I appoint Ormisd lord over thee. After the nine thousand years Ormisd shall rule, and what he wishes that shall he bring to pass.'"

The Mahometan writers were all subsequent to the time of the Sassanidæ. For this reason their evidence is not noticed. That of the Syrians is less full than that of the Armenians. Hence it is believed that the preceding notices, though anything but exhaustive, give a fair and sufficient notion of Zoroastrianism as a living creed at its zenith.

As a living creed at the present moment, Zoroastrianism is held by a few Parsis in Kirman, a few in Khorasan, and a great many more (the bulk of the faith) in Guzerat. In respect to its scriptures—

The Vendidad is a dialogue between Oromasdes and Zoroaster. The Yashna and Vispared are liturgies. The Khurdavesta is also a liturgy. The Yasts are minor and more fragmentary compositions.

There are, of course, in the Persian language several works which treat of Zoroastrianism, and which increase the bulk of the Parsi literature. Others, of which the Bundehesh is the chief, are in what is called Pehlevi. The language, however, of the religion of real life is the Gujerati, in which the Parsiism of India embodies its teaching, and conducts its controversies; for there are, at least, two sects—that of the Khadimi and that of the Rasami—who differ on a question analogous to that of the old and new styles in England. One admits, the other denies, the intercalation of a month. There are other elements of controversy besides, as will soon be seen.

The Parsiism of the present time has much that reminds us of Judaism. It makes few proselytes. It is not a religion for a poor man. Its adherents are chiefly mercantile. It differs, however, from Judaism in having never developed itself into any other religion; so that the creed which should stand in the same relation to the Zendavesta that Christianity does to the Old Testament is non-existent. This isolates Parsiism even more than Judaism is isolated.

The doctrines themselves are taken from the Zendavesta, and it cannot be said that the contents of the Zendavesta itself are unexceptionable. The apparent purity of a simple elementary worship, with a matter so suggestive of spirituality as fire for its main object, excited the imagination of the first investigators of the religion of the ancient Persians. The Parsi scriptures themselves, though not without better things, are full of angels and observances, of impossible epochs and absurd developments. That these are not taken *verbatim et literatim* speaks well for the present state of thought amongst the Parsis. The extent to which a freedom of interpretation existed (provided that it did exist, and was not evolved by the occasion) might not have been known had not the creed come within the sphere of the activity of the Bombay missionaries. These having got into controversy with the Parsis, found them ready to take their own part. I know the arguments of their defence only through the work of their arch-antagonist, the Rev. John Wilson, of the Scottish Church, which puts them in the light of eclectic critics rather than servile bibliolaters. They explain away their angels by making them abstractions, and excuse their ceremonies by reducing them to symbols. In short, they rationalize.

Thus—it is objected that they worship Feruher or Angels.

Answer by Dosabhái. "*Faruhar* means *johar*. They call that *johar*, which is in English called *Essence*. It is a *mantak*, or logical word. In Arabic, they apply *johar* to an article which is composed of its own substance; and they apply the word *araz* to an object which is composed of another object. Take for example the sun and sunshine:—The *johar* is the sun and the sunshine is *araz*. Take another example, of wood, and a chair:—the wood is *johar* and the chair is *araz*, for the chair is made from wood, and if there were no wood, there would be no chair."

Whether the trains of reasoning hereby suggested are strictly Zoroastrian or not is unimportant. Let them be ever so opposed to the original doctrine, Parsiism is still a creed, of which all that can be said is that its modern form differs from its ancient. In the fifth century, Zoroastrianism persecuted. In the nineteenth, it rationalizes.

## CHAPTER XXVIII.

**The Ancient Languages of Persia and India.—The Persepolitan of the Cuneiform Inscriptions.—The Caubul Coins.—The Pali Inscriptions.—The Sanskrit and Pali of Literature.**

THE next step in the ethnology of Persia and India is the consideration of those languages of which we have the oldest specimens, and of which the influence has been greatest. They all belong to one and the same class.

The language of this class that has commanded the greatest attention is, undoubtedly, the Sanskrit. Sanskrit, however, is by no means the most convenient name for the class; nor is the Sanskrit language the most convenient to begin with. The most convenient form of speech to begin with is what may be called

*The Persepolitan.*—The following is a sample at large from an inscription on the tomb of Darius at Naksh-i-Rustam, according to the text and translation of Sir H. Rawlinson:—

1 Baga wazarka Auramazdá, hya im
2 ám bumim adá, hya awam asm
3 ánam adá, hya martiyam adá, h
4 ya shiyátim adá martiyahyá,
5 hyá Dár(a)yavum khsháyathiyam ak
6 unaush, aivam paruwanám khsháyath
7 iyam, aivam paruwanám framáta
8 ram.

The Great God Ormazd, (he it was) who gave this earth, who gave that heaven, who gave mankind, who gave life (?) to mankind, who made Darius King, as well the King of the people, as the lawgiver of the people.

Many inscriptions in the same language are found elsewhere, *e.g.* at Behistun, at Hamadan, and at Van. As a general rule, they occur in conjunction with two others in different languages. Whenever they do this, they take what may be called the place of honour, *i. e.* when the columns are arranged horizontally they stand at the left hand, so as to be read first, and, where there is a grouping round a centre, it is in the centre that the present language finds its place. Again, on a Persepolitan monument it stands alone. It is with good reason, then, that Sir H. Rawlinson considers that this is the primary language of the Achæmenian dynasty—a language of which the other members of the trilingual inscriptions are translations. Whether it be Persian rather than Mede is another question. It is safe to call it the language of the first inscriptions. It is safe, too, as well as convenient, to call it Persepolitan, inasmuch as, in Persepolis, it is found by itself.

In respect to its matter, it is the edicts of the Achæmenian kings which this language more especially embodies; the most important of which is that of the Behistun inscription. In respect to its structure it is closely akin to the oldest Sanskrit. There is no evidence, however, to it having ever been spoken in India, nor yet in the east of Persia. It is on the Kurd frontier, and in Fars, that samples of it most abound. It is only in inscriptions, and only in the cuneiform characters that it is found. Whether the Persepolitan inscriptions give us the oldest compositions in the class of languages to which they belong is uncertain. Most Sanskrit scholars would say that they do not. It is certain, however, that they are the oldest compositions that bear a date. Next to these come

*The legends of the Caubul coins.*—The kingdom which,

after the death of Alexander the Great, was founded in the north-east of Persia is better known through its coins than its historians. Of the former, some thousands have been deciphered. They show that the nearest successors of Alexander ruled as Greeks, their names being Greek and the legends on their coins being Greek. Letters and legends, however, other than Hellenic soon appear, and a series of coins, some bearing native, some bilingual, inscriptions follows. The mintage then degenerates, the names become barbarous, and the signs of a fresh dynasty of conquerors from Scythia show themselves. All, however, that is not Greek in the way of legend, belongs to the same class as the Persepolitan inscriptions on the one side and the literary Indian on the other. The fullest history of the dynasties in question is that of Professor Wilson, in the Ariana Antiqua. He calls the alphabet Arian.

*The Pali of the oldest inscriptions.*—Cotemporary with the earlier but older than the later Caubul coins, are certain inscriptions on pillars at Dauli and Girnar, known most especially through the papers of Prinsep; one of which gives us what will be noticed more fully in the sequel, the famous edict of Priyadasi, prominent and conspicuous in the real or supposed history of Buddhism. The language is a form of the Pali; the date of the inscription the reign of Sandracottus, or Chandragupta, the cotemporary of Seleucus.

Whether the inscriptions of the last two alphabets give us the oldest forms of the language to which they belong is uncertain. Most Sanskrit scholars would say that they do not. It is certain, however, that, next to the Persepolitan, they are the oldest compositions that bear a date.

Whether they give us the oldest alphabets is also un

certain. It is only certain that they give us the oldest documents on which an Indian alphabet appears.

*The language of the Sassanian coins, &c.*—The coins and inscriptions of the Sassanian kings exhibit a language of which it is unsafe to say much. It has affinities with the ones preceding. But it has also prominent Semite elements. The coins themselves are, of course, politically speaking, Persian. The alphabet, however, is Semitic. It contains no vowels, and only eighteen consonants. The legends which it embodies have, of course, a definite date. They range over the fifth, sixth, and seventh centuries.

Now come the compositions which, whether older or newer than the ones which have preceded, have no dates.

These fall into three great divisions:—(1) the Sanskrit, (2) the Pali, and (3) the Zend of the written literatures as opposed to the language of the inscriptions.

1. *The Sanskrit.*—The language of those numerous, long, and important compositions, of some of which further notice will be taken when we treat of the Brahminic literature of India, is the Sanskrit; the Sanskrit with its Devanagari alphabet, its fuller forms, and (along with other characteristics) its dual number, as opposed to the Pali. Of the Sanskrit, some forms are older than those of the literary language in general and some newer. Some present archaisms, some degenerations.

*The Sanskrit of the Vedas* is older than that of the great mass of the Sanskrit literature. How much is another question.

*A Pracrit* is a form of speech which, to explain *obscurum per obscurius*, bears the same analogy to the Sanskrit that the Lingua Rustica of ancient Rome may have borne to the pure Latin of Cicero. Or it may be compared to the Megarian dialect in the Acharnenses. Or it may be compared to the Gascon French in Molière; or to the Bolognese, and other dialects, introduced upon the Italian stage side by side with the purer Tuscan. It is in the Hindu dramas where the Pracrits are to be found; and it is women and servants who chiefly speak it.

*The Kawi* will be noticed when the influence of India upon Java, and

*The Fan*, when the influence of India upon China, is considered.

2. *The Pali.*—The scriptures of Tibet, Mongolia, Pegu, Ava, Siam, Kambojia, and Cochinchina, so far as they are composed in the learned or holy language of the Buddhist creed rather than in the vernacular of the several countries, are not in Sanskrit, but in Pali—Pali, the language of the Buddhism of the south of India. How far it was the language of Buddhism altogether, especially of the Buddhism of the north, is another question.

3. *The Zend*, or *language of the Parsi scriptures.*—This is a form of speech which requires more criticism than it has found. The matter which it exhibits is supposed to be older than the time of the Sassanidæ; the form only in which it appears being attributed to that dynasty. Under the Arsacidæ learning and religion had declined. There was a general knowledge of Zoroaster and his doctrines; but the Zoroastrian scriptures were wanting. So the old men with the long memories were looked up, and the Zendavesta, with its congeners, was constructed from their dictation. The result of this is a book discovered in India, in the seventeenth century, in a language different from that of the Sassanian coins, but akin to the Persepolitan and the Sanskrit. The alphabet, however, is not Indian—or rather it is and it is not. The letters are the letters of the Sassanian

legends adapted to writing; but the principles upon which they are applied are those of the Indian alphabet. They have eight or nine vowels—additions. In other words, the alphabet of the Sassanian coins consists of eighteen, the alphabet of the Parsi scriptures of forty-two characters.

*The language of the glosses to the Zendavesta.*—In the same letters as the Zend, *i. e.* in letters which represent the Sassanian inscriptions in a cursive form, are to be found certain glosses to the Zendavesta, which are neither Sassanian nor Persian proper, nor yet Gujerati, nor yet, exactly

*The language of the Bundehesh* (a work on the mythology of the Zendavesta), though closely akin to it, and written in the same characters.

That the preceding forms belong to the same class has already been stated. It should now be added that the Sanskrit and Pali are Indian rather than Persian; the Persepolitan Persian rather than Indian; the rest Persian in some respects, Indian in others, *e. g.* the Caubul legends are Pracrit in the way of language; whilst their alphabet is, in some respect at least, Semitic. On the other hand, the Zend alphabet is, in some respects, Indian, while the language itself is Persepolitan, rather than either Sanskrit or Pali. More, however, will be said on this head when the alphabets of India, &c., come under notice. More, too, when the origin of the present Persian and the modern dialects of India is considered.

## CHAPTER XXIX.

On the Languages akin to the Tamul.—The Telinga.—The Tamul proper. —The Canarese.—The Cúrgi.—The Malayalam.—The Tulu, or Tulava. —The Ghond.—The Khond.—The Eastern Kol.—The Rajmahal.— The Tamul elements of the Brahúi.

THE languages which form the subject of the present chapter are the languages akin to the Tamul. Between these and the languages akin to the Sanskrit there is a strong contrast. The further we go into the ethnology of India, the clearer this will be seen. The languages of the last chapter were dead; the languages of the present are living.

The earlier writers (and *early* in Indian ethnology means the writers of the beginning of the present century) certainly undervalued them. The habit, too, of speaking of them as the languages of Southern India is inconvenient; for, in ordinary parlance, few of us make Southern India to begin at the Ganges. Mysore and the Carnatic, the Madras Presidency and the Canara country are southern in every sense of the word. Bombay, too, is in the southern half of India, if we begin with Cashmir. Yet the Rajmahal hills are north of Bombay, and the Rajmahali form of speech is Tamul—the word, of course, being taken in a general sense. Add to all this the Tamul elements of the Brahúi, and the reasons against localizing the great family to which that name applies increase. So far from being South Indian, it is not exclusively Indian.

It is Persian as well. The origin of the Brahúi has nothing to do with this view. We are simply looking to the actual distribution of the Tamul tongues in space, as they exist at the present moment. We are simply guarding against the influence of certain expressions which may lead us to under-estimate its extent.

The reasons for giving prominence to the forms of speech now coming into view are less manifest; indeed, the practice of doing so is anything but general. Yet nothing is clearer than the geographical contact between the languages of India and those akin to the Tibetan along the whole range of the Himalayas. Along the whole range of the Himalayas, from Cashmir to the end of Asam, the two groups touch each other definitely and directly; no intermediate language intervening. All that is not Tibetan, Nepaulese, or Burmese, is Hindu; all that is not Hindu is Burmese, Nepaulese, or Tibetan. Such the general character of the frontier. In its details we may fairly presume there has been a difference. What if the Tibetan or Nepaulese tongues have once extended further south, so that the Hindu dialects have encroached upon them? Nepaul, at the present moment, is Bhot. May not the parts south of Nepaul once have been the same? What if the history of the Hindus in the north of Hindostan be that of the English in England, the Nepaulese and Tibetans representing the Welsh of Wales? In such a case the whole valley of the Ganges may once have been, more or less, Bhot. More than this. There may have been a time when (for the eastern half of India at least) the southern frontier of the Tibetan, and the northern frontier of the Tamul, areas touched each other. What if the Ganges separated them, even as the Rhine separated Gaul from Germany? I do not, at present, say that this was the case; I only point out the bearings of the Tibetan tongues upon the ethnology of India. I add, too, that in one point, at the present moment, the distance between the two extremities of the two areas is not more than sixty miles as the crow flies. In the parts to the north and north-east of Calcutta the monosyllabic languages of the Garo hills are spoken to within a short distance of the northern bank of the Ganges. In the parts west of Calcutta the Rajmahal hills actually abut upon the river from the south. Yet the Rajmahal area is Tamul. Again—the original language of Kooch Bahar has its southern frontier a little to the north of Agra; to the south of which populations reasonably believed to belong to the Tamul family make their appearance.

*The Telugu, Teloogoo, Telaga, Telunga,* or *Telinga,* is spoken from Chicacole on the north to Pulicat on the south, extending in the interior as far as the eastern boundaries of the Mahratta districts; so as to be the vernacular language for upwards of fourteen millions of individuals in the northern Circars, and in parts of Hyderabad, Nagpúr, and Gondwana. The drainages of the Kistnah and Pennaur rivers are within the Telinga area. The great stream of the Godavery has Telinga districts on each side of it. A third or more of the eastern Ghauts is Telinga. Then there are the Telinga populations of the parts beyond the proper Telinga area, chiefly in the Tamul districts—Naiks, Reddies, &c. Of these there may be a million; yet it is doubtful whether the Telinga populations are either the most enterprizing or the most civilized of their class. With a smaller population there is, at the present moment, more activity amongst the speakers of

*The Tamul.*—Whether this was always the case is another question. The energy of the latter population is measured by the extent to which Tamul servants, Tamul labourers, Tamul tradesmen, are to be found beyond the proper boundaries of their language, working hard, pushing their fortunes, making money. This is considerable. As the parts on each side of the Godavery are Telinga, the districts which the Cavery waters are Tamul. Madras is Tamul, Pondicherry is Tamul, Tranquebar is Tamul, Negapatam is Tamul, the Carnatic is Tamul. In fact, the Tamul language succeeds and replaces the Telinga about Pulicat, a little to the north of Madras, and is spoken all along the coast of Coromandel to Cape Comorin. It then turns to the north, and constitutes the vernacular of the southern part of the Rajahship of Travancore, giving way to the Malayalim in the parts about Trevandrum. Inland, it extends to the Ghauts and Nilgherries—say to the parts about Coimbatúr. It is the language of a vast plain; contrasted in this respect with the Telinga, which is spoken over a varied surface, sometimes level, oftener broken.

Ten millions is the number given to the speakers of the Tamul tongue. They are not, however, confined to the district just indicated. There are Tamul settlers in Ceylon, especially in the north-western parts of the island. The coolies of the coffee plantations are generally Tamul all over the island. There are numerous Tamul merchants in the capital; and "ere long," writes Mr. Caldwell, "the Tamilians will have excluded the Singalese from almost every office of profit or trust in their own island." The majority of the domestic servants and camp-followers, even in the Telinga portions of the Presidency of Madras, are Tamul, and whatever may be the vernacular dialect, the Tamul is current in all the military cantonments of Southern India. Cannanore is in the Malayalim, Bangalore in the Canarese, Bellary in the Telugu, Secunderab in the Hindostani, countries; nevertheless, the language which (if not heard oftenest) is, at least, thoroughly understood, is the Tamul. Then there are the Klings in Pegu, in Penang, and in Sincapore. These, as a general rule, are Tamul. So are the emigrants to the Mauritius. Of course they have been compared to the Scotch, also to the Greeks. They may or may not be like them. If they were not active and energetic the comparison would never have been made.

The Tamul, being a language long cultivated, is known in two forms—an ancient or literary, a modern or colloquial.

The literary Tamul is called the Shen Tamul.

The colloquial Tamul is called the Kodun Tamul.

West of the Telinga, west of the Tamul, and in the central table-land of Southern India, is spoken the vernacular language of Seringapatam and Mysore.

*The Canarese, Kannadi,* or *Karnataka.*—Mysore is its centre. Yet it touches the coast in the district of Canara between Goa and Mangalore, a district to which it is scarcely indigenous, but one in which it has succeeded the Tulava, a language that will soon come under notice. On the east it nowhere even approaches the sea. Nor is it the only language of Canara. Beside it there is the Tulava. Beside it is the Malayalam of the southern frontier. Beside it is the Konkani of the northern frontier—the Konkani, which is a dialect of the Mahratta, and, as such, strongly contrasted with the other three forms of speech. In the Nizam's country it reaches as far north as Beder, the frontier between it and the Mahratta being, in many districts, eminently irregular.

There are two stages, or forms, of the Canarese, even as there were two forms, or stages, of the Tamul. The ancient or literary dialect exhibits a difference of inflexion in several notable details—a difference of inflexion, not merely of words.

*The Coorgi*, or language of Coorg and Wynaad, is a dialect of the Canarese.

Including the Coorgis, the number of individuals who speak the Canarese may amount to 5,000,000.

*The Malayalam*, if we allowed ourselves to refine upon its affinities, would possibly find its place immediately in contact with the Tamul. It is the Tamul with which it comes in the closest geographical contact. Like the Tamul it is a language of the extreme south. It has been imagined to be of special Tamul origin. It is, however, a separate substantive language, possibly more akin to the Tamul than its other congeners—but no Tamul dialect.

The Malayalam is the language of the western side of the coast of Malabar. On its east lies the Canarese; on its north the Tulava; on its south the Tamul. The Tamul succeeds it at Trevandrum, the Tulava and Canarese of Canara, about Mangalore. It stretches over about six degrees of latitude, but only in a narrow strip between the Ghauts and the sea. It is the vernacular of Cochin, and the northern and middle parts of Travancore.

*The Tulu, Tuluva*, or *Tulava* is spoken by no more than 150,000 souls. It succeeds the Malayalam about Mangalore, and reaches, northwards, the Mahratta frontier about Goa. Like the Malayalam, it covers but a strip between the Ghauts and the ocean. It is said to resemble both the Malayalam and the Canarese, the latter most.

The following are, according to Caldwell, the writer from whose Dravirian Grammar the preceding details are exclusively taken, the statistics of the above-mentioned languages.

| | | | |
|---|---|---|---|
| 1. Tamul is spoken by | | . . | 10,000,000 |
| 2. Telinga | ,, | . . | 14,000,000 |
| 3. Canarese | ,, | . . | 5,000,000 |
| 4. Malayalam | ,, | . . | 2,500,000 |
| 5. Tulu | ,, | . . | 150,000 |
| | | | 31,650,000 |

The previous forms of speech constitute a natural group—a natural group, and not a very large one. They all belong to the Dekhan. They are all spoken by populations more or less Hindu. They are all the languages of the civilized Indian. Their area is continuous; in other words, they are all in contact with each other, and their frontiers join. There is nothing between the Telinga and the Tamul, the Tamul and the Canarese, the Tamul and the Malayalim. Their area is continuous.

The forms of speech that now come under notice, though in all essentials closely allied to the preceding, in some respects form a contrast rather than a counterpart to them. They are spoken by the ruder, rather than the more civilized, sections of the Indian family. They are spoken beyond the Dekhan as well as within it. They are spoken in the hill and jungle rather than in the town and village. They are spoken by either actual pagans or imperfect Hindus. For the purposes of literature they have been wholly neglected. There is not a native alphabet amongst them. Finally, their area is, in many places, either actually discontinuous or very irregular, *i. e.* they are separated, or nearly separated, from each other by languages of either a different family or a different branch of the same. The level country is Hindu both in creed and language. The mountain which it encompasses is other than Hindu in language, and pagan in the way of creed.

*The Ghond.*—This is the language of that portion of India which is marked in the maps as Gondwana; or, if not in the white district, of its hillier and more impracticable portions. Like most of the localities which preserve, in fragments, the older populations of a country, it is a watershed. The northern feeders of the Godavery, and the south-eastern of the Nerbudda, take their origin in the Ghond country, of which, the greater part lies considerably to the north of the most northern portion of Telinga area, and of which the northern frontier, is (in the way of language), Hindu, the western and south-western Mahratta. As the region, however, to the south and south-east of Gondwana has been but imperfectly explored, I am unable to say whether it is absolutely isolated. It may or may not touch certain parts of Telingana. Again, it may or may not, touch the western portions of the

*Sour, Khond,* and *Kol areas.*—Word for word, Sour is Sairea, a name which will appear in the notice of Bundelcund and elsewhere. It is no native term, but one by which certain Hindus designated certain populations different from themselves. It indicates, then, a negative character; from which it follows that the populations to which it applies may or may not be allied; the affinity or the difference being, in each instance, determined by the special circumstances of the case. It is necessary to be familiar with the distinction, in order that we may not be misled by names.

Word for word, Khond is Ghond, a name which has already appeared. It is no native term, but one by which certain Hindus designated certain populations different from themselves.

Word for word, Kol is Kúli, a name which will appear in the notice of Gujerat or elsewhere. It is no native term, but one by which certain Hindus designated certain populations different from themselves.

The Sours, Konds, and Kols are the Orissa analogues of the Gonds of Gondwana. They occupy the fastnesses of the eastern Ghauts rather than the more complicated ranges of the centre. They run in a rough kind of parallelism to the sea; their direction being vertical, *i. e.* from north to south rather than horizontal, *i. e.* from east to west. At the same time they run sufficiently inland to touch parts of Gondwana; so that the distinction between the present group and the preceding is, probably, artificial; Gondwana, for the most part, having been approached from the west, the Kond country from the east; Gondwana having been treated as an eastern district of the Mahratta country, the Kond region as a western portion of Orissa.

It is the Kond section that is best known; both in respect to its proper ethnology and its geography. It is this last alone which now lies under notice. The Konds are found as far north as 20° N. L., and as far east as the sea-coast. This brings them to the parts about Ganjam, about Kuttak, Juggernáuth, and the Chilka Lake. Southwards they extend below Chicacole; portions of the Vizagapatam district being Kond. This is within the Telinga area.

The Sours (wholly within Telingana) extend from the southern frontier of the Konds to the Godavery.

The Sours to the south—the Konds in the centre—the Kols to the north—this is the distribution northwards.

*The Rajmahali mountaineers.*—These are the occupants of the Rajmahal hills in the neighbourhood of Bogilpur. How far their area is continuous with that of the northern Kols is uncertain. It is only certain that the numerous dialects of the Gonds, Konds, Kols, Sours, and Rajmahalis, are, at one and the same time, connected with each other, and connected with the Telinga, the Canarese, the Tulava, the Malayalim, and the Tamul.

*The Brahúi.*—The Tamul elements of the Brahúi have already been noticed. The details of the Brahúi occupancy will be noticed in the sequel.

# CHAPTER XXX.

Relations of the languages akin to the Tamul.—Relations of the languages akin to the Sanskrit.

*The languages akin to the Tamul.*—The affinity of these is the one suggested by their geography. Their nearest congeners are the Tibetan and Burmese. The Tamul forms of speech, however, are in a higher stage of development. They are what is called agglutinate; *i. e.* they exhibit inflections; but those inflections can, for the most part, be reduced to separate words incorporated with the main term. Doing this, they stand in the same relation to the languages of the so-called monosyllabic class on the south, that the Turk, Mongol, Tungús, and Ugrians stand on the north and west. Whatever relation they may have with these last is indirect. In agreeing with them in structure, *i. e.* in their stage of development, they are their analogues, not their congeners. Whether there may not be direct (but intrusive) Turanian elements in India is another question.

*The languages akin to the Sanskrit.*—These are all truly inflectional rather than agglutinate, *i. e.* they are in the condition of the Latin and the Greek with their cases and tenses, rather than in that of the English or French with their prepositions and auxiliary verbs which have replaced them, or that of the Burmese and Tibetan wherein they have yet to be fully developed.

The Sanskrit, then, and its congeners are inflectional, after the manner of the languages of Europe, and, being this, stand in strong contrast to all the Tamul dialects, which are (as aforesaid), after the fashion of the Turk and Fin, agglutinate.

There is, then, a contrast here. There is another and a stronger one when we pass over to the field of the monosyllabic tongues. With the Tibetan, with all the Nepaulese dialects, and with the Burmese, the Sanskrit differs more decidedly than with the Tamul. Both these contrasts are important. They make us ask the following question:—If the Sanskrit be unlike its neighbours on the south, if it be more unlike its neighbours on the north, and if it be equally foreign to the frontier languages on the east, what is it like? What is it like, and where are its congeners? They are not to be found on the frontier of India; so that the Sanskrit comes from the north and west rather than from the south and east.

*The Sanskrit language.*—Westwards lie the Persian localities; the localities for the language of the cuneiform inscriptions, and perhaps of the Zend. Can these be in what we may term their proper *situs, i. e.* in geographical contact with the languages next akin? One of these is the Arabic, which is as little like the Sanskrit as are the Turk and Mongol. Another is the Armenian, which is somewhat more like, and another, the Iron, which is decidedly like the modern Persian. None, however, are the nearest congeners to either the Sanskrit or the Zend. To find these we must go westward, beyond the Black Sea and the Hellespont; beyond the Don. We must enter Europe. The nearest congeners to the Sanskrit are the languages of the Russian empire; then those of Rome and Greece; then those of Germany. Changing the phrase, the Sanskrit belongs to the same class with the Sarmatian, the classical, and the German tongues; a class to which some (perhaps most) philologues add the Keltic. The ordinary (but exceptionable) name for this group is Indo-Germanic (or Indo-European); the languages which belong to it being spoken in Germany (or Europe) and in Hindostan. Its most eastern division is the Sarmatian, which falls into two branches—the Slavonic and the Lithuanic, the latter lying east of the former. Now, without doubt, the affinities of the Sanskrit are closer with the Lithuanic than with any other language on the face of the earth. It is not what we expect *à priori*. Still, it is the case.

I should add, however, that this is not the usual language of philologues; who, generally speaking, are satisfied with making the Sanskrit Indo-European, without deciding to which of the other members of the class it has the greatest affinity. I look upon this as the cause of much error; inasmuch as it is evident that to search for the origin of a language that is equally allied to half a dozen others (unless, indeed, it stand in the centre of them) is a waste of learning and acumen. Next to the Lithuanic, the Sanskrit is most like the old Slavonic; which is, again, the most eastern member of *its* class.

The Sanskrit is more closely allied to the Lithuanic than to aught else. In making the comparison, however, one very important fact must be remembered. The oldest specimen of the Lithuanic is no older than A.D. 1500. In Sanskrit there are compositions 2000 years old. The Sanskrit, in fact, is in the stage of the Latin and Greek. The Lithuanic, on the contrary, though not exactly in the modern condition of the Spanish or Italian, is, nevertheless, in an advanced stage. It has, doubtless, had inflections, which, like those of other languages, have existed and have died out—died out before the language was reduced to writing, and before their existence could be recorded. In some respects, then, the Latin and Greek are more like the Sanskrit than is the Lithuanic, inasmuch as they are in the same stage, the stage wherein inflections are numerous. Nevertheless, the real affinities are Lithuanic. Those with Germany are less close. Those with the Keltic tongues more remote still.

Here we pause for the present, and pass on to a new class of facts.

## CHAPTER XXXI.

The languages akin to the Hindí.—The Kashmeri.—The Hindí.—The Gujerati.—The Bengali.—The Udiya.—The Mahratta. Sectional and Intermediate Forms, &c.—Migratory Populations and Trades.—The Gypsies.—The Bhil Dialects.—The Hindostani.

If the Sanskrit and the Pali be dead languages, and if the languages akin to the Tamul be limited to the areas which have been described (and they *are* so limited), what are the living forms of speech in those parts of India which lie north of the Dekhan and west of the Gond and Kond countries? What, indeed, are the forms of speech for certain tracts east of Gondwana? What is the language of Bengal? What is the language of the natives of Orissa itself, who are other than Kond? What is the language of Oud, of Delhi, of the Rajput country, of the Desert and the whole drainage of the Indus, of Gujerat, of the Mahratta country? It was not Sanskrit. Sanskrit, like Latin, has ceased to be spoken. It was not Telinga or Canarese. Canarese and Telinga belong to the Dekhan.

There is a class of languages which we may describe, as we have described the Pali, the Telinga, and their respective congeners. There is a class of languages the members of which may be said to be akin to the Hindí. Saying this we use a circumlocution. There are reasons, however, for doing so. That they are akin to the Hindí and to each other no one denies. That they belong to *one* of the two groups which have preceded no one denies either. That they are Tamul rather than Sanskrit many deny. That they are Sanskrit rather than

Tamul some deny, some doubt. It is best, then, to describe them as Hindí, or akin to the Hindí.

So much for the term. The group itself is dealt with as a separate class, not because it belongs to neither of the preceding, but because it is doubtful to which of the two it should be referred.

At the same time the group is, from a certain point of view, a natural one. All the languages it contains agree in giving the following contrasts. As compared with the Sanskrit they are poor in inflections; even as the Italian, when compared with the Latin, shows poor. As compared with the Tamul tongues, they abound and over-abound in words of Sanskrit origin; even, as compared with the Dutch or the Danish, the English abounds in Latinisms. It is unnecessary to say to what difference of opinion these conditions may give rise. There is the claim for the Sanskrit, and there is the claim for the Tamul, origin of the languages of northern India, with authorities and arguments on both sides. The highest authorities, and the greatest number of advocates, are for the Sanskrit. Whether the best arguments are in the same predicament is another question.

The dialects of the present group are numerous, and some of them will be noticed as we go on. At present it is convenient to enumerate the following six languages—for separate substantive languages they are usually considered to be.

1. The Cashmirian of Cashmir.

2. The Brij Basha, or Hindí.

3. The Gujerati, or Gujerathi, of Gujerat.

4. The Bengali of the lower Ganges, the *valley* of Asam, and parts of Sylhet and Chittagong.

5. The Udiya of Orissa.

6. The Mahratta or Marathi of Aurungabad, &c.

I give these divisions as I find them, adding that, though convenient, they are, by no means, unexceptionable. In the first place, the difference between a language and a dialect has never been satisfactorily explained: so that neither term has yet been defined. It will be seen, ere long, that there are several other forms of Indian speech, of each of which, though we may say with truth that it is more Hindí, more Bengali, or more Marathi than aught else, we cannot say that it is a Marathi, a Bengali, or a Hindí dialect. For this reason it is inexpedient to give the numbers of individuals by which each tongue is spoken. And it is also inconvenient to say whether such and such languages are mutually unintelligible. It is only certain that whatever difference may exist between any two is exaggerated rather than softened down when they are written. This is because the alphabets, though all of Sanskrit origin, differ from each other in detail.

Of the six languages under notice, the Cashmiri, the Gujerati, and the Udiya, are spoken not only over the smallest areas, but by the fewest individuals; the largest areas being those of the Marathi and Hindí, the largest mass of speakers being those of the Bengali language. It is the Bengali which has the greatest tendency to extend itself beyond the frontiers of India; the Bengali of Asam and Chittagong being the form of speech which is more especially encroaching upon the Tibetan and Burmese areas.

The languages that lie in the closest contact with the members of the Tamul group are the Marathi and Udiya. The affinities of the Cashmirian with the Dard tongues are decided.

I guard against the notion that the difference between the six tongues of the foregoing list is greater than it really is. A little more Sanskrit or a little less; a little more Persian or a little less; a Telinga or a Canarese element more or less; an alphabet of more or less detail —in these points and the like of them consist the chief differences of the languages akin to the Hindí.

I guard, too, against the notion that the preceding list is exhaustive. Before Hindostan has been traversed we shall hear of such sectional and intermediate forms as the Jutki, the Sindi, the Punjabi, the Haruti, the Marwari, the Konkani, and others; of all whereof thus much may be said—

1. That they are allied to each other and to the Hindí.

2. That they are not akin to the Sanskrit in the manifest and unequivocal way in which the Sanskrit, Pali, and Persepolitan are akin to each other.

3. That they are not Tamul or Telinga in the way that the Canarese, the Kond, &c., are Canarese, Tamul, and Telinga.

*Necdum finitus Orestes.*—There are certain populations which drive trades that requre movement from one part of the country to another, trades like those of the drovers, knife-grinders, and the like, in England. Most of these have a mode of speech more or less peculiar. They will be noticed hereafter. Meanwhile, it may be laid down, as a general rule, that their dialect is that of the country to which they more especially belong, *i. e.* more Hindí than Tamul in the Marathi, &c., more Tamul than Hindí in the Canarese, &c., countries.

*The Gypsy language.*—That this is Indian is well known. What are its affinities, Tamul or Hindí? Hindí. Hence it belongs to the present group.

*The Bhíl, &c., dialects.*—In habits the Bhíls, the Wárálì, the Kols of Gujerat, and other allied tribes, are, on the western side of Gondwana, what the Sours, the Konds, and the Kols of Bengal are on the eastern. All are believed, on good grounds, to be of the same blood. At the same time, the language of the first is akin to the Hindí; just as the Cornish is English, though the blood of the Cornishman is Welsh. The Welshman, however, has preserved what the Cornishman has lost, *i. e.* the characteristic of language. *Mutatis mutandis,* this is what is believed, on reasonable grounds, to be done by the Konds and Bhíls, &c. On the eastern side of India the language and blood coincide. On the western the blood is southern, the language northern—the language Marathi, the blood more or less Canarese and Telinga.

The only form of speech that now stands over for notice is

*The Hindostani.*—This is the language of the Mahometans of Hindostan. It is essentially and fundamentally Hindí, but it comprises more Persian and more Arabic words than any of the true vernaculars. It is written, moreover, in Arabic characters.

# CHAPTER XXXII.

India as an influence.—Its action upon Tibet, Ava, &c.—Upon the islands of the Indian Archipelago.—Brahminism and Buddhism.

IMPORTANT as are the great polytheist mythologies of Greece and Rome in the history of art and literature, they have been but little influential in the history of the world at large. They may safely be ignored in the present chapter, which is devoted to a short notice of what may be called the six great creeds of mankind, viz. Judaism, Christianity, Mahometanism, Parsiism, Brahminism, and Buddhism. All these agree in being the religions of a lettered language; so that their doctrines can be expounded, their canons embodied, and their controversies conducted by means of writings more or less permanent, more or less capable of both multiplication and diffusion. When this is the case, creeds both increase in stability and become susceptible of development. They become measures of the multiplicity of ways in which the human mind can employ itself upon transcendental subjects, and they also grow into historical influences and determine the moralities or immoralities of nations. The division, then, between the lettered and unlettered religions is natural. As for the unwritten superstitions of the ruder varieties of mankind, it is convenient to denote them by the general name of paganism. It is also convenient to call the paganism of Asia and Europe shamanism; that of Africa fetichism. It is convenient to do this. I do not say that it is strictly scientific.

That the six great lettered religions fall into groups is manifest. The first three are in decided and palpable relations to each other, connected by their common monotheism, connected by their common recognition of several prophets and patriarchs. They belong to the west rather than the east, to those parts of the world where northern Africa and western Asia come in contact. The languages of the countries in which they arose were Semitic; and Semitic is the language of two of their scriptures, the Old Testament and the Koran.

In like manner Buddhism and Brahminism are connected; connected both in the doctrines which they convey and the language in which those doctrines are embodied. They belong to the east rather than the west, and they originated in those districts where Persia, Central Asia, and India join. The languages in which they are embodied are closely allied; indeed, they are a dialect of one language rather than separate forms of speech. The alphabets which represent them differ. So do the Arabic and the Hebrew. So do the Hebrew and Samaritan. This agreement in speech, combined with a difference of expression, is a common phenomenon in the history of religions.

What Brahminism and Buddhism are in the matter of language that is Parsiism also. Whether Zend or Pehlevi, the speech of the fire-worshippers was akin to that of the Indian rituals. The Zend and Pehlevi alphabets, however, are other than Indian. That there are Parsi elements in the Indian mythology is well known. It is well known, too, that from actions and reactions between the creeds of Judæa and Chaldæa, there is something Parsi (the word is used in its widest sense) in Judaism, something Judaic in Parsi.

As a religious influence, Parsiism is either stationary or retrograde. It is not dead like classical polytheism. It is only deficient in development. Its history, however, I believe to have been important; for I believe that in Turkistan, in Mongolia, in parts even of China and Siberia, not to mention many districts of Caucasus, there was, before the diffusion of the present Buddhist and Mahometan theologies, a more or less imperfect fire-worship.

Of the western religions, Judaism, of the eastern, Brahminism, are what may be called passive, *i. e.* they care little to propagate themselves abroad. What is Brahminism out of India? Who are Jews except the children of Israel? The religions for the Gentiles are the remaining three.

I have not made these remarks solely and wholly for the sake of either suggesting analogies or exhibiting the sketch of a classification. I have rather made them as preliminaries to a special fact connected with India as an influence on the history of the world. India, beyond the area of Hindostan, is chiefly a great religious influence so far as it is Buddhist; just as the western or Semite religions are chiefly forces so far as they are either Christian or Mahometan. Yet India, at the present moment, is no Buddhist country at all. Neither are Palestine and Asia Minor Christian. Yet it was in them that Christianity arose. The country that propagates a creed is not always the country that retains it.

The country that propagates a creed is not always the country that originates it. Neither Greek nor Latin Christianity originated in either Greece or Rome.

There is no Buddhism, *eo nomine,* in continental India at the present moment; though there is plenty of it in the island of Ceylon, and remains of it, as well as existing modifications, on the mainland.

There is no Buddhism, *eo nomine*, in continental India, at the present moment.

Is Buddhism, then, Indian in its origin? It is not safe to affirm even this. Fair reasons (to say the least of them) can be given for believing that, originally, Buddhism was foreign to the soil of Hindostan.

What, then, is its connection with India? It developed itself on the soil of that country and from that country it diffused itself.

It spread from two points, from the north and from the south. Of the Buddhism of the north, the Sanskrit rather than the Pali was the vehicle, and the route by which it diffused itself was Nepaul, Tibet, Western China, Mongolia, and Japan.

With the Buddhism of the south, the island of Ceylon is more especially connected. Its vehicle was the Pali rather than the Sanskrit, and the countries over which it spread were Pegu, Burma, Siam, and Kambojia.

With the creed went the alphabet and with the alphabet the civilization.

Hence, it is India to which nine-tenths of the civilization of the eastern part of continental Asia is due.

Indian also is the earliest civilization of the more civilized parts of the Indian Archipelago; though, at the present moment, the details of their older creeds and literatures are obscure. Mahometanism, except in a few places, has superseded the religion introduced from India. The island of Bali, however, is at this moment Indian. So is a small district in Java. Amongst the Battas of Sumatra; amongst the Philippine islanders; amongst the rude tribes of the interior of the Malayan peninsula; amongst even the Dyaks of Borneo the paganism is, by no means, pure and unmixed. On the contrary, it always exhibits Indian elements. Perhaps it may be styled a degraded Hinduism.

I am not prepared to say how far this peculiar offset

of the Indian religion is Buddhist rather than Brahminic, or Brahminic rather than Buddhist. It is sufficient for it to be Indian. Being this, it helps us to the measure of the influence of India as a civilizing power.

As such, India is what she is, only so far as she is either Buddhist or Brahminic. How far are Buddhism and Brahminism the indigenous growths of the Indian soil?

Whatever may be the best manner of exhibiting a series of recognized and undoubted historical details, it is manifest that for the purposes of *investigation*, the right points to begin with are those that are well defined, whether in time or place. In geography we look for accurate latitudes or longitudes; in archæology for ascertained dates.

Upon this principle, in attempting a sketch of the early history of the two great religions of India, I shall begin as I began with the Sanskrit and Pali records; *i. e.* with the facts that bear dates.

The notice of Herodotus can scarcely be called the notice of a religion. It is rather the account of an abominable social practice. Still, as it has its religious aspect, I give it.

The notice of Herodotus, to all appearance, rests upon the accounts given to the author by certain informants in either Persia or Babylonia.

It is to the effect that the land of the Indians was wide in extent, and heterogeneous in respect to its occupants; that a multitude of tongues was spoken within its boundaries; that some of the Indians were nomads, some Ikhthyophagi; that these last dwelt in the marshy swamps of the Delta of Indus; that they ate their fish raw. In all this there is rudeness and barbarism. So there is the following account of the Padæi. They dwelt to the east of the Ikhthyophagi, and were eaters of flesh. This, however, was raw. When any one was sick, the men of his acquaintance would kill him, provided he were a man. If she were a woman, the females would do the same. This they did in order to enjoy a feast; for all that were killed were also eaten; and, as the ailment spoilt the quality of the flesh, it was in vain that the future victim protested against being treated as a patient. He was killed and eaten, say what he might about being in health.

The Kalatii, we are told in another part of the Herodotean account, ate their parents. Whether these were the same people as the Padæi is uncertain. It is only certain that they shrunk with horror from the idea of burning their dead.

Another tribe (name unknown) abstained from the slaughter of animals, and fed only upon vegetables. The sick they carried to some lone spot in the wilderness and left to die. They showed their rudeness in other matters as well. They kept themselves, however, independent. They "dwelt at a distance from the Persians, towards the south, and never obeyed Darius." Meanwhile the northern part of the Persian frontier gave signs of civilization. A city named Kaspatyros* was near the Paktyan land (Πακτϋικῆ χωρῆ) and not far from the districts which yielded gold. The men that held it were the most warlike of the Indians, and their manners were like those of the Bactrians.

That, word for word, Padæi is Batta,† has long been surmised. That, tribe for tribe, the Batta are the descendants of the Padæi is by no means certain. All that can fairly be inferred from the name is that certain Indians called certain tribes of their frontier by that name. Word for word, Vaddah is the same as Batta. A rude

* Also written *Kaspapyros*.

† The name of a population in Sumatra

tribe in contact with an Indian population—this (and no more) is what comes of the roots *P-d, B-t,* or *V-d.*

Word for word, Kaspatyrus may or not be Cashmir. Place for place, the two localities certainly coincide.

The next notices represent the knowledge derived from the Macedonian conquest. They make it clear that, when that event took place, there were asceticism and philosophy in India. Before the Macedonian conquest there were, *iis nominibus*, Brachmani, Sarmani, and Gymnosophistæ. These observed practices, more or less, Buddhist and Brahminic (either or both), practices out of which either Buddhism or Brahmanism might evolve itself; practices which either the Buddhist or the Brahmin may claim as evidence to the antiquity of his creed. Brahminism, however, and Buddhism are one thing, practices out of which either or both may be developed are another. At the same time, or but a little later, we find evidence to a tenderness for animal life and to a difference between Brahmins and non-Brahmins.

*Laws of the Brahmins which are in India.*—Again, among the Indians, the Brahmins, among whom there are many thousands and tens of thousands, have a law that they should not kill at all, and not revere idols, and not commit fornication, and not eat flesh, and not drink wine, and among them not one of these things takes place. And there are thousands of years to these men, lo! since they govern themselves by this law which they have made for themselves.

*Another law which is in India.*—And there is another law in India, and in the same clime, belonging to those, which are not of the family of the Brahmins, nor of their doctrine: that they should serve idols, and commit fornication, and kill, and do other abominable things, which do not please the Brahmins. And in the same clime of India there are men that by custom eat the flesh of men, in the same manner as the rest of the nations eat the flesh of animals. But the evil stars have not forced the Brahmins to do evil and abominable things; nor have the good stars persuaded the rest of the Hindoos to abstain from evil things; nor have those stars which are well arranged in their places which it is proper for them, and in the signs of Zodiac which relate to humanity, persuaded those who eat the flesh of men to abstain from using this abominable and odious food.

This is from Bardesanes. Whether the facts just given constitute Brahminism is another question. It is certain that they fail to give us much that is Brahminic, *e. g.* Suttí, and the Brahminic system of incarnations, &c.

I should add that the Caubul coins exhibit certain signs or symbols of both (? either) Brahminism or Buddhism.

What Brahminism really is in full is to be found only in the practices and literature of the creed. The Brahminism, however, of the present time, and the Brahminism of the oldest works in the Sanskrit language, are different things. The oldest works in the Sanskrit are—

*The Vedas.*—The Vedas are hymns that formed either the part or the whole of an actual or possible ritual, the deities which they invoked being what is called elemental, *i. e.* personifications of earth, fire, water, the meteorological forces, and the like. Indra, for instance, (or the firmament,) conquers the Vrita, (or vapours,) with the Maruts, (or winds,) as allies.

An Ashtaka is a book; a Sukta is a hymn. Out of the 121 Suktas of the third Ashtaka, forty-four are addressed to Agni. Word for word, Agni is the Latin *ignis*, the Slavonic *ogon;* its meaning being *fire;* fire, however, personified, spiritualized, deified. Sometimes the attributes are obscure, and the language mystical; sometimes, instead of a series of epithets, we have a legend or an allusion to one. Sometimes it is Agni alone that is addressed; sometimes it is Agni in conjunction with some other personification.

1. I glorify Agni, the high priest of the sacrifice, the divine, the ministrant, who presents the oblation (to the gods), and is the possessor of great wealth.

2. May that Agni, who is to be celebrated by both ancient and modern sages, conduct the gods hither.

3. Through Agni the worshipper obtains that affluence, which increases day by day, which is the source of fame and the multiplier of mankind.

4. Agni, the unobstructed sacrifice of which thou art on every side the protector, assuredly reaches the gods.

5. May Agni, the presenter of oblations, the attainer of knowledge; he who is true, renowned, and divine, come hither with the gods!

This is a fair sample of the simpler style of invocation. The following supplies a contrast by being more mystical:—

1. I, Agni, am by birth endowed with knowledge of all that exists; clarified butter is my eye; ambrosia is my mouth; I am the living breath of threefold nature, the measure of the firmament, eternal warmth; I am also the oblation.

2. Agni, thoroughly comprehending the light that is to be understood by the heart, has purified himself (by the three) purifying (forms), he has made himself most excellent treasurer by (these) self-manifestations, and has thence contemplated heaven and earth.

Large as is Agni's share of the invocations of the third Ashtaka, that of Indra is larger; forty-eight Suktas being addressed to Indra, or the firmament, either singly or conjointly:—

1. Come, Indra, and be regaled with all viands and libations, and thence, mighty in strength, be victorious (over thy foes)!

2. The libation being prepared, present the exhilarating and efficacious (draught) to the rejoicing Indra, the accomplisher of all things.

3. Indra, with the handsome chin, be pleased with these animating praises: do thou, who art to be reverenced by all mankind, (come) to these rites (with) the gods.

4. I have addressed to thee, Indra, the showerer (of blessings), the protector (of thy worshippers), praises which have reached thee, and of which thou hast approved!

5. Place before us, Indra, precious and multiform riches, for enough, and more than enough, are assuredly thine!

6. Opulent Indra, encourage us in this rite for the acquirement of wealth, for we are diligent and renowned!

7. Grant us, Indra, wealth beyond measure or calculation, inexhaustible, the source of cattle, of food, of all life.

8. Indra, grant us great renown and wealth acquired in a thousand ways, and those (articles) of food (which are brought from the field) in carts!

9. We invoke, for the preservation of our property, Indra, the lord of wealth, the object of sacred verses, the repairer (to the place of sacrifice), praising him with our praises!

In the fourth Ashtaka there is somewhat less of a monopoly, though the shares of both are large.

The Maruts are the winds, and, next to Indra and Agni, they have the most hymns addressed to them.

1. The Maruts who are going forth decorate themselves like females: they are (gliders through the air), the sons of Rudra, and the doers of good works, by which they promote the welfare of earth and heaven: heroes, who grind (the solid rocks), they delight in sacrifices!

2. They, inaugurated by the gods, have attained majesty, the sons of Rudra have established their dwelling above the sky: glorifying him (Indra) who merits to be glorified, they have inspired him with vigour! the sons of Prisni have acquired dominion!

3. When the sons of the earth embellish themselves with ornaments, they shine resplendent in their persons with (brilliant) decorations; they keep aloof every adversary: the waters follow their path!

4. They who are worthily worshipped shine with various weapons: incapable of being overthrown, they are the overthrowers (of mountains): Maruts, swift as thought, intrusted with the duty of sending rain, yoke the spotted deer to your cars!

5. When Maruts, urging on the cloud, for the sake of (providing) food, you have yoked the deer to your chariots, the drops fall from the radiant (sun), and moisten the earth, like a hide, with water!

6. Let your quick-paced smooth-gliding coursers bear you (hither), and, moving swiftly, come with your hands filled with good things: sit, Maruts, upon the broad seat of sacred grass, and regale yourselves with the sweet sacrificial food!

7. Confiding in their own strength, they have increased in (power); they have attained heaven by their greatness, and have made (for themselves) a spacious abode: may they, for whom Vishnu defends (the sacrifice) that bestows all desires and confers delight, come (quickly) like birds, and sit down upon the pleasant and sacred grass!

8. Like heroes, like combatants, like men anxious for food, the swift-moving (Maruts) have engaged in battles: all beings fear the Maruts, who are the leaders (of the rain), and awful of aspect, like princes!

9. Indra wields the well-made, golden, many-bladed thunderbolt, which the skilful Twashtri has framed for him, that he may achieve great exploits in war. He has slain Vritra, and sent forth an ocean of water!

10. By their power, they bore the well aloft, and clove asunder the mountain that obstructed their path: the munificent Maruts, blowing upon their pipe, have conferred, when exhilarated by the soma juice, desirable (gifts upon the sacrificer)!

11. They brought the crooked well to the place (where the Muni was), and sprinkled the water upon the thirsty Gotama: the variously-radiant (Maruts) come to his succour, gratifying the desire of the sage with life-sustaining waters!

12. Whatever blessings (are diffused) through the three worlds, and are in your gift, do you bestow upon the donor (of the libation), who addresses you with praise; bestow them, also, Maruts, upon us, and grant us, bestowers of all good, riches, whence springs prosperity!

Then there are the Aswins, or the inferior suns; Ushas or the dawn: Varani, which is, word for word, Uranus; Mithras, and other deities of greater and less importance, the majority of which are elemental, meteorological, or telluric. Yupa, the post to which the sacrificial victim is bound, has also a hymn:—

1. Vanaspati, the devout, anoint thee with sacred butter at the sacrifice; and whether thou standest erect, or thine abode be on the lap of this thy mother (earth), grant us riches.

2. Standing on the east of the kindled (fire), dispensing food (as the source) of undecaying (health) and excellent progeny, keeping off our enemy at a distance, stand up for great auspiciousness.

3. Be exalted, Vanaspati, upon this sacred spot of earth, being measured with careful measurement, and bestow food upon the offerer of the sacrifice.

4. Well clad and hung with wreaths comes the youthful (pillar); most excellent it is as soon as generated; steadfast and wise venerators of the gods, meditating piously in their minds, raise it up.

5. Born (in the forest), and beautified in the sacrifice celebrated by men, it is (again) engendered for the sanctification of the days (of sacred rites); steadfast, active, and intelligent (priests) consecrate it with intelligence, and devout worshipper recites its praise.

6. May those (posts) which devout men have cut down, or which, Vanaspati, the axe has trimmed, may they, standing resplendent with all their parts (entire), bestow upon us wealth with progeny.

7. May those posts which have been cut down upon the earth, and which have been fabricated by the priests, those which are the accomplishers of the sacrifice, convey our acceptable (offering) to the gods.

Of the mass of the Vedas an idea may be formed from the following *data*. A single hymn is called a *sukta*. So many suktas make an *anuvaka*, so many anuvakas an *adhyáya*; so many adhyáyas an *astaka*, ogdoad, or book, forming an eighth of the whole Rigveda. The third volume of Wilson's translation comes to the middle of the whole, so that the Rigveda alone gives six volumes of hymns. But the Rig is only one out of four Vedas; for besides it there is the Sama-veda; there is the Yagur-veda; and there is the Athava-veda—four in all. The Rig-veda, however, is the chief, containing nearly all the important matter of the rest; the Athava-veda being later in date than the other three, to which it forms a sort of supplement. These four compositions form the *Sanhita*, or text. The Sanhita itself, with the hymns it embodies, forms the *mantra*, or ritual, a ritual upon which there are notes and supplements.

Without being a Veda, in the strict sense of the term, the *Brahmyanas* are Vedaic. So that here we have another series of works; themselves incomplete without *Vedangas* (in which the grammar of the Vedas is explained) and *Upanishads*, which are a sort of supplement.

Few works are less metaphysical than the Vedaic hymns. This, however, does not prevent the existence of a *Vedanta* philosophy. The connection, however, lies chiefly in the name. Wherever there is tendency to rationalism anything can be rationalized.

It is not for nothing that this list of works, more or less Vedaic, has been given. That the Vedas are a root out of which much has grown is a fact of great importance in our criticism. Dates they have none. Failing these, what can we have recourse to? We must take a measure of the extent to which the original hymns have developed a system, and then ask at what rate such developments proceed.

*The Institutes of Menu.*—Later than the Vedas, and in many respects different from them, are the Institutes of Menu. These give us the legal, social, and political, rather than the poetical and religious, aspects of Brahminism. The Brahminism, too, is of a more advanced growth; containing much for which the Vedas have been appealed to in vain. It contains, for instance, the doctrine of cast.

*Sir Graves Haughton's Translation.*

1. For the sake of preserving this universe, the Being, supremely glorious, allotted separate duties to those who sprang respectively from his mouth, his arm, his thigh, and his foot.

2. To Brahmins he assigned the duties of reading the Veda, of teaching it, of sacrificing, of assisting others to sacrifice, of giving alms, if they be rich, and, if indigent, of receiving gifts.

3. To defend the people, to give alms, to sacrifice, to read the Veda, to shun the allurements of sensual gratification, are, in a few words, the duties of a Cshatriya.

4. To keep herds of cattle, to bestow largesses, to sacrifice, to read the scripture, to carry on trade, to lend at interest, and to cultivate land, are prescribed or permitted to a Vaisya.

5. One principle duty the Supreme Ruler assigns to a Súdra; namely, to serve the before-mentioned classes, without depreciating their worth.

6. Man is declared purer above the navel; but the Self-Creating Power declared the purest part of him to be his mouth.

7. Since the Brahmin sprang from the most excellent part, since he was the first born, and since he possesses the Veda, he is by right the chief of this whole creation.

8. Him, the Being, who exists of himself, produced in the beginning, from his own mouth, that having performed holy rites, he might present clarified butter to the gods, and cakes of rice to the progenitors of mankind, for the preservation of this world.

9. What created being then can surpass Him, with whose mouth the gods of the firmament continually feast on clarified butter, and the manes of ancestors, on hallowed cakes?

10. Of created things, the most excellent are those which are animated; of the animated, those which subsist by intelligence; of the intelligent mankind; and of men the sacerdotal class.

11. Of priests those eminent in learning; of the learned, those who know their duty; of those who know it, such as perform it virtuously; and of the virtuous, those who seek beatitude from a perfect acquaintance with scriptural doctrine.

12. The very birth of Brahmins is a constant incarnation of Dherma, God of Justice; for the Brahmin is born to promote justice, and to procure ultimate happiness.

13 When a Brahmin springs to light, he is borne above the world, the

chief of all creatures, assigned to guard the treasury of duties, religious and civil.

14. Whatever exists in the universe, is all in effect, though not in form, the wealth of the Brahmin; since the Brahmin is entitled to it all by his primogeniture and eminence of birth.

15. The Brahmin eats but his own food; wears but his own apparel; and bestows but his own in alms: through the benevolence of the Brahmin, indeed, other mortals enjoy life.

16. To declare the sacerdotal duties, and those of the other classes in due order, the sage Menu, sprung from the self-existing, promulged this code of laws.

17. A code which must be studied with extreme care by every learned Brahmin, and fully explained to his disciples, but must be taught by no other man of an inferior class.

18. The Brahmin who studies this book, having performed sacred rites, is perpetually free from offence in thought, in word, and in deed.

19. He confers purity on his living family, on his ancestors, and on his descendants, as far as the seventh person; and He alone deserves to possess this whole earth.

*The Epics.*—A nearer approach is made to the existing form of Brahminism in the Ramayana and the Mahabharata; the Ramayana being the name of a poem which gives us the exploits of Rama, whilst the Mahabharata is a narrative of the Great War.

That both are later than the Vedas is evident from not only the general character of the details, but from the fact of both the Vedas and the Vedangas being mentioned by name in their text. The more a man knows of them the wiser and better he is represented to be. The hero of the Ramayana is Rama, who is Vishnu incarnate. The scene lies in Oud. The subject is the conquest of such parts of India as, at the time when the poem was written, belonged to Brahminic India; of Lanka, or Ceylon, most especially. That an island in the south is reduced at an earlier period than the interjacent portions of the continent to its north is remarkable. It suggests the idea of ships and sailors.

The following is the opening of the Ramayana as translated by Wilkins:—

I salute Kama, the beautiful, the elder brother of Bukshmuna, the illustrious Kughoo, the husband of Seeta, the descendant of Kukootstha, full of clemency, a sea of excellencies, the friend of Brahmans, the virtuous one, the sovereign, devoted to truth, the son of Dusharutha, him whose body is blue, the benign, the delight of the universe, the glory of Kughoo's race, Kaghava, the enemy of Kavuna.

Victory to Kama, the glory of Kughoo's race, the increase of Koushulya's happiness, the destroyer of the ten-headed, to Dusharutha, whose eye is like the water lily.

I salute Valmeeki, the kokila, who, mounted on the branch of poesy, sounds the delightful note kama, kama, Kama. Salutation to the lord of the Moonis, the blessed, the Tupushee, the abode of all knowledge. To this Valmeeki salutation.

Valmeeki, the chief of the Moonis, devoted to sacred austerities, and the perusal of the Veda, the incessant Tupushee, pre-eminent among the learned, earnestly inquired of Naruda, Who in the universe is transcendent in excellence, versed in all the duties of life, grateful, attached to truth, steady in his course, exuberant in virtues, delighting in the good of all beings? Who is heroic, eloquent, lovely, of subdued anger, truly great? Who is patient, free from malice, at whose excited wrath the gods tremble? Who is great, mighty in preserving the three worlds? Who devoted to the welfare of men? The ocean of virtue and wealth. In whom has Hukshmee, the complete, the beautiful, chosen her abode? Who is the equal of Urida, Unula, Soorya, Indoo, Shukra, and Oopendra? From you, O Naruda! I would hear this. You are able, O divine Sage, to describe the man. Naruda, acquainted with the present, the past, and the future, hearing the words of Valmeeki, replied to the sage: Attend: the numerous and rare qualities enumerated by you, can with difficulty be found throughout the three worlds; not even among the Devtas have I seen any one possessed of all these. Hear: he who possesses these, and virtues far beyond, a full-orbed moon, a mine of excellence, is of Ishwakoo's race, and named Kama; of regulated mind, temperate, magnanimous, patient, illustrious, self-subdued, wise, eminent in royal duties, eloquent, fortunate, fatal to his foes, of ample shoulders, brawny arms, with neck shell-formed, and rising cheeks, eminent in archery, of mighty energy, subduing his enemies, with arms extending to the knee, manly, of fine-formed head and open front, of mighty prowess, whose body is exact in symmetry, of hyacinthine hue, who is full of courage, with eyes elongated, his cest circular and full, who is fortunate, imprinted with auspicious marks, versed in the duties of life, philanthropic, steadily pursuing rectitude, sapient, pure and humble, contemplative, equal to Prujapati, illustrious, supporting, the world, subduing his passions, the helper of all, the protector of virtue, skilled in the Vedas and Vedangas, deep in all the Shastras, strong, acquainted with the secrets of nature, practising every duty, penetrating, amiable to all, upright, ample in knowledge, of noble mind, ever attended by the good, as the ocean by the rivers, the companion of truth, social, the only lovely one, Kama, the seat of every virtue, the increaser of Koushulya's joy, profound like the deep, immovable as Heemaluya, heroic as Vishnoo, grateful to the sight as the full-orbed moon, in anger dreadful as the conflagration, in patience like the gentle earth, generous as Dhanudc, in verity ever unequalled. By these his matchless virtues he conferred felicity on his subjects, and therefore is known by the name Kama.

The Mahabharata is the Great War waged between the Yadava and the Pandava dynasties; the scene being laid in the parts about Ujein. The uniformity of style and composition is said to be less in the Mahabharata than in the Ramayana; so that some parts of the former poem are older or newer than others. The fictions in both are supernatural, impossible, outrageous. In both the chief deity is Vishnu.

*The Puranas.*—The Puranas are compositions in the form of dialogue, between certain enquirers and Brahma, upon points of cosmogony and early history—also upon the attributes and actions of the three great deities; of Siva and Vishnu most especially, both incarnate. They (I follow Wilson almost *verbatim*) are derived from the same system as the Epics. They represent, however, modifications of opinion and feeling. They repeat and expand the epic cosmogony. They give special importance to new divinities; Vishnu and Siva most particularly. They give new legends. They are possibly founded upon earlier compositions. The word *Purana* means *old.* A typical Purana is, according to the lexicon of Umura Sinha, *Pancha-lackshanam,* or that *which has five characteristic topics.* These are—

1. Cosmogony.

2. Secondary creation, or the destruction and renovation of worlds.

3. Genealogies of Gods and patriarchs.

4. Reigns of the Manus, or periods called Manwantaras.

5. History of the kings of the Solar and Lunar families.

The existing Puranas scarcely meet the conditions here implied. Yet they meet them, perhaps, half way.

The Puranas are eighteen in number. Of these the best known, as well as the most important, is the Vishnu Purana, accessible to English readers through the translation of Wilson. It is the great repertorium for the elements of Brahminism in its working form.

The Upa-puranas are minor compositions, akin to the full Puranas both in matter and in form. They may be as few as four, as many as eighteen.

The "Vishnú Puráná has kept very clear of any particulars from which an approximation to its date may be conjectured." Wilson refers it to the eleventh century.

Now comes the notice of the general character of the Sanskrit literature. The best preliminary to the classification of this is a general view of the literature of Greece. In some shape or other *every* form of Sanskrit literature has its equivalent in that of Greece. In some shape or other *most* forms of Greek literature have their correspondents in Sanskrit. Are there Epics in the language of Stesichorus? So are there in that of Parasara. Was there a New Comedy in Greece? There was something very like it in India. The nearest analogues of the Vedas (respect being had exclusively to the class of compositions to which they belong) are, perhaps, the Homeric and Orphic hymns, by no means the only hymns of Greece. The Greek equivalents to the laws of Menu, though they have not come down to us in their full form, have had a real existence on the soil of Greece. Subject for subject, the authors of the Puranas dealt with the same kind of questions that the Greek logographers investigated. *Mutatis mutandis*, the same applies to the grammarians and lexicographers. Both are conspicuous in India;

both in Greece—Alexandrian Greece, however, rather than Athenian. And where there were grammarians and lexicographers, there were there geometricians also; in Ægypt as in India, in India as in Ægypt. There was science in both countries. There was, also, in both, philosophy. The Vedanta philosophy of India has already been noticed. It has its counterpart in Platonism and Neo-platonism.

*Buddhism.*—Buddhism is one thing. Practices out of which Buddhism may be developed are another. It has been already suggested, that the ideas conveyed by the terms Sramanæ, and Gymnosophistæ are just as Brahminic as Buddhist, and, *vice versâ*, just as Buddhist as Brahminic.

The earliest dates of specific Buddhism are of the same age as the earliest dates of specific Brahminism.

Clemens of Alexandria mentions Buddhist pyramids, the Buddhist habit of depositing certain bones in them, the Buddhist practice of foretelling events; the Buddhist practice of continence; the Buddhist Semnai or holy virgins. This, however, may be but so much asceticism.

He mentions this and more. He supplies the name Bouta; Bouta being honoured as a god.

Porphyry tells us of an important point wherein the Brachmans and the Samanai differed. The former were born to the dignity; the latter elected. This shows that though both may have been in the same category as to their ascetism, there was a difference between them; a difference which exists at the present day.

Cyril of Alexandria states that there were Samans (whom we may now especially connect with the cultus of Bouta) in Bactria.

From Cyril of Jerusalem we learn that Samnaism was, more or less, Manichæan, Manichæanism being, more or less, Samanist. Terebinthus, the preceptor of Manes, took the name Baudas. In Epiphanius Terebinthus is the pupil of Scythianus. Suidas makes Terebinthus a pupil of Baudda, who pretended to be the son of a virgin. And here we may stop to remark, that the Mongol Tshingiz-khan is said to be virgin-born; that, word for word, Scythianus is Sak; that Sakya Muni (compare it with Manes) is a name of Buddha. Even so cautious a speculator as Professor Wilson admits that Buddha may be the gentile name Bhot. I think that he might have maintained that such was actually the case. Its *quasi*-synonym Sakya bears just the same relation to the word Sak or Sakæ. Be this as it may there was, before A.D. 300,

1. Action and reaction between Buddhism and Christianity.
2. Buddhist buildings.
3. The same cultus in both Bactria and India.

Whether this constitute Buddhism is another question. All this and more may have existed, and yet the cultus to which it belonged have been just as far from Buddhism in the ordinary acceptation of the word, as modern Judaism is from Christianity, or the doctrine of the Sadducees from modern Judaism.

The Buddhist records themselves are—

1. *Chinese.*—The most that can be got from the earliest Chinese accounts is that in (say) the sixth century there was Buddhism in both China and India. The following is a piece of Chinese grammar for the Sanskrit.

| Chinese. | Sanskrit. | English. |
|---|---|---|
| Po'-po-ti | Bhavati | He is |
| Po'-po-pa | Bhavapa | They two are |
| Po'-fan-ti | Bhavanti | They are |
| Po'-po-sse | Bhavasi | Thou art |
| Po'-po-po | Bhavapa | You two are |

| Chinese. | Sanskrit. | English. |
|---|---|---|
| Po'-po-t'a | Bhavatha | You are |
| Po'-po-mi | Bhavami | I am |
| Po'-po-hoa | Bhavavak | We two are |
| Po'-po-mo | Bhavamah | We are |
| | NOUN. | |
| Pu-lu-sha | Purushah | Man |
| Pu-lu-shao | Purushau | Two men |
| Pu-lu-sha-so | Purushás | Men |
| Pu-lu-sha-tsic | Purushasya | Of a man |
| Pu-lu-sha-pien | Purushábhyam | Of two men |
| Pu-lu-sha-nan | Purushanám | Of men. |

2. *Northern.* — It has already been stated that the vehicle of the Buddhism of Nepaul and Tibet was the Sanskrit rather than the Pali language. In like manner, *mutatis mutandis,* the vehicle of the

3. *Southern*, or Cingalese, Buddhism was the Pali rather than the Sanskrit.

4. *Monumental.*—There are

*a.* Architectural,
*b.* Sculptural,
*c.* Sepulchral,
*d.* Inscriptional.

The literary documents are, *of necessity*, valid for the time at which they were written, and no other. They are, *of necessity*, valid only so far as they are evidence. What they tell us of the times previous to their composition may, or may not, be true. How far they are so depends on the details of each particular case. The *onus probandi* lies with the supporter of their accuracy. They contain a doctrine, a discipline, a philosophy, and a history. They are the scriptures of Buddhism, and from them must the nature of Buddhism, as a whole be ascertained. The doctrine, the discipline, and the philosophy are dateless. The historical portion gives us three Councils ; the latest of which took place about B.C. 153. I take this date as I find it. It tells us thus much—that earlier than B.C. 153 the work from which it is deduced could not have been composed. Common sense tells us that it need not have been composed even then. Who could write about the third council before it had met? This date is got from the Sanskrit authorities.

What applies to the Sanskrit applies, *à fortiori*, to the Chinese. Say that in the sixth century there was a voluminous mass of Chinese translations from the Indian. *Mutatis mutandis*, there was the same in the Christian world. There were translations from the Greek in Syriac, in Armenian, and in German. Yet the works from which they are translated were, each and all, at the the very least, fifty years later than the birth of our Saviour.

When Buddhism has so much in common with Christianity, and the Indian literature so much in common with the Greek, the question as to the probability of there being borrowings and lendings must be worked out with special attention to dates. A century more or less may seriously affect our results.

What applies to the Sanskrit is believed on good grounds to apply, *à fortiori*, to the Pali. The evidence that the Buddhist scriptures in this last-named language are newer than those in Sanskrit is less conclusive than it was in the case of the Chinese. Still it is satisfactory; so that, upon the whole, we may commit ourselves to the doctrine that no canonical works in Buddhism are older than the scriptures of northern India. That these are not older, and may be much newer, than B.C. 153, has already been stated.

Of monuments the most important are the Viharas or monasteries, and the Sthupas, or topes. Now, it is one thing to be a temple, or a tumulus; another thing to be a

Buddhist tumulus, or a Buddhist temple. It is one thing to be a king, another thing to be King Lear. Of records that are, at one and the same time, monumental, Buddhist, and undoubted, none are older than A.D. 300. *Non meus hic sermo.* The criticism of the Pali scriptures, the Viharas, the topes, and the cave-temples, along with nine-tenths (or more) of the preceding facts, is Professor Wilson's.

And now comes the notice of the famous Priyadarsi memorials. Dhauli is in Kuttak. Girnar in Guzerat. Kapurdigiri in Caubul. In each of these localities is a long and well-known inscription. It is the same, in the way of language and contents, in all. The inscriptions themselves are ancient. They contain the name of Antiochus. They are admitted, even by Wilson, to be, more or less, Buddhist. Be it so. It only shows the germs of the creed, not the full creed itself. It is true that, by certain assumptions, more than this may be got out of them. In a Singalese work some centuries later it is stated that Priyadarsi was Asoka; Asoka being a great propagator of Buddhism according to the historians of several centuries after his time. What, however, is the warrant for the identification? To say that *Priyadarsi* means *Asoka* is certainly a statement which may possibly be true. But it is not the *planus literalis et grammaticalis sensus* of the word.

As the Brahminic, or Sanskrit, literature reminds us of Greece, so does Pali Buddhism suggest comparisons with Christianity. It has its monachism, its councils—both conspicuous—I had almost said characteristic. If these resemblances are spontaneous they are very remarkable phenomena. Are they so? Are the presumptions in favour of their being so?

I can only say, in answer to this, that if we claim an

inordinately high antiquity for either Buddhism or Brahminism we must assume something that, in the eyes of the cautious critic, is illegitimate. To few of the monuments can we assign a truly historic date. Their epoch, then, is assigned on the score of internal evidence. The language is much more archaic than that of the Institutes, and the mythology so much simpler; whilst the Institutes themselves are similarly circumstanced in respect to the Epics. Fixing these at about 200 B.C., we allow so many centuries for the archaisms of Menu, and so many more for those of the Vedas. For the whole, eleven hundred has not been thought too little; which places the Vedas in the fourteenth century B.C., and makes them the earliest, or nearly the earliest, records in the world.

It is clear that this is only an approximation. Now, although all inquirers admit that creeds, languages, and social conditions, present the phenomena of *growth*, the opinions as to the *rate* of such growths are varied—and none are of much value. This is because the particular induction required for the formation of anything better than a mere impression has yet to be undertaken—till when, one man's guess is as good as another's. The age of a tree may be reckoned from its concentric rings, but the age of a language, a doctrine, or a polity, has neither bark like wood, nor teeth like a horse, nor a register like a child.

# CHAPTER XXXIII.

## The Alphabets of India.

THE alphabet of the very earliest specimen of the languages akin to the Sanskrit is cuneiform. It is found only in Persia. It belongs to the reigns of Darius and his successors.

The alphabet of the next earliest *dated* monuments is of the older Caubul coins; those of Eukrates and his successors. This is what is called by Wilson Arianian, or Arian. It is written from right to left, and, *pro tanto*, is Semitic. It is held (and that on reasonable grounds) to be an older form of what appears afterwards as Sassanian.

It is monumental, *i. e.* in capitals, and in a form adapted for coins and inscriptions rather than documents written *currente calamo*. It is monumental rather than cursive.

In a cursive form it comes out, later, as the Zend of the Parsi scriptures, &c. It has, however, taken additions—Indian in character. Still, it is so far Semitic as to run from right to left.

The alphabet of the oldest Pali monuments of the soil of India is that of the Dhauli and Girnar inscriptions. It has more than one character like those of the old Greek alphabet, and, like the old Greek alphabet, it is written from left to right. It appears, under modifications, in the coinage of the dynasties called Saurasthra, Gupta, and Rajput.

The alphabet of the oldest MSS. (which, it must be observed, are not Pali but Sanskrit) is called Devanagari. It is inscriptional rather than cursive, in so far as it consists of capitals. It is a modification of the inscriptional and monetary Pali. As such, it runs from left to right.

The alphabets of the written languages akin to the Hindí are all visibly and manifestly derived from the Devanagari.

The alphabets of the languages akin to the Tamul are derived from some form of some prototype of the Devanagari—scarcely from the actual Devanagari. They are rounded rather than angular, *i. e.* they are cursive rather than either inscriptional or capital.

The alphabets of the Indian archipelago will be noticed in their proper place.

On these facts two observations must be made :—

1. That the alphabets of the Greek type—for so we may call those that run from left to right—are of equal antiquity with those of the Semite type, or those that run from right to left.

2. That the alphabet of not only the oldest MSS., but that of the so-called oldest compositions in Sanskrit (the pre-eminently literary language of Brahminic India) is of Pali origin.

The details of the extent to which the right-to-left, or Arian, and the left-to-right, or Indian, alphabets are used concurrently are curious.

The legends of the oldest coins are Greek. Then comes the Arianian: then the Indian and Arianian concurrently.

The Girnar and Dhauli inscriptions are Indian. The

Kapur-di-giri inscription (which, in language and import, is the same as the other two) is Arianian.

The provisional hypothesis which best accounts for this concurrence runs thus :—

The left-to-right alphabet reached India *viâ* Asia Minor and Northern Persia.

The right-to-left reached it *viâ* Babylonia and Southern Persia.

## CHAPTER XXXIV.

The Frontiers of India and Persia.—The Paropamisans.—The Afghans.—The Caukers, &c.—The Brahúi and Bilúch.

I AM satisfied that the chief details of immediate ethnological importance to India are the details of its frontier. These are Persian. But the frontier of Persia is Asia Minor, and the frontier of Asia Minor, Europe.

*The Paropamisans.*—Of the Paropamisan boundary, the *minutiæ* on the west are obscure. The Huzara country is a British dependency. It is divided amongst numerous petty chiefs, *e. g.* the Khan of Turnoul, the chief of the Dhúnds, the chiefs of the Gukkurs, and others. They are (I believe) Mahometans. West of these occupancies lies the valley of

*Kaghan;* and west of Kaghan, on the very crest of the hills, the country of

*The Hussunzye;* whose name, at least, is Afghan or Patan.

I cannot say what, in these parts, is Afghan, what Paropamisan, what Indian proper.

*Afghanistan.*—That the Afghans themselves are far more heterogeneous in the matter of blood than of language is patent from more signs of intermixture than one. In the first place, there are few points in the map of Afghanistan whereof it is not said that the occupants are, more or less, recent and intrusive. The Ghilzyes, for instance, are derived from the Ghor mountains. That certain Berduranis have moved from west to east is specially stated, whether truly or otherwise is of no importance. The present observations merely go to prove the fact of there being presumptions in favour of the Afghan blood being mixed. The men themselves have no general name for their own country; *i. e* no name at once general and native, for Afghanistan is a Persian term. It is one thing for the mountains of Ghor to have contained Afghan settlements at an early period, another thing for them to have been the cradle of the race. Let it be admitted, for argument's sake, that the princes of Ghor belonged to the Afghan tribe of Suri, and that at so early a period that their dynasty was considered old even in the eleventh century. What does this show? Simply that there were Afghans in two districts; Afghans who, in the Ghor principalities, may as easily have been immigrants as indigenæ.

Add to this that the districts named Gour are no less than three in number. The king of one of them reduced "Raver and Kermessir, which separate Ghor from Hindustan." This is an extract from Herbelot, upon which the editor of the last edition of Elphinstone remarks that in *Raver* and *Kermessir*, names which, *totidem literis* and *totidem syllabis*, no longer exist, we may have the present appellations of the *Dawer* and *Gurmsir* districts. If so, Hindostan must have extended far westwards. Whether it did so or not, and whether (assuming it to have done so) the boundary was ethnological rather than political, is another question.

The Arabs call the Afghans Solimani. This I believe to mean the occupants of the parts about the Tukt-i-Soliman, who were probably neither more nor less than the first members of the group with whom the Mahometans came in contact. If so, India must have been entered on the south, *viâ* Biluchistan and Sind, rather than by the valley of the Caubul.

The locality, then, of the nucleus of the nation is still to be discovered. The language, I think, originated in the north-east, *i. e.* on the Paropamisan rather than the Carmanian frontier. The language, however, is purer than the blood. This is largely Tajik, not a little Mongol, largely (perhaps) Indian, very largely Turk. There are special statements that certain Afghan tribes, at a certain date, spoke Turkish. There is *garden* after *garden* named *bagh*, and more than one *hill* named *dagh*. There are the tribual names Othmankheil and Turcolaini, along with other terms less transparently Turk. The question, however, is suggested rather than exhausted. There is much blood in India which has come from Afghanistan, and much in Afghanistan which has come from Persia, Turkistan, and Mongolia.

*The Caukers,* &c.—I do not say that these are not Afghans. I only desiderate the evidence to their being such. They may be Persian, Biluch, Brahúi, Indian (wholly or partially), rather than truly Afghan.

*Biluchistan.*—As compared with the term Biluchistan, the term Afghanistan is clear and unambiguous. Afghanistan, whatever may be the details as to the descent of its occupants, is, at any rate, the region of the Pushtu language. *Mutatis mutandis,* Biluchistan should be the same. It is nothing, however, of the kind. It is pre-eminently a political designation. It means the country of the Biluches. But many of its occupants are Brahúis. Nor is this all. I know of no definite test which enables us to separate, in a thorough-going manner, the two populations. I hardly know which is the more important of the two. The four works that tell us most about them are those of Pottinger, Masson, Postans, and Burton. In the two last the view is taken from Sind, the conquest of which country is (apparently) attributed to the Biluch proper rather than to the Brahúis, the Kalora and Talpúr dynasties being simply called Biluch.

The inference from the notices of both Postans and Burton is, that, in Biluchistan, the Biluch family is the rule, the Brahúi the exception.

From this Masson, and, to a certain extent, Elphinstone suggest something very different. *Biluchistan* is, doubtless, the name of the country which Masson describes. Yet when he comes to detail, it is a *Brahúi* history that he investigates. The Sehrais, a Mahometan family from Sind, govern at Kelaut, until they are displaced by the Séwah (Hindus), who are, in their turn, expelled by the Brahúis.

Again, the Brahúi conquest is believed to have been effected under Kambar, of the Mirwari tribe. Now the *Mirwari* is the head tribe, the Khan-kheil as it would be called in Pustú; whilst Kamburani is the actual term for one of the primary divisions of the Brahúi name. From this we may infer, that Kambar (whether a real or hypothetical personage) was the hero of the dominant family. In accordance with this, it is fixed that the power of the descendants of Kambar should be supreme and hereditary, whilst from the two next tribes, the Raisani and the Zehri, Sirdars should be appointed, for Saharawan and Jhalawan respectively; these Sirdarships being, also, hereditary. Meanwhile, the Vizeers were to be Dehwaurs, or Tajiks. Time goes on until, at the beginning of the last century, Nazir Khan, the most energetic and intelligent of the Kelaut Khans, attempts (and that effectively) to introduce union and homogeneity into the Biluch community. The Rinds are settled in Saharawan, the Magazzi in Jhalawan. Kutch Gundawa is added to

Khanat. So is Shall. So is Mastung. So are Hurrund and Dajil. So are Kej and Punjghír. This is during the last days of the Kalhora dynasty in Sind. The history (it is Masson who gives it) is continued up to the present period; and throughout the whole of it the Khelat Khans are called Brahúis.

Again, in Ferishta, and doubtless, in other historians of India as well, there are numerous notices of a hostile nation called the Varahas; the particular portions of Hindostan which they attacked being the western States of Rajasthan.

All this gives to the Brahúi population of Biluchistan a much greater prominence than the name of their country suggests. The *name* suggests the predominance of the Biluches.

That the foregoing cautions against being misled by the name of the district are, by no means, unnecessary will soon become manifest. When Sind comes under notice we shall find it necessary to speak of, at least, one Biluch dynasty; that of the Talpurs. That the Talpurs were so far Biluch as to have come from Biluchistan may safely be asserted. Whether they were Biluches is another matter. What if they were Brahúis? I raise, rather than solve this question. The ethnological position of the tribes of Biluchistan must be determined by the circumstances of each individual case. I doubt whether it can always be determined at all. Physical appearance is something: but the physical appearance of both the Brahúis and the Biluches varies. Language, too, is something; but it is especially stated that the blood and the language by no means coincide. And here the Biluch tongue preponderates. I find no evidence of any Biluch tribes having unlearned their own tongue and adopted the Brahúi. I find decided evidence, however, of certain Brahúis being in the habit of speaking Biluch. The khans and sirdars of the Mingalls and Bizunjus do so. It would be vulgar to use the Brahúi.

I find, too, that this latter language is said to be peculiar to Jhalawan and Saharawan. Now, admitting that these are the chief Brahúi localities, we must be convinced that there is much Brahúi blood beyond them.

Again, it is probable that certain Brahúis may have adopted the Jutki and Sind dialects.

That certain Rinds (Biluches) have done so, is specially stated by Masson; who (along with others) tells us that their physical form is, more or less, Indian; at any rate, that it differs perceptibly from that of the Nharui tribes of the west. What, then, I ask, is the evidence that the Rinds are Biluch at all? Their form is Indian; their language Indian. They come, indeed, from Biluchistan —but so do some of the Brahúis and some of the Juts.

What is the evidence, &c.? I ask this for information. I do not say that it is wanting. I think it very likely that it can be adduced. I only suggest that it is wanting. At present the Rinds are Biluchistanis (*i. e.* men of a country named after the Biluches), rather than Biluches in the proper sense of the word.

The typical Biluches, then, are the Nharui tribes of the west; and the typical Brahúis certain tribes of Saharawan and Jhalawan. The others are, to all appearance, more or less, the exhibitors of mixed characteristics.

These characteristics may be derived from several quarters; from Central Asia, from Arabia, from Persia, from Caubul, from India.

*Central Asiatic elements.*—These may be either Turk or Mongol. Laying aside the doctrines suggested by the local names, especially Seistan (Segistan), (which is

Sakastene, or the country of the Sakæ) as well as those implied in the term Indoscythæ, let us look at Masson's list of the Brahúi, and Pottinger's of the Biluch, tribes. The first gives the names Sâka and Minghal; both referable to the Western Provinces. That Saka is Sakæ is suggested by Masson himself. Can Minghal be Mongol? Possibly. That Mekran is not beyond the confines of the Mongol world is shown in the following genealogy. The Numris of Luz trace their origin to Samar the founder of Samarkand, who had four sons—Nerpat, the father of the Numris and Jukias; Bopat, the father of the Bhats of Jessulmer; Gajpat, father of the Chura Rajputs; and Aspat, father of the Tshagatai—the Tshagatai being, of all the Turks, the most mixed-up with the Mongols. Indeed, to suppose that the two words are synonymous is as legitimate here as in India, where (as is well known) the empire founded by Baber, is called the empire of the Great Mogul, *i. e.* Mongol. Yet Baber was a Tshagatai Turk, and no Mongol at all.

Let, then, the Brahúi name *Mingall* be considered as a probable form of *Mongol*—word for word. Whether it stand for a Turk tribe or a tribe from Mongolia, in the strict sense of the term, is another question. The names of both Tshingiz-khan and Timur are known in the parts about Kelaut.

*Arabian.*—I lay but little stress upon the so-called tradition of the Biluches that they came from Arabia. I have elsewhere suggested that Arabia may mean the *Arabius fluvius,* and the promontory of *Arabat* in their own immediate neighbourhood. In this, too, it is possible that we may find the origin of the name of the *Arab* Gudur, a Luz tribe. On the other hand, the Arab conquest of Sind, and the parts to the west of the Indus, in the first century of the Hegira, is a historical fact, so that, over and above a certain amount of imaginary, there may, also, be some real, Arab blood in Biluchistan.

*Persian.*—The Nushirvanis of K̇haran (it is Masson who speaks), along with the Rajputs of Udipur, trace their origin to Nushirvan. Such the doctrine. *Valeat quantum.* It shows, at least, Persian ways of thinking. In like manner the Shirwani Brahúis believe that their forefathers came from Shirwan, which they may easily have done, or have not done.

The Mehmasani bear a Kurd name. So do the Lari; though not one exclusively Kurd. So do the Kurds, *eo nomine* and *totidem literis.* The Kurds of Dasht Bedowlat, Merv, and part of Kutch Gundava, are divided into

| | |
|---|---|
| The Made Zai | The Saltag Zai |
| —— Shudan Zai | —— Shadi Zai |
| —— Zirdad Zai | —— Massutari. |

Word for word, *Zai* appears to be the Afghan *Zye.*

*Caubul.*—The Kaidrani of the hills about Khozdar appear in Masson's list as Brahúis.

I have found them, however, treated as Biluches, as Afghans, and as a population neither Afghan nor Biluch. There are two divisions of the name, the occupancies of which are separated from each other.

The Bizunji are, in like manner, called Brahúi, yet the name appears elsewhere, and that beyond the Brahúi area.

*Indian.*—That the Jatuks of Masson's Brahúi list are Juts is suggested by Masson himself. It is also suggested by Masson himself that the Kalmatti of his Brahúi list are Sindis.

Then there are the tribes that appear both as Biluch and Brahúi.

Also the Langhow tribe, the members of which are said

to be enfranchised slaves of the Rinds; a fact, however, which is not incompatible with their being Brahúi in blood.

And now, premising that I, by no means, consider that the above-named exceptions are conclusive, and that I have exhibited them chiefly for the sake of making out a case in favour of the blood of the Brahúi and Biluches being more or less mixed, and with the view of inducing others to go minutely into the analysis, I give the remainder of Masson's list.

*In the Western Provinces.*

| | |
|---|---|
| Mirwari | Sanghur |
| Gitshki | Hallada |
| Homarari | Rodahi |

Rakshani (?)

*In Saharawan.*

| | |
|---|---|
| Raisani | Mahmudshahi |
| Sirperra | Bangul-zai |
| Ghazghi | Shekh Husseini |
| Samalari | Sunari. |

*In Jhalawan.*

| | |
|---|---|
| Zehri | Saholi |

Lutiani.

So much for the details of the Brahui name as opposed to the Biluch.

The details of the Biluch name, as opposed to the Brahúi, are as follows.

The first division is into the western and the eastern Biluches, the western Biluches being named Nharúi; the eastern, Mugsi and Rind.

*The Nharúi.*—The Nharúi list contains seven names, three of which may be other than Biluch.

1. *The Rukshani.*—In Masson the Rukshani are made Brahúi.

2. *The Mings.*—Word for word, this seems to be Mingul.

3 *Kurd.*—This is the name for the tribes of Bushkurd, Kohuki, and Mydani; tribes which are, probably, Kurd in blood as well as in name.

To the following four tribes no exception is taken. They are, probably, true Biluches.

| | |
|---|---|
| The Sajadi | The Urbabi |
| —- Khasogi | —- Mullikah. |

They lie to the south of Seistaun, between the Brahúi frontier and the Kurd districts; these last leading to the truly Persian province of Kirman.

By "true Biluches" I mean men whose language neither is nor has been either Brahúi or Jut, and who are, in other respects, Persian rather than Indian, and Biluch rather than either Afghan or Kurd.

I have already noticed the statement that the Rinds, to some extent at least, speak Jutki. To what extent? Burton writes that the Domki, Magasi (Magazzi Mugsi), Burphat (Bulfat), Kalpher (Kalpur), and many other smaller tribes, speak the hill language; the hill language meaning the Biluch. Meanwhile, the Rinds, Talpurs, Murris, Chandiya, Jemali, and Laghari speak "either Jatki or the hill-tongue; and their selection depends upon the district they inhabit." The Bulfat, however, are specially connected with the Numris, who are Sindi in speech. Again—the "Jataki is also called Siraiki from Siro, or Upper Sind, where it is commonly spoken by the people, and Belocki (Biluch) on account of its being used by several of the Biluch clans settled in the low country. The Langha or Sindhi bards seem to prefer it to their own language, and many well-educated natives, especially Belochis, have studied it critically and composed works in it." All this goes for the Rinds being Indian rather than Persian in speech. All goes to the suggestion of the following question—is there any better reason for making them Biluch than the fact of their coming from Biluchistan?

Be this as it may, there is a certain number of tribes that belong, or are supposed to have originally belonged, to the Khanat of Kelaut rather than to India proper, and who are other than Afghan as well as other than Brahúi in speech. Their manners and religion—predatory and Mahometan—are Biluch; their language and physiognomy more or less Indian. Their political importance is considerable, inasmuch as they lie along the whole of the Dera Ghazi Khan frontier, beginning where the Afghans end and extending into Sind.

The most northern of these, after the Khetrans, whose place is ambiguous, are—

*The Khusranis*, on the hills, and

*The Mutkanis*, on the plains. Then follow

*The Bozdars*, of whom there are, at least, the following sections—

| | |
|---|---|
| The Seharni | The Jelalani |
| — Suwarni | — Chandiah |
| — Gulamani | — Shahani. |

The Bozdars are both mountaineers and occupants of the lower country.

*The Lúnds*, and

*The Khosahs*, on the plains. Khosa is a Rajput name.

*The Lagaris.*

*The Ghurkanis.*—These occupy Hurrund and Darjil, falling into

The Lushari | The Durkhani, and
The Chakri.

*The Drishuks*, a peaceable, and

*The Murri*, a warlike, tribe;

*The Mazaris*, and

*The Bugtis* (both powerful), succeed; south of whom the Brahúi name appears.

All the preceding tribes belong to the British frontier; either on or within it.

Behind the frontier, especially in Kutch Gundava, lie

| | |
|---|---|
| The Dumki | The Puzh |
| — Pugh | — Kullúi, |

and others. These appear in both Masson and Pottinger, and, by both authors, they are especially stated to be Rind, *i. e.* Rind rather than Mugsi.

*The Magazzi* of Masson seem to be the Mugsis of Pottinger. Of the Magazzi, however, all that is said by the former author is that they are the inveterate enemies of the Rinds. Pottinger, on the other hand, gives the following list of their tribes:—

| | |
|---|---|
| The Lashari | The Musari |
| — Matyhi | — Kukrani |
| — Burdi | — Isobani |
| — Unurs | — Jullani |
| — Nari | — Turbundzye |
| — Kullunderani | — Jekrani |

The Jutki.

The Jekrani are probably Rind; the Jutki, Juts in the proper sense of the term. The Musari and the Lashari have already appeared. They were among the tribes of the frontier (Lusharis and Mazaris). Upon the whole, it seems that the Rind area is Kutch Gundava rather than the valley of the Indus, the Mugsi area the valley of the Indus rather than Kutch Gundava. The details, however, are very obscure.

But little has to be said concerning the archæology of the Brahúi country. It contains but few ruins, and none of any very great importance. Of coins, but few have been found within its limits; of inscriptions (I believe) none. That some, however, exist is specially stated. It should be remembered, however, that, with the exception of Pottinger and Masson, few Europeans have, at one and the same time, explored the country, and given an account of their explorations. Hence the statement that "of its Greek rulers we have no vestiges," is one which future discoveries may not improbably modify. A city was founded in Arachosia by Demetrius. Near Kelaut are the sites of three towns—of Sorra Bek, of Kuki, and of a third with an unknown name. These, however, seem to have belonged to the times of the Kalifat.

At Mehara, in the hills, to the east of Kelaut, are a few caves and cave-temples; also the remains of what is called a city of the infidels (Kafirs); also walls and parapets of stone—works of the infidels too. Hinglatz, in Luz, is a sacred spot, visited by both Hindu and Mahometan pilgrims. It is in the eyes of the latter, at least, the shrine of the Bíbí Náni = the Lady Mother. It is suggested by Wilson that, word for word, *Nani* is *Nanaia*, the name of a goddess, which appears on many of the Caubul coins.

Let us now assume, *provisionally*, that the Brahúis are Indian, and ask (such being the case) what are the western boundaries of India? Where does it begin?

If the Brahúis be as Indian as their language is believed to make them, and if the Gitshki and Minguls, and Rakshanis, be Brahúi, the Indian area must be carried as far north as Noshky, and as far west as Punghír and Kij. If so, half Mekran is Brahúi. Noshky touches the Baraich districts of Shorabuk, and all but touches Seistaun. It is watered by the river Kaiser. It is the occupancy of the Rakshanis, upon whom the Minguls from the parts about Kelaut have encroached. They reside in tents.

Panjghur, an agricultural district, is cultivated by the Gitshki; as is Kij—after which begins the territory of the Imaum of Muskat on the south, and Persia proper on the north.

That India, then, in some shape or other, has a great extension westward is manifest. It shows itself long before we get to the Indus. Indeed, it is by no means easy to say where India begins or Persia ends.

## CHAPTER XXXV.

Foreign influences in India.—Bacchic (?).—Assyrian (?).—Persian.—Turanian.—Macedonian.—Arab.—Afghan.—Turk (Tshagatai).

Of the invasions of India, the chief are

1. *The conquest by Bacchus.*—Whether this be so purely mythic as is generally believed will be considered in the sequel. Say, however, that it is ever so much so. The belief in its existence shows, at least, that Greece and India were contained in the same world of fiction. Now, where there is a community of fiction there are also other points of contact—direct or indirect.

2. *The conquest by Semiramis.*—This, if real, would introduce Assyrian influences.

3. *The Persian conquest.*—In order for any part of India to have become a part of the empire of Darius conquest from Persia must have been effected.

4. *Turanian conquest.*—If no conquest from Turania had been effected the term Indo-scythæ would be non-existent.

5. *The Macedonian conquest*, ending in a permanent occupation of Bactria, has already been noticed. This brought Greece upon the Indus.

6. *The Arab conquest.*—In the forty-fourth year of the Hejra, the Mahometans appear on the frontier of India—the Mahometans of the Kalifat, Arabs in language and nationality. Their impression, however, is but slight. They invade, and retire from, Multan; but the occupancy

is partial, and the withdrawal early. They also invade Sind, but not, in the first instance, effectually.

Forty-eight years later, in the reign of Walid, begin what may be called the campaigns and conquests of Mohammed Casim, a brave, skilful, and successful general. They end in the reduction of Multan and Sind. How much further his arms penetrated is doubtful. There is a notice of his having begun a march toward Canuj, in which he succeeded in reaching a place which seems to have been Udipur. His actual conquests, however, we limit to the above-named countries, the countries most immediately on the Persian or Afghan frontier. I imagine that his army was largely recruited from Persia, it being expressly stated that it was raised at Shiraz. A.D. 711. A.H. 92.

The conquests of Casim were made over to his successor, in whose family they remained for about thirty-six years, when a native insurrection, of which we do not know the details, ended in the ejection of the Mahometans and the restoration of Sind and Multan to the Hindus. This state of things lasted 250 years—from 750 to 1000, there or thereabouts.

*The Turk conquests.*—The first undoubted Turk dynasty in India was founded A.D. 1000—say when Canute was King of England. Its founder's name was Mahmud. He was governor of Korasan under the Samanid successors of the Caliphs. His chief town was Ghuzni, so that he is called Mahmud of Ghuzni, or Mahmud the Ghuznivid, he and his descendants forming the Ghuznivid dynasty. His father was a Turk, Sebek-tegin (a Turk compound) by name. He was originally a slave, his patron and predecessor in the occupancy of Ghuzni having been a slave also; also a Turk.

Such the dynasty. The country from which India was

invaded, the kingdom of this dynasty, was Caubul. It was in the parts about Ghuzni that Alp-tegin first found the nucleus of his empire. One historian states that he had with him, when he first attempted his independence, 3000 Mamelukes; and a Mameluke, at this time, would be a Turk, not (what he is now) a Circassian, or something else of mixed blood and no definite extraction. He would, doubtless, too, have numerous additions from the Ghuzni district itself, and these would be chiefly Afghans. Let us say, then, that the bulk of what Mahmud of Ghuzni, or his father, Sebek-tegin, may have called the army of India, was Turk and Afghan, without going too minutely into the question as to how far the two terms mean the same thing. I imagine, too, there must have been in it Persians, Lughmanis, and perhaps Biluches.

The hostilities that led to the Ghuznivid conquest of India began with Sebek-tegin, but the conquest itself was the work of Mahmud. The opponents to both were the Rajputs of western and northern Rajasthan.

The descendants of Sebek-tegin held India from the death of Mahmud, A.D. 1030, to that of Khusru Malik, A.D. 1186. They were all Turk on the father's side at least—probably on the mother's as well. The succeeding dynasties are all Turk.

Tamerlane retired from India A.D. 1399. For two months after Tamerlane's departure there was anarchy, then the rule of a chief named Ekbal, then the restoration of Mahmud; who is succeeded by another chief, Doulat Khan Lodi, who, at the end of fifteen months, is expelled by the governor of the Punjab. This takes place fourteen years after Tamerlane's departure; during, however, Tamerlane's lifetime.

It is as a subordinate to Tamerlane that the governor of the Punjab, who expels Doulat Khan Lodi, affects to govern. His name is Khizr Khan, and he is a native of India, probably an Indian rather than a Turk. If he has no Turk blood at all in his veins, he is the first ruler of India without it. He is, moreover, a Syud, *i. e.* a descendant of Mahomet, so that he and his three descendants constitute what is called the Syud dynasty. Soon after his seizure of Delhi, his original province, the Punjab, revolts, and his family has to struggle for it during the whole duration of the dominion.

The Syud dynasty ruled thirty-six years, *i. e.* from 1414 to 1450, when Ala-u-din, the fourth of the family, makes over his capital and titles to

*An Afghan*, Behlol Khan Lodi, the first ruler of the house of Lodi. The kings that this house gave to India were three in number—by name Behlol Lodi (already mentioned), Secander Lodi, and Ibrahim Lodi, under whose reign India was invaded by

*The Tshagatai Turk*, Baber, the founder of the empire of the Great Mogul. As a Tshagatai, Baber came from the Mongol frontier; the extent to which Mongol elements entered into his army being indicated by the name of the dynasty.

Since the time of Baber the foreign influences have been Portuguese, Dutch, French, and English.

## CHAPTER XXXVI.

General view of the divisions of the population of India.—Cast.

I NOW bid farewell to the numerous preliminaries by which the notice of the populations of India proper has been preceded, and I use the term India proper because, in the forthcoming chapter, no notice will be taken of the Paropamisans and the Brahúi. Ethnologically, indeed, they are Indian; geographically, they are Persian.

They ought not, perhaps, to be excluded. The objects, however, of the present work are mixed. If it were more purely scientific than it is, I should claim them for Hindostan. The Hindostan, however, of the forthcoming notices extends no further westwards than Cashmír, the Punjab, and Sind.

*Qui bene dividet, bene docet.* For our *primary* division the best basis is language, either actually existing or reasonably inferred. This gives us;

1. The populations whose languages, as now spoken, are Tamul rather than Hindi, along with such Bhils and Kols as are believed to have unlearnt their own tongue and to have adopted that of their neighbours. It also comprises (though the evidence to their belonging to this group is capable of great improvement) the Mairs, Minas, Moghis, and some others;

2. The populations whose languages are Hindí rather than Tamul, the chief of which are the Cashmírian, the Hindí itself, the Bengali, the Uriya, the Gujerathi, and the Marathi.

Are the forms of speech the best basis for our *minor* divisions? I think not. I think it better to take in more characteristics than one. I also think it better to form our groups by type rather than definition. If these views be right, the classification will explain itself.

1. In the extreme north-west, Cashmír stands by itself. It is largely Mahometan. It is Paropamisan as much as it is Indian. It is a land without (or with a *minimum* of) casts.

2. The next division is less simple. Like the first it is largely Mahometan. It is also Sikh. It is by no means sharply defined on its frontier. So far as it is Hindu (and it is so to a very great extent) it is Kshetriya rather than either Sudra or Brahminic. Its area is nearly, but not wholly, commensurate with the extension of the Rajput dynasties, present or past, patent or inferred.

3. The third contains the pre-eminently Brahminic districts along the Ganges, from Oud to Bengal inclusive. It also contains the area of the Uriya language.

4. The fourth contains the populations that occupy the southern slope of the Himalayas, in contact with the Bhots of Tibet, Nepal, Sikkim, Butan, and Asam.

5. The fifth gives us the Marattas, who are Sudras rather than either Kshetriyas or Brahmins.

And here we may notice the meaning of the word *cast*. When two sections of the same group, class, or division, refuse to intermarry, there is an approach to it. There is an approach to it when the intermarriage is other than reciprocal, *i.e.* when a man of one section may take his wife from another, though wives, similarly situated, may not take husbands.

There is an approach to it when individuals of different sections may not eat together; or when they will not eat food cooked or served by one another.

There is the same when mutual contact is eschewed.

There is the same when certain branches of the population are limited to the exercise of certain trades, crafts, or professions, and when (as, of necessity, must be the case) these trades, crafts, or professions become hereditary.

When one class is, in any one of these ways, separated from the other, an approach to cast is the result. When several principles of separation are united the approach becomes nearer.

Nearer still does it become when, in addition to these forms of mutual repulsion, the cohesion of the several members of the same class is strengthened by common ceremonies, legends, beliefs, prejudices, and genealogies, real or hypothetical.

Let all this take place, and let certain classes be held more honourable than others, cast becomes more decided. The higher classes avoid, despise, abhor the lower.

Let the number of classes be great, and the degrees of dignity will be numerous. There will be a highest and a lowest.

All this is cast, and of all this there is more in India than in any other part of the world. There are approaches to it, however, in most countries.

In most of the reports and memoirs upon Hindostan, lists may be found of the casts of the several districts. They are often long ones. They differ, too, from one another. In many cases they do this simply because the languages are different. In essentials they agree. They chiefly consist of the names of trades. There is the cast of cultivators, gardeners, fishers, porters, sweepers, and the like—some high, some low. The lists, however, are long, and the casts are numerous.

The lists are long and the casts are numerous when we

look at the realities of Indian life as it exists at the present moment. And, except that in a ruder condition of society, the division of employments was less, the lists of the earliest historical period are long also.

*Theoretically*, however, the number of casts is four.

1. There is the priestly cast, or that of the Brahmins.

2. There is the warrior cast, or that of the Kshetriyas.

3. There is the Vaisya class, or that of the merchants; and

4. There is the lowest class, or that of labourers—the Sudra class.

The outcasts are of no class at all. The commonest name for these is Pariah.

The origin of these is given in an extract from the Institutes of Menu, already laid before the reader.

I doubt, notwithstanding, whether this fourfold generality was ever an historical fact.

I think that priests, soldiers, merchants, and labourers were Brahmins, Kshetriyas, Vaisyas, and Sudras only in the way that apes, lions, horses, and hogs are Quadrumana, Carnivora, Solidungula, and Pachydermata. In ethnology, as in zoology, it is the species only which has a tangible definite existence. The genus lies in the mind of the contemplator.

In ethnology, however, as in zoology, the genus and species may coincide. In India this is done by the class of Brahmins. Whatever else a Brahmin may be, he is a member of a privileged order. Hence arises the observation of one of the classical authorities on India to the effect that India is the land, not of four, but of one superior, and many subordinate, casts. To a certain extent, the terms Rajput and Kshetriya coincide. The Vaisyas, however, are pure *entia rationis*.

The Mahratas are called Sudras. This can but mean

that they are neither Brahmins nor Rajputs; at any rate, no fact in history is more patent than their activity, courage, and success as soldiers.

The extent to which the rules of cast press upon individuals can never be laid down in generals. The details of each case regulate it. The most stringent restraints can be set aside by actual lawlessness. The Pindarris, for instance, who were armed robbers, but at the same time so numerous as to resemble an army rather than a banditti, found no difficulty in recruiting themselves from all classes. The Sikhs, again, and the several members of the casts which they left upon conversion, keep up both domestic and social arrangements, and marry and are given in marriage with each other. The view on the part of the Hindus of their neighbourhood (who, it should be remarked, are not of the strictest) is, that it is a political confederation of which their converted brothers have made themselves members. On the other hand, the cases are numerous where the violation of the laws of cast are unnaturally strict; and that without defeating themselves. They are so (for instance) in Nepal, as will be seen when that country comes under notice. Cast, then, is easily lost or easily regained as circumstances dispose.

Upon the origin of so peculiar an institution much speculation has been expended—some, perhaps, wasted. Many maintain that, wherever it occurs, there has been invasion and conquest. If so, it implies the juxtaposition of two hostile nations, and tells a tale of intrusion, resistance, subjugation, slavery, contempt. That this is a possible, and not an improbable, mode of developing such an institution as cast is clear. Whether it be the only one is doubtful. There is cast, in some degree or other, all over the world. Hereditary privileges are cast. Monopoly of employment, continued from father to son, is cast. Social exclusiveness is cast. The tribe-system and the cast-system are often contrasted, and it is true that the circumstances under which the two are evolved are, for the most part, different. Yet there are tribes who assume a superiority over the rest, and refuse to intermarry with them. Again—the tribe and the municipality are contrasted. But what is the tribe whereof the members have certain occupations but cast?

Thus far we have considered cast as a condition and as an effect. But what is it as cause? Assuredly, it is a great ethnological force. Let the business of a jockey, on one side, or of a pugilist, on the other, become, even in England, hereditary, and it is clear that the one will give big, the other small, men. In like manner, though in a less degree, Brahminism must encourage one physiognomy, Sudraism another. We are justified, then, in taking cognizance of cast even where it may not coincide with original ethnological differences.

## CHAPTER XXXVII.

### Populations whose Languages are akin to the Hindí.—Cashmír.

Cashmir is a basin rather than a valley; the bottom of a lake rather than the holm of a river.

The physical form of its occupants is that of the Paropamisans.

On the side of Tibet, its frontier is decided and definite; by which I mean that the whole of Cashmír is Cashmírian. No fragments of any earlier occupancy have been discovered within its frontier. On the east, it stands contrasted with the more purely Hindu countries of Kistewah, and the Sub-himalayas in general. The difference, however, here is one of degree rather than kind

On the west the details are obscure; the exact extent to which the parts interjacent to Cashmír and Swaut are Cashmírian, Afghan, or Dard being unknown.

The language is quite as much Paropamisan as Hindí. This, however, is the language of common life rather than the language of literature and polite society. The literary language is Persian. As far, however, as the Cashmírian is written, it is written in a character derived from the Devanagari.

Word for word, Cashmír is believed (and that on reasonable grounds) to be Caspatyrus, or Caspapyrus. So that the notices of the country are early.

Cashmírians beyond the limits of Cashmír are numerous, for the population is industrial and commercial.

They are also numerous in Tibet, where intercourse and intermarriage between the two populations are by no means uncommon.

In the way of politics, Cashmír is Sikh, having been so since 1831; in creed, however, it is Mahometan, the Mahometanism being mixed. To a certain extent, it is, like that of Persia, Shiite. To a certain extent, it is, like that of Afghanistan, Sunnite, for between the break-up of the Mogul and the rise of the Sikh power, Cashmír was a portion of the Durani dominion. That many of the converts have been forcibly made is stated by good authorities, and the fact seems likely. It is certain that, at the beginning of its history, Cashmír was one of the strongholds of Brahminism; at the same time the reign of the first Mahometan king belongs to the fourteenth century. His descendants and successors reign till (about) the end of the sixteenth century; when Cashmír, ceasing to be independent under kings of its own, becomes one of the *subahs* of the Mogul empire. As such, it is the least part of itself. Pukhli and Bajowr belong to it. So does Swaut. So do Caubul and Zabulistan. I mention this to show that, even in the way of politics, its connections have run westwards.

*Description of Cashmír by Abulfazel.*

The whole of the *subah* represents a garden in perpetual spring, and the fortifications with which Nature has furnished it are of an astonishing height, so that the grand and romantic appearance cannot fail of delighting those who are fond of variety, as well as they who take pleasure in retirement. The water is remarkably good, and the cataracts are enchantingly magnificent. It rains and snows here at the same seasons as in Tartary and Persia; and during the periodical rains in Hindostan, here also fall light showers. The soil is partly marshy, and the rest well-watered by rivers and lakes. Violets, roses, narcissuses, and innumerable other flowers, grow wild here. The spring and autumn display scenes delightfully astonishing. The houses, which are built of wood, are of four stories, and some higher, and they are entirely open, without any court-yard. The roofs of the houses are planted with tulips, which produce a wonderful effect in the spring. In the lower apartments are kept the cattle and lumber; the family live in the second story; and the third and fourth stories are used for warehouses. Earthquakes are very frequent here, on which account they do not build their houses of brick or stone, but of wood, with which the country abounds. Here are, however, many ancient idolatrous temples, built of brick and stone, some of which are in perfect preservation, and others in ruins. Here are various woollen manufactures, particularly of shawls, which are carried to all parts of the globe. Although Cashmir is populous and money scarce, yet a thief or a beggar is scarcely known amongst them. Excepting cherries and mulberries, they have plenty of excellent fruits, especially melons, apples, peaches, and apricots; grapes, although in abundance, are of few kinds, and those indifferent. In general they let the vines twist round the trunks of the mulberry trees. The mulberry trees are cultivated chiefly on account of the leaves for the silkworms, little of the fruit being eaten. The silkworms' eggs are brought from Kelut and Little Tibet, but those of the first place are best. The inhabitants chiefly live upon rice, fish, fresh and dried, and vegetables, and they drink wine. They boil the rice over night, and set it by for use for the next day. They dry vegetables, to serve in the winter. They have rice in plenty, but not remarkably fine. Their wheat, which is black and small, is scarce, and *mowng*, barley, and *nakhud* are produced, but in small quantity. They have a species of sheep, which they call *Hundoo*, resembling those of Persia, the flesh of which is exceedingly delicious and wholesome. The inhabitants wear chiefly woollen clothes, an upper garment of which will last several years. Their horses are small, but hardy and sure-footed, and they are very cheap. They breed neither elephants nor camels. Their cows are black and ugly, but yield plenty of milk, of which is made good butter. Every town in this *soobah* has as many handicraftsmen as are found in the large cities of other countries. They have no fairs, all their goods being sold at regular shops. In their cities and towns there are neither snakes, scorpions, nor other venomous reptiles. Here is a mountain called Mahades, and every place from whence it can be seen is free from snakes, but the country in general abounds with flies, gnats, bugs, and lice. Sparrows are very scarce, on account of the general use of pellet bows. The inhabitants go upon the lakes in small boats to enjoy the diversion of hawking. They have partridges; the elk is also found here, and they train leopards to hunt them. Most of the trade of this country is carried on by water, but men also transport great burdens upon their shoulders. Watermen and carpenters are professions in great repute here. Here dwell a great number of Brahmins.

Cashmír is the only portion of Hindostan of which there is a native history. When Akbar "led his victorious standards into the region of perpetual spring, the natives presented him with a book called Raj Turungi, written in the Sanskrit language, and containing the history of the princes of Cashmeer for 4000 years back." Akbar ordered it to be translated into Persian. The original text has since been procured, and as it is "the only Sanskrit composition yet discovered to which the title of history can with any propriety be applied," it has commanded no little attention. An elaborate essay upon it by Professor Wilson * gives us a clear view of its general character. It gives us, too, not a few of its details. It gives us, too, a view of the authorship. At any rate, it gives us the names and approximate dates of four authors. The first of these is Calhana, who quotes as predecessors Suvrata, Narendra, Hela Raja, Padma Mihiri, and Sri Ch'havillacára, along with Nila Muni, a purana. The history of Calhana begins with the fabulous ages, and comes down to A.D. 1027. The author himself is believed to have lived about the middle of the following century. Then follows

Jonah Raja, author of the Rájávali, who begins where Calhana ends, and, himself, ends A.D. 1410; followed by

Sri Várá, whose Sri Jaina Rájá Taringíní continues the Rájávali down to A.D. 1477.

The fourth part was added by the order of Akbar. It brings the work down to the time of that monarch.

It is the history of Cashmír as an independent Mahometan kingdom, that this latter part of the work, more especially, delivers. It is a domestic history; *i. e.* its range is a narrow one. The political horizon, a single mountain-basin, must needs be limited. It comprises Tibet, Kashgar (or the Paropamisan countries), Budukshun, and part of Caubul. Of Indian principalities, the little rajahship of Kistewah is Cashmír's nearest neighbour, and it is into Kistewah that the Cashmírian

* In the Transactions of the Asiatic Society, vol. xv.

captains are most particularly in the habit of retreating when defeated. Of external enemies the most formidable are the Turks, by whom invasion after invasion is effected; the way lying over the Baramula pass. Of internal movements the chief are made by the Chuk, Reigna, and Magrey—names which I give as the names of either actual tribes or of something more or less tribual. The Chuks are probably, word for word, the Gukkers.

Mahometanism was introduced as early as A.D. 1341. It took root, however, but slowly and imperfectly, until the end of the century, when Ali, a Syud, who had incurred the anger of Timur, fled from his native city of Hamadan (A.D. 1388), and, attended, it is said, by 700 others, settled in Cashmír. His son, a fugitive also, introduced 300 more. And now the zeal for making proselytes burned bright and hot, and shrines multiplied, and persecution set-in. The Hindu temples were either burnt or thrown down. The Hindu devotees were forced to abjure their religion. Industry, however, was encouraged, and Cashmír became, under its independent princes, what Abulfazel described it. The Rishis, a set of Mahometan ascetics, numbered, in the reign of Akbar, about 2000. They have since either simply decreased, or become wholly extinct. So much for the times described by the last three authors of the chronicles of Cashmír.

The work of Calhana may or may not be trustworthy for the times immediately preceding those of the author. The mass of his statements is fabulous.

Most of the kings bear Indian names. Some, however, are specially stated to be Turks; whilst, in one of the very oldest and most decidedly fabulous dynasties, the title of each and all of the kings is the Turk adjunct, *khan*. One of these Turanian kings introduced Buddhism. Eventually, however, Brahminism prevailed.

Older, however, than either of the great Hindu creeds, was the worship of Nagas or snake Gods. Abulfazel relates that he found carvings of snakes in seven hundred places—these being objects of respect.

"Whether," writes Wilson, "the Cashmirian worship of snakes was mystical, at least in the earliest ages, may be questioned. There is likewise reason to suppose that this worship was diffused throughout the whole of India, as besides the numerous fables and traditions relating to the *Nagas*, or snake gods, scattered through the Puránas, vestiges of it still remain in the actual observances of the Hindus. It seems not improbable that the destruction of the whole serpent race by Janaméjaya, the son of Paricshit, recorded in the Puránas as a historical fact, may in reality imply the subversion of the local and original superstition, and the erection of the system of the Vedas upon its ruins." The *cultus* itself was old. A strange passage in Strabo tells, that "Abisarus fed two serpents (δράκοντας); one of which was 80, the other 140 cubits long." Again, Taxiles showed Alexander an enormous snake, which he reverenced as the symbol of Dionysus.

These notices (from Wilson) are not given for nothing. Like so many other phenomena, they point westwards. Stories connected with snakes appear twice in Gardiner's account of the Kafirs. Stories connected with snakes appear more than once in the mythology of Persia: prominent amongst which is that of Iblis and Zohauk—Iblis tempts Zohauk, a youth who, until the time of his temptation, is well disposed and virtuous, to the committal of gross crimes, and to the indulgence of an epicurean sensuality. Taste after taste is gratified. Every day something newer and more delicate than the luxuries of the day before appears at table; and that with the promise that "to-morrow there shall be something more delicious still." Pampered and corrupted, Zohauk now asks Iblis how he can show his gratitude. "By allowing me to kiss your naked shoulder." So Zohauk stripped, and Iblis kissed, and from the spot between the shoulder-blades, which he touched with his venomous and deceptive mouth, sprang two black snakes. Some time after this happened, Iblis, in the garb of a physician, visited Zohauk, and prescribed as the only means of preventing him from being gnawed into nothing by the serpents, a daily meal of human brains. So Zohauk fed the snakes; even as did Taxiles.

Now Zohauk was a usurper, the true king being Jamshid, for some time a fugitive in Zabulistan; for some time a wanderer in Caubul—in both places a drinker of wine.

Of Jamshid's family is the famous champion Rustam, who fights against (*inter alios*) the great Turanian champion Afrasiab, in Caubul, in Segistan, in Zabulistan and elsewhere.

There is nothing new in the notice of these numerous fictions. It is well known that they constitute the basis of the great poem of Firdausi—the Shah Nameh; wherein the stories of Jamshid, Feridun, Kavah the blacksmith, Zohrab, and others form a cycle. There is nothing new in the notice of them. There is no reason for mentioning them on their own account. The fact that claims attention is that of their localization in the Paropamisus—on the Paropamisus itself and on each side of it, in Cashmír as well as in Afghanistan, in Afghanistan as well as in Cashmír.

In both countries Jamshid is a real name. It was borne by one of the kings of Cashmír. It is borne, at the present time, by one of the tribes of the Hazarehs, or Afghans. Suhauk, too (word for word Zohauk), is the name of another of them. Forts, of which the building is attributed to Rustam, are common over the whole district. Finally, either Chitral or Kafiristan is the so-called wine-cellar of Afrasiab.

In the notice of Hwantsian, Cashmír stands prominent. His account contains a long story of a serpent that lay in the middle of the lake. Of the draining of the lake the following legend is native.

The country was entirely covered with water, in the midst of which a demon, Jaladeo, resided, who preyed upon mankind, and seized upon every thing and person he could meet with in the neighbouring regions. It happened, at length, that Cashef, the son of Marichi, and according to some accounts, the grandson of Brahmá, visited this country, and having spent some time in pious abstraction on mount Sumar, turned his attention to the desolated appearance of the earth, and inquired its cause: the people told him of the abode of Jaladeo in Sati Sar, and his predatory incursions upon them. The heart of Cashef was moved to compassion, and he took up his residence in Noubadan, near Hirapur, for a thousand years, employing that period in religious austerities; in consequence of which Mahádeo appeared to him, and assented to his prayers for the extirpation of Jaladeo; Mahádeo accordingly sent his servants Vishnu and Brahmá to expel the demon. Vishnu was engaged in the conflict one hundred years, when finding that the mud and water afforded a secure retreat to the Deo, he at last made the chasm at Baramouleh, by which the waters were drained off, the demon exposed, taken, and slain, and the country recovered and rendered habitable; being thence called Cashef-Sir, or the Mountain of Cashef.—*Asiatic Researches*, vol. xv. p. 94.

The first of the following tables gives us the comparison between the Cashmírian and the Paropamisan forms of speech: the second the words common to the two chief Paropamisan dialects, the Cashmírian, and the Hindi.

(1.)

| English. | Cashmíri. | Arniya. | Khajunah. |
|---|---|---|---|
| *Man* | manu | rag | hir |
| —— | —— | moash | er |
| *Woman* | zanana | kamri | gus |
| —— | —— | kamedi | —— |
| *Head* | kalah | sur | yetes |
| *Eye* | akh | ghakh | ilchin |

| English. | Cashmíri. | Arniya. | Khajunah. |
|---|---|---|---|
| *Ear* | kan | kad | iltumal |
| *Nose* | nast | naskar | gomoposh |
| *Mouth* | aso | diran | gokhat |
| *Tooth* | dand | dond | gume |
| *Hand* | atha | hast | gurengghar |
| *Foot* | khor | pang | goting |
| *Blood* | rath | le | multan |
| *Sky* | nab | asman | ayesh |
| *Sun* | aftab, suraj | —— | sa |
| *Moon* | tsandar | —— | balans |
| *Star* | tarah | satar | aso |
| *Fire* | nar, agan | ag, ingar | phu |
| *Water* | ab, pani | auqr | chil |
| *River* | bulwit | sin | sindha |
| *Stone* | khain | —— | dhan |
| *Tree* | kulu | kan | —— |
| *Wood* | zun | jin | gashil |
| *One* | ak | i | han |
| *Two* | zih | juh | altas |
| *Three* | trah | trui | usko |
| *Four* | tsor | chod | walto |
| *Five* | panz | push | sundo |
| *Six* | shah | chui | mi-shando |
| *Seven* | sat | sut | talo |
| *Eight* | ath | ansht | altambo |
| *Nine* | noh | neuhan | huncho |
| *Ten* | dah | jash | tormo. |

(2.)

| English. | Cashmíri. | Shina. | Arniya. | Punjub, &c. |
|---|---|---|---|---|
| *Air* | hawe | —— | hawa | hawa |
| *Arrow* | kan | kon | —— | kaneru |
| *Blood* | —— | lohel | —— | lohu |
| *Daughter* | —— | dhi | —— | dhi |
| *Ear* | kan | kund | —— | kan |
| *Earth* | —— | birde | —— | prither |
| —— | —— | —— | bhum | bhumi |
| *Eye* | ach | achhi | ach | akh |
| *Fire* | agan | agar | ag | ag |
| *Foot* | —— | pa | pang | pan |
| *Grass* | ghaso | kats | —— | ghas |
| *Hair* | wal | —— | balo | bal |
| —— | —— | —— | sur | sar |

| English. | Cashmíri. | Shina. | Arniya. | Punjab, &c. |
|---|---|---|---|---|
| *Honey* | manch | macchhe | —— | makhir |
| *Leaf* | —— | patta | —— | patta |
| *Milk* | dod | dudh | —— | dudh |
| *Moon* | tsandar | yun | —— | jun |
| *Mouth* | aso | asi | —— | —— |
| *Name* | —— | noma | —— | nam |
| *Night* | rat | rat | —— | rat |
| *Nose* | —— | —— | naskar | nasika |
| *Snow* | shin | hin | him | him |
| *Son* | —— | pucha | —— | putr |
| *Star* | tarah | taro | satar | tara |
| *Stone* | —— | bat | —— | patthar |
| *Sun* | —— | suri | —— | suraj |
| *Tooth* | dand | dhuni | dond | dand |
| *Wood* | —— | katho | —— | kath |
| *Right hand* | dachin | dachin | —— | dakhin |
| *Red* | —— | lolo | —— | lal |
| *Behind* | pat | pato | —— | pit |
| *Strait* | synd | sunth | —— | sidha |
| *Dry* | hok | sukho | —— | sukha |
| *Hard* | —— | koro | —— | karha |
| *Hot* | tat | tatto | —— | tatta |
| *Large* | bod | baro | —— | bara |
| *Ripe* | —— | pakko | —— | pakka |
| *Thick* | —— | tulo | —— | tula |

That the Khajunah is the least Indian of the Paropamisan forms of speech has already been stated.

## CHAPTER XXXVIII.

**Populations whose language is akin to the Hindí.—The Rajput and Jut division.—The Sikhs.**

The second division is, in the way of creed, Sikh, Hindu, and Mahometan.

In the way of cast, its noblest tribes are Kshetriya rather than either Brahminic or Sudra; though, of course, in the Sikh and Mahometan districts, the spirit of cast is abated.

The chief form of speech is the Hindí, of which the dialects are numerous—the Hindí, rather than the Bengali, Uriya, or Marathi.

Its area is bounded by Cashmír, Afghanistan, Biluchistan, the Ocean, and the Vindya mountains—there or thereabouts. In the north, it approaches the Himalayas, in the east and north-east the Jumna—sometimes touching it. In the east its boundaries are obscure. They lie beyond the Chumbul, beyond the Sind, and, in some cases, beyond the Betwa.

This contains—

1. The valley of the Indus.
2. The Desert.
3. The hilly districts of the Aravulli range, and the drainage of the south-western feeders of the Jumna.
4. The drainage of the rivers that fall into the gulfs of Kutch and Cambay.
5. The Peninsula of Gujerat.

Politically speaking, it contains the Punjab, Sind, the proper Rajput country, Gujerat, and other districts of less importance and prominence.

On the east it is Hindu; on the west, Sikh and Mahometan.

As this difference of creed is attended with a difference of nomenclature, it is necessary to be on our guard against being misled by terms. As a general rule, a Rajput is a Hindu. As a general rule, a Jut is a Mahometan. As a general rule, a Jut is a peaceable cultivator. For all this the Jut may be, in blood, neither more nor less than a converted Rajput; and, *vice versâ*, the Rajput may be but a Jut of the ancient faith. That other differences have been effected by this difference of creed is likely. The difference between arms and tillage as a profession, the difference between a haughty autonomy, and a submissive independence, are sure, in the course of time, to tell upon the temper and the features. That they have done this in the cases before us no one doubts. At the same time, it is safe to maintain that, before the introduction of Mahometanism, the difference between the Jut and the Rajput was but slight. That the Sikhs are, *mutato nomine*, and, *mutatâ fide*, with few exceptions, Juts is a matter of ordinary history.

*The Punjab.*—The notices of some of the populations of the valley of the Indus are well nigh as old as those of the river itself. This was crossed by Alexander: so that the kings who opposed him were Punjab sovereigns. Such were Porus and Taxiles.

Lower down the stream lay the dominions of kings whose names end in *-khan*—Musi*canus*, and Oxy*canus*.

Later in time comes the name Indoscythæ.

Memorials of the kingdom founded by the successors

of Alexander, have been found on the eastern side of the Indus—though less abundantly than in the valley of the Caubul river.

Word for word, *Multan* is supposed to be the country of the *Malli*.

In the way of physical geography, the Punjab falls into the hill-country, and the low-country. The hill-country (the details of which are imperfectly known) belongs to the remnant of the Great Sikh Empire, rather than to Britain. It was left to Gulab Singh.

On the southern frontier of Cashmír lie what were once the petty independencies of Prúnch, Rajour, &c.; now parts of Gulab Singh's dominion. They are Mahometan rather than either Hindu or Sikh. The rajahship of Jumma, the original territory of Gulab Singh, is Sikh.

The parts marked in the map as the country of

*The Bumbas* is but little known. I cannot say in what respect the Bumbas differ from another population with whom, both geographically and ethnologically, they are connected, viz.,

*The Kukkars.*—Word for word, this is Cauker; and it is a name which occurs frequently in the Mahometan historians. It seems to be the general name for the mountaineers of the Salt range, and the ranges to the north. That occupants of districts like these are hard to conquer, is what we expect *à priori*. We find that it was their habit to harass the armies of most of the invaders from the west. The Kukkars and Bumbas form a natural division of the Punjab population. So do the inhabitants of the level country.

Essentially these are (Jits) Juts—*i. e.* they are Jut in blood, language, and physical form; though not, wholly, Juts *eo nomine*. They are Sikhs rather than Mahometans;

but, before they became Sikh, they were Jut in every sense of the word.

The Sikh sect came into existence in the latter half of the fifteenth century, its founder, Nanak Shah, having been born in the district of Lahore, A.D. 1469. He was both the founder of a sect himself, and the father of a founder, inasmuch as one of his two sons, Dherm Chand, took to asceticism and originated the sect named, at first, Udasi; but afterwards (and now) Nanak Putrah, or sons of Nanak. It is one of the existing Sikh sects. Nanak was a devotee, a philosopher, and a writer. The first of the Sikh scriptures, the Adi Grunt'h, was composed by him. He saw with equal pain the bigotry of the Mahometan, and the superstition of the Hindu. He wished to replace both by a pure and charitable monotheism. Yet his means were conciliatory. He dealt tenderly with absurdities of both belief and practice. He was a man of peace rather than war.

(2.) Guru Angaa succeeds him; himself succeeded by (3) Amera Das, succeeded, in his turn, by (4) Ram Das: who leaves his authority to

(5.) Arjunmal, who, adding to the chapters of the original Adi Grunt'h, puts the whole into form, and gives shape and consistency to what is now a definite and important creed—the creed of a sect which up to this time has comported itself quietly, mildly, inoffensively. But Arjunmal is murdered by the Mahometans; and

(6.) Har Govind succeeds him. But not as the head of a peaceable population. The anger of the Sikhs is awakened, and a long series of hostilities, destined, in the end, to overthrow all the Mahometanism of the Punjab, now commences. Every Sikh now wears steel. Every Sikh is a zealot, and a soldier. Har Govind, priest militant and prophet captain, wears two swords, "the one to revenge the death of his father, the other to destroy the miracles of Mahomet." He has converted a race of peaceable enthusiasts into an army of fiery soldiers. In 1644 his grandson

(7.) Har Ray succeeds him; succeeded by

(8.) Har Crishn, succeeded by

(9.) Tegh Behadur—These are the days when Aurungzeb is emperor; no good days for any new sect; least of all for one that has set itself against the Koran. The Sikh power is broken—partly by the strong hand of the emperor, partly by internal dissensions. In the days of Aurungzeb and Tegh Behadur, miracles are wrought by the Sikh *gurus* or priests, especially by Har Crishn, and Ram Ray. Tegh Behadur himself is murdered: even as Arjunmal was murdered. Like causes, like effects. Out of the blood of Arjunmal rose the awakened spirit of the Sikhs, under Har Govind. Out of the blood of Tegh Behadur rises the power of his son,

(10.) Guru Govind—When his father died he was a stripling; but he devoted himself to revenge. Like the Pindari and Mahratta chieftains, Guru Govind opened the ranks of his army and the gates of his faith to all comers. Nanak wished to abolish cast, and taught that before God all men were equal. It was a saying of Guru Govind's, that the four tribes of Hindus, the Brahmins, the Kshetriyas, the Vaisyas, and the Sudras, would, like lime, betel-nut, betel-leaf, and catechu, become all of one colour when chewed. The name Sikh he changed into Singh (Lion), a name first assumed by the Rajputs. He required that every man should bear arms, should wear a blue dress, should let his hair grow, and should use, as a part of his salutations, Glory to the Guru (spiritual leader). The Grunt'h, or book of the scriptures, was to be his law, his duty obedience to his chief, his pleasure war. It is Govind himself—priest, soldier, and poet—who writes the following :—

Cripál rages, wielding his mace: he crushed the skull of the fierce Hyat Khan. He made the blood spurt aloft, and scattered the brains of the chief, as Chrishna crushed the earthen vessel of butter. Then Nand Chand raged in dreadful ire, launching the spear and wielding the sword. He broke his keen scymitar, and drew his dagger, to support the honour of the Sondi race. Then my maternal uncle, Cripál, advanced in his rage, and exhibited the skilful war-feats of a true Cshatriya. The mighty warrior, though struck by an arrow, with another made a valiant Khan fall from his saddle; and Saheb Chund, of the Cshatriya race, strove in the battle's fury, and slew a blood-thirsty Khan, a warrior of Khorasan.

* * * * * * *

The blood-drinking spectres and ghosts yelled for carnage; the fierce Hetala, the chief of the spectres, laughed for joy and sternly prepared for his repast. The vultures hovered around, screaming for their prey. Hari Chund (a Hindu chief in the emperor's army), in his wrath, drawing his bow, first struck my steed with an arrow; aiming a second time, he discharged his arrow; but the deity preserved me, and it passed me, only grazed by my ear. His third arrow struck my breast; it tore open the mail and pierced the skin, leaving a slight scar: but the God whom I adore saved me. When I felt this hurt, my anger was kindled; I drew my bow and discharged an arrow; all my champions did the same, rushing onwards to the battle. Then I aimed at the young hero and struck him. Hari Chund perished, and many of his host; death devoured him who was called Rájá among a hundred thousand Rájás. Then all the host, struck with consternation, fled, deserting the field of combat. I obtained the victory through the favour of the Most High; and, victorious in the field, we raised aloud the song of triumph. Riches fell on us like rain, and all our warriors were glad.

Hero as he is, Govind finds it necessary to yield to the superior power of Aurungzeb; and becomes a fugitive, a wanderer, a madman. He had written to the emperor thus: "You make Hindus Mahometans, and are justified by your laws. I, on a principle of self-preservation, will make Mahometans Hindus. You may rest in fancied security. But beware, I will teach the sparrow to strike the eagle to the ground." The latter part of the vaunt was never realized. Many a Mahometan, however, was made a Hindu. The proselytes fall into four divisions, retaining, as Sikhs, the distinctive appellations as Mahometans. Two of these are founded on their pedigree, two on their country:—

| | |
|---|---|
| Syud Singh | Mogul Singh |
| Sheikh Singh | Patan Singh. |

The latter part of Govind's life is obscure. He was the last ruler of the Sikhs who was, at one and the same time, a religious chief, and universally acknowledged to be such. The number ten was fated, and Govind was the ninth from Nanak. He was the last head of a united Sikhdom. His friend, however, and follower, Banda, availed himself of the confusion which set-in after the death of Aurungzeb, plundered the country, and defeated some of the minor Mahometan chiefs, especially Foujdar Khan, governor of Sirhind, and murderer of the infant children of Govind. Quarter was neither asked nor given. The wife and children of the murderer were slaughtered. There was an indiscriminate massacre in Sirhind; there was the same, or sadder, bloodshed, when the province of Saharanpur was invaded. The buried dead are said to have been disinterred; the unburied were mutilated and exposed to wild beasts.

The power as well as the temper of these savage sectarians has become formidable; but it is broken. The following notice of the death of Banda and his followers is from a Mahometan, and an enemy.—"They not only behaved firmly during the execution, but would dispute and wrangle with each other, who should suffer first. Banda was at last produced, his son being seated on his lap. His father was ordered to cut his throat, which he did without uttering one word. Being then brought nearer to the magistrate's tribunal, the latter ordered his flesh to be torn off with red-hot pincers, and it was in those moments he expired; his black soul taking its flight by one of those wounds, towards the regions for which it was so well fitted." A proof that Banda, with all his authority and bravery, was no true religious chief to the whole Sikh sect is found in the fact of some writers having considered him a heretic. He departed from more than one of the institutions of Nanak, and he put to death some of Govind's most devoted followers for not doing as he did.

The extirpation of the Sikhs is now attempted. The remnant flies to the hills. Yet, thirty years afterwards, when Nadir Shah invades India, we find them descending upon the plains.

In 1805, the country, according to Sir T. Malcolm, who, being with the army under Lord Lake, describes what he saw and heard, was weak, distracted, disunited. There were different districts, and different chieftaincies in the country between the Beas and Ravi. "Runjít Sinh of Lahore, Futteh Sinh of Aliwal, and Jud'h Sinh of Ramgadia, are the principal chiefs."

How familiar are, at least, two of the names, now! The consolidation of the Sikh power under Runjít Singh, and its subsequent overthrow, are events that have taken place before our eyes.

The Punjab is a district wherein the traces of either anything Tamul from the south, or anything Bhot from the north, are at a *minimum*. We cannot, indeed, say that they exist at all. At the same time, we cannot say that they do not.

Of recent intrusion there has been abundance. The extent to which the valley of the main stream of the Indus, is more or less, Afghan and Biluch has already been noticed. Turk names (Hissar, &c.) of geographical localities are numerous. Upon the whole, however, the

Punjab has been a country to pass through rather than to settle in.

*Bahawulpur* (*Daudputra*).—This is one of the preeminent Biluch districts of India,—whatever that word may mean; the Biluch intrusion being recent. The creed is chiefly Mahometan, the older elements of the population Jut.

## CHAPTER XXXIX.

Populations speaking either the Hindí or languages akin to it.—The Rajput and Jut divisions.—Sind.—Kutch.—Gujerat.

INDIA, even when we take no account of the Brahúis, and limit ourselves to the prolongations of the Sind population, extends far into Mekran.

The special Sind tribes do this. So do

*The Juts, Jits, Jauts.*—Word for word, all these forms are the same; though they apply to populations between which there are some notable differences both in respect to habits and creed.

In the parts beyond the India frontier, in parts of Caubul and Biluchistan, a population more or less sporadic and gypsy-like, bears the name. Of this we take no notice.

In the Punjab the term is Jit; the Punjab being pre-eminently a Jit occupancy, and the blood of the Sikhs being (as aforesaid), for the most part, Jit.

Sind, along with a portion of the Desert, is the chief occupancy of the Mahometan Juts; the congeners of whom, with the same name, extend over the greater part of Rajputana; until at Bhurtpore and Dholpore we find an actual Jaut dynasty.

The Juts of Kutch Gundava have already been noticed. The Juts of Sind are Mahometan cultivators—numerous and peaceable descendants of the first converts. They fall into divisions and subdivisions, called *khum*, a term which re-appears with a similar meaning in Burma. The camel is the chief animal of the Sind Juts, who live together in large communities, sometimes with fixed, sometimes with movable, dwellings. Sometimes they hire themselves to the Biluch landowners as agricultural labourers.

*Sindis to the west of Sind.*—As far within the limits of Mekran as Hormara, on the Kalamat creek, lives a small tribe which believes that it came originally from Sind. Whether this be true is uncertain. It is only certain that considerably to the west of Cape Monze a Sindi population is to be found.

*The Med.*—This is the name for the maritime and fishing tribes for the eastern coast of Mekran. The Meds fall into four divisions—

| | |
|---|---|
| The Gazbur | The Jellar Zai |
| — Hormari | — Chelmar Zai. |

These may or may not be in the same category with the Kalamatti tribes.

*The Numri.*—This name is sometimes spelt Lumri. It is that of the chief population of the small province of Luz, one of the numerous dependencies of the Khanate of Khelaut. The minute details of the Numri group differ. The most specific account, however, is the following.

| | | Fighting Men. |
|---|---|---|
| The Jamutri | division can muster | 600 |
| — Shuru | ———————— | 200 |
| — Burah | ———————— | 300 |
| — Shukh | ———————— | 100 |
| — Warah | ———————— | 100 |
| — Mungayah | ———————— | 300 |
| | | 1600 |

The Arab Gudur tribe is, perhaps, other than Numri;

inasmuch as it professes to be, what its name suggests, Arabian in origin.

The Numri is the chief population of Luz. But it is not confined to the province. The Jokías and Jukrias of Sind differ from the Numri in their political relations only. The Numri are Mahometans.

*The Chuta.*—On the upper and middle part of the Hub river, which falls into the sea at Cape Monze, lies a rugged district occupied by the Chuta, whose origin is said to be Sumrah, whose dress is Brahúi, whose manners are pastoral, whose houses are huts. They are, probably, in the same category as the Numri.

They bring us to Sind proper.

The history of Sind gives the following periods :—

(1.) From the earliest times to the Mahometan conquest.—During this period the invasion of Alexander took place; one of the results of which was the descent of the Indus by Nearchus. But, before this, Turanian occupancies had been effected, and Indoscythæ is the name of one portion of the Sind population.

(2.) From the Mahometan conquest to the end of the Ghuznevid dynasty.—The Mahometan conquest was one of the conquests of the Kalifat. This means that the conquerors were Arabs rather than Persians or Afghans. Under Mahmud of Ghuzni the influence would be both Afghan and Turk.

Of the Sumrah and Summa dynasties which succeeded, the latter, at least, appears to have been Hindu. At the present time there are few or no Kshetriyas in Sind; consequently few or no Rajputs. The Summa chiefs, however, conquered Kutch. Now, Kutch is, to a great extent, Rajput. More than this, some of the Rajput families affect a Summa, or Sind, origin. Jam, a Bhot word, was the title of the Summas, who were overthrown by Shah Beg

Arzhun, prince of Candahar, A.D. 1519. Soon after which Mirza Isa Tirkhan, a military adventurer, raised his family to power. The prince of Candahar seems to have been an Afghan; Isa Tirkhan, a Turk. The next were—

*The Kaloras* and *Talpuras.*—Long before A.D. 1736 the power of the central Government had been diminished, and the protection of its distant States had become impossible to the descendants of Akbar and Aurungzeb. Meanwhile, the descendants of one Adam Shah, of the Kalora tribe, who, in the fifteenth century, had imbibed fanaticism from the teaching of a holy man, Mian Mahomed Mikidy, had become powerful, both in religious influence and in secular possessions. They had appropriated lands belonging to others, and had defended their appropriations by the sword. They were a set of fighting, formidable fakirs. In 1717 Mian Nur Mahomed had obtained from Mahomed Shah the title of the Friend of God, and the government of Sewestan. By '36, he was, to all intents and purposes, the ruler of Sind.

By A.D. 1768 the Kalora dynasty was overthrown by the Talpurs.

In 43 the British replaced the Talpurs.

At the present moment Sind is the least Indian part of India. The extent to which it has admitted foreign influences has been suggested by the preceding sketch of its history.

The Sindi form of speech falls into dialects and subdialects, each of which approaches the language of its neighbourhood. Thus the Siraiki of Upper Sind contains numerous Jutki words; whilst the Kutch dialect has Gujerati elements; and a third dialect, belonging to the Thull, or Desert, and spoken as far as Jessulmir, has borrowed from, or given to, the Marwar. It is the language of the Shikari (hunters) and Dedhs (tanners), who are said to have their own peculiar scriptures called Pali, written in a peculiar character. The Lar form of speech is the purest, Lar being Lower Sind.

| English. | Sar. | Lar. | Punjabi. |
|---|---|---|---|
| *Man* | maru | —— | manas |
| —— | murs | —— | —— |
| *Woman* | zal | mihri | gharwali |
| *Head* | matho | sisi | sir |
| *Hair* | war | jhonto | bal |
| —— | choti | —— | —— |
| *Eye* | ak | —— | akh |
| *Ear* | kan | —— | kan |
| *Hand* | hath | kar | hath |
| —— | chambu | —— | —— |
| *Foot* | per | —— | pao |
| *Mouth* | wat | —— | mukh |
| *Tooth* | dand | dandan | dand |
| *Tongue* | jhibh | —— | —— |
| *Day* | dink | —— | din |
| *Night* | rat | —— | rát |
| *Sun* | sijj | adit | suraj |
| *Moon* | chandr | —— | chand |
| *Star* | taro | —— | tara |
| *Fire* | bar | jando | ag |
| —— | —— | jeru | —— |
| *Water* | pani | —— | pani |
| —— | sandaro | —— | —— |
| *Tree* | wanper | —— | rukh |
| *Stone* | rahan | —— | hatar |
| —— | khod | —— | —— |

Among the subordinate populations of Sind are

*The Moana* or *Miani.*—A Miani is a boatman, a fisherman, and a Mahometan—strongly built and dark skinned. Many of the Miani, like the Chinese, live on the water, rather than by its side. When occupants of a town, the Miani have a separate quarter. Their women are lax and handsome; an inordinate portion of them being courtesans and dancing girls. The name re-appears in

Kutch. The Meyanna, however, of the Meyanné district in Kutch, are robbers by profession, and but half Mahometans in creed. A section of them called Munka neglects circumcision. When a Munka dies a bundle of burning grass is laid on his face previous to interment.

*Arab families.*—Syuds, or descendants of the Prophet, Kurayshi, or descendants of the ancient Koreish, Alawi and Abbasi, descendants of Ali and Abbas, are all to be found in Sind.

*Meman.*—The Memans, numerous about Hyderabad, Sehwan, and Kurraché, are industrious, well informed, and sharp bargainers. I do not know their special characteristics, or whence they get their name. They are Mahometans.

*The Khwajo.*—The Khwajo are heretics, holding the Ismaelite creed. They amount to some 300 families, and are believed to be of Persian origin.

*The Sidi.*—Under the Amírs there was a considerable importation of slaves from the eastern coast of Africa. The trade has now either ceased or decreased. The full-blood African is called Sidi; the half-blood, Gaddo; the Quadroon, Gambrari.

*The Khosa* fall into two divisions. The first contains those of Upper Sind, who are peaceable cultivators. The second is represented by a body of robbers, who, within the present century, left Sind, and betook themselves to the Desert, where they joined the Sodha in their forays, being numerous, bold, and well mounted.

Sind leads to

*Kutch.*—Of actual Juts, *eo nomine*, Kutch contains few or none. Their analogues, however, and perhaps their congeners, are

*The Katti.*—A Katti is a herdsman, occupant of the districts of Pawur, Puchur, and Parkur, or the parts on the north, rather than the south of Kutch, resembling in dress, habits, and dialect,

*The Ahir*, with whom, however, he does not intermarry.

*The Rehberi.*—Neither the Ahir nor the Rehberi, still less the Katti, refuse to eat with Mahometans. Their widows are free to form second marriages.

The Rajputs are either Jareyas or Waghelas. The Waghela Rajputs, or the Rajputs of the district of Wagur (the most eastern part of Kutch), are few in numbers, and unimportant in respect to their influence. A few families represent their original power; for powerful they were before the rise of the Jareyas. They resemble the Rajputs of Gujerat, except that they are somewhat less scrupulous. This is what we expect from their neighbourhood and relations; for the leading Rajputs of Kutch, the Jareyas, are half Mahometan. They eat food cooked by Mahometans, and swear by Allah.

Some, indeed, are stricter, and adhere to the *cultus* of Vishnu. The general character, however, of the Jareya Hinduism is lax. The more a Jareya venerates Vishnu the more he abstains from spirits and indulges in opium. The nearer he approaches the Mahometan the less he takes of opium, and the more of spirits. The two vices seem to stand in an inverse ratio to each other. In both of them few; in one almost all, indulge. Every village has its still, sometimes applied to sugar, sometimes to dates, sometimes to carrots. The Jareya wakes to drink and drinks to sleep. His bard, a musician (*bhat* or *lunga*), amuses him during the waking intervals with song or story. His wives intrigue. It is in vain that, after the strictest fashion of the Mahometans, they are secluded. They intrigue with high and low. They intrigue and do worse. In no part of India is female infanticide more general than in the Jareya districts. Sometimes it is effected by means of opium, sometimes by drowning the infant in milk, sometimes by smothering. The father hears that his wife has been delivered, and that the child is in heaven. So he bathes and asks no questions. Should the mother hesitate or delay, he declares his resolution not to enter her house as long as the child lives.

In respect to female infanticide but too many of the Mahometans act after the manner of the Rajputs; with whom they agree in blood, and differ only in creed.

To the north of the Waghela district lies Parkur, an oasis, and, in cases of attack, a place of refuge. Its one poor town, and its twenty poor villages, represent the power, such as it is, of the Sodha Rajputs, or the Rajputs of the Desert, between Kutch, Sind, and Jessulmir. Less Hindu than even the Jareya, the Sodhas are distinguished by their creed only from the Mahometans of their area and neighbourhood. They are herdsmen, poor and unlettered. They intermarry with the Rajputs around them, but not with each other. And they give their daughters, who are remarkable for their beauty, to the Mahometans. In doing this, they show themselves in a strong contrast to the Jareyas, with whom the birth of a girl child is not only a misfortune, but the cause of a crime. The Sodha practice, on the other hand, like that of the Circassians, makes capital out of the female part of the family. The Rajput father sells. The Mahometan husband buys.

A Sodha gives his daughter or sister one day in marriage, and has no scruple, the next, in driving-off the cattle of his bridegroom.

*The Chawrah.*—The geographical names Kurrir, Khori, and Kawra, appear in the parts to the north of Kutch, and I have little doubt as to their being connected with that of the population so-called, a population occupant of Kutch, reduced in power, and limited in numbers; a population, however, which has some imperfect Rajput rights, though practically subordinate to the Jareyas.

Kutch leads to

*Gujerat.*—The area of the Gujerathi language begins to the west of the Little Desert. • This assumes that the language of the occupants of that district is either Kutchi or Sindi. If it be not, the Gujerathi extends somewhat further westward. In Kutch itself it is the language of business and literature, though not the vernacular of the people. To the east and north-east of the Run it is spoken on both sides of the lower Lúni, though to what extent inland is uncertain. In Marwar the dialect changes; and I presume (without being certain) that the language of the Bhíls of Sirohi is other than Gujerathi. In the Rewa Kanta the population is Kol, the exact details of the Kol philology being uninvestigated. Along the coast, however, the language is, to a certainty, Gujerathi. So it is on the neck of the peninsula. So it is on the neck of the peninsula of Kattiwar. So it is in Cambay, and a great portion of the Surat collectorate. Here, however, change begins. In Durhampur and Bundsla, petty States to the south-east of the town itself, the Marathi shows itself. Both languages, however, are in use. In Penth, still further to the south, (though at the same time to the north of the Damaun river,) the language is "Marathi with numerous Gujerathi words."

Between the Little Desert, Marwar, and the Gulf of Kutch, lies a mass of extremely small States.

Four of these are Mahometan, viz. Pahlunpúr, Radhunpúr, Warye, and Terwara.

Four are Rajpút, viz. Thurad (*cum* Morwara), Wao, Soeghaum, Deodur, and Suntulpúr (*cum* Charchut).

Two are Kol, or Kúli—Bhabhur and Kankruj.

In the north-eastern parts of Pahlunpúr the language approaches the Marwari. Again—though the larger portion of the area is Mahometan in respect to its dynasties, the decided majority of the population is Hindu; the Gujerati, rather than the Hindostani, being the language of even the Mahometan minority. In Suntulpur there is a Ahir population. Terwara and Deodur, though Rajput in the way of politics, are as thoroughly Kuli as Bhabhur and Kankruj. The Kols affect a Rajput origin, and explain their loss of cast by the fact of their ancestors having made marriages of disparagement. The Kols, too, where they come in contact with the Bhíls, look upon themselves as the superior people.

In Pahlunpúr the Mahometans are from either some other part or from Afghanistan, the ruling family itself being Patan. Of the other two divisions—the Sheiks and Synds—the former call themselves after the name of the country from which they came, and are Behari, Nagori, or Mundori Mussulmauns, according as they came from Behar, Nagore, or Mundore. Others, of Rajput origin, are Purmas, Chowras, and Rahtors. The Boraks speak Arabic. The Mehmans are descended from the Sind Lohanas.

Amongst the Hindus the Brahmins are—

1. Owdich Brahmins
2. Suhusra Owdich
3. Meywara Brahmins
4. Omewul Brahmins
5. Sirmali Brahmins.

To which add certain half-bloods, who have lost cast by marriages of disparagement.

The Kshatryas are either Rajputs or Banians.

The Rajputs are—

1. Purmar
2. Solunkhi
3. Gohil
4. Chowra
5. Waghela
6. Chowan
7. Rathor
8. Diol
9. Rana
10. Jhalla
11. Deora.

The Banians are—

1. Visa Sirmali
2. Uswal
3. Pirwal
4. Dussa Sirmali
5. Pancha
6. Wussawul Nagra
7. Dussawul Nagra.

Of the Sudras, the most important class is that of the Kúmbi, or cultivators, who fall into the Leora, the Arjuna, and the Kurwa divisions.

That the Kuli affect a Rajput origin has already been stated. Hence they take Rajput patronymics, and are—

1. Rathor Kúli
2. Waghela Kúli
3. Solunkhi Kúli
4. Songhurra Chowan
5. Dabi Kúli
6. Mukwana Kúli.

These details may serve as a sample of the complexities of Indian ethnology—in the parts under notice more complex than usual. Sind, Gujerathi, Bhíl, Kuli, Rajput, and Mahometan populations, meet in the parts between Marwar and Kattiwar; Kattiwar being the name for the country of the Katti, the peninsular portion of Gujerat.

For this, the newer occupants are Rajputs, the older Ahirs, Katti, and Babrias, *i. e.* what we have observed in Kutch repeats itself here. In Jhalawar the Rajputs are of the Jhala branch. They either take their name from, or give it to, the district. In Hallar they are Jareyas, guilty here, as elsewhere, of female infanticide. The Rajah of Purbunda in Soruth is a Jetwa Rajput. Gohilwar is the occupancy of the Gohillas, whose name is conspicuous in the history of Marwar. When the

Rahtors from Canuj invaded Marwar, they found the Gohillas in the land, and ejected them from it. The result was the settlement in Gohilwar. This may be a true history, or it may merely be a hypothesis founded upon the appearance of the name in two places.

In most, perhaps in all, of the districts of the peninsula there are Katti. Their chief locality, however, is, as the name suggests, the central district of

*Kattiwar proper.*—The Katti of Kattiwar proper consider themselves to be descended from Khat, who was produced by Kurrun. Kurrun struck his rod on the ground, and out came Khat. The function of Khat was to steal certain cattle from Berat or Dholka. He afterwards married the daughter of an Ahir in the district of Powar, between Sind and Kutch. He had eight sons. His descendants seek their fortune and join the Charun who are doing the same. They reach the town of Dhauk, the chief of which was Walla Rajput, who marries one of their women, and becomes a Katti. From Walla come the Shakayut, or chief nobles; the other division consisting of the Urtia (Ourteea) or inferiors. The Katti then went to Kutch, moving thence under a leader who saw the sun and took advice from it, in a dream. They, then, came into their present occupancy which was (till then) held by Ahirs and Babrias. They expelled

*The Babrias,* who still give their name to Babriawar, a district on the sea-coast, south of Kattiwar proper, in which they are the chief inhabitants; poor, rude, predatory; less predatory now, however, than they have been. The Babrias are said to be the offspring of an Ahir with a Kuli woman. They intermarry with the Ahirs.

*The Sidi of Muzuferabad,* or *Jafarabad.*—Muzuferabad is the fort of Babriawar. The governor is always a Sidi, *i.e.* an African in blood, and a slave in origin. The details of the history by which they became independent sailors are unknown.

*The Mher* pretend to be Rajputs, their claim being doubtful. In every village belonging to the Rana of Purbunder there is a certain number of Mhers, who are charged with its defence. They are supported by grants of land. They breed horses and camels; the males of which they give to the Rana. They were formerly exempted from paying taxes; their personal services being all that the State required. At present, however, they are taxed—though lightly.

A portion of the Purbunder army, the militia, consists of these Rebharis and Mhers. A portion consists of foreign mercenaries, chiefly from Arabia and Mekran. So that

*Arab* and *Mekrani* elements are to be considered in the ethnology of western Gujerat.

*The Mian* occupants of the fortified town of Mallia, are said to have been introduced into the district of Muchukund from Waghur, having originally come from Sind. This may be a historical fact, or it may be a mere inference from the name. The Mian under notice are predatory Mahometans.

Of the Ahir and Rebhari notice has already been taken.

The Isthmus is more Bhil and Kol than the Peninsula, the petty States of Dunduka, Runpur, and Gogo, being more especially Bhil. In Dholka there is a considerable amount of Mahometanism.

The parts between the Suburmuti and the Mahi contain Kulis; the fewest of which are in Neriad, the most in Bijapur.

The parts between the Mahi and the Nerbudda are Bhil and Rajput; Bhil and Rajput, but not without Mahometan elements. Some of the districts belong to the Company, some to the Guikowar, some to Sindia's territory. Some are independent. Some are mere village chieftaincies.

The parts between the Nerbudda and Tapti are Bhíl; Bhíl and Rajput, but not without Mahometan elements. Rajpîpla, to the north-east of Surat, is, pre-eminently, a Bhíl area. So are the more impracticable districts of the collectorate of Surat, or the parts between the Tapti and the Damaun Gunga; in which, however, we pass (as already stated) from the Gujerathi to the Maratta area.

As a rule, Kandeish is Bhíl, so that its details will be given when that population comes under notice.

## CHAPTER XL.

Populations speaking either Hindí or a language akin to it.—The Rajput and Jut divisions.—Rajputana, Rajwarra, or Rajasthan.

Tod, who takes the Rajput districts as he found them when he wrote, gives the following boundaries,—

1. To the north—the sandy desert beyond Bikanir.
2. To the south—the Nerbudda.
3. To the west—the Mahometan districts on the Indus.
4. To the east—the river Sind, a feeder, from the south of the Ganges.

This gives us Bikanir, Jessulmir, Marwar, Mewar, Ajmir, Jeypúr, Búndi, Kotah, and Malwa, and other districts of less importance; altogether a very considerable portion of India.

It also leads us to ask the import of the word Rajput in its stricter sense. In any other country but a country of casts, like India, Rajputana would be a land of tribes; one or more of which possessed (or claimed) a superiority over the others. In India it is this, with the phenomena of cast superadded.

The highest tribual division seems to be a *kula*, word for word, the Afghan *kheil*. A *kula* contains so many *sachas*; a *sacha* so many *gotras*. The races are thirty-six in number, some being of solar, some of lunar, descent. The Rajputs of Mewar, as they exist at the present moment, are Rajputs of the Sisodía division; Sisodía being the name of a *sacha*. The *kula* to which it belongs is the Gehlot, or Grahilot—Suryavansi (Solar or Sun-born) in blood, and attached to the Lord of Chitor. Silladitya, the last prince of Gujni, leaves a posthumous son named Grahaditya, whence Grahilot, or Gehlot. In the sixth century this name is replaced by Ahar; the Aharya dynasty ruling in Chitor. Chitor, however, they leave in the twelfth century, under two brothers, Rahup and Mahup. Rahup settles in Dongurpur, where, at the present moment, his descendants, the Aharya Rajputs, are to be found. Meanwhile, Mahup fixes himself in Sísodía. All this seems to be mere logography. What, however, are the real facts? Out of the twenty-four *sachas* into which the Gehlot *kula* is divided, eight are "almost extinct," eleven are "small and obscure." In Dongurpur there are some Aharyas; in the Desert some Mangulías; in Marwar some Piparras; in Mewar the proud and powerful Sísodías. The following legend shows how mythologies degenerate. Colonel Tod, our authority, is speaking of a part of Mewar.

In these wilds an ancient Rana of Cheetore had sat down to a *gote* (feast), consisting of the game slain in the chase; and being very hungry, he hastily swallowed a piece of meat to which a gad-fly adhered. The fly grievously tormented the Rana's stomach, and he sent for a physician. The wise man (*bèd*) secretly ordered an attendant to cut off the tip of a cow's ear, as the only means of saving the monarch's life. On obtaining this forbidden morsel, the bèd folded it in a piece of thin cloth, and attaching a string to it, made the royal patient swallow it. The gad-fly fastened on the bait, and was dragged to light. The physician was rewarded; but the curious Rana insisted on knowing by what means the cure was effected; and when he heard that a piece of sacred kine had passed his lips, he determined to expiate the enormity in a manner which its heinousness required, and to swallow boiling lead (seesa)! A vessel was put on the fire, and the metal soon melted; when, praying that his involuntary offence might be forgiven, he boldly drank it off; but lo! it passed through him like water. From that day the name of the tribe was changed from Aharya to Seesodia.

Such is the Gehlot *kula*. That of the Agnicula is more complex. Before falling into *sachas* it divides itself into four primary branches—

1. The Pramara, with thirty-five *sachas;*
2. The Purihana;
3. The Chaluk, or Solankhi;
4. The Chohan.

To the Purihanas belong—

*a.* The Sodha;

*b.* The Sumra;

*c.* The Omutwarra families; all real—the two former being found in (or on the frontier of) Sind, the latter in a district so-called.

The Yadu *kula* stands in contrast with the Gehlot in being of Lunar rather than Solar origin. It contains—

The Bhattis of Jessulmír, amongst whom is a belief that their ancestors came from Zabulistan, a Turk district;

The Jareyas of Kutch;

The Yadu of Kerowli, a small State on the Chumbul;

The Sumaicha of Sind converted to Mahometanism.

The Rahtor *kula* contains twenty-four *sachas*. Its original occupancy was Canúj. It is at present a real and important dynasty in Marwar.

The Kutshwaha *kula* holds Amber or Jeypúr.

The Chohans, already mentioned as Agniculas (twenty-four *sachas*), rule in Bundi and Kotah. They also occupy parts of the Desert.

The Chaluks held Bhagelkund.

The Chawura or Chaura are in Gujerat. They are neither Lunar nor Solar.

All these are real families, whose pedigrees and pretensions are, in the latter part of their so-called annals, historical. Others, however, are, evidently, either fictitious or false. There is a *kula* called *Hun*, of which all we know is that *Hun* is what it is called.

There is a *kula* called Jit. This, however, is neither more nor less than the denomination of that widely-spread group of tribes which has already been noticed.

Nearest to Sind and the Punjab lies

*Jessulmír*, a true Rajput district, the Rajputs being of the Bhat section. The cultivators, however, are, as is expected, Jut.

*Bikanir*, Jut and Rajput, differs from Jessulmír chiefly in the real or supposed origin of its nobles, the Rajputs of Bikanir being Rahtors from Marwar, who entered the country under a chief named Bika; whence the name Bikanír.

*Bhutnair*, on the northern frontier of Bikanír, is, probably, one of the more especially Turanian parts of India. It lies on the road from the Indus to the Ganges, and, as such, is likely to have been important in the eyes of the invaders. A little to the east stands Hissar, Turk in name. The opponent of the earlier Rajputs was Chugti (Tshagatai) Khan.

In the notices of the wars of the Jessulmír frontier the name Barahi continually occurs. Word for word, this is Brahúi.

The Pokurna Brahmins of these parts are of suspicious purity. The bridegroom buys his bride, Turk fashion. The horse has amongst the Pokurnas undue and un-Indian importance. The bridle is an object of real or feigned respect. So is a pickaxe; for the Pokurna Brahmins are said to have earned their rank by digging the great Pokurna reservoir.

*Marwar*.—From Bikanír Bhutnair—from Marwar Bikanír—this is the order of invasion. Bika was a Rahtor Rajput of Marwar. Like all the countries already mentioned, Marwar is, more or less, Jut. But this it may be without being other than Hindu. It is, however, something more than Jut. It is Maruwár, Marústhan, or Marudesa—not the country of Death (as has been argued), but the country of the Mairs.

In the thirteenth century, *i. e.* A.D. 1212, eighteen years after leaving Canúj (mark the multiples of six), Seoji and Saitram, Rahtor Rajputs, invaded the country of the Gohillas and other Hindu populations, occupants of the valley of the Lúny; occupants, too, of the western skirts of the Aravulli, but not occupants of the range itself. There were Brahmins amongst them, *e. g.* the Palla Brahmins, who invoked the aid of the strangers against certain Mair tribes of the contiguous hills. The help was given. Land was appropriated. The original Brahmins were made uncomfortable in a land once their own. Others, too, besides them, got oppressed and ejected; so that, in the course of time, the district of Marwar became Rajput. Mundore first, and afterwards Jodpur, were founded as capitals.

The most numerous of the inhabitants of Marwar are the Juts. Colonel Tod considered that they formed about five-eighths of the population, the Rajputs forming two-eighths. The chief Brahmins are of the Sanchora class.

*Amber* or *Jeipur*.—Mewar, like Marwar, is Jut and Rajput. Mewar, like Marwar, is, more or less, other than Hindu. The Minas are to Mewar as the Mairs are to Marwar.

Beyond the Chumbul, the pure Rajput character is less prominent. Beyond the Chumbul, there has been contact with either the Gonds or a population akin to them. There has, also, been the Brahminism of the north bank of the Ganges. There has, also, been the subsequent intrusion of the Mahrattas. This excludes the parts about Gwalior (Sindia's territory), and Bundelcund, from the Rajputana of Tod, though, in many respects, they are truly Rajput.

*Bhurtpur* and *Dholpur* are Jaut.

*Bhopal.*—Partly on the drainage of the Ganges and partly on that of the Indus, Bhopal is, more or less, a watershed; and as it is in physical geography so is it in ethnology. It is Hindu and Gond; so much so, that I find the statement that the boundary between Gondwana and Malwa ran through the metropolis; one gate belonging to one district, the other to the other. Some part of the population of the hillier districts is Gond at this moment. The bulk is Hindu; but the Nawaub is a Mahometan of Afghan blood, and so are many of his subjects.

*Rewas* (*Bagelcund*).—That the Rajputs extended thus far is a matter of history. The soil, however, is essentially and originally Gond.

*Malwa* is Rajput in the north, Bhíl and Mahratta on the south.

## CHAPTER XLI.

Populations speaking either Hindí, or a language akin to it.—Delhi, Allahabad, Bahar, Bengal, Orissa.

BIKANÍR and Bhutnair are Rajput. In the parts, however, to the north a change takes place,—a change both in way of ethnology and physical geography. The limits of the Sandy Desert are passed, and the distance between the drainages of the Ganges and the Sutlej decreases. The foot, too, of the Sub-himalayan hills is approached. The watershed, however, between the two great rivers is insignificant.

The political geography is complicated. To the south lies the frontier of the Rajput country; to the north the territory of the Raja of Bisahur; to the north-west the Sikh frontier; to the south-west Delhi; in the centre the small Rajaships of Puttiala, &c.

With the district in question begins Gangetic Hindostan, as opposed to the India of the Desert and the Indus. The distance from Afghanistan, Biluchistan, and the Paropamisus, has increased. Bahar and Bengal are approached.

The district is important in the way of history. It is the point towards which so many of the invaders of India made their way. It was at Paniput where the decisive battle between the Mahrattas and the Patans was fought. It was in the parts about Thanesar that the army of Mahmud of Ghuzni was met by the army of Anungpal of Jeypur.

The name Hissar points to a Turk, the name Hurriana to an Iranian, occupancy.

More than this, the two small, but famous rivers, the Sersúti and the Caggar, find their channels in the sands of Hurriana; the Sersúti being, word for word, the Seraswati, and the Caggar being identified with the Drishadwati; these in their turn being the rivers upon which the Institutes of Menu place the first occupancy of the Brahmins, or Brahmaverta. The sacro-sanctitude of rivers (impossible in the Desert and kept within moderate limits on the water-system of the Indus,) now becomes conspicuous. The Ganges throughout its course is holy. Its feeders to the north are holy also. They are holy in the eyes of both the Hindu and the Bhot. Was it not said, when the Kooch, Bodo, and Dhimal were under notice, that the Pantheon of those semi-pagan populations consisted in the deities of the streams and streamlets of their irriguous countries? And will it not be seen, when we come to Oud, that, at the present moment, both Mahometans and Hindus believe that to swear by a river is to take the most binding of oaths?

That a natural group begins in these parts is true. And it is also true that it is pre-eminently Brahminic. In no part of India do the members of the holy class bear so great a proportion to the rest of the population as in the districts about to be noticed. At the same time no decided line can be drawn. Still less can Rajput blood and Rajput modes of thought be excluded. In many respects Oud is one of the most Rajput countries of India. It is the seat of the great Solar and Lunar dynasties. What the Sersúti district is in Menu, that is Oud in the Ramayana.

Neither must a great amount of Mahometanism be

ignored. Though no portion of the present area be Mahometan after the fashion of Sind, the fact of Delhi having been the metropolis of the Great Mogul is important.

To recapitulate—

In the eyes of the author of the Institutes the parts about the Seraswati were the first occupancies of the Brahmin.

In the eyes of the military critic they are the parts for which a foreign army would, most especially, make its way.

In the eyes of the actual historian they are the localities of the first Turk and Mongol occupancies.

What all this points to is evident. The parts about the Sersúti are the terminus of the high road to India, and beyond the Sersúti the pre-eminently Indian parts of India begin.

The district, however, which first comes under notice is somewhat exceptional.

*Rohilcund.*—The name is Hindu, the area to which it applies Hindu and Afghan. Roh, in the Punjabi dialect, means a hilly district, and denotes the eastern frontier of the Biluch and Patan countries. The western boundary of Dera Ghazi Khan is called Roh. The Rohillas, then, of Rohilcund are Patans or Afghans. The settlement was made in the beginning of the last century. At the present time the majority of the population of Bareilly (and perhaps of the country round) is Mahometan rather than Brahminic.

*Canúj.*—Less important, at the present moment, than Delhi, Agra, Allahabad, and the other great cities of the Doab, Canúj claims attention from its antiquity, and from the name it gives to the chief division of the Brahminical cast. Before the Ghuznevid conquest, it was the metropolis of a large empire, which the Rahtor Rajputs believe to have belonged to their ancestors. The Canúj (Canacubya), Brahmins and the Ujein Rajputs are the noblest divisions of their respective classes.

*Oud.*—Brahminic, Rajput, and Mahometan, Oud, along its northern frontier, is Sub-himalayan, *i. e.* it touches Nepal. Whether there are Bhot elements in Oud will be considered in the sequel.

*Bahar.*—Bahar, or the kingdom of Magada, is the mother-country of the language of the Buddhist scriptures—the Pali. In (say) the seventh century, or the time when the Chinese traveller Hiouen Thsang visited India, Buddhism was, if not the dominant creed, at least, on a par with Brahminism. At the present time, Bahar is one of the least Buddhist parts of Hindostan.

In north Behar Bhot elements present themselves.

In Delhi, in Agra, and in Allahabad, the language is Hindí; being spoken in the greatest purity about Agra. In Bahar it changes character. Still it is Hindí rather than Bengali.

*Bengal.*—The Bengali form of speech belongs to the provinces from which it takes its name, from which it has extended itself both into Asam and Arakan; where it has encroached upon the Burmese and Tibetan. That it is bounded on the north by the Kooch, Bodo, Dhimal, Garo, Aka, Abor, Dofla, and other dialects, has already been suggested in the notice of those tribes. In Sylhet and Tippera the Bengali is similarly intrusive.

From the number of individuals by whom it is spoken, and from its geographical contiguity to the Indo-gangetic peninsula, the Bengali is, perhaps, the most important of Indian languages.

In the district of Midnapúr, it is succeeded by

*The Uriya of Orissa*, into which some of its dialects are believed to graduate. To the back of the Uriya area lie the Khond, to the south the Telinga, districts, the latter of which begins at Ganjam. At Baurwah, however, to the south of that town, the Uriya re-appears. At the same time, it is pronounced Telinga-fashion; in other words, *d* replaces *r*, and U*r*iya and Ge*r*h, become U*d*iya and Ga*d*da.

Of all the forms of speech akin to the Hindí the Uriya is most unimportant. It is spoken but by few individuals. It is but slightly cultivated. The work that has the most pretensions to originality is a poem on the conquest of Conjeveram. The rest of the literature consists of translations.

Of Bengal, Gour was the capital, and it is believed to have been the capital of an important empire; of an empire which spread itself, both towards the north and towards the east: towards the east most especially—Asam being conquered from Bengal. From Bengal, also, must have spread the Brahminism of Munipúr and Arakan.

Of Orissa the political influence has been but slight.

In the way of physical form, it may safely be said that the best features and the stoutest limbs are to be found within the area of the Hindí dialects. This means that the men of Oud, Allahabad, &c., are better-made than those of Bengal. Oud, however, and Allahabad, &c., lie higher up the river. That the muscular power of the Bengalis is but slight is generally, if not universally, stated; indeed, extreme effeminacy, both in the way of their *physique* and *morale*, is attributed to them. In the *turai* this attains its *maximum*. In the *turai*, however, there is a difference of blood. This may or may not exist in the sunderbunds; which are inhabited by but few occupants, and those unhealthy; sufferers from fever, sufferers from ague, sufferers from dysentery, sufferers from cutaneous disorders.

According to Stirling the men and women of Orissa are even inferior to the Bengalis.

Of both we may say, with safety, that the language is Indian. Of neither can we safely say that the blood and language coincide. The lower Ganges but just separates the northernmost members of the Tamul, from the southernmost members of the Bhot, stock. There are the Kols and Sontals in the Rajmahal hills. There are some miserable undersized Sontals in the jungles of Midnapúr. They are tribes denominated impure in Dinajpur, the district in which stood the ancient Gour metropolis. There is a tract in Purnía called Gondwara. In the Mechpara districts of Rungpur there are both Bodos and Garos. Surely, then, there is a mixture of blood in both Bengal and Orissa; and that mixture is three-fold.

In Bengal, too, and in Orissa, the military element (by which I mean that cast which has elsewhere been called Rajput and Kshetriya) notably decreases. There are Brahmins in both districts; and these numerous. There are Sudras; who are numerous also. There are mixed classes and impure classes—numerous as well. But the analogues to the Rajputs are few. The nearest approach to them is in what is called the militia of Orissa; wherein the landowners take the appearance of petty feudalists, and can call into the field a certain number of armed followers. It is, however, specially stated, that the blood of these fighting-men is mixed; some being of Telinga, some of Mahratta, some of Afghan, some of Khond origin.

| English. | Bengali. | Asam. | Uriya. |
| --- | --- | --- | --- |
| *Man* | manushya | manuh | minipo |
| *Tooth* | danta | dant | danto |
| *Head* | mastak | mur | motha |
| *Hair* | kesh | —— | balo |
| —— | chul | suli | —— |
| *Mouth* | mukh | mukh | muho |
| *Eye* | chhakhyuh | soku | akhi |
| *Ear* | karna | kan | kan |
| *Hand* | hát | hát | hato |
| *Foot* | had | bhori | goro |
| *Blood* | rakta | tez | rokto |
| *Day* | din | din | dino |
| *Night* | ratri | rati | rate |
| *Sun* | surjya | beli | surjiyo |
| *Moon* | chandra | jun | chando |
| *Star* | tara | tora | tora |
| *Fire* | agni | jui | nina |
| *Water* | pani | pani | pani |
| *Stone* | prastan | hil | pothoro |
| *Tree* | gachh | gosh | gochcho. |

*Bundelcund* and *Sindia's country.*—Of the districts to the south of the Ganges, between the proper Rajput country on the west, Orissa and Bengal on the east, and Gondwana on the south, I say but little. Sindia's country and Bundelcund are the most important of them. Their ethnological character is mixed; the elements being what we expect from their geographical relations. To the north lie the southern portions of the Doab, Allahabad, and Bahar; to the south and east decided Gond districts; to the west a region as decidedly Rajput Such being the case, it is safe to say thus much—that

1. The parts to the west of the Chumbul are chiefly Rajput with superinduced Mahratta elements;

2. The parts to the east of the Soane are chiefly Kol;

3. The actual valley of the Ganges is in the same category with the districts on the opposite side;

4. The Gondwana and Mahratta frontiers are, more or less, Mahratta and Gond.

The language is an outlying form ot the Hindí: the creed Brahminic. The Jains, however, begin to show themselves; increasing in numbers and importance as we move towards the south and south-west; being numerous in Central India, numerous in the Mahratta countries, and pre-eminently numerous in the area of the Tulava language on the Mahratta and Canarese frontiers.

## CHAPTER XLII.

Populations whose language is either Hindí or akin to it.—The Sub-himalayans.

This division is, by no means, wholly natural. It contains the northern members of the two last sections. A Punjabi, on the edge of Tibet, is still, in most respects, a Punjabi. A Bengali on the frontier of Butan is, in most respects, still a Bengali. We cannot even say that the physical conditions of its area are uniform. That the range of the Himalaya is a mountain-range is true; but it is not true that the soil and climate of its slope are the same throughout. The high levels at the head-waters of the five rivers are one thing. The jungles of the parts above the lower Ganges are another.

The real character of the class lies in the nature of its ethnological frontier. From Cashmír to Upper Asam the populations with which the Hindu comes in juxtaposition, are Tibetan, Bhot, or Burmese. The phenomena of the line of contact justify the formation of the present class; a class which for the purposes of investigation is, to say the least of it, eminently convenient.

The general history of the populations under notice is, for the western portion of their area at least, just what we expect, *à priori*, from the face of the country. The face of the country is like that of Little Tibet—so many valleys—so many lords of the valley. We begin with a mass of petty Rajaships. By conquest or intermarriage they become confluent, and two or three smaller form one larger one. Eventually they get absorbed by the powers of their neighbourhood.

In the way, Kistewar, Hanur, &c., between Cashmír and the Sutlej, belong to Gulab Sing's dominion; whilst Gurwhal is divided between Great Britain and the Raja of Bisihur. Kumaon is wholly British; the parts to the east of Kumaon, Nepalese.

As a general rule, the blood of the Rajas and their descendants is either actually Rajput, or believed to be so. The creed, too, is, as a general rule, Brahminic. There is, however, something Sikh in the western and something Buddhist in the eastern districts.

Where both the physical conformation and the language are Bhot, we have, of course, an actual Tibetan or Nepalese. Where one only of these characteristics occurs, we have a possible one. Where, both being absent, we have Tibetan customs, Tibetan superstitions, or Tibetan names of places, we have the elements of an interesting investigation. That these *do* occur is a fact. I am unable, however, to give the details. Captain Cunningham finds Tibetan names beyond the limit of the existing Tibetan localities. Most writers have noticed instances of the Tibetan practice of polyandria in Kistewar, Sirmor, &c.

From Cashmír to the Sutlej, the frontier with which the Hindu area comes in contact is Ladaki—*i. e.* it is Ladakh, rather than Tibet proper, which overlies the hill-country belonging to Gholab Sing.

The Rajaship of Bisihur touches Kunawer and Hungrung.

Kumaon (which is British), and the forty-six Rajaships (which are Nepalese), underlie Tibet proper.

In eastern Nepal, in Sikkim, and in the parts beyond, lie,

between the Hindus and the Tibetans, an intermediate series of minor populations, Magar, Gurung, and the like. It is not necessary to give the details and order of these. It has been done already.

From Kumaon to Nepal proper, the language (a variety of the Hindí) is called *Khas*. In Nepal proper it is called *Parbatiya* or *Purbutti*, *i. e.* the *Highland* form of speech.

*Kumaon.*—Kumaon, being British, is known, in detail, through an elaborate report by Traill. In the northern districts the people are strong, but short, stout-built, and fair-skinned. In the south the colour is darker, the stature greater, the form more spare. In the intermediate districts the type is also intermediate.

Spirits, as a stimulus, are commoner in Gurwhal than in Kumaon. In both provinces tobacco is smoked by all but the high-class Brahmins, who substitute for it the inspissated juice of the hemp.

The Hinduism of Kumaon is of that imperfect kind, which leaves room for innumerable vestiges of the original paganism to show themselves. Every village has its own especial deity, and, humbler than the Hindu temples (but not less venerated) their shrines are found over the whole country. The region, too, of spirits is both wide and populous. The individual who has died a violent death may revisit the earth as a *Bhút*, to haunt his posterity through many generations, and to be appeased by sacrifices and offerings. The bachelor who, without getting married, dies at an advanced age, becomes a will-of the-wisp, or *Tola*, whose society is shunned even by his brother spirits; for which reason he is only seen in lone places. The ghosts of men killed in hunting haunt the forests in which their deaths occurred, and these are *Airi*. To hear the voice of an Airi (and it may be heard hallooing to its dogs) is to become obnoxious to some future misfortune. The *Masan* are the ghosts of young children, buried instead of being burnt. The Masán haunt villages in the shape of wild animals. The Acheri are the ghosts of young children also; but of females. They it is who love the lonely mountain-top, better than the inhabited village—but only during the daytime. At dusk they descend to hold revel. To meet with a train of Acheri is death. Neither is it safe to cross the spots where the revels are usually held, even in the daytime, and when they are not there. The intruder may get molested; especially if she be a female, or wear any red in her dress; for red is the colour that the Acheri most especially dislike. Numerous optical phenomena that present themselves under certain atmospheric conditions, in mountainous countries, are attributed to the Acheri.

The village-gods are, in name at least, Hindu. Some of these are obnoxious to men, some to women, some to children, some to cattle. Ruma, one of them, moves from place to place riding on a rock, never molesting men, but by no means sparing females. Should he take a fancy to one her fate is fixed. She will be haunted by him in her dreams, pine and die.

The *Bogsa* is a sorcerer, endued with the property of becoming a wild beast at will. Lycanthropia, then, or its analogue, is a Kumaon superstition; as is the belief in the evil eye.

Kumaon, though now British, is an acquisition from Nepal; so that, in reference to its political history, it must be looked upon as a portion of the

*Nepalese Empire.*—This falls into two extremely natural divisions; a western and an eastern. The former, originally containing Kumaon, now contains what may be called the districts of the forty-six Rajaships.

I speak of forty-six Rajaships. The reader, however, will find more than forty-six names. This is because the exact details of the nomenclature are not known. The number, however, is forty-six.

I shall also speak of these forty-six petty Rajaships being divided into two primary groups; one containing twenty-two, the other twenty-four, districts. Here, however, as before, there will be some unimportant uncertainties as to the distribution. The majority will belong decidedly and undoubtedly to one of the two divisions. For the parts, however, where they meet there will be a few doubtful, or equivocal, names.

The twenty-two will be called, as they are in many maps, the Baisi; the twenty-four, the Chaubisi, Rajas.

Of the two divisions, the Baisi is more western. It begins when we leave Kumaon for Nepal. The Chaubisi group extends from the eastern frontier of the Baisi to the parts about Kathmandu, or Nepal proper; Nepal in the limited sense of the term; Nepal, the occupancy of the Newar.

The list is as follows:—the Rajaships being taken in their order from west to east. Those at the beginning of the list are most undoubtedly Baisi, those at the end most undoubtedly Chaubisi. The doubtful ones are those of the middle.

*Baisi and Chaubisi Rajaships.*

| | | |
|---|---|---|
| 1. Yumila | 8. Bangpai | 15. Palabang |
| 2. Acham | 9. Rughun | 16. Khungri |
| 3. Duti | 10. Muiskot | 17. Bingri |
| 4. Cham | 11. Satatala | 18. Piutana |
| 5. Dipal | 12. Malaneta | 19. Gajal |
| 6. Chhinachin | 13. Dang | 20. Jahari |
| 7. Jajarkot | 14. Salyana | 21. Bilaspur |

| | | |
|---|---|---|
| 22. Roalpa | 31. Argha | 41. Dhor |
| 23. Malebum | 32. Kachi | 42. Gajarkot |
| 24. Kalagong Ghurikot | 33. Gulmi | 43. Rising |
| | 34. Palpa | 44. Ghiring |
| 25. Balihang | 35. Garahang | 45. Tanahung |
| 26. Gutum | 36. Poin | 46. Lamjun |
| 27. Dharma | 37. Satahung | 47. Tarki |
| 28. Galkot | 38. Birkot | 48. Musikot |
| 29. Isma | 39. Nayakot | 49. Gorka. |
| 30. Durkot | 40. Kaski | |

Of these the most important are, Malebum, Yumila, and Gorka. Malebum belongs to the debateable land between the two divisions. The Raja of Yumila was a sort of Kaiser, or emperor, to the rest. They all, or nearly all, acknowledged his supremacy. They took from him the *tika*, or mark of authority. They allowed him to interfere in their private quarrels when the balance of power was endangered. On the other hand, they yielded as much actual obedience as their inclinations, regulated by their power of resistance, prompted. Still, the Raja of Yumila was the Raja paramount. Besides admitting the supremacy of a head, the chiefs formed amongst themselves subordinate confederations. Thus; Lamjun marched with Tanahung and Kaski; Tanahung being followed by Dhor, and Kaski by Satahung. Birkot, in like manner, headed Garahang, Poin, and Nayakot. And so acted others towards others. There was a league called Athabhai, or the eight, another called Satbhai, or the seven, brothers. The brotherhood, in these cases, might be real or imaginary.

In regard to its constituent population, the Rajaship of Yumila is the most Bhot, about one-fourth being Hindu, and three-fourths Tibetan.

Yumila, so far as it is other than Hindu, seems to be, to a great extent, Tibetan.

Malebum, so far as it is other than Hindu, seems to be, to a great extent, Gurung.

In Malebum, however, we find the name Jareya; it being believed that an impure chief of that name had once great power in Malebum. His daughter married a Gautamiya (Buddhist) Brahmin, by whom she had twenty-two sons, *i. e.* the twenty-two Rajas of the Baisi group.

The term Jareya points to Rajasthan; indeed, Rajput blood (either real or pretended) still continues to be the rule.

In the ordinary maps Malebum is the most conspicuous name for these parts. It is, in reality, the name of the State, which, until the rise of the Gorka dynasty, was the head of the forty-six Rajaships.

As Malebum and Yumila rose at the expense of the petty States around them, Gorkha rose at the expense of Malebum and Yumila.

Gorkha, so far as it was other than Hindu, seems to have been chiefly Magar. The details of its history, as a sovereign dynasty, are given by both Hamilton and Kirkpatrick.

Of the Hindus of Nepal, the blood seems to be, for the most part, either Rajput or Brahminic. The descendants of a Brahmin father and a native mother take high rank in Nepal. Lower than their fathers, higher than their mothers, they take the rank of Kshetriya; bear the title of the father and wear the thread.

The Khas fall into divisions, being Thâpa, Bishnyat, Bhandari, Karki, Khânkâ, Adhikari, Bisht, Kunwar, Baníah, and the like. They fall, too, into sub-divisions, *e. g.* the

| | |
|---|---|
| Bagyal | Gagliya |
| Takuryal | Suyal |
| Palami | Maharaji |
| Laminchanya | Khulal |
| Powar | Sunyal |
| Ghimirya | Khapotari |
| Gudar | Parajuli |

Deoia

are members of the Thâpa.

Akin to the Khas, yet differing in the real or supposed details of their origin (inasmuch as their fathers were Kshetriyas rather than Brahmins, and their mothers Hindu rather than Nepalese), the Ekthariah fall into the

| | |
|---|---|
| Burathoki | Bohara |
| Raya | Chiloti |
| Ravat | Dangi |
| Katwal | Raimarjhi |
| Khati | Bhukhandi |
| Maghati | Bhusal |
| Chohan | Khutal |
| Boghati | Dikshit |
| Khatil | Pandit |
| Bavan | Parsai |
| Mahat | Chokhal |
| Barwal | Chohara |

Durrah

sections; differing only in the details of their origin from the Thakuri, whose blood is royal, their ancestors having been the dynasts of some petty principality. The divisions of the Thakuri, are

| | |
|---|---|
| Sahi | Sena |
| Malla | Singh |

| | |
|---|---|
| Maun | Hamal |
| Chohan | Ruchal |
| Chand | Jīva |

Rakshya.

These details will not have been superfluous if we allow them to stand as a sample of the division and subdivision, which both the soil and the social system undergo in countries like Nepal—where the systems of both cast and tribe meet, and where the physical geography gives us hill and valleys.

*Populations of doubtful or equivocal position.*—The difficulties of determining the exact details of the Indian and Bhot (or Nepalese) frontier have already suggested themselves. Sometimes there is the loss of some notable characteristic, such as creed or language. Sometimes there is an actual intermixture of blood. Physical form, our best guide, is by no means, infallible. A Bhot from the higher Himalayas is, undoubtedly, a different being from a Rajput or Brahmin. But who will say that a Bhot from the jungles or the *turai* is the same, in skin and feature, as his congener from the snow-levels, or that he is so very different from the Kol, or Khond? Our best authority, on these matters, Mr. Hodgson—zoologist and physiologist, as well as philologue—by no means commits himself to any very trenchant lines of demarcation; indeed, he has, on one occasion, shown great and laudable candour in admitting that a certain language belonged to the Bhot group, whereas the physical conformation of the men who spoke it had been previously described by him as Tamul.

Beginning at the Sutlej, and moving eastwards, we find the following populations belonging to the class under notice. To each and all of them the following questions apply—Are they in the same category with the lower class Hindus? Or are they in the same category with the Che-pang, Dhimal, and Bodo tribes? Or are they a *tertium quid?*

*Chumars.*—These have already been noticed. They occupy parts of Kunawer; and (Bhot fashion) practise polyandria.

*Domangs.*—In the same districts as the Chumars. Word for word, Domang is

*Dom.*—The Doms of Kumaon have already been noticed. So have the

*Rawat* of the same country.

*The Tharu.*—These are the occupants of the *turai*, or belt of forest at the foot of the Himalayas. The Tharu first show themselves in Oud, and extend far eastwards.

In the western half of Nepal, and on the alluvia of the rivers which form the Gunduk, lie

1. The Denwar
2. — Durri
3. The Kumhal
4. — Manjhi
5. The Bramho.

These have been described by Mr. Hodgson as dark-skinned, light-limbed, oval-faced, and high-featured men; more like the Khonds than the Tibetans or Nepalese. They consider themselves Hindus; and belong chiefly to the Magar frontier.

Further to the east, where the Nepalese populations are Murmi, Limbu, and Kirata, and where the Hindus are the Hindus of north Bahar, lie (along with certain Tharus, whom they resemble) the

*Gangai*, chiefly in Morang; the

*Bhawar*, an impure tribe, once dominant; the

*Batar*, and the

*Aniwar*, once extended far beyond the frontier of Bahar. The

Rajbansi Kooch have already been noticed. They are succeeded by the Dhimal, Bodo, and Gharo; congeners of whom must originally have extended to the Ganges, or even beyond it. It is with Bengalis, on one side, and the Lepchas and Lhopa, on the other, that these most especially come in contact.

That the whole of Asam, even where the language is Bengali, and the creed Brahminic, is Bhot or Burmese in blood, has already been stated.

The heterogeneous character of the tribe and cast names of Nepal requires a special analysis. The lists given above are only a few out of many. What is general, what special; what natural, what artificial, should be distinguished.

## CHAPTER XLIII.

### The Mahrattas.

THE present section is pre-eminently a natural one; differing, in many significant respects, from all the preceding. In the first place, the Mahrattas are the most southern members of the group to which they belong. In the next, they belong to a broken, if not a mountainous, country. Deserts like those of Bikanir, alluvia like those of the Gangetic districts, find no place within the Mahratta area. At the same time, none of its levels are so high as the mountain-basin of Cashmír.

Again, the Mahratta country faces the sea; the sea that connects India with Persia, Arabia, Africa, and Europe. It will, therefore, not surprise us if we find African and Mahratta elements in contact.

The main *differentiæ*, however, lie in the relations of the Mahrattas to the populations whose language is akin to the Tamul. Up to the present time, the northernmost members of this class appear as intruders upon the proper Hindu areas. That they are not this we reasonably infer; the inference being that the intrusion has been on the other side. It was the Bhíls and Kols who were the aborigines, the Rajputs and their congeners who were the strangers. At the same time, as the map now stands, the Kol and Bhíl districts take the appearance of exceptional prolongations from the south. Their occupancies indent the Hindu and Gujerathi frontiers. They ly, however, indent them.

Now, instead of merely indenting the Mahratta districts, the aboriginal localities surround them. There are both Bhíls and Kols to the north of the northernmost Mahrattas. There are Kols in Gujerat, and there are Bhíls in Rajputana. There were Bhíls, indeed, on the very edge of the valley of the Indus. That in some cases the Mahratta language comes in direct contact with both the Hindí and the Gujerathi, is true. But it is also true that, as a general rule, its northern frontier is Bhíl and Kol, its eastern, Gond and Telinga, its southern, Tulava and Canarese.

The physical form of a Mahratta is most usually contrasted with that of the Brahmin and the Rajput; by the side of which it shows to disadvantage. As a general rule, writes Elphinstone, the lowest of the Rajputs wear an air of dignity. As a general rule, the highest of the Mahrattas comports himself meanly. The latter, however, are hardy and active, and, if somewhat undersized, well-proportioned. Their skins are dark, and their features irregular. The best commentary, however, upon their physical and moral constitution is their history.

They are Sudras (so-called) rather than either Kshetriyas or Brahmins. The fact of their being so has, perhaps, disparaged their personal appearance. They should be compared, not with the Rajputs and Brahmins, but with the lower casts in general of the rest of India.

Their language is, undoubtedly, in the same category with the Hindí, whatever that may be, *i. e.* its affinities are with the Gujerathi and Bengali, rather than with the Tamul and Telinga. It is, however, a somewhat outlying member of the class; so much so, that, in the hands of those writers who deny the Sanskrit origin of the group in question, the Mahratta has been the chief instrument of criticism. "The others are what the Mahratta is; and the Mahratta is more Tamul than Sanskrit." Such is the train of reasoning.

The alphabet is a derivation from the Devanagari, which it closely resembles. It does this because it has been but recently adopted. The literature it embodies is unimportant.

The historical area of the Mahrattas is far wider than the ethnological. Its extension, however, is recent. It began in the reigns of Shah Jehan and Aurungzeb, being founded by Sivaji, whose blood seems to have been mixed, *i. e.* Rajput as well as Mahratta. He was the son of Shahji, who was the son of Maloji, who was the son of Bapji, who was the husband of a lady of the very respectable Mahratta family of the Bhonslay. Maloji entered the service of a chief who, though, perhaps, in fact a simple Mahratta, had fair pretensions to some Rajput blood. At any rate, he bore himself as a man who is, at once, proud and practical. When Shahji, a child, was presented to him, his own daughter (a child also) was also in his presence. "What a fine couple they would make," was his observation—heard by Maloji, and hoarded-up in the treasure-house of his memory until some years had passed, and a public occasion brought him before his chief, and gave him an opportunity of reminding him of what he called a betrothal of his (the chief's) daughter to his (Shahji's) son. As Shahji had risen in the world, his version of the story was admitted, the marriage was effected, and Sivaji, the most prominent hero of all India, was the offspring. If the details of his career are withheld from the reader, it is not because they are foreign to ethnology. The biography of the representative men of the ruder portions of mankind is pre-eminently an ethnological subject. The life, however, of Sivaji belongs to Indian history in general. In the way, however, of extending the political power of his nation, his father did a little before him. He carried it southwards. In the service of, and (perhaps) second in command to, the Raja of Bejapúr, he received a grant of land and power in the Carnatic. This brought him to the parts about Madras, where the Polygar of Mudkul was at war with the Raja of Tanjore. Shahji joined the former, helping him to conquer his opponent; quarrelled with him about the spoils; defeated him; so that the descendants of Shahji were Rajas of Tanjore when that district became a British dependency. Sivaji himself turned his sword northwards. At first the captain of an organized body of banditti, then the zemindar of Punah, then a self-imposed potentate to the districts of his immediate neighbourhood, he is invited by Aurungzeb to join him in the war against his brothers. He plays his own game, however, and refuses to connect his fortunes with those of the imperial bigot; of whom, however, it was his future fate to hear and see more than enough. He plays his own game; with the Raja of Bejapúr as his first opponent. From him he wins more than one valuable fortress. He, then, takes the important towns of Kalian and Surat, extending his power to the sea. An Indian navy is first heard of in the days of Sivaji. It is, however, employed against him. We shall notice it in the sequel, when the sub-African districts of the western coast of India come under notice; when the Sidis of Abyssinian blood appear as elements of the heterogeneous population of Hindostan. The eventful life, however, of Sivaji draws towards its close, and he dies master of the whole of the Konkan, and of a large block of territory in the interior. This he leaves in a strong position, and in an aggressive attitude; fresh and full of vigour, and (as such) strongly contrasted with the decrepit empire of the Moguls. It was eminently a Hindu rather than a Mahometan organization.

The Mogul empire is breaking up. It has strength enough to reduce the kingdoms of Bejapúr and Hyderabad; but not strength enough to defend them against the Mahrattas. Neither are the southern districts of the Rajput country free from the Mahratta inroads. Berar on the Gond, and Kandeish on the Bhíl country, are plundered. Meanwhile, the districts of Aurungabad, Beder, and parts of Berar, are consolidated by the Nizam-ud-Mulk into a kingdom destined to retain the title of the founder, but not destined to be held by his successors. The dominion of the Nizam will become Mahratta. The founder, however, of the name was a Turk, Kulich Khan, son of Ghazi-ud-Khan. The Turks, who had been introduced into India by the conquest of Baber, were simply Moguls. The Turks who, from time to time, were introduced as mercenaries, were distinguished as Turani (or Turanian) Moguls. Kulich Khan was the chief of the Turani Moguls of the Dekkan. He effects the separation of the Nizam districts from the empire. He fails to keep them free from the Mahrattas, who, about the same time, conquer Gujerat.

A.D. 1732. The empire grows weaker and weaker. Delhi is sacked by Kuli-Khan.

A.D. 1745-47. A few years later the power of the Rohilla Afghans is established in the immediate neighbourhood of the capital, and Rohilcund becomes the seat of disturbance and the source of danger. Indeed, the Afghan aggressions have a double origin, Rohilcund and Afghanistan itself. The Durani dynasty is rising in power; and the two representatives of the Patan name unite in hostility to the Moguls. The weakest of the successors of Akbar calls in the treacherous aid of the Mahrattas, who now find their way to the parts beyond the Ganges, to Allahabad, to Delhi, to Oud. They make common cause with the Rohillas: quarrel with them; make common cause again. Still they are essentially antagonistic to the Duranis. The latter win the great battle of Paniput; with which ends the history of the Mogul India. A.D. 1760.

The area of the Mahratta language extends along the coast from the Damaun Gunga river to Goa—there or thereabouts. In the interior, however, it is spoken somewhat further to the north—indenting the Gujerat area, upon which it seems to have encroached. Eastward it extends into Hyderabad and Berar, where it comes in contact with the Gond and Telinga. Southward it is bounded by the Tulava and Canarese.

The Mahratta blood must be, to a great extent, Bhíl.

The Mahratta creed is, to a great extent, Jain.

The foreign settlements on the Mahratta area are numerous. These are chiefly

*Parsi*, as in Gujerat.

*African*, as in Cambay and Jinjira.

The Africans of these parts agreeing with those of Sind, in being called Sidi,* are, in other respects, very different. They are not only free but dominant. In the time of Aurungzeb, the admiral of the fleet was a Sidi.

*Jewish.*—In Kolaba.

*Portugueze*, chiefly in Sawuntwara, and the parts about Goa.

In the way of politics, the Mahratta area is very variously distributed. It contains several petty (very petty) independent States. The greater part of Portugueze India is Mahratta.

* Also Hubshesh.

The Guicowar, Sindia, and Holcar territories, are the same.

Specimen of the language.

| English. | Marathi. | Gujerathi. | Hindostani. |
|---|---|---|---|
| *Man (homo)* | manúsh | jana | ādmi |
| —— *(vir)* | purush | mānus | mard |
| *Woman* | baiko | bāyadī | randī |
| *Head* | doksheh | māthum | sir |
| *Hair* | kes | nimālo | bāl |
| *Eye* | doleh | ānkh | ānkh |
| *Ear* | kan | kān | kān |
| *Nose* | nakh | nāk | nak |
| *Mouth* | t'hond | mohodum | munh |
| *Tongue* | jib | jubh | jībh |
| *Tooth* | dant | dānt | dānt |
| *Hand* | hat | hāth | hāth |
| *Foot* | paie | pag | pānw |
| *Sun* | suria | sūraj | sūraj |
| *Moon* | tshundr | chānd | chānd |
| *Star* | tshandaní | tāro | tārā |
| *Day* | vuas | din | din |
| *Night* | ratr | rāt | rāt |
| *Fire* | vistú | āg | āg |
| *Water* | panni | pānī | pānī |
| *Tree* | dzad | jhāda | per |
| —— | bruksh | —— | —— |
| *Stone* | duggud | patthar | patthar. |

The numerals, like those of the Bengali, Uriya, &c., are Hindí.

# CHAPTER XLIV.

The populations whose language is akin to the Tamul.—The Rajmahali mountaineers.—The Kols.—The Khonds.—The Sours.

It has already been stated that the Tamul populations and their congeners have been called the natives of *southern* India. It has also been suggested that this term is inaccurate. That the parts about Cape Comorin are Tamul is true; and true it is that the Dekkan, or southern half of India, is what may be called Tamiliform. But it is by no means true that these districts constitute the whole of the Tamul area. This extends not only far beyond them, but far beyond them *to the north.* At one point it actually touches the Ganges, and that *at the present time*, and in an unequivocal manner. More than this, it all but touches the southern limit of the Bhot and Burmese areas—a fact to which attention has already been directed. The occupants of

*The Rajmahal hills*, on the southern bank of the Ganges, in the parts about Bogilpur, have long been known as a population whose language and manners differ from that of the ordinary Hindu of the districts around. In the Asia Polyglotta, a specimen of their dialect stands by itself, isolated on all sides, *i. e.* with no Hindu, no Tamul, no Tibetan affinities—the Garo being isolated also. No wonder. When the Asia Polyglotta was written, the Tamul class was limited to the south of India, the Khond, Gond, and Kol forms of speech being wholly, or all but, unknown.

The extent to which it agrees with these may be inferred from the following comparison of the pronouns.

| English. | Rájmahal. | Tamul, &c. |
|---|---|---|
| *I* | en | nân, en |
| *Thou* | nin | nin |
| *He, she, it* | ath | âta |
| *We* | nam | nâm |
| —— | om | ôm |
| *Ye* | nina | nim |
| *They* | awar | avar |
| *This* | îh | î |
| *That* | âh | â |
| *Here* | ino | inge |
| *There* | âno | ange. |

For a long time the Rajmahali mountaineers were the terror of the neighbouring districts. They robbed, they levied blackmail. A strong bamboo bow with a poisoned arrow was their weapon. With this they made themselves formidable to the Mahometan powers, troublesome to the Company. With this they defended their dense jungles, or rather the jungles defended them. Every arrow was unseen, certain, fatal. The Company failed in their measures of coercion, as the Mahometans had failed before them.

Kindness was then tried, and it was successful. The epitaph of Cleveland, bearing date 1784, records that "without bloodshed or the terrors of authority, employing only the means of conciliation, confidence, and benevolence, he attempted and accomplished the entire subjection of the lawless and savage inhabitants of the jungleterry of Rájamahal, who had long infested the neighbouring lands by their predatory incursions, inspired them with a taste for the arts of civilized life, and attached them to the British Government by conquest over their minds, the most permanent, as the most rational, mode of dominion." The tomb on which it is inscribed was erected at Bhagulpur by order of the Governor-General and Council of Bengal.

The skin of the Rajmahalis is dark, their face broad, their eyes small, their lips thicker than those of the men of the plains. That features of this kind suggest a variety of illustrations is what we expect *à priori*. "The Rajmahali physiognomy is Mongol," writes one. "The Rajmahali physiognomy is African," writes another.

The creed is, more or less, Hindu; its Hinduism being of an imperfect and degenerate character. *Bedo* is one of its gods; word for word, the *Batho* of the Bodos; word for word, the *Potteang* of the Kukis; word for word, *Buddha*. Their priesthood, like that of the Bodos, consists of Demauns and Dewassis; men whose functions have been already explained.

The nearest congeners to the Rajmahali mountaineers are the speakers of

*The Uraon* dialects, whose occupancy is the hilly country to the south and south-east. Word for word, *Uraon* seems to be *Uriya*.

| English. | Uraon. | Rajmahali. |
|---|---|---|
| *Man* | alla | male |
| *Head* | kuk | kupe |
| *Hair* | chutti | tali |
| *Ear* | khebda | khetway |
| *Eye* | khan | khane |
| *Blood* | khens | kesu |
| *Bone* | khochal | kochal |
| *Foot* | dappe | kev |
| *Hand* | khekhah | sesu |
| *Sun* | dharmi | ber |
| *Moon* | chando | bilpe |
| *Star* | binka | bindeke |
| *Fire* | chek | chiche |
| *Water* | um | am. |

*The Kols.*—That Kol is a word which is applied by the

Hindus to certain populations distinguished from themselves, and that it is also a term of general application, has already been stated ; the Kols of Gujerat having been brought under notice when the ruder tribes of western India commanded our attention. Word for word, the two names are identical. Between the eastern Kols of Monghir, Ramgurh, Chuta Nagpúr, Gangpur, Sirgujah, and Sumbhulpúr and the Uraon and Rajmahalis the chief difference seems to be that of dialect.

The divisions and subdivisions of the Kol name are numerous.

*The Sontals*, indigenous to Chuta Nagpur and the parts about Palamow, have, since the beginning of the present century, intruded themselves into some of the Rajmahali occupancies, which now contain two separate populations, allied to each other, though speaking languages which are said to be mutually unintelligible. It was with these northern and intrusive Kols that the recent disturbances arose. Like Kol, the name Sontal is found in western, as well as eastern, India. There was a Sontalpúr in Gujerat.

According to the Sontal mythology, the first two mortals bore the names of Pilchu-hanam and Pilchu-brudhi, one being a male, the other a female; being also brother and sister to each other, and the children of a duck's egg. A deity named Lita, or Marang Buru, brought them together as man and wife. In Orissa, this Lita, or Marang Buru, is very specially worshipped, and that both privately, as a domestic deity, and in public, by means of feasts and festivals. Of this god there is a stone image at Sikar-ghat, a place of resort and ceremony. It stands on one of the feeders of the Ganges, which receives in its waters, twice a year, a bone of some deceased Sontal, thrown in by one of the surviving relations, who makes a pilgrimage to the spot for the purpose of doing so. Other ceremonies accompany this act—lustral, or purificational, in character.

Maniko is the elder brother of Marang Buru, and is invoked once a year by the Naikis (mark the word) or priests, who sacrifice to him fowls—Bodo and Dhimal fashion. His sister's name is Jaherera.

Connected with every Sontal village is a grove called Jaher, in which the Manjhi-hanam, or the founder of the village, is periodically worshipped.

The domestic gods are called Odah-Bonga. Bonga means deity. Abge Bonga is the name of a god who is worshipped twice a year. The offerings to him consist of rams, he-goats, and red cocks, upon which all the males (but none of the females) regale themselves—burning the leavings.

Rankini, a bloody-minded female, is said to be occasionally propitiated by human sacrifices.

The Sontals swear by the skin or by the head of the tiger. They swear also by their gods and by the lives of their children.

*The Ho.*—The Ho are the best known of all the Kols; not, however, because they have been visited by the greatest number of Europeans, but because they have been made the subject of a valuable monograph by Lieutenant Tickell in the Journal of the Asiatic Society of Bengal.* The parts about Singbhúm are their locality.

The Ho are locomotive agriculturists; *i. e.* they sow the soil, and work it with the hoe; but are unskilled in the art of manuring. Hence, the lands on which they settle soon become exhausted, and fresh clearings are required. Their villages, too, are small, though the houses of which they consist are well-built. The walls are of

* Vol. ix. part ii.

mud, but strong and solid. The roofs are of thatch, well laid on. The veranda is supported by wooden pillars, rudely carved. The residence of the family consists of three rooms, one for eating, one for sleeping, one for stores. The outhouses are at a little distance; some for pigs, some for poultry, some for servants.

The Ho dress but lightly, some of them wearing next to nothing. The women work. The men hunt—or rather hawk; for falconry is both their business and their pastime. The bow is the chief weapon.

A Ho bridegroom buys his bride; or rather, his father buys her for him, the price being so many head of cattle. Whether, however, the match is to take place at all depends, to an inordinate extent, upon the omens that the parties concerned meet in their way from house to house. Should anything unlucky present itself, a sacrifice of fowls is made, and prayers put up to Singbonga (of whom more will be said hereafter), to the effect that, if the parties still wish to be united, better omens may attend their next negotiation. After looking over Captain Tickell's list of evil auguries, I wonder that Ho marriages ever take place. It contains almost everything that either runs or flies. If a vulture, crow, magpie, oriole, woodpecker, jackall, hare, bee, snake, &c., pass behind the negotiator, there will be a death. If a certain kind of ichneumon drag a certain kind of spider across the road, the bride will be dragged away by a tiger the first time she goes out for wood or water. If a hawk seize a bird, the same. If a certain kind of vulture fly singly, or in front of its flock, death to one of the four parents—death to the bride's parent if the village of the bride, to the bridegroom's if his village, be the nearest—death to a father if the bird be a male, to the mother if a female. If the great wood-hawk hover overhead, death to both mother and son at childbirth. Should a branch fall from a tree, death. The dung-beetle rolling dung portends hard work and little reward. Such are a few of the evil omens. There are some good ones to set against them. Upon the whole, however, the signs of bad luck preponderate. That the marriages are attended by feasts is what we expect *à priori*. There are feasts and ceremonies as well. There are ceremonies, too, at the birth of children, at the naming of them, at burials. There are ceremonies in abundance; but of a definite recognized priesthood very little. The following is a Ho dirge:—

> We never scolded, never wronged you;
> Come to us back;
> We ever loved and cherished you, and have lived long together
> Under the same roof;
> Desert it not now!
> The rainy nights, and the cold blowing days, are coming on;
> Do not wander here.
> Do not stand by the burnt ashes; come to us again!
> You cannot find shelter under the peepul when the rain comes down.
> The saul will not shield you from the cold bitter wind.
> Come to your home!
> It is swept for you, and clean; and we are there who loved you ever;
> And there is rice put for you; and water;
> Come home, come home, come to us again!

Dead bodies are interred, and gravestones placed over them. This, however, is insufficient to keep down the spirits, which are believed to walk about during the day, and to keep within-doors at night. A certain spot, upon which is placed an offering, is kept clean for them. According to the Ho mythology—

> Ote Boram and Sirma Thakoor, *i. e.* Sing Bonga, or God, were self-created. Sing Bonga is the sun. After them the moon was self-created.
>
> Ote Boram and Sirma Thakoor then made the earth; after that they clothed it with grass, trees, rocks, water; they then made cattle, which were first born in Bogo Bochee; after them all wild animals. They then made a little boy and a little girl, at the bottom of an immense

ravine, and as they had no houses to live in, the gods told them to inhabit a huge crab's cave (Katkomoá). They grew adult, and Sing Bonga came to see them every day, and called them his grandchildren; but at length seeing no hopes of any progeny, from their extreme simplicity, he taught them the art of making Eely (rice beer), the use of which caused those sensations, which were in due time the means of peopling the world.

After the creation of man, Sing Bonga, or the sun, married Chandoo Omol, or the moon, from whence sprung four sons and numerous daughters. Now the four sons kept with their father, and the daughters lived with their mother, and as the sun rose every day, with his four hot, fiery sons in addition, the whole world began to burn; and all the animals and man perishing with heat, entreated the moon to save them: so the moon resolved within herself to destroy the sun's sons, and went, and accosting the father, said, "Our children do much harm to the world, and will soon destroy your labour. I am determined to eat mine; do you also devour yours." The sun promised he would follow the moon's example; and so when she hid all her daughters, and came and told him she had devoured them, he destroyed and eat all four of his children; after which the moon released her daughters from confinement. This artifice so enraged the sun, that he drew his sword and cut the moon in half, but repenting afterwards of his anger, allowed her to get whole in certain days, though she still remained condemned to be in half at others, and so she remained, and all her daughters, with her, which are the stars.

Now, some time after the first man and woman had lived together and known each other, Sing Bonga came down and asked them what progeny they had; they say unto him, "Grandfather, we have twelve sons and twelve daughters." These twenty-four lifted up their voices and said, "Great grandfather, how can we brothers and sisters all live together?" Sing Bonga said, "Go you and make preparations and make a great feast, rice and buffaloes' flesh, and bullocks' flesh, goats, sheep, pigs, and fowls of the air, and vegetables;" and they did so: and when the feast was prepared, Sing Bonga said, "Take ye two by two, man and woman, that which shall please you most, and that shall ye have for share, to eat all the days of your life, apart from the rest, so that none shall touch his brother's share."

And so when the feast was prepared, the first pair and the second pair took buffaloes' and bullocks' flesh, even as much as they could carry, and these became the Kol and Bhoomij race; then a pair took the rice; and other pairs, male and female, rice and vegetables, and these became Bramins, Rajpoots, Chuttries, and other Hindoos; and others took away the goat's flesh and fish, and became other kinds of Hindoos; the Bhooians took the shell-fish. Lastly, when nothing was left but the pigs' flesh, came two pair and took it away, and these are Sontals and Koormees to this day; and when all the feast was cleared away, there remained one pair who had nothing, and to them the Kols gave of their share, and these are Ghassees to this hour.

And so all these went and lived separately, and peopled the world, and multiplied exceedingly, and Sing Bonga taught those who lived in far countries other languages, and he gave people of different trades their implements.

And after this from the Kols, from their senior house, sprung the English, who also eat of bullocks' flesh. But they are the senior children, and the Kols the junior!

And after the world was peopled, Sirma Thakoor destroyed it once, with the exception of sixteen people, because people became incestuous, and unmindful of God, or their superiors.

Wicked men are born again as dogs, pigs, or lizards. Suttees never are born again, but remain burning for ever in their pits, and come out at night, wandering about, still burning. Good people after death are born again in some better condition in life than formerly. And this order of things will remain for ever and ever.

When men die, their spirits go to the Sing Bonga, who asks them how they have lived, and judges them. The wicked he whips with thorny bushes, and sometimes buries them in great heaps of human ordure, and after a while sends them back to be born in this world as dogs, cats, bullocks, lizards, &c. The good man he sends back to be born a still greater and better man than he lived before, and all that he had given away in charity, Sing Bonga shows him heaped up in heaven, and restores it to him.

Other deities are Nagé Erra, Desa Uli, Marang Bonga, and Pangúra, his wife—village gods;

Chanala Desum Bonga, whose wife is also Pangúra, the god of married women;

Horaten Ko, a god of the roads;

Mahli Bonga and Chandu Omol;

Jaer Buri is the wife of Desa Uli.

Pigs and fowls are the chief offerings. Idols are wholly wanting. There is singing, dancing, and drinking at the festivals, some of which degenerate into orgies. Of domestic worship there is not a little. Every case of sickness involves a sacrifice, and an application to the soothsayer. That the Ho is eminently addicted to superstitions is clear. Whether he be more so than the rest of the rude world is doubtful.

The name for a Ho tribe is *kílí*—word for word, the Afghan *kheil.* A man cannot marry a woman of his own *kílí*, nor eat with a man of a different one.

*The Bendkars.*—The Bendkars form a single tribe consisting of about 300 individuals, their occupancy being the Bendkar Buru or the Bendkar hills. These lie to the north of Keonjur and the south of Kolehan.

The Bendkars speak either the Ho or the Uriya; are half Hindus; worshippers of Kali; eat neither pork nor beef; drink water from a Ho's hand, but will eat with neither Ho nor Hindu. They burn their dead.

KOL DIALECTS.

| English. | Singbum Kol. | Sontal. | Bhumij. | Mundala. |
|---|---|---|---|---|
| *Man* | ho | horh | horro | horl |
| *Hair* | ub | ub | ub | up |
| *Head* | bo | buho | buho | bohu |
| *Ear* | lutur | lutur | lutur | lutur |
| *Eye* | met | met | met | med |
| *Blood* | myun | myun | myun | myun |
| *Bone* | jang | jang | jang | jang |
| *Foot* | kata | suptijanga | kata | kata |
| *Hand* | thi | thi | thi | tihi |
| *Sun* | singi | singmanal | singi | singi |
| *Moon* | chandu | chandu | chandu | chandu |
| *Star* | epil | ipil | ipil | ipil |
| *Fire* | sengel | sengel | sengel | singil |
| *Water* | dah | dah | dah | dha |
| *One* | mi | midh | moy | miha |
| *Two* | barria | barria | barria | baria |
| *Three* | apia | pia | apia | apia |
| *Four* | upunia | ponia | upuria | upnia |
| *Five* | moya | monegotang | monaya | moria |
| *Six* | turia | turingotang | turrya | turia |
| *Seven* | iya | iairgotang | * sath | * sath |
| *Eight* | irlia | iralgotang | * ath | * ath |
| *Nine* | area | aregotang | * nou | * noko |
| *Ten* | gelea | gelgotang | * das | * dasgo. |

As far as I can judge from some short vocabularies from

* Hindu.

Gondwana, the affinities of the Kol dialects (of which the Ho is one) run westwards rather than eastwards, whereas

*The Khond* dialects extend east and south, in the direction of Orissa and the Telinga frontier. Fuller and more elaborate than Lieut. Tickell's paper on the Ho is that of Captain Macpherson on the Khonds; or rather on their religion, their human sacrifices, and their female infanticide. It is the great repertorium for our knowledge of the superstitions of the so-called aborigines of India. Pagan we can scarcely call them, inasmuch as, in the following notices, it is impossible to overlook the existence of ideas introduced from both ordinary Hinduism and Parsiism. The chief Khond deity, Bura Pennu, created for himself a consort whose name was Tari. He also created the earth. He walked abroad upon the earth—Tari, his wife, with him. But her affections were cold, and when Bura asked her to scratch the back of his neck for him, she refused. There were other causes of quarrel as well, but this refusal was one of them. And now Bura determined upon creating beings that should truly and warmly serve and love him, and, to this end, he made man. Tari opposed him as much as she could, but not effectually.

Man, when made, was pure, good, and healthy. But Tari envied his purity, goodness, and health, and sowed the seeds of sin and evil, "as in a ploughed field." Physical evil Bura met by antidotes, but moral evil he left mankind free to either choose or reject. A few rejected it at once and from the first. To these Bura said, "Become ye gods! living for ever, and seeing my face when ye will, and have power over man, who is no longer my immediate care." The greater part, however, chose evil, and had it as mankind has it now.

Tari, then, is the evil, Bura the good principle; and

whilst the sect of Tari holds that she will eventually win, the sect of Bura believes in the final prevalence of good Meanwhile, the struggle goes on, the weapons being hail, and rain, and wind, and lightning, and thunder. The comet of '43 was watched by the Kols with intense interest. They took it for a new weapon.

The first class of the minor gods of the Khond Pantheon is the offspring of Bura and Tari, and their offices (which may be collected in detail from the subjoined list) are to meet the primary wants of man—wants originating out of the introduction of evil. There are

Pidzu Pennu = the God of Rain.

Burbi Pennu = the Goddess of New Vegetation and First Fruits.

Petterri Pennuthe God of I ncrease and Gains.

Klambo Pennu = the God of the Chase.

Loha Pennu = the Iron God, *i. e.* the God of War.

Sundi Pennu = the God of Boundaries. These are invoked in all ceremonials next to Baru and Tari.

The sinless men, who, having at once and from the first rejected evil, were taken up by Bura, form the next class. They are tutelary to the different Khond tribes.

The third class consists of deities sprung from the gods of the other two—*e. g.*

Nadzu Pennu = the Village God.

Soro Pennu = the Hill God.

Jori Pennu = God of Streams.

Idzu Pennu = House-god.

Munda Pennu = Tank God.

Suga Pennu = God of Fountains.

Gossa Pennu = God of Forests.

Kutti Pennu = God of Ravines.

Bhora Pennu = God of New Fruits.

Dinga Pennu, the Judge of the Dead, is the only one of the Dii Minores who does not reside on the surface of the earth, or a little above it; for the ordinary habit of the other deities is to move about in atmospheric space, invisible to human eyes, but not invisible to the eyes of the lower animals. Of the spirits, then, Dinga Pennu is one; but he is not one of the spirits that walk abroad upon the earth. He resides in the region beyond the sea, where the sun rises, upon a rock called Grippa Valli = the Leaping Rock. It is smooth and slippery, "like a floor covered with mustard seed," and a black unfathomable river flows around it. To this the souls of men speed after their death, and take bold leaps in order to get on it. Hence its name. Some of these leaps succeed, but the greater part fail, in which case the limbs may be broken, or the eyes knocked out by the attempt, and when this happens, the deformity thereby contracted is communicated to the body next animated. Upon Grippa Valli sits Dinga Pennu writing the register of the deeds of men, and casting-up the account of their good and evil actions. Should he adjudge immediate beatification, the soul passes at once to the world of happy spirits. Should the evil, however, outweigh the good, it is recommitted to earth, and sent to its own proper earthly tribe to be re-born. Men have four souls. First, there is the one which is capable of happy communion with Bura. Secondly, there is one attached to the tribes on earth, and, in each particular tribe to which it belongs, it is re-born as often as it dies. Upon the birth of a child the priest determines who it is whose soul, having previously departed in death, has thus returned. Thirdly, there is a soul that is punished for sins done in the flesh; and, fourthly, there is one that dies with the body. Under such a thorough system of metempsychosis as this is, it is only natural for the different degrees of earthly prosperity or adversity to be looked upon as so many degrees of reward or punishment. Hence, the inflictions most dreaded are neither more nor less than the penalties of a former course of vice. Of these the most terrible are poverty, bodily deformity, epilepsy, cowardice, and the want or loss of male offspring. The chief sins are—

1. To refuse hospitality.
2. To break an oath or promise.
3. To speak falsely, except to save a guest.
4. To break the pledge of friendship.
5. To break an old law or custom.
6. To commit incest.
7. To contract debts, the payment of which is ruinous to a man's tribe, the tribe being responsible.
8. To skulk in time of war.
9. To divulge a public secret.

The chief virtues are—

1. To kill a foe in public battle.
2. To die in public battle.
3. To be a priest.

To these add, amongst the sacrificing tribes,—

To be a victim to the Tari.

A strong feeling of pedigree, blood, or tribe, is indicated in this code, and it is no wonder that, in all feastings and ceremonies, a long array of ancestors is invoked. Neither is the belief wanting that the kindest and worthiest of the departed spirits may be prevailed upon to intercede with Dinga Pennu for a discretionary and merciful exercise of his formidable jurisdiction.

It has been stated that Dinga Pennu, the judge of the

dead, is the only one of the Khond Dii Minores who does not inhabit either the earth or the atmospheric space immediately above it. He does not do this. Neither do Tari and Bura. but they are no Dii Minores; but on the contrary, the parents of the Pantheon. The remainder, then, are of the earth, but not earthly. They are shaped, too, as human beings, though their tissues are other than human. They have bodies of human form, but of ethereal texture. And they have also human passions, out of which legend upon legend has been evolved.

Such is the general view of the Khond divinities. The general view of their cultus is as remarkable for what we miss in it as it is for what it displays. There are no Khond temples. There are no Khond images. The stream, the grove, the rock, the glen, with the sky only above them, constitute the Khond shrines. The Khond priest is called Janni. Of the Janni there are two classes; one exclusively priestly, the other free to do anything but fight.

Deferring, for awhile, the notice of the cultus of the two primary divinities, Bura and Tari, I lay before the reader a sketch of the more curious amongst the rituals for the worship of the divinities of the second and third orders,—the worship of the beatified and deified beings, who, choosing good rather than evil, were taken up to Bura, at the beginning being unfrequent and (probably) simple.

The first two may be taken together. Pidzu Pennu is the God of Rain, and Burbi Pennu the Goddess of New Vegetation. Their functions being easily confused, their rites are similar. When Pidzu Pennu has to be invoked, the elders traverse their village and cry "Vessels Ho!" which means that vessels of arrack are to be brought out. These are carried to the tree or stone sacred to *Burbi*

Pennu. Pidzu Pennu then comes upon the priests when the offerings are deposited under the tree, and the meeting is seated, and the great Janni, with two minor assistants, performs the following worship apart.

The Janni first calls on Bura and Tari, and then on Pidzu Pennu, and all or most of the other gods, who (it is hoped) will exert their influence with him. Then follows the prayer, after which they kill the sheep, and either give its flesh away or leave it on the field. The liquor they drink. The Janni stays a little longer than the rest, in case any god may have to question him concerning any omission or imperfection of the ceremonial. "If we have unconsciously omitted to do honour on this occasion to any god, we pray of the other deities to intercede for us, and pacify him."

The God of Increase and Gain is Petterri Pennu, worshipped at seed-time. A rude car is made of basket-work and bamboo. This the Janni drags to the head of the tribe that takes precedence, and obtains from him a little of each kind of seed and some feathers. Having made a circuit of the village with a like object, the car is then accompanied to some appointed field by the young men of the village beating each other and the air with sticks. The seed thus carried out is the share of the evil spirits, who are held to be driven out with the car. The next day a hog is killed, and Petterri Pennu invoked. After this the hog is eaten; only, however, by the elders; for the young men went afield with the car. They have, however, their revenge for their exclusion, and waylay the feasters on their return, pelting them with jungle fruit. On the third day the head of the chief tribe sows his seed, after which the rest may do so too.

A stone in the neighbourhood of each village is dedicated to Klambo Pennu, on which the huntsman lays offerings, and also sharpens his axe or arrow, Klambo Pennu being extreme to mark any neglect of himself, or any violation of the rules of the chase.

*Loha* = *Iron*, and Loha Pennu, the god of war, is, literally, the Iron God. In the grove sacred to Loha Pennu is buried a piece of iron, or an iron weapon. When war threatens it appears above the surface, emerges further on the eve of battle, and subsides when peace is made. Loha Pennu, however, presides only over the wars between Khonds and enemies other than Khond, or (at any rate) over those between different tribes. Quarrels within the tribe he leaves alone. The offering of a fowl, rice, and arrack, within the precincts of a holy grove and in the presence of the assembled warriors, precedes the invocation to Loha Pennu.

And now, when all have snatched up their arms, the priest commands silence, and recites a hymn, concluding by the words "Arm and march." They march, and the priest accompanies them to the enemy's boundary, over which an arrow is shot, by some one indicated by the divining sickle. Thirdly, a branch of some tree growing on the enemy's soil is cut off, and carried away to the spot where the exsertion of the iron indicates the invisible presence of Loha Pennu. Here it is clothed like one of the enemy, and, with certain invocations, thrown down on the symbol or shrine of the divinity. The enemy has full time given him for the completion of similar rites.

The declaration, then, of a Khond war is a matter of no small form and ceremony. So, also, are the overtures for peace and the ratifications of treaties. When one of the two belligerent parties is weary of war, the intervention of some friendly or neutral tribe is requested. If this be successful, a kind of mixed commission of two old men on each side is appointed in order to ascertain the will of Loha Pennu as indicated by certain divinations. In a basket of rice an arrow is placed upright. If it remain so, war proceeds. If it slant, the ceremonies that bring in peace are continued. The population makes a procession. The priest, with rice and two eggs, calls on Loha Pennu. They now fill a dish with hog's fat, and place a cotton wick in it. They light this, and if the flame be straight, the augury is for war; if not, for peace.

The peace-dance is one of long duration, and frantic excitement.

Sundi Pennu, the God of Boundaries, may be invoked by two hostile parties on the same occasion, inasmuch as, *ex vi termini*, he is common to them both. He may not, however, be so invoked on the same day. Hence, when a quarrel as to boundaries arises, there must be at least two days before the fighting begins, for (as has been seen in the case of Loha Pennu) it is part and parcel of the military code of the Khonds for each belligerent to allow the other time for his ceremonies.

Of the ceremonials for the divinities of the third class the two selected for notice are those for

1. The Village God, Nadzu Pennu.
2. The God of Fountains, Sugu (or Sidruju) Pennu.

A stone under a cotton tree is the place of worship for Nadzu Pennu. The tree is planted when the village is founded, and when the village is founded the priest says to the tree, "I bring you by order of Bura Pennu, who commanded us to build the village, as did also ——and—— and——" (naming some ten or twelve divinities).

The people feast and the tree is planted.

A day or two afterwards the Janni meets the villagers again, when an old man, stupid and clownish for the occasion, gets up, with him, the following dialogue:—

*Old man.*—What, I pray you, may be the meaning of the planting of this stick?

*Janni.*—If you don't know, friend, you must assuredly be a great block —a mere jungle-stick, yourself. And how, O friend block, may I ask, did you find legs to bring you hither? You must have acquired them in some wonderful way. But since you are come to us, I will enlighten you, and make a man of you. Know, then, that when Boora Pennu first ordained that villages should exist, he gave us the tree which you now see planted, for a model in all these respects. That our families should spread like the branches of this great tree, strongly and widely. That our women should resemble its lovely and glowing red flowers. That, as the birds are attracted by the love of those sweet flowers, so the youths of neighbouring tribes should come, attracted by our young daughters. That, as of the flowers of this tree not one falls barren, but all unblighted bear fruit, so should it be with our women. That our sons should, in their youth, be rough, sharp, and keen, like the young branches of this tree, which are covered with thorns; but that, as those thorns disappear with age, so should they become smooth and cool when youth is past. And lastly, this tree is given us as an example that we should live as long as it, a most long-lived tree. Boora Pennu thus ordained, and gave us this model tree.

*Old man.*—And for what purpose, I pray, is this hog (or buffalo, as the case may be)?

*Janni.*—One places things which are of value on a stand. We place flesh upon leaves, rice in vessels of earth or of metal; a man rests upon a couch; and this animal is an offering upon which the commands of the deity may rest.

The victim is then killed, and some of its dung mixed with straw and put on the tree-top.

When a spring dries up no divinity is the object of more earnest prayer than Sugu (or Sidruju) Pennu, the God of Fountains. Failing in his ordinary invocations, the Janni takes the cocoon of a silkworm, empties it, and, at the dead of night, repairs, at the risk of his life, to some spring, situate in a different village, or belonging to other proprietors, and tries to wile away its waters to his own dried-up water-course. To this intent he mutters prayers or spells, fills the cocoon, and walks back. At the well which has gone dry, the elders of the village await him—the elders, but no women or youths. The scanty contents of the cocoon are now poured into it, and a sheep or a hog is sacrificed to Sugu Pennu. If all goes favourably a stream of water will have passed from the full well to the empty one, underground, and along the line that the priest took in his way back.

Salo = a cattle-pen, and kallo is the name of a certain spirituous liquor. Hence, the Salo-kallo is the liquor prepared in the cattle-pen, or the Feast of the Cattle-pen-liquor. It is a great yearly festival, and Bura Pennu is the divinity in whose honour it is held. Every branch of every tribe, every member of every village celebrates it, and it is at the time of the rice-harvest that such celebration takes place. It lasts five days; during which the celebrators eat freely, and over-freely, of the kennah, which is fermented rice, with intoxicating, stimulant, or narcotic properties. The Salo-kallo is a period of great licence. The most serious part of it consists in the recitation by the Janni of the doctrines or legends of the Khond Cosmogony, the origin of Evil, the Antagonism of Tari and Bura, &c. A hog is the sacrifice.

The next great festival in honour of Bura is the Jakri, or Dragging; the origin whereof is as follows:—

The woman, Umbally Bylee, appeared as a tiger, and killed game every other day, and all ate of it. There was at that time a fight between the people of Kotrika and those of Mundika. But it was private strife, carried on in womanish fashion, before the art of taking life and that of public battle were known. Umbally Bylee said, "I will kill any one of your enemies you please." They said to her, "Kill so and so;" and she went as a Mleepa tiger, and killed him. Then the people placed unbounded faith in her, and said to her, "Teach us this new knowledge, and show us the art of killing." She replied, "I will teach you; but thenceforward you must do one thing." And she accordingly taught the art of Mleepa to a few, so that they practised it; and she then said, "Now you must worship me by the sacrifice of men, or the earth shall sink beneath your feet, and water shall rise in its place, and I will abandon you." The earth heaved terribly—as some think, from the wrath of Boora Pennu; some, in obedience to the power of the Earth Goddess. Fear filled the minds of all, and, as directed, they set up a pole beyond the village, and brought human victims, and all was prepared for the sacrifice. But now the God of Light sent a god bearing a mountain, who straightway buried Umbally Bylee therewith, and dragged forth a buffalo from the jungle and said, "Liberate the man, and sacrifice the buffalo. I will teach you the art of Mleepa in every form." And he taught that art, and the art of public war.

So, the buffalo having been dragged from the jungle, the festival took the name of the Dragging.

But what is *Mleepa?* Mleepa is a kind of tiger. The ordinary animal is believed by the Khonds to be good rather than bad, a friend rather than an enemy. This is because when he hunts down some other wild animal, and eats only a part of it, the Khond, who may find the remainder, has the benefit of its predaceous propensities. It is only when it is other than an ordinary animal that the tiger kills men; when it is either a tigriform man, or, perhaps, even Tari herself metamorphosed. Tigers of this kind are *Mleepa* tigers.

Tari is malevolent and must be propitiated, and in the necessity of appeasing an evil-minded, rather than in the spontaneity of feeling that delights in doing homage to a kind being, lies the chief difference between the worship of Tari and Bura. In other respects, what applies to the one applies to the other also. The sect of Tari, like that of Bura, believes that the latter has provided remedies for the consequences of the introduction of evil; but it holds that these remedies are only partial, incomplete, and insufficient, that although the soul after death may enjoy happiness under Bura, the body during life may be sorely afflicted by the ill-nature of Tari.

Such earthly good as Tari permits is on the express condition of her being worshipped with human sacrifices, upon which she feeds. The sacrifices are made periodically and publicly, also on certain occasions by individuals. The tribe, the subtribe, the village, may offer them. At the periodical sacrifices each head of a family procures a shred of the human flesh. The victims are provided by the tribe, each member contributing according to his means. When special occasions demand a special victim, whoever furnishes it receives its value, and is exempted from contribution for the next time of offering. Should an individual lose (say) a child, carried off by a tiger, the tiger will be held to have been Tari, and the priest will be invoked. After certain formulæ he will declare that Tari must be pacified, and the father will bind himself to find a victim within the year—a victim called *Tokki*, or *Keddi*, by the Khonds themselves, *Meriah* by the Oriyas. The Tokki, to be acceptable, must be the full and unimpeached property of the offerer, acquired by purchase. It is better still if his father has been a victim before him, or if he has been devoted to the gods as a child. The purchase of victims is made from the men of one of two casts, the Panwa (or Dombanga) and the Gahinda, some of such wretches being attached to each village. They procure them by kidnapping from the Hindus. Sometimes they sell their own offspring. A long interval may elapse between the purchase of a victim and its immolation.

*The Tokki* (or *Keddi*), being brought blindfold to the village for which he is destined to become the offering, is lodged with its head-man, in fetters if an adult, at liberty if a child; and here he is honoured as a being consecrated and hallowed, and, on the whole, scarcely unhappy. Everyone welcomes him, and should he grow, and have intercourse with any of the village females, the father or husband is only too thankful for the distinction. Sometimes a female, herself a victim, is specifically awarded to him, along with a portion of land and stock. The condition of the parents is now inherited by the offspring, and the children of such unions are liable to be sacrificed, when called, which is not always. Escape is rare, nothing being more sedulously inculcated on the victim than the conviction that his death will bring him to immediate happiness, his flight to certain and well-deserved misfortune. And now the time of oblation comes on. The victim, hitherto unshorn, has his hair cut off, and the village performs the ceremony called bringa. By this they make the vow that a sacrifice shall be effected. All wash their clothes and go out of the village, headed by the priest, who invokes Tari.

The first day and night of the festival thus horribly solemnized is devoted to drunkenness, frantic dances, and all kinds of impure excitement, excitement which it is deemed to be impious to resist. Upon the second morning the victim is led forth to some grove solemn and shaded, and never violated by the axe, and to some stream sacred because it flows through it. Such are the spots that so many superstitions love and choose; choose for the most unholy rites. A post is now sunk in the ground, and the victim fastened to it, anointed with oil and ghee, daubed with turmeric, adorned with flowers. So he remains till the third morning, when a little milk and sago is given him. At noon the barbarities by which he is deprived of life begin. His limbs are broken, for, as he must die unbound, he must also be prevented from escaping. The ritual varies—the following, the fullest, in the possession of Captain Macpherson, is given *in extenso*, notwithstanding its length.

*The Priest's Invocation.*

O Tari Pennu! when we omitted to gratify you with your desired food, you forgot kindness to us. We possess but little and uncertain wealth. Increase it, and we shall be able often to repeat this rite. We do not excuse our fault. Do you forgive it, and prevent it in future by giving us increased wealth. We here present to you your food. Let our houses be so filled with the noise of children that our voices cannot be heard by those without. Let our cattle be so numerous that neither fish, frog, nor worm may live in the drinking ponds beneath their trampling feet. Let our cattle so crowd our pastures that no vacant spot shall be visible to those who look at them from afar. Let our folds be so filled with the soil of our sheep that we may dig in them as deep as a man's height without meeting a stone. Let our swine so abound that our home fields shall need no ploughs but their rooting snouts. Let our poultry be so numerous as to hide the thatch of our houses. Let the stones at our fountains be worn hollow by the multitude of our brass vessels. Let our children have it but for a tradition that in the days of their forefathers there were tigers and snakes. Let us have but one care, the yearly enlargement of our houses to store our increasing wealth. Then we shall multiply your rites. We know that this is your desire. Give us increase of wealth, and we will give you increase of worship.

After this each individual present asks for what he wishes; and the priest continues :—

Umbally Bylee went to cut vegetables with a hook. She cut her finger. The earth was then soft mud; but when the blood-drops fell it became firm. She said, "Behold the good change! cut up my body to complete it!" The people answered, "If we spill our own blood we shall have no descendants. We will obtain victims elsewhere. Will not the Dombo and the Gahi sell their children when in distress? and shall we not give our wealth for them?" and they prayed thus :—

"May the gods send the exhausted Dombo, his feet pierced with thorns, to our door! May the gods give us wealth."

Their prayer was answered. They procured and sacrificed a victim. The whole earth became firm, and they obtained increase of wealth. The next year many victims came for sale, and the people thanked the gods, saying, "You have sent us victims, and have given us wealth." Thenceforward the world has been happy and rich, both in the portion which belongs to the Khonds, and the portion which belongs to Rajahs.

And society, with its relations of father and mother, and wife and child, and the bonds between ruler and subject arose. And there came into use cows, bullocks, and buffaloes, sheep, and poultry. Then also came into use the trees and the hills, and the pastures and grass, and irrigated and dry fields, and the seeds suitable to the hills and to the valleys, and iron and ploughshares, and arrows and axes, and the juice of the palm-tree, and love between the sons and daughters of the people, making new households. In this manner did the necessity for the rite of sacrifice arise.

Then, also, did hunting begin. A man brought in a rat, a snake, and a lizard, and inquired if they were fit to eat. Then the Earth Goddess came and rested on the Janni, and said to him, "Give names to all the wild animals, distinguishing those that are fit and those that are unfit for use, and let men go to the jungles and the hills, and kill the sambur and spotted deer, and all other game, with arrows and with poison." And men went to hunt.

While hunting, they one day found the people of Darungabadi and Laddabarri (tribes of the Souradah Zemindary, adjacent to Goomsur, which do not offer human sacrifices) offering sacrifice. Their many curved axes opened the bowels of the victims, which flowed out. They who went to the hunt said, "This ceremony is ill-performed. The goddess will not remain with you." And the goddess left these awkward sacrificers, and came with our ancestors. These people now cut trees only. The deity preferred the sacrifice at the hands of our forefathers, and thenceforth the whole burden of the worship of the world has lain upon us, and we now discharge it.

Tari Pennu in this way came with our ancestors. But they at first knew only the form of worship necessary for themselves, not that necessary for the whole world. And there was still much fear; and there were but few children, and there were deadly snakes and tigers, and thorns piercing the feet. They then called upon the Janni, to inquire the will of the goddess, by the suspended sickle. He said, "We practise the rite as it was first instituted, worshipping the first gods. What fault, what sin is ours?" The goddess replied, "In a certain month, wash your garments with ashes, or with stones; make kenna; purchase a child; feed him in every house; pour oil on him and on his garments, and ask for his spittle; take him into the plain, when the Earth Goddess demands him; let the Janni set him up; call all the world; let friendship reign; call upon the names of the first people; cut the victim in pieces; let each man place a shred of the flesh in his fields, in his grain store, and in his yard, and then kill a buffalo for food, and give a feast, with drinking and dancing to all. Then see how many children will be born to you, how much game will be yours, what crops, how few shall die. All things will become right."

We obeyed the goddess, and assembled the people. Then the victim child wept, and reviled, and uttered curses. All the people rejoiced, except those with whom the child had dwelt, and the Janni. They were overwhelmed with grief; their sorrows prevailed entirely over their expectations of benefit, and they did not give either their minds or their faith to the gods. "The world," said they, "rejoices, we are filled with despair;" and they demanded of the deity, "Why have you instituted this miserable heart-rending rite?" Then the Earth Goddess came again and rested upon the Janni, and said, "Away with this grief. Your answer is this: when the victim shall weep, say to him, Blame not us, blame your parents who sold you. What fault is ours? The Earth Goddess demands a sacrifice. It is necessary to the world. The tiger begins to rage, the snake to poison, fevers and every pain afflict the people; shall you alone be exempt from evil? When you shall have given repose to the world, you will become a god, by the will of the gods."

The victim answers :—

Have you no enemies, no vile and useless child, no debtor to another tribe who compels you for his debts to sell your lands; no coward who in time of battle skulks with another tribe? Have you none of these to seek out and sacrifice?

*The Janni.*—We have acted upon quite different views. We did not kidnap you on the road, nor while gathering sticks in the jungle, nor when at play. The souls of those whom you would have us sacrifice can never become gods. They are only fit to perish by epilepsy, falling in the fire, or by ulcers, or other dread diseases. Such sacrifices would be of no avail. To obtain you, we cleared the hill and the jungle, fearless of the tiger and the snake. We stinted ourselves to fill your parents, and gave them our brass vessels; and they gave you to us as freely as one gives light from a fire. Blame them! Blame them!

*The Victim.*—And did I share the price which my parents received? Did I agree to the sale? You now tell me this. No one remembers his mother's womb, nor the taste of his mother's milk; and I considered you my parents. Where there was delicate food in the village, I was fed. When the child of any one suffered, he grieved; but if I suffered, the whole village grieved. When did you conceive this fraud, this wickedness to destroy me? You, O my father, and you,—and you,—and you,—O my fathers! do not destroy me.

The Mullicko, or chief of the village in which the victim was kept, or his representive, now says :—

This usage is delivered down to us from the first people of the first time. They practised it. The people of the middle time omitted it. The earth became soft. An order re-established the rite. Oh, child, we must destroy you. Forgive us. You will become a god.

*The Victim.*—Of this your intention I knew nothing; I thought I was to pass my life with you. I assisted to build houses and to clear fields for my children. See! there are the palm-trees I planted. There is the mowa tree I planted. There is the public building on which I laboured —its palings still white in your sight. I planted the tobacco which you are now eating. Look behind you! The cows and the sheep which I have tended look lovingly at me. All this time you gave me no hint of my intended fate. I toiled with you at every work with my whole mind. Had I known of this doom, I had still toiled, but with different feelings. Let the whole burden of my soul's grief, as I remember the past, lie upon you.

*The Chief.*—You are about to become a god. We shall profit by your fate. We cannot argue with you. Do you not recollect that, when your father came to claim your uncompleted price, you snatched up a shining brass vessel; that we said, "That is your father's," and you threw it at him, and ran away amongst the sheep? Do you not recollect the day on which we cut your hair, devoting you to sacrifice? And do you not recollect that when many were sick, and the Janni brought the divining sickle, he declared "The earth demands a victim?"

Then several persons around say, "I should have told you, and I, and I;" and several give answers such as "I thought of our hard labour to acquire you, which had been wasted, had you escaped from us;" and,—"You might have known all well."

*The Victim.*—It is true I did observe something of this; but your aged mothers, and your wives, and your beautiful children, my brothers and sisters, assured me that you were humane, and would never kill one so useful and so beautiful as I. "They will rather," said your mothers and children, "remembering your acts and your ways, sell these fields, and these trees, and that tobacco, to procure a substitute." This I believed, and I was happy and laboured with you.

*The Chief.*—We cannot satisfy you. Ask your father, who is present. I satisfied him with my favourite cattle, my valuable brass vessels, and my sheep, and with silken and woollen cloths, and axes. A bow and arrows, not four days old, I gave to his fancy. Your parents, forgetting your beauty, forgetting the pleasure of cherishing you, turned their hearts to my cattle and my brass vessels, and gave you away. Upbraid them. Heap imprecations upon them. We will curse them with you, imprecating upon them—that all their children may be similarly sacrificed. That they may lose, within the year, the price for which they sold you. That they may have a miserable and forlorn old age, lingering childless and unfed. That when they die in their empty house, there may be no one to inform the village for two days, so that, when they are carried out to be burned, all shall hold their nostrils. That their own souls may afterwards animate victims given to hard-hearted men, who will not even answer their death plaints consolingly. Curse them thus, and we will curse them with you.

The victim will now turn to the Janni, saying:—

And why did you conceal my fate? When I dwelt with the Mullicko, like a flower, were you blind, or dumb, or how were you possessed, that you never said, "Why do you cherish, so lovingly, this child—this child who must die for the world?" Then had I known my doom and leapt from a precipice and died. Your reason for concealment—living as you do apart from men, is—that you thought of yourself. "I am great. The whole world attends on my ministrations." But, world, look upon him! What miscreant eyes! What a villainous head, with hair like a sumbully tree! And see how enraged he is! What a jabber he makes! What a body he has got, starved upon worship which depends upon men's griefs!

—A body anointed with spittle for oil! Look, O world! Look, and tell! See, how he comes at me, leaping like a toad!

The Janni replies:—

Child! why speak thus? I am the friend of the gods; the first in their sight. Listen to me. I did not persuade your father or your mother to sell you. I did not desire the Mullickos to sell their fields to acquire your price. Your parents sold you. These Mullickos bought you. They consulted me, inquiring, "How may this child become blessed?" The hour is not yet over. When it is past how grateful will you be to me! You, as a god, will gratefully approve and honour me.

*The Victim.*—My father begot me; the Mullickos bought me, my life is devoted, and all will profit by my death. But you, O Janni! who make nothing of my sufferings, take to yourself all the virtue of my sacrifice. You shall, however, in no respect profit by it.

*The Janni.*—The Deity created the world, and everything that lives; and I am his minister and representative. God made you, the Mullicko bought you, and I sacrifice you. The virtue of your death is not yours, but mine; but it will be attributed to you through me.

*The Victim.*—My curse be upon the man who, while he did not share in my price, is first at my death. Let the world ever be upon one side while he is on the other. Let him, destitute and without stored food, hope to live only through the distresses of others. Let him be the poorest wretch alive. Let his wife and children think him foul. I am dying. I call upon all—upon those who bought me, on those whose food I have eaten, on those who are strangers here, on all who will now share my flesh—let all curse the Janni to the gods!

*The Janni.*—Dying creature, do you contend with me? I shall not allow you a place among the gods.

*The Victim.*—In dying I shall become a god, then will you know whom you serve. Now do your will on me.

The cruelties of the absolute immolation are now drawing nearer and nearer still, and, in a few minutes, the victim will be torn to pieces, quivering with life, by the fanatic and maddened crowd around him. The exact spot for the sacrifice has been determined beforehand, *i. e.* the night previous, and by a strange kind of divination. A number of persons are sent in the dark with sticks in their hands, and with orders to probe and poke some portion of the ground about the village in order to find a crack or opening, for such is the spot indicated by the Earth Goddess as the exact locality for the sacrifice. This being found, a short post is fixed in it, in the morning. Round this they place four larger ones, and in the middle the victim. The arm of a growing tree is now riven half-way down, and the victim, forced into the cleft, like Milo, is left for it to close on him; the natural elasticity of the timber being assisted by ropes round its open extremity. These the priest, with his assistants, draws tighter and tighter. He then wounds the victim slightly with an axe, and leaves him to the crowd. They throw themselves on him, and strip the flesh from the extremities and trunk, leaving the head and intestines untouched.

Such are the usual rites; subject, however, to variations in the way of detail. In one district the victim is slowly burnt to death, with horrible cruelties besides. A low stage with a roof-like ridge is raised, and the victim fastened to it. Fire is then applied in such a manner as to make him writhe and struggle up and down the two slopes alternately. The more tears he sheds the more abundantly will Tari allow a supply of rain. The next day he is cut to pieces.

None but the worshipper can approach the victim. Strong parties guard his remains against wild beasts the night after the sacrifice, and, the next day, the chief and priest consume them along with the whole carcase of a sheep, on a funeral pile. The ashes are scattered over the fields, or made into a paste, and plastered over the barns and granaries.

Two formalities are indispensable:—

1. To the father or seller of the victim, as the case may be, a *dhulj* is given. This is a bullock, equivalent to a payment in full satisfaction of all demands.

2. A bullock is sacrificed and made a feast of, with the following prayer to Tari:—

O Tari Pennu! You have afflicted us greatly; have brought death to our children and our bullocks, and failure to our corn;—have afflicted us in every way. But we do not complain of this. It is your desire only to compel us to perform your due rites, and then to raise up and enrich us. We were anciently enriched by this rite; all around us are great from it; therefore, by our cattle, our flocks, our pigs, and our grain, we procured a victim and offered a sacrifice. Do you now enrich us. Let our herds be so numerous that they cannot be housed; let children so abound that the care of them shall overcome their parents—as shall be seen by their burned hands; let our heads ever strike against brass pots innumerable hanging from our roofs; let the rats form their nests of shreds of scarlet cloth and silk; let all the kites in the country be seen in the trees of our village, from beasts being killed there every day. We are ignorant of what it is good to ask for. You know what is good for us. Give it to us.

When the victim has been cut to pieces, the deputies, who have been sent from the several villages to receive a shred of its flesh, return home. At home, the few who have remained behind, keep fast till their arrival. The bearer of the flesh rolls it up in the leaf of the guglut tree, and, when he gets near the village, lays it on a cushion of grass, and deposits it in the place of the public meetings. He then divides and subdivides it amongst the heads of families, saying:—

O Tari Pennu! our village offered such a person as a sacrifice, and divided the flesh among all the people in honour of the gods. Now, such a village has offered such a one, and has sent us flesh for you. Be not displeased with the quantity, we could only give them as much. If you will give us wealth we will repeat the rite.

Other formulæ and feastings defer the full completion of the ceremony until the fourth day from the return of the Janni and his distribution of the flesh. A buffalo is then slaughtered and feasted on, its inedible parts being left for the spirit of the victim (Tokki, Keddi, or Meriah). Nor is this all. A year afterwards a hog is sacrificed to Tari Pennu with this invocation: "O Tari Pennu! up to this time we have been engaged in your worship, which we commenced a year ago. Now the rites are completed. Let us receive the benefit."

The practice of female infanticide amongst the Khond tribes is at least as common as that of human sacrifices; indeed, there is no part of the population where it is utterly unknown and unpractised. At the same time some sections of the population are more infanticidal than others. Of these the most conspicuous are certain of the sect of Bura—not of Tari, as we might at first expect. To such an extent is the practice carried among the more extreme adopters of it, that, except when a mother's first child is a girl, no female infant is allowed to live. So deadly is the effect of this pernicious custom that villages of more than a hundred houses may occasionally be seen without a single female child.

The religious view of the practice is as follows:—Bura found so little comfort in his own wife, Tari, that he came to the conclusion that women were only to be tolerated as necessary evils, and gave his instruction, advice, or injunctions to mankind accordingly. He gave them, in short, an express admonition to bring up as many females as were necessary for the good of society, and no more.

Other reasons lie in the belief that the amount of soul assigned by Bura to a given generation is limited, and that the less there is for women the more there is for men.

Is it because the social position of the woman is unnaturally low that this practice of female infanticide thus predominates? By no means. So far from the condition of Khond females being bad, or even indifferent, the very reverse is the case. They have many and high privileges, privileges which are believed to be the highest and most numerous amongst the tribes that most especially practise infanticide.

One of these privileges is a very near approach of polyandria. Whilst infidelity on the part of a married man is punished by fines and other penalties, little or no constancy is required on the part of the wife. A wife, too, may quit her husband, and take another, at any time, except when she is *enceinte*, within a year of her marriage, or within a year of the birth of a child. Nor is this all; her property goes with her, being re-claimed by her father. But the tribe at large is answerable for the debts of its individual members. Hence, when wives are capricious the community suffers. "To any man but a rich and powerful chief, who is able to make large and sudden restitutions, and to his tribe, a married daughter is a curse. By the death of our female infants before they see the light, the lives of men without number are saved, and we live in comparative peace."

*The Sours.*—Long as have been the notices of the Kols and Khonds, they are but extracts from still more elaborate descriptions. Of the Sours I can give no such accounts, having no *data* of equal or even approximate magnitude to refer to. As a general rule, they are said to form the third or (counting the Uraon and Rajmahalis) the fourth section of one great class, the so-called aborigines of the eastern Ghauts, as opposed to the Bhíls and Kols of the west, and the Gonds of the centre. With these they, in all probability, agree in most of the points wherein they differ from the ordinary Hindu. Their area begins where that of the Khonds ends, and is extended as far south as the Pennaur—there or thereabouts. It is succeeded by that of

*The Chenchwars*—an allied population, lying along the mountains that run southward, between the Kistna and the Pennaur.

In one important respect both the Sours and the Chenchwars differ from the Khonds, Kol, and Uraon. They lie within the true Tamul area, and, so doing, present no notable contrast, in the way of language, to the populations around them. Their languages are represented by the following lists, in which the Chentsu (word for word Chenchwar) presents the most Hindu forms—indeed, as far as the following list is evidence, it is actually Hindí.

| English | Khond. | Savara. | Gadaba. | Yerukala. | Chentsu. |
|---|---|---|---|---|---|
| *Man* | lokka | mandra | lokka | mumisam | manus |
| *Head* | tlavu | abobumu | bo | talayi | mund |
| *Eye* | kannuka | amu | ollo | supan | ayenkhi |
| *Ear* | kirru | luv | nintiri | soyi | kan |
| *Mouth* | sudda | amuka | tummð | vayi | mu |
| *Tooth* | ahamu | ajagna | ginna | pallam | dat |
| *Blood* | rakko | miyamo | yignam | regam | lahu |
| *Bone* | pasu | ajagna | vondramgoyi | yamaka | had |
| *Hand* | kaju | asi | titti | ky | hat |
| *Foot* | vestamu | aji | adugesananu | keru | khoju |
| *Day* | vujjagu | tamba | simmya | pammaru | din |
| *Sky* | mudengi | agasa | konda | menu | sarg |
| *Sun* | bela | vuyu | singi | beruli | bela |
| *Moon* | layidi | vonga | arke | tarra | masu |
| *Star* | sukala | tute | tsukka | tsukka | bhudaka |
| *Fire* | nade | togo | sungol | nerupu | agin |
| *River* | jodi | nayi | roggilu | aru | ladi |
| *Stone* | viddi | aregna | birel | kellu | paththar |
| *Tree* | mranu | anebagna | sunabbo | chede | gats |
| —— | —— | —— | —— | marom | —— |
| *One* | rondi | aboy | vokati | vondu | * yek |
| *Two* | jodeka | bagu | rendu | rendu | * duyi |
| *Three* | tinigota | yagi | mudu | mume | * tin |
| *Four* | sari | vonji | nalugu | nalu | * char |
| *Five* | panchu | mollayi | ayidu | anju | * panch |
| *Six* | —— | kudru | aru | aru | * chhe |
| *Seven* | * sata | gulji | yedu | yegu | * sat |
| *Eight* | * ata | tamuji | yenimide | yettu | * ath |
| *Nine* | * nogatta | tinji | tommidi | ombadu | * lo |
| *Ten* | * doso | galliji | pade | pottu | * das. |

As for the Kol forms of speech, they seem to extend considerably towards the west, inasmuch as more than one of the dialects from Gondwana, and (as such), *eo nomine*, Gond is decidedly Kol. Such are the Cúr and Chunuh

* Hindí.

specimens. The details, however, of the line of demarcation are obscure.

*The Gonds.—Mutatis mutandis,* what applies to the Sours and Chenchwars applies to the Gonds—they are Kol, Khond, or Uraon in the points wherein they most especially differ from the Hindus. Of the details of their creed we know but little. Of the poetry or legend the following is a sample:—

*Sandsumjee's Song.*

Sandsumjee's song hear, O Father.
Six wives he took, Sing-Baba not born,
Seventh wife took, by her Sing-Baba was conceived.
Of her pregnancy Father was not informed.
Departed Father, his kinsfolk being assembled together.
For this reason to some one it happened to offer a sacrifice to a God.
Hereupon Sing-Baba began to be born.
Small wife was sleeping, the other six were there.
Said they, grain basket's mouth into her head let us introduce.
In our house child is born,
So said, so done, into mouth her head introduced,
And Sing-Baba was born.
Sing-Baba having taken up, into buffaloe's stable threw,
And a puppy instead placed,
And said, a puppy is born.
A puppy having brought forth,
Crows to frighten they set her,
Sing-Baba, buffaloes said, that him let none hurt,
Nor blow strike, and into his mouth milk having poured him suckled.
The six wives said, let us go and see him, is he living or dead?
Sing-Baba was playing.
Thence indeed having taken him into cows' stable threw.
The cows said Sing-Baba let no one hurt
Or blow strike, into his mouth milk pouring him suckled,
Therefore information they sent to seek, is he living or dead?
Sing-Baba was playing.
Thence having taken well into threw.
On the third day having gone to see, is he living or dead?
Sing-Baba there indeed was playing.
Thence indeed having taken, tiger's path upon.
They threw him, tiger's female and male were coming;
Sing-Baba's cries they heard.
Tigress compassion felt, "my child it is."

Having said so, took him away. Their den came to and their pups
from apart set,
Meat bringing their pups to feed
Their pups weaning, with milk Sing-Baba suckled,
So continuing to do, Sing-Baba grew up.
One day his mother her whelps
Together brought, and to whelps began to say
Yourselves among together stay, fight not.
The third day Sing-Baba said, my body is naked
To me a dhoty, dohur, and pugrey give.
She going Bazar road seated remained.
A muslin-maker and cloth-maker that way came
Having got up ran, they their bundles having thrown away fled,
She having taken up brought Sing-Baba took and put on
And his mother's feet kissed,
Staying staid then one day indeed began to say
That to me a bow give. She again went
Seated remained a sepoy armed with a bow that way came.
She ran having cried out. Bow thrown away, he fled.
She having it came and to Sing-Baba gave;
Sing-Baba big brother little brother together played.
Birds shot big brother little brother to them gave to eat
So continuing to do, Sandsumjí home returned with his friends
And Sandsumjí began to say has any one become inspired, let him
arise;
God into any one not entered? Then Sing-Baba inspiration received.
Sing-Baba was coming, big brother little brother together were
Coming came, in the midst was a bráhman
Him Sing-Baba required to get up, he refused;
Big brother became angry, the bráhman eat up
Sing-Baba the image took up.
All began to say, that you who are you?
He said that you the buffaloes and cows ask
And to his little brother said, mother go and call.
He ran and called.
These three species before the punchait assembled came.
Then Sing-Baba said that them question,
From them they asked, this one who is he?
First the buffaloes said this Sandsumjee's son is.
They said, you how understand? These said
In our house two days staid. How did he remain?
These said thy six wives having taken into our house to kill threw
And there not injured, then cow's house into threw
From these asked, How into your house Baba came?
The cows said, At our house two days stayed.
These six wives thence having taken into well threw,

There indeed not injured, thence taking I know not where took.
Sing-Baba they questioned that thence you went where?
He said of my mother ask.
They mother-tigress asked
You where found? She said
On my road these six wives threw away?
I having taken brought, my whelps weaning,
Milk him suckled and here there with prey
My young fed. All-understood, tigress'
Feet embraced, and her a God established.
And these six wives to this Tigress gave.
That day Sing-Baba illustrious became
And Tigress indeed as a God established became.
Of Sandsumjee Baba this song is,
Of Bhirry bamboo jungle Bhirri the song is.

In the original the first ten lines run thus:—

Sandsumjee-na sáka kuyát, ro Bábán,
Sark ask kítur, Sing-Baban hilló púttúr,
Yirrún ask kítúr, awító Sing-Bábán autarietúr.
Aulár yétana Baban púnwakê.
Taksítún Baban, tunwa pari sumptó kiáló
Bariké bouke aie penk putta sika.
Hikké Sing-Baban putti-lé-ai latur.
Loro askna sowatí, sarún mutta.
Awítun, koti aunáté tulla dúrissí, "assun inga chawa putti,"
Ud it, ahé kint annáté tullatún durritún.

*The Kol* or *Kúlis of Gujerat*.—These differ from the Ghonds, &c., in speaking a language, that (in the present state of opinion) is held to agree with the Hindí rather than the Tamul; in other words, they are tribes who, from being in closer contact with the Gujerati, and Mahratta Hindus, have either unlearned their own tongue, or adopted so many Hindí words as to disguise it. Miscellaneous notices concerning them have already been given.

*The Mairs*.—These seem to be the Kols, Bhíls, Khonds, or whatever else we choose to call them, of Marwar, as

*The Minas* are those of Mewar;

*The Moghis* being those of Amber or Jeypur.

That their occupancy is the hill country rather than the plains, and that it reaches the Ganges has already been stated. They are the hill men of the Aravulli.

*The Bhíls.*—These also have already been mentioned. They extend far towards the north. In the desert to the north and north-west of Marwar, they approach the frontier of Sind.

In Marwar itself they are numerous. Between Sirohi and Udipur they constitute the chief population, being the occupants of a hilly district, in small communities under leaders with the title *Rawut*. The Rawut of Oguna, when Tod was in his country, could muster as many as 5000 bows. He was in all but name independent, paid no tribute, obeyed no one. One of the Colonel's men, who penetrated into these parts, found that the Lord of the Mountain was dead, his men abroad, his widow alone in the hut. He told his story, and asked for a passport. This was an arrow from the quiver of the late chief. It carried the bearer safe through the whole country. The symbolic power of the arrow has already been noticed. Mahmúd of Ghuzni was told what it meant in Turkistan, when he held his dialogue with the Tshagatai chief.

In Malwa the Bhilalahs are Bhíls, with a certain amount of real or reputed Rajput blood. They "combine the pride and pretensions of the Rajput, with the cunning and roguery of the Bhíls, and appear to be, without exception, a debauched and ignorant race, often courageous from constant exposure to danger, but invariably marked by an equal want of honour and shame. Many remarkable instances of their being of this character came within my knowledge. The Bhillalah and Sundi chiefs were the only robbers in Malwa, whom under no circumstances travellers could trust. There are oaths of a sacred but obscene kind amongst those that are Rajputs, or who boast their blood, which are almost a disgrace to take, but which they assert the basest was never known to break before Mundrúp Singh, a Bhilalah, and some of his associates, plunderers on the Nerbudda, showed the example."*

The great centre, however, of the Bhíls is Kandeish, itself the alluvium of a river, but encompassed with mountains. To the north lies the Satpura range, the watershed to the Nerbudda and the Tapti. To the south the Satmalla and Ajunta ranges give an easterly spur to the Ghauts. This is what the Bhíl country is in the way of physical geography. Politically speaking, the space between them is bounded by portions of the Guicowar, by portions of the Holkar, and by portions of the Nizam territory. Three agencies, however, are British.

1. The north-west } Bhíl agency.
2. — north-east }
3. — southern }

The Bhíl districts take in a portion of the area between the Ghauts and the sea,—the Daung or Dang country, a land of forest and jungle. Hence, we must be prepared to hear of the Dang Bhíls. So we must of the Satpura (or northern), and Ajunta (or southern) Bhíls. The Mahabarata mentions the Bhíls. The Mahometan histories of Gujerat and Malwa mention them. The Kandeish records say little about them. The inference is, that the latter are late in date; in other words, that all Kandeish before it was Mahratta, was Bhíl, rude and unlettered. Another fact in favour of this view is the circumstance of many Bhíl tribes being Mahometan. This means that Mahometanism was the first powerful influence that acted on them. In Baglan, to the north and north-west,

* Malcolm's Central India, vol. ii. p. 156.

they are cultivators. There are Bhíls in Bugswara, on the other side of the Ghaut. The general title of a Bhíl chief is Naik. Few Naiks belong to an old dynasty.

It was under Aurungzeb that the majority of the Mahometans became proselytes, of whom many relapsed. This should teach us to look for traces of an abortive Mahometanism amongst them.

They are agricultural rather than industrial or commercial. They are graziers rather than farmers. Yet they are scarcely to be called graziers or herdsmen. They are rather the analogues of the sub-Himalayan tribes like the Kooch and Bodo, who are locomotive agriculturists. They sow and reap, but before they reap or sow they clear the land by burning the trees upon it. They clear and manure. They then crop and exhaust. They exhaust and leave. A great deal is said about the extent to which, when disease or accidental death is superstitiously accounted for, they are ready and willing to migrate. I think that the exhaustion of the soil may have something to do with their readiness. They are hunters and fowlers, their architecture being of the rudest. Their huts are compared to bee-hives. This means that they are low and rounded, made of wattles. The village system is fully developed among them. The Jagla is the head of the village, the Naik of the tribe. The village watchman is, by theory, appointed by the Naik; by practice, by the head man of the village.

The chief Mahometan Bhíls in Kandeish are—

*The Turví*, on the north-east; well-made, fair-complexioned.

*The Nirdhi*, to the south, on the Ajunta range.

Then, in the scale of civilization, come

*The Mutwari*,

*The Burda,*

*The Dorepi,* and

*The Khotíl,* of the north-west, baskét-makers, cultivators, and gum-collectors. It is to the wax and gum collectors in general that the term Khotíl is applied. Then come, ruder still, allied in wildness, but separate in occupancy,

*The Nahal,* on the Turvi frontier.

The Bhíls drink. They marry as many wives as suits. They rob. They reverence their chiefs. They swear on a strangely-foul mixture of salt, cow-dung, and joware. They have the credit of keeping oaths thus sworn. They play on an instrument which Scotchmen compare to the bagpipe.

The Kalapurruj, Durio, Naiko, and Chowdri are Bhíls, who, from the western side of that jungly part of the Ghauts which is known as the Dang Forest, have spread themselves over some of the lower levels, especially over parts of Bugswara. They are small-made, bright-eyed, dark-skinned; shy and locomotive; skilled in the use of the bow; professors of sorcery. Their chief respect they show to trees and stones remarkable for either size or shape. The death of a child, a cow, or even a few fowls, will make a whole family migrate from the village in which it took place to some less ill-omened spot.

*The Wárâli.*—The Wárâli have Marathi names and speak the Marathi language. When asked What are the names of your wives? the answer was, "We never mention the names of our wives." When further pressed, each man gave the name of his neighbour's, no one that of his own wife. Girls marry at twelve or thirteen, boys at sixteen or seventeen. The dialogue, conducted by Dr. Wilson and the Rev. J. Mitchell on one side, and some Wárâli of the parts about Umargaum in Havoli pergunna (a Portugueze dependency) on the other, from which the preceding statements have been taken, thus proceeds:—

Do you give any instructions to your children? Yes, we say to them, Don't be idle, Work in the fields, Cut sticks, Collect cow-dung, Sweep the house, Bring water, Tie up the cows.

Do you give them no more instructions than these? What more do they need?

Don't you teach them to read or write? No Wáralís can either read or write.

Do you give them any instructions about God? Why should we speak about God to them?

What God do you worship? We worship Wághiá (the lord of tigers).

Has he any form? He is a shapeless stone, smeared with red lead and ghí (clarified butter).

How do you worship him? We give him chickens and goats, break cocoa-nuts on his head, and pour oil on him.

What does your God give to you? He preserves us from tigers, gives us good crops, and keeps disease from us.

But how can a stone do all this for you? There is something besides the stone at the place where it is fixed.

What is that thing? We don't know; we do as our forefathers showed us.

Who inflicts pain upon you? Wághiá, when we don't worship him.

Does he ever enter your bodies? Yes, he seizes us by the throat like a cat, he sticks to our bodies.

Do you find pleasure in his visits? Truly, we do.

Do you ever scold Wághiá? To be sure we do. We say, You fellow, we have given you a chicken, a goat, and yet you strike us? What more do you want?

Do you never beat Wághiá? Never.

Whether do you bury or burn your dead? We burn them.

What interval occurs between the death and the burning? We allow no interval when the death occurs during the day. When it occurs during the night, we keep the body outside till the break of day.

Why are you so hasty in the disposal of your dead? Why should we keep a corpse beside us?

Where does the soul go after death? How can we answer that question?

When a man dies in sin, whither does he go? How can we answer that question?

Does he go to a good place, or a bad place? We cannot tell.

Does he go to heaven or to hell? He goes to hell.

What kind of a place is hell? It is a bad place; there is suffering in it.

Who are in hell? We don't know what kind of a town it is.

Where do good people go after death? They go to Bhagaván.
Don't they go to Wághiá? No, he lives in the jungles.
Where is Bhagaván? We don't know where he is, and where he is not.

The Warali believe that the country which they now occupy has always been theirs. A line drawn from Damaun to Jowar cuts their country. So does a line drawn from Jowar to the Dhano creek. In many places they come within a few miles of the sea. This means that the hills which give its southern feeders to the Damaun and its northern to the Surya rivers are Wáráli. Some belong to British, some to Portugueze, India; some to the independent State of Jowar. The tribual system prevails amongst them, the tribes being numerous. There are, amongst others, the

| | |
|---|---|
| Ravatia | Meria |
| Bantria | Wangad |
| Bhangara | Thakaria |
| Bhavar | Jhadava |
| Sankar | Kharbat |
| Pileyane | Bhendar |

Kondaria, &c.

No man marries a wife of his own division.

*The Kathkuri* or *Katodi*.—These take their name from the *kath* or *cat-echu*, of which they have almost the exclusive preparation. They are small and dark, with low foreheads and curly hair. They have a belief that they are descended from the monkeys and bears which Adí Narayun, in his tenth incarnation of Rama, took with him for the destruction of Rawun, king of Lanka. Him he conquered. Meanwhile, the promise was made to his ursine and simious allies that in the fourth age they should become human beings. They object to mentioning the name Rama, except on their death-beds;

when they mutter it as long as they can. The Dhor Kathkuri eat the flesh of the cow. The Mahratta Kathkuri, though they abstain, have no natural repugnance to it. They abstain because if they did not they would be forbidden to enter a Hindu village. We have the names of five of their tribes—

| | |
|---|---|
| 1. Helam | 3. Gosavi |
| 2. Powar | 4. Jadavi |
| 5. Sindhi. | |

These are Hindu.

They acknowledge the existence of a supreme being named Tsher. They have their domestic gods and goddesses. They practise incantation, and encourage the awe with which the Hindu regards their imprecations; for a Hindu believes that a Katodi can transform himself into a tiger.

The women are on an equality with the men. Their marriages are conducted without the intervention of any Brahmin. The bride chooses her husband. A few twigs are stuck on the heads of the couple. A few words of ceremony are muttered. A feast follows, at which anything or everything may be eaten, and at which much is drunk, for the Kathkuris are amongst the least temperate of the Mahratta populations, and most of what they earn by their catechu goes to the shop of the Parsi liquor-merchant. They name their children on the fifth day, generally giving an ordinary Mahratta name. The dead are burned. If wood be wanting, they are buried along with a pot of rice. Some time after the interment the bones are taken up and burned. Persons dying of cholera are always buried first, their bones being burnt afterwards.

Like the gutta-percha hunters of the Malayan peninsula. the Katodi have a sort of slang of their own.

| English. | Katodi of Kolaba. | English. | Katodi of Kolaba. |
|---|---|---|---|
| *Call* | akh | *Hawk* | moregai |
| *Boiled rice* | anuj | *Take* | lí |
| *Hedgehog* | abída | *Give* | wope |
| *Kite* | alav | *Turban* | salu |
| *Crab* | kírlú | *Dog* | súna |
| *Fowl* | kúkdai | *Boy* | sora |
| *Iguana* | gohur | *Girl* | sori |
| *Arrow* | chúmbotí | *Crow* | hadia |
| *Munjus* | nagúlia | *Man* | hodus |
| *Crane* | bugad | *Woman* | hodis. |

The miserable huts of the Katodi stand outside the villages. The brown-faced monkey is one of the few animals whose flesh they hesitate to eat. They say that it has a human soul.

*The Mhars*, like the Katodi, live on the outskirts of villages, and are abhorred by the Hindus. They cut wood and grass. They measure land. They remove carcases from the towns, eating those of buffaloes and bullocks.

## CHAPTER XLV.

The Telinga, Canarese, Tulava, Malayalam, and Tamul districts.

WHEN the Mahratta area, on one side, and the Uriya, on the other, have been left behind us, the continuous and homogeneous character of the remaining population can no longer be overlooked. There is no longer a question as to whether the proportion of Sanskrit vocables in the languages be sufficient to either disguise their character or effect a transformation. Whatever may be meant by Hindu affinities, the affinity itself is now out of sight. Neither are there any populations like the Kols and Bhíls, the Mairs and Minas; where the language and blood are believed to differ, the former belonging to the north, the latter to the south. All south of the Mahratta and Uriya districts is, in speech at least, either Tamul or Tamuliform.

There are derivatives from the Sanskrit in abundance; but these derivatives are not only foreign to the original language in the way that the French of the Norman conquest is foreign to the speech of England, but are admitted, on all hands, to be so. The creed, however, is Hindu.

The creed in the Tamul districts is Hindu, even as it is Hindu in Rajputana or Bengal.

But it is not wholly and exclusively Hindu in either Bengal or Rajputana. Neither is it in the Dekkan. There are mountains and forests in both areas, and the mountain and the forest have ever been the fastnesses in which the older creeds, the older habits, the older physiognomies, and the older dialects of a country, resistant to the encroachments that change the ethnology of the level plains, longest linger. The analogues of the Kol and Khond, the Wáráli and Katodi, are numerous in southern India. In southern India, however, their language belongs to the same class as that of their more-civilized neighbours, and (so doing) fails to create contrasts. To some extent, however, contrasts exist; and, to some extent, they will be noticed.

Again—in even the most Hindu parts of the districts under notice there are customs and beliefs which, if found at all in the other parts of India, are, by no means, very prominent and characteristic. In other words, there is Hinduism in the south in abundance, but there is also much that appears to be other than Hindu—other, and apparently older.

As a general rule, the Tulava and Malayalam countries exhibit extreme forms of the Telinga, Canarese, and Tamul peculiarities.

As a general rule, such peculiarities as appear in an extreme form in the Tulava and Malayalam districts, and in a moderate one in Canara and Malabar, are to be found, in some shape or other (either fragmentary or rudimentary), in northern India. This means that the differences are differences of kind rather than degree.

At the same time, the Dekkan is Indian in the way that Brittany is Parisian, or Wales English. The political relations and the creed agree. The blood disagrees to a great extent, the language to a greater extent still.

Of predial slavery there is more in Tamuliform India than in Hindostan proper.

So there is of the Jain, or semi-Buddhist, creed.

So there is of the Sudra cast, as opposed to the Kshetriya and Brahminic.

So there is of what may be called, for want of a better name, the *no-cast* system. Few Asiatic terms are commoner in Europe than the word *Pariah.* It is generally translated *outcast.* But, as the past participle of the English for the Latin word *jacio,* and the Portugueze word *cast* have no etymological connection, and as the link between the two words is *nil,* and as their relationship is neither closer nor more distant than that between the English word *sparrow-grass* and the Latin *asparagus,* the correspondence is no correspondence at all, and the translation is exceptionable. Hence it is best to speak only of Sudras and the classes below them. Now the Sudras are the chief cast of the Dekkan, the Sudras being, according to theory, the lowest of all casts. In a Brahminic district this inferiority is possible. In a Kshetriya district it is possible. In a Vaisya district (if such a thing existed) it would be possible also. But what in a district where the Sudras themselves are dominant? It is improbable, to say the least. The lowest man in his own country always discovers an inferior in a strange one. As parasites are fed upon by parasites; as the lowest depth leads to a deeper still; as—but why go on with metaphors? The Sudras are powerful in southern India; and their inferiors are, perforce, other than Sudra. In their own eyes they are the lowest of four casts. If so, their serfs and slaves must be of no cast at all. Such is the Sudra view. The Pariahs are below them—*ergo,* the Pariahs are without cast.

But what say the Pariahs? Do they ignore the principle of cast? By no means. In the first place, there is the great right and left hand struggle, as bitter as was that of the green and blue factions of the Constantinopolitan

Circus, as to whether they or the Pallas move on such or such a side at such and such processions. Then there are some half-dozen lower groups with members of which no Pariah will intermarry or eat. But each of these groups is equally exclusive. What is the true interpretation of this? This has already been suggested. The four great divisions are *genera;* the minor classes, whose name is legion, are *species*. If the Pariahs are anything, they are instances of a fifth *genus*. *Outcasts* or *abjects* they may be. They are not men *without cast.*

Whatever they are, they are the most numerous, *eo nomine*, at least in southern India—in southern India, where the standard of the highest is but low; in southern India, where the magnates are Sudra.

The characteristic, however (if it be one), which has commanded the most attention is that of polyandria. In the present work it has already been noticed. It is Tibetan and Tamul, but it is North American as well. It is more or less African. It is more or less a practice of many countries. I am unwilling to give it a general character. I prefer to exhibit a few concrete instances. Amongst the Moylar of the Tulava country, a widow, tired from celibacy, but restrained from re-marriage, may go to a temple and eat some rice. She may then choose between living in the temple or out of it. If she decide upon being an indweller, she takes a piece of cloth and a daily allowance of rice. She then is bound to sweep the temple, fan the idol with a yak's tail, and submit herself to the embraces of men of her own cast only. The sons of Brahmin women are called Moylar. They wear the Brahminical thread, and employ themselves about the temple. The girls are given in marriage to them.

The out-door prostitutes (for this is what they really

are) may cohabit with any one of pure descent. They pay, however, a sum not exceeding half a pagoda to the temple.

Compare this with the accounts given by Herodotus of the practice in the Assyrian temples.

In the Malayalam country the Nairs are Sudras—Sudras, but often soldiers. They fall into eleven classes, of which three are superior to all the rest, and, more or less, on an equality with each other. Thus, a Kirit may marry the daughter of either a Sudra or a Charnadu, whose profession is akin to his own. The fourth class, however, are palanquin-bearers, and the tenth and eleventh are potters or weavers. The men take their wives before they arrive at puberty. After consummation, husband and wife live apart, the latter in the house of her mother so long as she lives, and in that of her brother afterwards. Doing this, she is free to cohabit with any one she chooses; with any one or with any number of ones. It is only necessary that her lovers be her equals or superiors in cast. The consequence is, that no Nair son knows his own father, and *vice versâ*, no Nair father knows his son. What becomes of the property of the husband? It descends to the children of his sisters. The eldest male manages the landed property. The personal is divided. A man's mother manages his house; when she dies, his eldest sister. Brothers, as a matter of course, live under the same roof. Should one separate from the rest, he takes a sister with him. This is the *descensus per umbilicum*,—part and parcel of polyandria; polyandria being Nair, but not Nair exclusively.

The purity of cast is continually impaired; where is it not? But there are ways and means by which a partial reparation is effected. In many cases the original difference is of no notable amount; and when this is the case, the offspring follows the condition of the lower of its parents. If the mother be higher than the father, the father's cast is the child's also. If the father be the higher, the child goes to the side of mother.

But what if the difference be great? In this case it is of no importance, provided that the father be the higher of the two progenitors. But if it be the mother, suicide or abortion is the result,—we may almost say the remedy. When the abandonment of cast is on the side of the female, so that a woman of either high or middle rank has conceived by a man of the lower (and that such cases actually happen, is the express statement of Mr. Caldwell), the child never sees the light. The miserable mother either destroys herself, or procures abortion.

| English. | Tamul. | Malayalam. | Canarese. | Telugu. |
|---|---|---|---|---|
| *Man* | al | al | alu | al |
| *Head* | talei | tala | tale | tala |
| *Hair* | mayir | talamudi | kudala | ventruka |
| *Ear* | kadu | kada | kivi | chevi |
| *Eye* | kan | kanna | kannu | kannu |
| *Mouth* | vayi | vaya | bayi | noru |
| *Tooth* | pal | palla | kallu | pallu |
| *Bone* | elumbu | ella | eluvu | emika |
| *Blood* | udiram | chora | netturu | netturu |
| *Egg* | muttei | mutta | tatti | gaddu |
| —— | —— | —— | motti | —— |
| *Day* | pagal | pagal | hagalu | pagalu |
| *Night* | ira | rav | iralu | reyi |
| *Sky* | vanam | manam | banu | minnu |
| *Sun* | pakalon | surya | hottu | poddu |
| *Moon* | tingal | tingal | tingalu | —— |
| *Star* | vanmin | minjawna | chukki | chukka |
| *Fire* | neruppu | tiyya | benki | nippu |
| *Water* | tanni | vellam | niru | nillu |
| *River* | aru | puzha | hole | eru |
| *Stone* | kal | kalla | kallu | rayi |
| *Tree* | sedi | chedi | gida | chettu |
| —— | maram | maram | mara | —— |
| *Village* | ur | tara | halli | uru |
| —— | —— | desam | uru | —— |

| English. | Tamul. | Malayalam. | Canarese. | Telugu. |
|---|---|---|---|---|
| *Snake* | pambu | pamba | havu | pamu |
| *I* | nan | gnan | nanu | nenu |
| *Thou* | ni | ni | ninu | nivu |
| *He* | avan | avan | avanu | vadu |
| *She* | aval | aval | avalu | ame |
| *It* | adu | ada | adu | adi |
| *We* | nam | gnangal | navu | memu |
| *Ye* | nir | ningal | nivu | miru |
| *They* | avar | avara | avaru | varu |
| *Mine* | enadu | enre | nannadu | nadi |
| *Thine* | unadu | ninre | ninnadu | nidi |
| *His* | avanadu | avanre | avana | vadidi |
| *Our* | namadu | nangade | nammadu | madi |
| *Your* | umadu | ningade | nimmadu | midi |
| *Their* | avarudu | avarude | avarudu | varidi |
| *One* | onru | onna | ondu | vokati |
| *Two* | irandu | renda | eradu | rendu |
| *Three* | munru | munnu | muru | mudu |
| *Four* | nalu | nala | nalku | nalugu |
| *Five* | anju | anja | ayidu | ayidu |
| *Six* | aru | ara | aru | aru |
| *Seven* | ezhu | ezha | elu | edu |
| *Eight* | ettu | etta | entu | enimidi |
| *Nine* | ombadu | ombada | ombhattu | tommidi |
| *Ten* | patta | patta | hattu | padi. |

When the details of the superstitions of the independent tribes and the lower casts shall have been investigated, an inkling towards the original mythology of Southern India will become possible. A belief in *pysachi*, or spirits; a veneration of a black stone, and a Shammanist diabololatry are the chief phenomena towards which our present imperfect evidence points. There is also a deity named Buta to whom fowls are offered, every man being his own priest, just as is the case with the Bodo and Dhimal.

It is one thing to be a Pariah, or a man of such low cast as to be contemned by the Sudra. It is another thing to be the analogue of the Bhil or Kol. Of these last the chief occupancy is the Nilgherry Hills and the range between them and the Mahratta frontier. The Nilgherry Hills, however, are the parts which have been best investigated. They give us

*The Tudas.*—Infanticide polyandrists, who are few in number, and less Hindu than their neighbours:

*The Kohatars.*—Occupants of the lower ranges, and eaters of beef:

*The Curumbars,* Curumars, or Curbs;

*The Irular*—(compare the name *Warali*), and

*The Budugurs*—all fragmentary, pagan, and semi-pagan populations. In the Tuda creed the black stone has a prominent place. The fuller form of the word is Tudava, apparently, word for word, Tulava.

*The Malearasar.*—These are the analogues to the Tudas, &c., in the hills of the Malayalam country.

*Specimen of Language.*

| English. | Tuda. | Kohatar. | Budugur. | Curumbar. | Irular. |
|---|---|---|---|---|---|
| *Man* | al | ale, manija | manija | manisha | manisha |
| *Woman* | kuch | pemmage | hennu | hennu | ponnu |
| *Head* | madd | mande | mande | mande | tele |
| *Eye* | kann | kannu | kannu | kannu | kannu |
| *Ear* | kevvi | kive | kive | kive | kadu |
| *Tooth* | parsh | palle | hallu | hallu | pallu |
| *Mouth* | bor | vai | bai | bai | vai |
| *Blood* | bach | netra | netru | netaru | latta |
| *Bone* | elf | yelave | yellu | yellu | yellambu |
| *Foot* | kal | kalu | kalu | kalu | kalu |
| *Hand* | koi | kei | kei | kei | kei |
| *Day* | nal | nale | dina | dina | nalu |
| *Sun* | birsh | potte | hottu | hottu | podu |
| *Moon* | teggal | tiggule | tiggalu | tingla | nalavu |
| *River* | pa | pevi | holla | niru | palla |
| *Water* | nir | nire | niru | niru | dani |
| *Fire* | nebb | —— | kichchu | kichchu | tu |
| —— | dilth | dije | —— | —— | tee |
| *One* | vadd | vodde | vondu | vondu | vondu |
| *Two* | ed | yede | yeradu | yeradu | erndu |
| *Three* | mudu | munde | muru | muru | muru |
| *Four* | nank | nake | nalku | nalku | naku |

| English. | Tuda. | Kohatar. | Budugur. | Curumbar. | Irular. |
|---|---|---|---|---|---|
| *Five* | utsh | anje | eidu | eidu | eindu |
| *Six* | ar | are | aru | aru | aru |
| *Seven* | el | yeye | yellu | yellu | yettu |
| *Eight* | ett | yette | yettu | yettu | yettu |
| *Nine* | anpath | vorupade | vombattu | vombattu | vombadu |
| *Ten* | path | patte | hattu | hattu | pattu. |

Of these, the Budugur and Curumbar are somewhat more Hindí than the rest; the Tuda being the most peculiar.

## CHAPTER XLVI.

Ceylon.—The Maldives and Laccadives.—Migratory and other populations of Continental India.

In one important point Ceylon differs from Continental India. It is, to a great extent, Buddhist. In Continental India there was only an approach to Buddhism. In Ceylon it actually exists, *eo nomine*, and with its own proper literature; a literature of which the Pali, rather than the Sanskrit, is the vehicle.

That there were traces of what was called Diabololatry, or Devil-worship, in Southern India has already been stated. When Siva entered the country (so runs the doctrine), he found himself unable to extinguish the ancient worship of the aborigines, without, to a certain extent, allying himself with it. So he made himself his own son, named Vira Bhadra, whose wife Bhadra Cali is the patroness and mother of the present Shanars, whose business it is to cultivate the palmyra tree, and whose cast is one of the very lowest. They belong to the Continent. Their *cultus*, however, illustrates that of the Singhalese.

When an offering to a devil has to be made, a devil-dancer is sought out from either the head men of the villages, or from some amateur devotees who are often females. There is no regular priesthood. The officiating individual dresses himself as some particular devil, with cap and bells, horns and drum, and, above all, a bow. On the frame of this bow a series of bells is fastened, the bow resting on a pot, and being struck by a plectrum. One musician strikes the string, another produces the bass note out of the brass pot, a third beats cymbals. Meanwhile the devil-dancer gradually works himself into a frenzy; when he is supposed by the lookers-on to have the powers of the devil he represents. As a present deity they worship him, tell him their grievances, reveal their wants, implore his oracles. This is the Shamanism of Southern India, as exhibited by the Shanars of Tinevelly.

In Ceylon there is a diabolical literature or liturgy.

I.

Come, thou sanguinary Devil, at the sixth hour. Come, thou fierce Devil, upon this stage, and accept the offerings made to thee!

The ferocious Devil seems to be coming, measuring the ground by the length of his feet, and giving warnings of his approach by throwing stones and sand round about. He looks upon the meat-offering which is kneaded with blood and boiled rice.

He stands there and plays in the shade of the tree called Demby. He removes the sickness of the person which he caused. He will accept the offerings prepared with blood, odour, and reddish-boiled rice. Prepare these offerings in the shade of the Demby tree.

Make a female figure of the planets with a monkey's face, and its body the colour of gold. Offer four offerings in the four corners. In the left corner, place some blood, and for victims a fowl and a goat. In the evening, place the scene representing the planets on the high ground.

The face resembles a monkey's face, and the head is the colour of gold. The head is reddish, and the bunch of hair is black and tied. He holds blood in the left-hand, and rides on a bullock. After this manner make the sanguinary figure of the planets.

II.

O thou great devil Maha-Sohon, preserve these sick persons without delay!

On the way, as he was going, by supernatural power he made a great noise. He fought with the form of Wessamoony, and wounded his head. The planet Saturn saw a wolf in the midst of the forest, and broke his neck. The Wessamoony gave permission to the great devil called Maha-Sohon.

O thou great devil Maha-Sohon, take away these sicknesses by accepting the offerings made frequently to thee.—The qualities of this devil are these: he stretches his long chin, and opens wide his mouth like a cavern: he bears a spear in his right hand, and grasps a great and strong elephant with his left hand. He is watching and expecting to drink the blood of the elephant in the place where the two and three roads meet together.

Influenced by supernatural power, he entered the body of the princess called Godimbera. He caused her to be sick with severe trembling sickness. Come thou poor and powerless devil Maha-Sohon to fight with me, and leave the princess, if thou hast sufficient strength.

On hearing these sayings, he left her, and made himself like a blue cloud, and violently covered his whole body with flames of fire. Furiously staring with his eyes, he said, "Art thou come, blockhead, to fight with me who was born in the world of men? I will take you by the legs, and dash you upon the great rock Maha-meru, and quickly bring you to nothing."

Thou wast born on Sunday, the first day of the month, and didst receive permission from the King of Death, and didst brandish a sword like a plantain-leaf. Thou comest down at half-past seven, to accept the offerings made to thee.

If the devil Maha-Sodon cause the chin-cough, leanness of the body, thirst, madness, and mad babblings, he will come down at half-past seven, and accept the offerings made to him.

These are the marks of the devil Maha-Sohon: three marks on the head, one mark on the eye-brow and on the temple; three marks on the belly, a shining moon on the thigh, a lighted torch on the head, an offering and a flower on the breast. The chief god of the burying-place will say, May you live long!

Make the figure of the planets called the emblem of the great burying-place, as follows: a spear grasped by the right hand, an elephant's figure in the left hand, and in the act of drinking the blood of the elephant by bruising its proboscis.

Tip the point of the spear in the hand with blood, pointed towards the elephant's face in the left hand. These effigies and offerings take and offer in the burying-place,—discerning well the sickness by means of the devil-dancer.

Make a figure of the wolf with a large breast, full of hairs on the body, and with long teeth separated from each other. The effigy of the Maha-Sohon was made formerly so.

These are the sicknesses which the great devil causes by living among the tombs: chin-cough, itching of the body, disorders in the bowels; windy-complaints, dropsy, leanness of the body, weakness and consumptions.

He walks on high upon the lofty stones. He walks on the ground where three ways meet. Therefore go not in the roads by night: if you do so, you must not expect to escape with your life.

Make two figures of a goose, one on each side. Make a lion and a dog to stand at the left leg, bearing four drinking-cups on four paws—and make a moon's image, and put it in the burying-place.

Comb the hair, and tie up a large bunch with a black string. Put round the neck a cobra-capella, and dress him in the garments by making nine folds round the waist. He stands on a rock eating men's flesh. The persons that were possessed with devils are put in the burying-place.

Put a corpse at the feet, taking out the intestines through the mouth. The principal thing for this country, and for the Singalese, is the worship of the planets.*

That the more impracticable districts of so large an island as Ceylon should contain the analogues of the Bhíls, Kols, Khonds, and their congeners, is what we expect *à priori*. We also expect that the analogues of the Pariahs and the so-called outcasts will be forthcoming. There is Buddhism in Ceylon it is true, and it is also true that the Buddhist creed is opposed to many distinctions upon which Brahminism insists. At the same time there is enough of the latter to develope the ordinary phenomena of Hinduism, and these exist to a considerable extent. The population which, on the strength of its pagan or semi-pagan wildness, has commanded the most attention, bears the name Vaddah, a name which is, more or less general, and which is apparently of Hindu origin. It certainly applies to a very rude class of Singhalese. Whether, however, they represent the aborigines of the island, or whether they are the equivalents to the Pariahs, is uncertain. I know of no monograph that gives us the details of their creed. I learn, however, from Dr. Rost, who has kindly favoured me with more than one valuable fact relating to the population under notice, that their language varies but little from the common Singhalese. Now, the common Singhalese is far more Sanskrit than either the Tamul or the Malayalam; far more Sanskrit

* From Callaway's "Translation of the *Kolán Nattannawa*."

than any member of the class to which those languages belong.

| English. | Singhalese. | Sanskrit. | Pali. |
|---|---|---|---|
| *Man* (*homo*) | manushyayâ | jana | jana |
| —— —— | minihâ | manush | —— |
| —— (*vir*) | purshayâ | purusha | puriso |
| —— —— | pirimiyâ | —— | —— |
| *Woman* | strî | strî | itthi |
| —— | gäni | —— | —— |
| *Head* | oluwa | siras | siro |
| —— | isa | —— | —— |
| *Hair* | isakê | kesa | keso |
| *Eye* | äsa | —— | —— |
| —— | aksiya | akshi | akkhi |
| —— | net | chakshuh | —— |
| *Ear* | kana | —— | —— |
| *Nose* | nâhe | nāsā | nāsā |
| *Mouth* | kata | mukham | mukham |
| *Tooth* | data | danta | danto |
| *Tongue* | dîwa | jihva | jivhā |
| *Hand* | ata | —— | hattho |
| —— | hastaya | hasta | —— |
| *Foot* | patula | —— | —— |
| —— | pâdaya | pada | pādo |
| *Bone* | ashtiya | —— | —— |
| —— | ätiya | —— | —— |
| *Blood* | le | lohitam | lohitam |
| —— | rudhiraya | raktam | —— |
| *Day* | dawasa | dinam | dinam |
| *Night* | ratriya | rātri | rātti |
| *Sun* | ira | sūrya | sūriyo |
| *Moon* | handa | chandra | chando |
| *Star* | taruwa | tārā | tārā |
| —— | târukawa | —— | sitārā |
| *Fire* | ginna | agni | aggi |
| —— | gindara | —— | —— |
| *Water* | diya | udakam | udakam |
| —— | diyara | —— | —— |
| —— | watura | jalam | jalam |
| *Tree* | gaha | vriksha | rukkho |
| *Stone* | gala | prastara | pāshana |
| *One* | ek | eka | eko |
| *Two* | de | dwi | dwi |
| *Three* | tun | tri | ti |

| English. | Singhalese. | Sanskrit. | Pali. |
|---|---|---|---|
| *Four* | hatara | ehatur | chatu |
| *Five* | pas | panchan | pancha |
| *Six* | ha | shash | chha |
| *Seven* | hat | saptan | satta |
| *Eight* | ata | ashtan | attha |
| *Nine* | nama | navan | nava |
| *Ten* | daha | dasan | dasa. |

*The Rodiyas.*—A better claim to stand as the representatives of a primitive population can be put in for the Rodiyas,* who exhibit a striking dissimilarity "in their physical characteristics, being much more robust and vigorous." They are found only in the interior, and that as a sporadic population, sometimes in one district, sometimes in another, their numbers being inconsiderable—a thousand (perhaps) in all.

| English. | Rodiya. | English. | Rodiya. |
|---|---|---|---|
| *Man (vir)* | gäwâ | *Hand* | dagula |
| *Woman* | gäwî | *Blood* | latu |
| *Head* | keradiya | *Sun* | îlayat teriyangê |
| *Hair* | kaluwäli | *Moon* | hapa teriyangê |
| *Eye* | lâwatê | *Stars* | hâpangawal |
| *Ear* | irawuwê | *Fire* | dulumû |
| *Nose* | irawuwa | *Water* | nilatu |
| *Mouth* | galla | *Tree* | uhälla |
| *Tongue* | galagewunu | *Stone* | boraluwa. |

That this gives us a wide departure from both the Singhalese and the dialects more espccially connected with the Hindí is as manifest. At present, however, it is the only representative of its class.

*The Maldive* and *Laccadive islanders.*—In language they approach the Singhalese proper, or the Singhalese with its Hindu elements. Their alphabet, however, is Arabic.

* See Paper by Simon Casie Chitty, Esq., in Journal of the Ceylon Branch of the Royal Asiatic Society, vol. xi.

| English. | Maldivean. | English. | Maldivean. |
|---|---|---|---|
| *Man* (*homo*) | mihung | *Mouth* | aga |
| —— (*vir*) | firihenung | *Eye* | lo |
| *Woman* | anghenung | *Day* | duas |
| *Head* | bo | *Nigh* | re |
| *Hair* | istari | *Sun* | iru |
| *Hand* | aitila | *Moon* | hadu |
| *Foot* | fiyolu | *Star* | tari |
| *Tongue* | du | *Fire* | alifang |
| *Tooth* | dai | *Water* | feng |
| *Nose* | nefai | *Tree* | gas. |

The chief aliment is from the cocoa-nut-tree; the cocoa-nut-tree and fish.

In all parts of India there are numerous populations of settlers, or colonists, rather than true natives. There are, for instance, Tamul labourers in Ceylon, Telinga families in the Tamul and Canarese countries, Canarese in the Mahratta districts, and *vice versâ*. What occurs, more or less, in most parts of the world occurs to an inordinate extent in Hindostan. The details, however, of these settlements lie beyond the pale of our present inquiry.

Then there are the locomotive, or migratory classes—analogues of the travelling tinkers and pedlars of Europe, analogues to the gipsies of Europe. In Britain the gipsies are wanderers without fixed habitations; whilst, at the same time, they are more abundant in some parts of the island than others. They have no very definite occupation; yet they are oftener tinkers and tinmen than aught else equally legal. They intermarry with the English but little. All this is cast, although we may not exactly call it so. Then, again, they have a peculiar language, although it is so imperfectly known to the majority of the British gipsies as to have become well-nigh extinct.

Of the chief of the tribes in question a good account

is given by Mr. Balfour. This list, however, which is as follows, may be enlarged.

1. *The Bunjaras,* or *Bunjarris.*—Lumbari is another name for the population. So is Gohur. According to Balfour the latter is the name by which they designate themselves. This is probable; since it means, in their language, *man.* They are bullock-owners; and as the bullock is the chief beast of burden, they are grain-merchants. Their communities are called Tanda, their chiefs Naik. They affecta Rajput descent, and fall into the four following divisions.

*a. Rahtor,* on the head-waters of the Wurda on the Gondwana frontier; the field of their operations extending to Mysore south, and the Concan west.

*b. The Burtiah,* to the east of the preceding, from Chicacole to Nellore.

*c. The Chouhan,* in Mysore.

*d. The Powur,* in Orissa, and on the east of Gondwana.

Akin to the Bunjaras are—

2. *The Multanis* of the parts about Aurungabad, who emigrated from Multan in 1739. They are Mahometans.

3. *The Beopari* are also carriers and traders of the Deccan.

4. *The Hirn-shikari,* or *Hirn-pardi,* who call themselves Bhouri, are hunters. They fall into the following tribes, two of which bear Rajput names:—

1. Rhator, or Mewar
2. Chouhan
3. Sawundia
4. Korbiar
5. Kodiara.

The chiefs of their communities are called Howlia; their festivals Holi. They steal as well as hunt.

5. *The Tarremuki.*—This is what a class of wandering tinkers call themselves; being also called, by others, Ghissari, Lohar, and Bail-kumbar.

6. *The Korawa.*—In Bejapur, Hyderabad, and Canara, the Bajantri or Gaonka Korawa are musicians, basket-makers, and, real or supposed, thieves, who tattoo themselves.

7. *The Bhatu* train themselves for the performance of feats of strength, which they wander from village to village to exhibit.

8. *The Muddikpur* earn a "living by catching fish with nets, and their women earn a little by knitting, and by tattooing the dark blue marks on the foreheads of the brahmins and lingaets; but their chief occupation is the exhibition of the transparencies used in representing the battles of the Panch Pandya, five brothers, whose exploits are, we believe, detailed in the Ramayana. The figures are painted on deer-skin with very brilliant colours, and the story being one the Hindu never tires in listening to, in every village after night-fall you may see the representation of the battles, and hear the Keeli Katr describing the heroes' deeds.

"Their females are very virtuous; and one woman has been known to give birth to twelve children. Reading and writing is unknown amongst them. Their dress and food are the same as the Hindus among whom they dwell.

"They live in square huts formed of grass sewed together, the whole being, perhaps, a rupee in value. These they themselves make, and carry with them at their periodical migrations, which custom renders obligatory every three months—a longer stay would, they say, subject them to some dire calamity; and as the third moon passes by, the spot that yesterday was a merry encamping ground, is to-day a desolate and unoccupied waste.

"The Muddikpur seem to have no idea of a Supreme being. They pay their devotions to the transparent figures with which the battles of the Panch Pandya are represented; the box of bamboo containing them is each morning placed on a part of the floor fresh covered with cow-dung; and on the lid being opened to expose the drawings, they burn frankincense, and bow down to the ground in worship:—'Oh Panch Pandya, by you we live, continue to give us our daily bread!'

"They are not restricted to one wife, and they bury all their dead, except lepers, whom they burn." *

9. *The Ramusis.*—Men of predatory habits in the Mahratta country, but Canarese or Telinga in speech and origin; like

10. *The Mangs*—also in the Mahratta country

11, 12. *The Thugs* and *Dacoits*, widely distributed, gang-robbers and thieves.

Last of all (premising that the preceding list is, by no means, exhaustive) I draw attention to—

13. *The Gipsies.*—That these, wherever found, and under whatever names they are described, are in physical form and language, Indians, is now well known.

(1.)

| English. | Gohurn. | Bowri. | Taremuki. |
|---|---|---|---|
| *Man* | gohur | mankhoe | lokro |
| *Woman* | gohurni | manussi | chali |
| *Head* | mathoe | goddo | mathoe |
| *Eye* | ankhi | dolo | dolo |
| *Nose* | nak | nak | nak |
| *Ear* | kan | kan | kan |
| *Hand* | hath | hatha | hath |
| *Foot* | pae | —— | pug |
| *Water* | pani | pani | pani |
| *Stone* | bhatta | bhattu | duggru |
| *Earth* | jami | bhoe | mattri |
| *Tree* | jharr | jhar | jhar. |

* E. Balfour on the Migratory Tribes of Central India. Journal As. Soc. Beng. vol. xiii.

(2.)

| English. | Korawi. | Bhatúi. |
|---|---|---|
| *Man* | amlún | múns |
| *Woman* | punjeri | jo |
| *Head* | —— | múndhi |
| *Eye* | —— | akhoe |
| *Nose* | —— | luk |
| *Ear* | —— | kunnu |
| *Hand* | —— | hut |
| *Foot* | —— | pae |
| *Fire* | nerpu | ugg |
| *Water* | —— | pani |
| *Stone* | kellay | pathar |
| *Earth* | tirri | bhui |
| *Tree* | muru | jhar. |

The wandering life of these, and other similar tribes, is not, by itself, sufficient to justify us in separating them from the other Hindus. But it does not stand alone. The fragments of an earlier paganism, and the fragments of an earlier language, are phænomena which must be taken in conjunction with it. These suggest the likelihood of the Gohuri, the Bhatti, and their like, being in the same category with the Khonds and Bhíls, &c., *i. e.* representatives of the earlier and more exclusively Tamul populations. If the gipsy language of England had, instead of its Indian elements, an equal number of words from the original British, it would present the same phænomena, and lead to the same inference as that which is drawn from the Bhatti, Bowri, Tarremuki, and Gohuri vocabularies, viz. the doctrine that fragments of the original population are to be sought for amongst the wanderers over the face of the country, as well as among the occupants of its mountain strongholds.

(3.)

| English. | Ramusi. | Mang. |
|---|---|---|
| *Eye* | kunnul | kewrja |
| *Teeth* | pundul | chawur |
| *Sun* | goanda | goanda |

| English. | Ramusi. | Mang. |
|---|---|---|
| *Moon* | phakut | goanda |
| *Fire* | dhupa | dhupa |
| *Water* | nidul | nir |
| *Stone* | ratul | upalla. |

The following is a list of words which, apparently, are slang terms :—

| English. | Bagwan. | Thug. |
|---|---|---|
| *One* | ungud | udanka |
| *Two* | duke | sheluki |
| *Three* | ruk | udanu |
| *Four* | phoke | pokú |
| *Five* | bút | molú |
| *Six* | dag | shely |
| *Seven* | puyater | pavitrú |
| *Eight* | mung | mungi |
| *Nine* | kone | tivsu |
| *Ten* | sula | avutaru |
| *Eleven* | ekla | ekpuru |
| *Twelve* | jewla | habru. |

*Foreign settlers.*—The classes just enumerated were Indian. The following, though occupant of the soil of India, are foreign to it. Some of them have already been mentioned. A long list, however, of alien elements will be given, in order that the very heterogeneous character of the ethnology of India may stand forth in its full due prominence.

1. *Persian.*—Parsis in Gujerat, Mekrani soldiers, &c.

2. *Biluch.*—In Sind and Bahawulpur.

3. *Patan* (*i. e. Afghan*).—In Rohilcund and parts of the Mahratta country.

4. *Arab.*—The Moplahs of the Mahratta and Tulava districts, savage, bigoted, and dangerous Mahometans.

5. *Jewish.*—The Beni Israel of Kolapur. The Jews of Cochin.

6. *Syrian* and *Persian.*—There is, probably, both Syrian

and Persian blood amongst the so-called St. Thomas Christians of Cochin.

7. *Armenian.*—In Calcutta, Dacca, &c.

8, 9. *Turk* and *Mongol.*—This is the blood of many of the royal families; also of many settlements originally military.

10. *African.*—The Sidi, &c.

11. *European.*—Portuguese, Dutch, Danish, French, English.

Of these, the Persians, Biluches, Patans, Turks, Mongols, Africans, and Portuguese, have most mixed themselves, by marriage, with the natives; the Jews and Armenians the least.

# CHAPTER XLVII.

Populations of the Malayan Peninsula.—Orang Benua and Malays proper. —Semang.—Sakai.—Johore tribes.—Orang Laut.

THE empire of Siam extends into the Malayan peninsula, and in the Malayan peninsula the character of the population changes. The language is no longer denominated monosyllabic, notwithstanding the existence of a great quantity of monosyllabic affinities. The physical conformation is no longer called Mongol or Mongolian, in the strict and more limited sense of the term; though it is often termed Mongoliform or Mongoloeid, *i. e.* like that of the Mongols. The chief points of difference may be collected from the details of what is forthcoming. I prefer leaving these to the acumen and attention of the reader to giving any general view of them. It would be neither difficult nor unsafe to say that, as a general rule, the Malay populations were darker in colour than the members of the neighbouring classes. It would be neither difficult nor unsafe to say that they were shorter in stature. Both statements might possibly be true if subjected to an average, of which, however, there is no chance. Both, however, might be false. It is undeniable that there are *some* Malays shorter than certain Burmese, or Tibetans, and it is probable that there are many. It is equally undeniable that there are *some* Malays darker in respect to their skin than *some* Chinese or Tunkinese. Yet it is also true that *some* are lighter than other members of the same stock. Again, the skull of the Malay is said to grow narrow towards the vertex; so that, with its prominent cheekbones and small chin, the Malay face resembles a lozenge or an ace of diamonds. That this is true of *some* Malays I by no means deny. It is true. I believe, of many. At the same time, the induction that such notices suggest is far from being sufficiently established. It rests on too small a number of observations.

The same criticism applies to the notices of the temper and disposition of the Malay tribes. Some are sullen, or at least, abundant in sullen individuals. Others, however, are cheerful; fond of music, fond of song. There is nothing in the moral and mental constitution of the Malay to justify any broad line of separation between them and their frontagers.

The real characteristic of the Malays is connected with the area which they occupy, and (so connected) is, in the first instance at least, rather a point of physical geography than proper ethnology. The Malays are the most insular population in the world. All Sumatra is Malay. So is all Borneo. With a slight change of type the Philippines are the same. The only Malays occupant of any portion of the continent are those of the narrow tongue of land which runs south of Siam till it ends in the island of Sincapore. This is the Malayan Peninsula—no island, but, as its name denotes, a near approach to one; and, as its name denotes, a Malay occupancy. Such proximity to the sea cannot fail to exert an influence on the habits and aptitudes of the occupants of the countries to which it appertains. It makes them mariners perforce, or, doing less than this, encourages maritime enterprize, maritime activity, maritime civilization. We must expect to find trading communities in such localities. We must not be surprised to find pirates. Malays, too, in outlying and distant areas must not surprise us. Malays, too, we may find in the middle of London; just as we find Indians from Calcutta, Madras, and Bombay; Malays who have formed part of some English ship's crew. More numerous still, both in Liverpool and London, are the Philippine islanders—short and thick-set men, with the dress and garb of an English or Spanish sailor. Walking behind one of these, we may fancy that it is a countryman of our own whom we are following. It is only when we see his face that we find the difference.

Much has been written about the excitability of the Malay character, and the influence of stimulants upon it, much about the state of madness into which a Malay may work himself when under the influence of an apparently uncontrollable passion he abandons himself to a violent animal paroxysm and runs amuck (*amok* is the native word) at all he meets; like the old Berserks of the Scandinavian sagas. That Malays do this is true, and it is, perhaps, true that they do it oftener than the individuals of other stocks. Yet the Chinese and many other populations do the same. The Chinese, too, and other nations are quite as capable as the Malays of gambling like madmen, and staking their whole personal possessions, their freedom, and even their life, on the strength and courage of a cock or quail.

It is the tribes, however, of the Malayan Peninsula rather than the great Malay group in general, which are now under notice—the tribes of the only portion of the old *continent* which have yet to command attention.

They fall into two divisions, (1) the pagan or semi-pagan, and (2) the Mahometan, the phenomena which have presented themselves in India being *re*-presented here. For "Hindu," read "Mahometan," and for

"Khond" or "Kol," read "Orang Benua," and, *mutatis mutandis*, the now familiar contrast between the occupant of the sea-side or fertile plain, on one side, and the mountain or forest, on the other, will reappear. In the more impracticable districts of the Malayan Peninsula traces of an original paganism are abundant. Engrafted upon this will be found traces of Indian influence, in the shape of Brahminic and Buddhist creeds; sometimes as purely Brahminic or Buddhist as in India itself, but oftener in either a fragmentary or rudimentary form,—fragmentary where it has been overlaid by a subsequent conversion to Mahometanism, rudimentary where it has not been strong enough to eradicate the aboriginal superstitions. The third series of influences is from Arabia, for the Malays, in the more limited sense of the word, are Mahometans.

With these preliminaries we may enter upon the details of the Mahometan and Pagan populations of the Malayan Peninsula; taking care to distinguish between them. The former will be called Malays, the latter Orang Benua.

*Orang* means *man*, whilst *benua* means *soil*, *land*, or *country*, so that *orang benua* means *men of the soil*. The words belong to the proper Malay language, and are applied by the Malays to the natives of the land around. In the present work they will be used even more widely than they are used in the Peninsula. They will be applied as a generic denomination to all the older tribes of the Peninsula, and to their analogues, or equivalents in the islands. They will be used, in short, much as the word aborigines is used in ordinary ethnography. Particular names, however, will be given to particular divisions of them. Of these the first and most northern contain—

*The Semang tribes.*—Semang is a Malay word; a word applied by the Mahometans of Keddah, Perak, Tringanu, and Salangore to the pagan tribes of the interior, a name, more or less, general and collective; a name, however, which is probably strange to the Semang themselves. That it is general and collective is inferred from the following divisions of the populations to which it applies.

1. The Semang Paya are those who reside on the borders of the morasses.

2. The Semang Bukit are the occupants of the hills.

3. The Semang Bakow love the neighbourhood of the sea, the creeks, and the districts where the mangrove grows.

4. The Semang Bila are somewhat less rude than the others, and approach the Malays in habits and civilization.

*The Sakai.*—The Sakai, like the Semangs, are known by their Malay name, and, like the Semang, are divided into classes.

1. The Sakai Bukit are, like the Semang Bukit, men of the hills and mountains.

2. The Sakai Jina, like the Semang Bila, are, more or less settled, and imperfectly civilized.

*The Halas,* though known by a different name, are, apparently a branch of the Sakai. They are, probably, the rudest members of the class. They tattoo the face and breast. They pierce, not only the ears, but the cartilage of the nose, inserting porcupine quills in the bore.

The little that is known of the Sakai religion is as follows:—

The superior Spirits are named Nyani, the inferior Pateh.

The latter are the cause of thunder; and hence, in a thunderstorm, the Sakai rush out of their houses, brandishing poles and sticks, and using similar means to frighten them.

A man and his wife are put in an arbour. The rest of

the company stand outside and sing. This invokes a spirit, who takes possession of the couple; indicating the fact by some mysterious noise. When this has been heard, the possessed pair come out, and say their say; every word of which is believed to be inspired.

| English. | Jurui. | Kedah. | Malay. |
|---|---|---|---|
| *Man* | teunkal | tumkal | orang |
| *Woman* | mabei | badon | perampuan |
| *Head* | kala | kay | kapala |
| *Eye* | med | med | mata |
| *Nose* | muk | muk | idong |
| *Mouth* | temut | ban | mulut |
| *Tongue* | litig | —— | ledah |
| *Tooth* | lemun | yus | gigi |
| *Ear* | pol | anting | telinga |
| *Hand* | tong | chas | tangan |
| *Foot* | chau | —— | kaki |
| *Blood* | koad | cheong | dara |
| *Bone* | gehe | aieng | tulang |
| *Sky* | —— | kael | langit |
| *Sun* | mitkakok | mitkakok | matahari |
| *Moon* | bulan | kachik | bulan |
| *Star* | —— | bintang | bintang |
| *Fire* | us | us | api |
| *Water* | hoh | bateao | ayer |
| *Tree* | kuing | chuk | poko. |

The Sakai are the Orang Benua of Pahang, or rather Sakai is the Pahang word for an aboriginal.

Between Pahang and Johore lies a *terra incognita,* covered with jungle and occupied by a population of dammer and rattan gatherers, whose habits have yet to be described, but which are probably those of the

*Orang Benua of the southern third of the peninsula, i.e. Johore.*—The great repository for the ethnology of the populations under notice, as well of many others, is the Journal of the Indian Archipelago, the chief authority being the Editor, Mr. Logan. From his paper upon what he calls the Mintira tribes of Johore, the whole of the following account is taken. Whether Mintira be the best and most convenient denomination is doubtful. Some of the tribes to which the description applies, are called Jakun, or Jokong, a name which has, for some time, been, more or less, current. It will be used in the present work when wanted. The name, however, is of less importance than the description. This is that of the pagan or semi-pagan Orang Benua of Johore.

The general form of government is patriarchal. Each tribe, village, or settlement is under the direction of an elder or Bátín. Under the Bátín come two subordinates termed Jennáng and Jurokrá. The Pawang is the equivalent to the priest, or physician. When a Bátín dies, the nearest relation presents his eldest son to be elected as his successor. If the tribe refuse him, the second son is put up; and if *he* be refused, a third. So on till the family is exhausted, and a fresh one tried. *Mutatis mutandis*, this applies to the Jennáng and Jurokrá also; except that the Bátín (and not the tribe at large) appoints them.

The social and political relations between the Orang Benua and the Malays are easily understood. We know beforehand what they will be. The Malay will despise the Orang Benua, the Benua hate the Malay. Nevertheless there will be some slight degree of intermarriage after the ordinary *jus connubii* of different populations. Malay men will take to themselves Benua wives far oftener than Benua men will take wives from the Malays. This means that there will be marriages of disparagement, in which it is more usual for the man to elevate the woman than for the woman to elevate the man. Children thus produced can scarcely be called half-bloods, so little is the difference between the two original stocks.

We know, too, what to expect commercially. The

Malays will buy and sell with the Benuas; but they will buy cheap and sell dear. They will be the only population that comes in immediate contact with them, and, they will take care and pains to keep others away.

The dress is no dress; but simply the *chawat*, a narrow strip of cloth passing between the legs, and fastened round the waist. Sometimes this is of cloth, but the ruder and more aboriginal material is a piece of beaten bark. The more general the use of the chawat, and the more primitive its fabric, the ruder the tribe. The women are the first to abandon it; substituting for it the *sarong* or Malay petticoat. For this reason the words *chawat* and *sarong* have almost a technical meaning. They will often re-appear; sometimes in speaking of countries where other terms are current.

The more elaborate ornaments are plain brass rings and bracelets. The ears are pierced; the size of the bore being, like the use of the *chawat*, a rough measure of the rudeness of the tribe. Sometimes there is a simple perforation; as large, perhaps, as a quill, but not much larger than the weight and size of the ring requires. Sometimes, a wooden plug, a rolled leaf, or a piece of cloth replaces it. Sometimes the hole is artificially and indefinitely enlarged by the insertion of wooden pins or rollers gradually increasing in size.

The teeth are filed.

The first of the stimulants is, perhaps, tobacco. The cigar into which it is rolled is called *roko*. The women smoke it as well as the men, and when they take it out of their mouth transfer it to their ear.

The characteristic of the dwelling-house is, that it is raised on posts or piles; sometimes driven in the ground, sometimes consisting of trees cut down. A rude ladder leads to an open doorway. The walls are of bark, the thatch of leaves, or rice-straw. Sometimes there are but three, sometimes no more than two sides. One in which Mr. Logan slept had only one. This was a break-wind—such as the aborigines had in Tasmania—rather than a house. A mat to sleep on is the most constant piece of furniture; pillows and curtains being rarer. Gourds of different kinds hold the water; though not exclusively. Amongst the articles of furniture in a comparatively well-furnished hut, I find two iron pans, two earthenware pots, two *santongs* (a kind of basket), *sarongs*, handkerchief, hair-pin, and brass rings.

Like so many other rude tribes, they find no difficulty in procuring fire by rubbing two pieces of wood together. In one stick they make a slight cavity or depression. Another they sharpen into an imperfect fit. A few quick revolutions give a light.

The dwelling-house, hut, or cabin, stands in a *ladang* or clearing; the clearance being made by means of fire. The spot is chosen, its *genii* propitiated by certain preliminary forms or offerings, and the trees that overshadow it felled, and left to dry. They are, then, burned. The plants that follow are the kledi, a substitute for the potato, different kinds of yams, a sort of water-melon, the sugar-cane, maize, rice, and tobacco. The men effect the clearance and the first plantation; after which the females do the work of weeding and watering. The chief fruit is the durian.

To this extent the Orang Benua are imperfect agriculturists. They are fishermen and hunters as well. The fish are chiefly taken in nets, eel-pots, and weirs—not by the rod and line, nor yet (I think) by the means of the bow and arrow, as is so often done in South America. Upon this point, however, I speak with hesitation. So many habits are common to the equatorial populations of the Indian Archipelago and America, that I am unwilling to hazard any negative statement.

The forest supplies snakes, which are not uncommon articles of food, monkeys, which are commoner still, deer, and wild hogs. These they catch in pitfalls, or hunt with dogs. The latter, the companion of man in so many countries, is found in every family. Sometimes there are several. So is the Malay cat. So is the domestic fowl.

For catching pigeons and other wild birds, they have several kinds of bird-lime.

After the body has been buried, a fire is lit over the grave, and kept up for three or seven nights to prevent the *hantu*, or spirit of the deceased, from crying underground. Another practice consists in placing a bamboo stake close to the nose of the corpse, so as to act as a sort of funnel for the gases engendered by the decomposition of the body to escape. It is chiefly confined, however, to children ; it being held, that should their integuments be allowed to burst the living mother would sympathize with them.

The most characteristic weapon is the sumpitan. With the tribes under notice it is about seven feet long, and made of bamboo. It is about three-fifths of an inch in diameter. This, however, is not thick enough for its length ; so it is enclosed in a larger one. Hence, the true instrument is a sumpitan within a sumpitan ; the bore being made by the hands of nature. The Dyak weapon is very skilfully contrived. It consists of a simple piece, artificially perforated. This difference between the natural and the artificial bore, will re-appear in South America. Some tribes will bore their own sumpitans : others cut them ready bored. The arrows are about ten inches in length ; tipped with the poisonous juice of the ipoh.

The mythology of what we may call the continental Malays will not command much of our attention at present. In more than one of the islands it will show itself in a fuller, and more instructive form. It is sufficient to say, that its basis is that of the paganism of the rude tribes of Ava, Siam, and Asam, the paganism of an untutored population of the inter-tropical districts of south-eastern Asia. More or less of it has been seen already; the samples being miscellaneous and fragmentary. The ethnologist regrets that they are thus exhibited. His *data*, however, are fragmentary and miscellaneous. He can only lay before the reader such facts as happen to have been recorded. It may be, however, that these are enough to convey a general idea—and a general idea of Asiatic paganism, whether northern or southern, whether eastern or western, in the form that it took before either Parsíism or Buddhism, Brahminism or Mahometanism, effected their respective modifications is all that in the present state of our knowledge is possible. And, in respect to the paganism under notice, it is a patent fact, as will be seen when we come to Borneo, that both Brahminism and Mahometanism have modified it.

In respect to physical form, one of our best authorities, the French missionary, M. Favre, was informed, in answer to his questions about the Jakuns of Johore, that they were darker than those of Pahang; in other words, that the latter were whiter and fairer than the former. They were as white as Europeans. They were numerous. They were also valuable as articles of commerce; selling well at the town of Pahang, and selling well at Siam. They were small, however, in size; though comely. The Malays formed parties to hunt them, and beat the forest for them just like Europeans at a deer-hunt. Are these simply fairer families than the allied populations, or are they, more or less, albino? Probably the former—"other persons who have seen this species of Jakuns, tell me that they are not so white as Europeans, but that they approach more to the colour of the Chinese, which is most probable."

In the immediate neighbourhood of the town of Malacca, the aboriginal population is but scanty, the whole number being, perhaps, under 400. M. Favre, who visited those of Reim, Ayer Baro, Gassing, Kommendar, Bukit Singhi, the river Muar, Pankalang kota, Poghalay, Sagu, Lemon, Segamon, and the river Pago, found amongst them traces of an intermixture of Portuguese, probably on the fathers' side. So at least he interpreted the following signs. After having been persuaded to visit the town of Malacca, they asked to be shown the upper part of the door of the fortress, on which they found the sculptured figures of a king and queen of Portugal. These they said were their ancestors. Many others, similarly questioned, said that they were the descendants of the Orang puti or white man; a statement that certain resemblances to the lower class of Malacca Portuguese confirmed; as did the highly probable report that more than once criminals or malcontents had fled from the city into the interior—betaking themselves to the bush, after the fashion of outlaws of every age and country. Add to this that more than one Portuguese term is said to be found in their vocabularies.

So much for the general statement as to their likeness to the Portuguese. When we come to the details we find it repeated. They are specially stated to be as tall as the common run of Europeans, and to be dark-skinned. On the other hand their hair is more frizzled, a point reminding us of the Semang.

Putting all this together I commit myself to the doctrine that some of the Orang Benua are darker, some lighter, than the average; some showing the ordinary departure from the current physiognomy under the influence of certain physical and social influences, and some doing so as an effect of actual intermixture. That they are fundamentally Malay I believe. Their traditions (or what simulates them) run to this effect.

But the ordinary Malays proper, who occupy the towns of the sea-coast, and the more practicable inland districts of Kedah, Perak, Pahang, Tringano, and Johore, of the Malayan peninsula, are, in general, by no means either savages or pagans; but, on the contrary, civilized Mahometans who have, as a matter of credible and reasonable history, brought their civilization from Sumatra. In respect to their settlement the tradition (or what passes as such) is as follows:—A.D. 1160, Sang Nila Utama, a descendant of Alexander the Great, founded Sincapore at the head of a Sumatran colony. About a hundred years later Tu Puttair founded Malacca from Sincapore. He had no women with him; so he took to wife a Jakun woman of Taba on the river Naning, and his companions followed his example. He was himself a Menankabaw chief, but his offspring were of mixed blood. This is, I believe, an explanation with circumstances originating out of the attempt to explain the relations between the Malays and Orang Benua, for that they are connected is believed, more or less, on both sides. There are Malays who connect their remote ancestors with the Jakuns, and Jakuns who believe that the Malays are descendants of their own distant forefathers. Nor is there anything in the Sumatran origin of the latter that militates against this view. Orang Benua may have left the peninsula for the island, developed a civilization in their insular locality, and then revisited the old country as settlers.

But why, if the population are really akin, should there be any doubt as to the kindred? Surely the Malays of Sumatra, if they were actually the descendants of certain pagans of the continent, would, despite the difference of creed, have recognized their ancestors.

By no means. Changes may have been effected in either of the two occupancies. Changes may have been effected in both. Let us look to what has happened in our own island in respect to our own relations with our congeners of Germany.

In the eighth century the Angles of Great Britain, themselves originally Pagan Germans, took an interest in the spiritual welfare of the so-called Old Saxons, a tribe of Westphalia, immediately related to their own continental ancestors; these Old Saxons having retained their primitive Paganism. The mission partly succeeded, and partly failed.

Now, if in addition to this partial success of the Angle mission, there had been a partial Angle colonization as well, and if, side by side with this, fragments of the old unmodified Paganism had survived amongst the fens and forests up to the present time, we should have had, in the relations of England and Germany, precisely what I imagine to have been the case with the Malayan peninsula and the island of Sumatra. Like Germany, the peninsula would have supplied the original stock to the island; but, in the island, that stock would have undergone certain modifications. With these modifications it would—so to say—have been *reflected* upon the continent—*re*-colonizing the old mother-country. But would the Christians from England have recognized in the pagans of Germany their cousins? In the time of King Pepin—possibly. In the time of Charlemagne—probably. In the time of the electors of Hanover—certainly not,—not at least, without that amount of literary knowledge which we as Englishmen possess, but which the Malays of Sumatra at the time of their separation, and the Jakuns, at the present time, are without.

Two divisions of the Orang Benua have a special interest.

1. *The Biduanda Kallang* of the parts about Sincapore. Their present locality is the banks of the most southern of the rivers of the peninsula, the Pulai. Thither they were removed when the British took possession of the island of Sincapore; of which they were previously the joint occupants—joint occupants, because they shared it with the tribe which will be next mentioned. They were boatmen rather than agriculturists. But they were only freshwater sailors; since, though they lived on the water, they avoided the open sea. They formerly consisted of one hundred families; but have been reduced by smallpox to eight.

Their priest or physician is called *bomo*, and he invokes the *hantu*, or deities, the *anito* of the Philippine Islanders, the *tii* of the Tahitians; and, probably, the *wandong* and *vintana* of Australia and Madagascar respectively.

They bury their dead after wrapping the corpse in a mat; and placing on the grave one cup of woman's milk, one of water, and one of rice; when they entreat the deceased to seek nothing more from them.

Persons of even the remotest degree of relationship are forbidden to intermarry.

The account of their physical appearance is taken from too few individuals to justify any generalization. Two, however, of them had the forehead broader than the cheekbones, so that the head was pear-shaped. In a third, it was lozenge-shaped. The head was small, and the face flat. The lower jaw projected; but not the upper—so that "when viewed in profile, the features seem to be placed on a straight line, from which the prominent parts rise very slightly."

2. *The Orang Sletar.*—The original joint-occupants of Sincapore with the Biduanda Kallang, were the *Orang Sletar,* or *men of the river Sletar;* differing but little from the former. Of the two families they are the shyer, and the more squalid; numbering about two hundred individuals and forty boats. Their dialect is Malay, spoken with a guttural pronunciation, and with a clipping of the words.

At the birth of a child they have no ceremonies; at marriage a present of tobacco and rice to the bride's mother confirms the match: at death the deceased is wrapped in his garments and interred.

Skin diseases and deformities are common; nevertheless, many of their women are given in marriage to both Malays and Chinese; but I know of no account of the mixed progeny.

A low retreating forehead throws the face of the Orang Sletar forwards, though the jaw is rather perpendicular than projecting.

# CHAPTER XLVIII.

**Retrospect.—Relative influence of the preceding populations upon the history of the world at large.—Zones of conquest.—Origin and diffusion of civilization.**

A RETROSPECTIVE view of the wide field over which our inquiries had carried us was taken when we passed from Asia to Europe, and when Africa had yet to come under cognizance. At the present moment, the islands of the Indian Archipelago, and the Pacific, along with New Guinea, Australia, and Tasmania, still stand over. So does the whole of America, the New World as it is often called; though, in many respects, it is no newer than Polynesia —indeed, scarcely so new. Old or new, however, the aforesaid areas still stand over for notice.

And, in one respect, they constitute (if not a new) at least, a different world. Until recently they have stood apart from the three old continents; and, even now, the influences are all on one side. There is action, but no reaction. There is giving but no taking. There is reciprocity in plenty; but to speak after the fashion of the Irish, it is wholly and exclusively on one side. The action, in the world's history, of the parts described upon the parts that have yet to be investigated, is at a *minimum*. The action of the parts that have yet to be investigated upon those that have already been described is *nil*. India and Arabia have acted upon Sumatra and Java, but how have Java and Sumatra affected either Arabia or India, either India or any other portion of the continent? The world of action and re-action is the world we have just surveyed, and, most assuredly, we can, with all propriety and convenience, pause and look back.

Our first retrospect was partial. It took-in Asia alone. Yet it was convenient. It gave a measure of the relative importance of, at least, four great classes, the Tungús, the Mongol, the Ugrian, and (above all in magnitude and influence) the Turk. But even this it gave incompletely. The Turks (to go no farther) had only a fraction of their history exposed. Did we not see, when India and Persia were under view, that, in both countries, Turk conquests had been effected? To have mentioned these, however, in the first instance, would have been to anticipate.

Then there are the Sarmatians—conquerors like the Turks. And the Germans—conquerors like the Sarmatians. And the Romans—conquerors too; conquerors and civilizers—great as a material, great as a moral power. And the Greeks—conquerors to a great, civilizers to a greater, extent. And the Arabs, and the Jews—the Semite populations in general.

Of these I shall take my view from a point in the region of theory. Let us look at certain physical conditions, and ask how far they may determine the comportment of the populations to which they apply.

That the cold and darkness of the extreme north are as unfavourable to the development of bodily strength as the enervating heat of the tropics is adverse to the strenuous and continuous exhibition of either physical or moral energy, is true as a matter of fact; no truer, however, as a fact, than the plain and patent inference from it in favour of the temperate zone being that which best promotes activity and enterprise. That it should do this is what we expect *à priori*. That it has actually done this is what we find from observation. A population lying midway between the Arctic circle and the tropic, provided that it felt the instinct of aggression and conquest (and what populations fail to feel it?), would strike as with a double-edged sword. To the north it would smite the poor and weak, the undersized and the ill-provided; to the south, the enervate and the opulent—loving peace not wisely but too well. The populations who thus create fear on both sides are, one and all, the occupants of an area which is as truly, in the way of history and ethnology, a zone of encroaching conquerors, as the temperate is a zone of a medium climate.

It is scarcely too technical to call it a zone of conquest. That the lines by which it is bounded shall exactly coincide with those that give the parallels of latitude is improbable. It is rather to be expected that they will run irregularly—like the isothermals. They do so. From the mouth of the Elbe to the mouth of the Amur the ethnological areas are as follows:—1. German, 2. Sarmatian, 3. Ugrian, 4. Turk, 5. Mongol, 6. Mantshú; concerning each of which the following general statements may be made.

Their occupants have effected encroachments upon the areas of their frontagers, both north and south: whereas, from neither the south nor the north has any one of the frontier populations permanently dispossessed the men of the middle zone.

In detail—

1. The limit of Germany to the north is the Arctic Ocean; on the very edge of which are to be found the Swedes and Norwegians of Scandinavia. On the south, the displacement of the older occupants has been less. France, however, is a German name: the Duchy of Beneventum was a Lombard occupancy: Catalonia is the land of the Goths: Murcia is the March. So nearly

has the whole of western Europe been overrun from Germany. What, however, are the Keltic, the Spanish, the Italian, or Greek occupancies in Germany?

2. Sarmatia, like Germany, is limited only by the ocean. Archangel is Russian, just as Hammerfest is Norwegian. Ragusa is Slavonic. The Slavonic elements in Greece have long commanded attention.

3. The Ugrian class is, at the present time, in such a fragmentary condition, that it appears to give an exception. Several Fin populations, however, have been decidedly intrusive and encroaching. Most especially have they extended themselves northwards. That the Finlander has encroached upon the Lap is evident from what is going on before our eyes at the present moment. That the Voguls and Ostiaks are from the south has already been suggested. That the Magyars of Hungary are from the north is a matter of history.

Now, however, the Ugrians are a broken stock. Who, however, are the men who have dispersed them? To what groups and latitudes do they belong? Very nearly to those of the Ugrians themselves. The Turks have encroached from the east: the Sarmatians from the west. Between the two, the once wide Ugria, like iron between hammer and anvil, has been denationalized. It belonged to a class of strong occupancies. Of that class, however, it was the weakest. It was the land of neither the horse nor the camel. With an inconsiderable sea-board, it had vast and almost impenetrable forests.

That, even in those parts of Russia where the speech is Slavonic, the blood is, to a great extent, Ugrian, has already been stated. Besides this—even now—the Fin of Finland is spoken within the Arctic Circle, the Magyar of Hungary, on the Danube.

4. There are, at present, Turks on the Mediterranean,

viz. the Ottomans. There are Turks on the Icy Sea viz. the Yakuts.

5. The north and south prolongations of the Mongol area are unimportant.

6. The Tungús tribes, however, have been eminently encroaching. The Mantshús have conquered China. Meanwhile, the northern coast of Siberia (as is inferred from the affinities between the Samoyed, and Jukahiri forms of speech) was once continuously Ugrian. At the present time there is no continuity at all. The Yakut Turks have broken-in on one part: Tungús tribes on another. Both touch the Icy Sea.

Such are the phenomena presented by the Old World. The New when it comes under notice, will give the same.

The several portions of the zone under notice differ from each other, chiefly in being (1) forest, (2) steppe, or (3) sea-board. Of the last there is the most in Europe; of the second in Asia. The Ugrians are pre-eminently the foresters. Of morasses and mountains the protective powers are less than is generally supposed. The Bask part of the Pyrenees, and Caucasus, doubtless, preserve not only an old population, but, also, one of its chief characteristics—language. So does Albania. The Romance, however, and the German of the Swiss Alps, are equally intrusive. So is the Hindí of the southern, and (apparently) the Bhot of the northern slope of the Himalayas.

If bodily force were the only factor in the valuation of the relative importance of the different divisions of mankind, our observations would now terminate. Without, however, mental activity it is of little avail even as a material power or a means of effecting conquests and encroachments. The Barbarians (as they are called) of the North (by which the Greeks and Romans meant

Central Europe) were always formidable. As long, however, as they were pure Barbarians, the effect of their inroads were evanescent. They were the permanent conquerors of great and consolidated empires only when they became tinctured with civilization.

Now the physical conditions of civilization are by no means those of the physical conditions of rude strength. Climate has something to do with them; soil something; sea-board more. In the mind, however, of the present writer, the prime impulse is given by the mutual contact of dissimilar populations with dissimilar wants. If so, civilization is the product of neither blood nor nationality. It is rather a result of the contact of more nationalities than one. The natural history, however, of civilization is one thing; anthropology and ethnology another; and allied, as the three subjects undoubtedly are, they still differ. Without, then, going into the physical part of the subject, I content myself with drawing attention to the historical importance of those great families whose occupancy is the parts where Europe, Asia, and Africa join; where a narrow neck of land separates the Indian Ocean from the great inland sea of Europe, and where the Nile from the south, and the Dnieper from the north, bring Sarmatia and Æthiopia within the same great commercial basin of the Mediterranean; in the eastern end of which I believe that civilization arose—the civilization of the world at large—native to the parts in question—native to no other part of the world beside.

Out of the many fictitious dualisms with which the so-called philosophy of history abounds, I believe this of the centre of civilization and the zone of material force to be real. If so, it tells us what to expect. A little consideration shows that it is easier for the hardier populations of the north to adopt the civilization of their southern frontagers than for the natives of the south to invest themselves with the robuster energies of the north—north and south here meaning Germany, Sarmatia, and Turkistan on one side, and Ægypt, Syria, Greece, and Italy on the other. Hence, when the so-called Barbarians adopted the arts of Greece and Rome, the situs of the great powers was changed.

*Turks* and *Sarmatians.*—As long as the civilization of the southern frontier of the middle zone was nascent or incomplete, the Turks and Sarmatians, whose ethnological history has yet to be duly investigated, were the great encroachers. To each, I believe that many of the pre-historic influences are to be referred—to the Turks much of the nationality of Asia Minor, Persia, Syria, Arabia, Northern Africa, and (not impossibly) Italy—to the Sarmatians much of what passes for Italian, Greek, German, Scandinavian, Median, and Indian. The details, however, of the evidence upon which these surmises rest are far too lengthy to find place. The author has exhibited them, more or less fully,* elsewhere. He would rather increase than diminish the areas of his previous speculations.

Since the civilization of the southern frontier (in the consideration of which Mahometan Arabia must not be overlooked) has been diffused, Germany, Slavonia, and the Romanized portions of Iberia and Keltikê, have given forth the predominant influences. All of which have superadded to the ruder elements of their original strength, the forces deducible from the art, the literature, the policy, the science of both Greece and Italy,—of Italy as acted on by Greece, of Greece as acted on by Phenicia and Ægypt—acted upon, itself an agent.

* Especially in *Native Races of the Russian Empire*, and the *Germania of Tacitus, with Ethnological Notes*.

*Germans.*—The ethnology of the Sarmatians involves that of the Germans, the original magnitude of their respective areas being a point upon which current opinion is open to grave exceptions. As a matter of history it was the Elbe which, in the time of Charlemagne, divided Germany from Slavonia; to the east of which river no German occupancy existed. I hold that in the time of Tacitus the relations of the two areas were the same; believing that the contrary opinion, in favour of all the nations whose names appear in the Germania of Tacitus being actually Germans, is utterly untenable. If so, the southern side of the Baltic was Sarmatian. If so, a Sarmatian conquest of Scandinavia, anterior to that effected by the Germans, is probable. How far there is actual evidence in favour of one is another question. In the mind of the present writer there is a great deal. That the Vandals were Slavonians rather than Germans, and that the actual Germans of the history of the Lower Empire were only Goths, so far as they intruded themselves upon the country of the Getæ are, in the mind of the present writer, both important facts, and facts that magnify the early importance of the Sarmatians, and diminish that of the Germans.

Indeed, the extension of the German influence has been effected almost wholly within the historical period, subsequent to the extension of the Roman Empire northwards; and, generally speaking, from points where Roman civilization had, more or less, established itself.

*Kelts.*—The test of language makes the Keltic one of the subordinate divisions of mankind; the populations which speak the Breton and the Welsh, the Manks or the Gaelic, being, one and all, in a fragmentary condition, and the individuals of which they consist being counted by the thousand rather than the million.

The test, however, of language applies but imperfectly to either Gaul or the British Isles, over each of which important areas the blood is certainly more Keltic than the speech. It is this in even the eastern parts of England and the northern parts of France. It is so in a still greater degree in the west of England, in Cornwall, in the Isle of Man, in Scotland, and in Ireland.

And here it may be remarked that in those districts where the blood and speech coincide, and where the strain is the purest, we find a perennial supply of elements which, when transplanted elsewhere, by means of emigration, cannot but fail to Kelticize the stock with which they come in contact. In America, the offspring of parents whereof one is English and the other Irish, may marry an aboriginal of Ireland, whose child may, in its turn, do the same. In this way the Kelt family, as tested by its genealogy, may increase; whilst, as tested by its language, it may fall off. Whatever may be its fate in this respect, it is clear that its outward and visible characters have not only a decided tendency to change, but that, these being lost, little is left but an abstraction. Hence the Keltic family, like the Ugrian, must be looked upon as the family of a diminishing area.

Like that of the Ugrians, the Keltic area has lain between two forces—the rude force of Germany, and the civilization of Italy. It was first broken by the former. Whilst Italy was barbarous the Kelts were formidable. Their extension, both eastward and southward, though overvalued, has been considerable. It was effected, however, when the civilization of Italy was but nascent.

The present work, however, is upon Descriptive Ethnology, rather than either the Philosophy (so called) of History or the Natural History of Civilization. If it were not so, the evidence in favour of the foregoing view would run over many pages. What has been already written is written solely with the object of combining the acknowledged influence of the great material powers, like those of Germany, Sarmatia, and Turkistan, as well as those of Greece, Rome, Syria, and Ægypt with a theory, or hypothesis, which places them in the condition of the elements of a generalization.